The Role of Affect in
Motivation, Development, and Adaptation

Volume 1

Pleasure Beyond the Pleasure Principle

EDITED BY

Robert A. Glick, M.D.
& Stanley Bone, M.D.

FOREWORD BY

Ethel S. Person, M.D.

Yale University Press New Haven & London

Published with assistance from the foundation established in memory of
Philip Hamilton McMillan of the Class of 1894, Yale College.

Designed by James J. Johnson and
set in Ehrhart Roman by
Brevis Press, Bethany, Connecticut.
Printed in the United States of America by
Edwards Brothers, Inc., Ann Arbor, Michigan.

Library of Congress Cataloging-in-Publication Data

Pleasure beyond the pleasure principle / edited by Robert A. Glick and
Stanley Bone.
    p. cm. — (The Role of affect in motivation, development, and
adaptation ; v. 1)
Includes bibliographical references and index.
ISBN 0-300-04793-2 (alk. paper)

1. Pleasure principle (Psychology)   I. Glick, Robert A., 1941-   .
II. Bone, Stanley.   III. Series.
BF175.5.P54P42   1990
152.4—dc20   90-36667
                                                       CIP

*The paper in this book meets the guidelines for permanence and durability of the Committee on
Production Guidelines for Book Longevity of the Council on Library Resources.*

1   2   3   4   5   6   7   8   9   10

To Aaron Karush

Contents

Foreword

Affects, so long neglected by virtue of the psychoanalytical preoccupation with the discharge and transformation of libidinal energy, have been, so to speak, rediscovered in the context of object relations theory and the increasing attention paid to the self and to issues of narcissism. The Columbia Psychoanalytic Center's series on affects is intended both as an acknowledgment of this shift and as a spur toward the task of more fully integrating affect theory into contemporary psychoanalysis. It is also a return to our institutional roots insofar as the founders of the Center, particularly Sándor Radó, emphasized the primary role of affects in behavior. We chose to begin this series with a volume on pleasure and pleasurable affects because of the core position of concepts of pleasure and pain in psychoanalytic theory.

Freud, translating into psychological terms the biologist's recognition that the pursuit of pleasure and avoidance of pain are primary survival mechanisms, posited hedonic regulation as the prime motivational agent in psychic life. In classical psychoanalysis, libido is viewed as the instinctual force that presses for gratification. Gratification leads to pleasure, nongratification to an increase in tension. Although hedonic regulation continues to be a central tenet in psychoanalysis, many analysts, on the basis of clinical observations and new data from child development, have begun to revise their concepts, recognizing sources of pleasure other than instinctual gratification and no longer necessarily viewing pain and pleasure as opposite or antithetical states. How one understands the sources and nature of pleasure and pain is, of necessity, related to theories of motivation (the question of what initiates and directs behavior) and to conceptions of the sources and functions of affects. Consequently, revisions in the way pleasure and pain are regarded have ramifications for psychoanalytic theory as a whole.

Even within Freud's own evolving thinking, the relations between pleasure and pain, affects, motivation, and neurotic symptomatology underwent significant changes and reversals. In his first theory of neurosis (formulated in the 1890s), he focused on the importance of negative affects and feelings engendered by traumatic experiences, believing that if these were denied expression (discharge), they would lead to symptom formation. In essence, Freud believed the cause of his patients' neuroses was the "fact" that they had been sexually seduced in childhood. These seductions had led to undischarged, unacceptable, and consequently repressed ideas, wishes, and feelings. Hysterical symptoms were the aborted expression of these "foreign bodies," the negative feelings and forbidden wishes that had been repressed in the unconscious.

But this period of early theorization ended dramatically with a complete reversal in Freud's thinking. Out of a spate of new insights, among them significant discoveries made during his self-analysis, he concluded that what he had believed were real seductions were in fact disguised wishful fantasies. With that momentous reversal, Freud began to rethink causality in the genesis of neuroses. Rather than the foreign-body theory (unacceptable wishes and feelings aroused by trauma and pressing for expression), he now posited that the driving force in all human behavior, normal and neurotic, was the sex drive in its largest sense, a drive that he named "libido." In this second phase of theory making, Freud postulated that the energy pressing for discharge in symptomatic behavior was an endogenous sexual one, not negative affects produced secondary to trauma, as he had originally postulated.

Because Freud believed it was the nature of the psyche to rid itself of tension (defined as the buildup of libido), he attributed all behavior and feelings to this dynamic. The psyche's inclination to homeostasis by way of this cyclical buildup and discharge was reified as the "principle of constancy." The related "pleasure principle" attributed pleasure to the discharge of libido and pain to its buildup. With the enunciation of these theories, Freud turned his attention almost entirely toward the internal world, away from the external experiential world. Affects and feelings were downgraded to drive derivatives isolated from ideational content, mere epiphenomena attached to the success or failure of drive discharge. Libido and its permutations, rather than life experience and affects, took center stage in Freud's understanding of motivation and behavior.

Today no one can deny the immense power of libido theory to "explain" any number of normal and abnormal phenomena. Over time, however, psychoanalytic theory has evolved (in the work of both Freud and his heirs) to reintroduce the importance of "reality," to address the nature of the complex interactions between the internal and external worlds, and to reinstate the theoretical importance of affects. Concomitant with these shifts, and in some ways prerequisite to them, is the revision in the way pleasure and pain are regarded.

While the pursuit of pleasure and the avoidance of pain are still regarded as central to understanding motivation, the concept of pleasure and its sources has been enlarged. On philosophic grounds alone, the definition of pleasure as relief from tension is too narrow to account for all its different forms. Distinguishing between two kinds of pleasure, C. S. Lewis calls those pleasures that are preceded by desire and realized by the gratification of that desire *need pleasures*. The pleasure that comes from the release of sensual tension would certainly be included in this group, as would the pleasure of drinking a glass of water when one is thirsty. The second group of pleasures, which Lewis calls the *pleasures of appreciation*, comprises experiences that are pleasurable in their own right, without prior need or tension—for example, the pleasure one takes in the fragrance of flowers. This pleasure may be great, but it is occasioned outside the self, not having been sought as a release from tension or the satisfaction of an appetite. The pleasures of appreciation do not gratify mounting needs; instead our appreciation comes unbidden, elicited by the object itself.

Nonetheless, analysts might argue that the pleasures of appreciation are essentially irrelevant, without the same potential for fueling motivation as the need pleasures, or as we call them, appetitive pleasures. This may well be true, although the pleasures of appreciation clearly figure heavily in the aesthetic sense. However, within psychoanalysis there are clinical findings that lead us to acknowledge still other kinds and sequences of pleasure that serve as motivational forces, and conversely, behaviors not so readily explained in terms of a simple pleasure principle (for example, phenomena as diverse as the pleasure of sexual foreplay and masochism). Some shift in the conceptualization of pleasure can be seen in Freud's later work.

By 1914 Freud had once again begun to revise his earlier concepts of pleasure, affects, and motivation. As is evident in his paper "On Narcissism: An Introduction" (*Standard edition*, 14:67–102), he had revived his interest in the experiential world of relationships and reinvoked his earlier idea that these relationships were the source of key feelings and fantasies. The first glimmers of what would evolve into object relations theory may be found in that same paper. Implicit in its discussion of ego ideal and narcissism is an emphasis on the importance of those affects relating to the self and a recognition that the regulation of narcissistic self-regard is crucial to well-being. Additionally, by 1926, in describing anxiety as a signal affect rather than as an alternate discharge pathway for blocked libido, Freud reinstated the idea that affects have motivational potential. But he never systematized his thinking about the differences between affects and drives, nor did he systematically explore the enlarged concept of motives and desires that his work on narcissism implied. It was not until long after Freud's death that the implications of his nascent insights into affects and into issues of narcissism and object relations would be more fully explored.

In contemporary psychoanalysis, Joseph Sandler (in *Psychoanalysis: Toward the Second Century*, Yale University Press, 91–110) focuses on the primacy of those affects relating to the self—self-esteem, self-regard, and pride—and their obverse, shame, humiliation, and embarrassment. Consequently, he views motivation as not only targeted at instinctual gratification but also directed toward the achievement of well-being and safety and the sense of having achieved an "ideal" state. Object relations theorists posit attachment needs and object seeking as motivational forces; they describe not only the way the external world becomes an internal representational world but also the way aspects of the internal world are projected onto the external world. In self-psychology, behavior is viewed as being motivated (at least in part) by the need for self-affirmation, by the innate propensity toward self-actualization. These various theories enlarge the psychoanalytic concept of motivational forces and introduce the idea of pleasures other than sensual. As a result, they are much better able to interpret phenomena previously difficult to understand (and so acknowledged by Freud), such as the repetition compulsion, masochism, and the negative therapeutic reaction.

From these newer theoretical perspectives, one is able to distinguish at least three kinds of pleasures that have the potential to motivate and modulate behavior: not only the sensual pleasures of instinctual gratification but also the pleasures of "two-ness"—that is, of interpersonal relationships—and those of self-affirmation. Within the classical canon, it may be argued that the pleasures of two-ness ultimately derive from sensual gratification: because our earlier sensual pleasures are so intertwined with the Other, the argument goes, our sense of well-being and even our sense of self become bound up with our ability to form relationships with an Other. Having learned who we are through our sensual connection with an Other, we find our sense of self inextricable from our intimate relationships.

However, there appears to be good evidence that pleasure in relationships is not secondary to sensual pleasure, but primary and of a different nature. Convincing evidence comes from observation of mother-infant interactions, in which the joyful playfulness between mother and infant appears quite distinct from the pleasure of sensual gratification. The pleasures of mutuality, attunement, and intersubjective communication are characterized by a sense of security and contentment rather than by any sense of relief (see Daniel Stern, chapter 1). In fact, we are able to distinguish those mothers who are responsive primarily to physical needs from those who are sensitive to intersubjective attunement as well. Consequently, the pleasures of two-ness must be granted independent status. In addition, it is in the affirmation of the self by the Other (and the corollary ability to influence the Other) that the budding senses of agency and self-regard are born—hence the pleasures of validating one's autonomy.

Within the panoply of pleasures there are cogent pleasures that attach to both mutuality (two-ness) and to those acts that affirm the self as separate, as autonomous—acts that enlarge the sense of self and that gratify such aspirations as the wish to be good. One derives pleasure from mastery, achievement, from doing good, from all those things that add to self-esteem and enlarge the sense of the self. These two kinds of pleasures, those of mutuality and of autonomy, are better understood within the theoretical context of narcissism, object-relations, the ego ideal, the ideal self, and the ideal state than within that of instinctual gratification.

Not only is there a variety of sources of pleasures, but in another departure from libido theory, pleasure and pain can no longer be conceived of as opposites.

All varieties of pleasure may be mixed with fear and pain. The pleasure in physical exercise is often linked to pain and the ability to push oneself beyond the pain into that high that only athletes can know. Aspiration has as its dark side failure or the fear of failure. The pleasure of anticipation is frequently a combination of fantasy, performance anxiety, and fear of disappointment. The joys of creativity are usually inextricable from the pain of suffering and strain; the final vision achieved may be dark and shattering. These observations find their neurophysiological corollary in the fact that there are separate brain centers for pleasure and pain, and their psychoanalytic corollary in the facts that motivation is complex and motives often contradictory (hence the frequent admixture of pleasure and pain).

Many, though not all, analysts have come to acknowledge that pleasures are more various than can be understood within the context of drive discharge. Moreover, pleasures such as love, enthusiasm, joy, and pride and unpleasures such as fear, anger, and guilt are the currency with which we deal in clinical practice. From the theoretical perspective, the pursuit of pleasures and the avoidance of unpleasure, as mediated through affective life, not only regulate current motivations and choices but are instrumental in organizing and shaping the self. As Aaron Karush, to whom this volume is dedicated, puts it: "the core problems of psychoanalysis are not instinctual in the classical sense but are better formulated as vicissitudes of the emergency emotions ... coupled with social influences that also figure strongly in the development of personality and psychopathology" (in *Psychoanalysis: Toward the Second Century*, Yale University Press, 1989, 76). Our revised understanding of pleasure mandates an overall paradigm shift in which object relations theory and some form of self-psychology are regarded as equal partners with drive theory and ego psychology, and experience and affective regulation are considered on a par with drives.

This volume was designed to bring together the latest, and sometimes divergent, thinking of psychoanalysts, academics, and scientists about our vital pleasures and their place in psychic life. Its editors, Robert Glick and Stanley Bone, have been extremely successful in conceptualizing and organizing what I believe to be a major contribution to our understanding of pleasures beyond the pleasure principle.

Ethel S. Person, M.D.
Series Editor

Columbia University Center for
Psychoanalytic Training and Research

Acknowledgments

The inspiration for this series on affects comes from Ethel S. Person, M.D., the director of the Columbia University Center for Psychoanalytic Training and Research. The gestation and eventual delivery of the project were skillfully guided by her wisdom and loving care; without her scholarship, vision, and tact, it would never have succeeded. The intellectual legacy of Columbia—its empiricism and critical approach to theory, its avoidance of dogma, its interdisciplinary tradition and openness to ideas outside psychoanalysis—are all reflected in Dr. Person's contribution here. We also wish to express our appreciation to Willard Gaylin, M.D., whose commitment to the understanding of human emotion has been a source of encouragement and guidance.

We are very grateful to Bernard C. Mendik, a generous benefactor and great friend of the Center. He has funded a series of symposia on the theory of affects in honor of Dr. Aaron Karush, who was director from 1971 to 1976. The first symposium was held on 4 April 1987 and provides the basis of this volume. We are especially appreciative that Mr. Mendik has given us this opportunity to honor Dr. Karush, who left his creative imprint on the Center in many ways: a critical and comprehensive evaluation of Freudian theory, a seminal study on the working-through process, and an investigation of ego strength. The work most relevant to this series, however, is Dr. Karush's interest in and contributions to understanding the relation of psyche and soma—the emotions and the body. For this and more we are pleased and proud to honor him.

We also thank Irwin Freeman of the Educational Fund of the Upjohn Corporation for providing additional support for the original symposium.

We wish to thank the members of the symposium committee, Doctors Harvey Chertoff, Deborah Hamm, Sherry Katz-Bearnot, David Lindy, Steven Roose, and Marvin Wasserman for their thoughtfulness and many hours of dedicated attention to the infinite details that were essential to making the symposium from which this volume came actually happen.

We owe much to many others who have given generously of their time, interest, and knowledge. We particularly thank Doctors Richard Druss, Gerald Fogel, Donald Klein, the late Robert Liebert, Roger MacKinnon, and Samuel Perry.

Many other people helped us to shape and clarify our ideas in the process of editing this volume. We are grateful to Michael Basch, Francis Cohen, Arnold Cooper, Abby Fyer, Jack Gorman, Lawrence Kolb, Michael Liebowitz, Donald Meyers, Helen Meyers, David Olds, and Sally Severino.

We are most appreciative of the tireless efforts and cool-headedness under fire of the Columbia Center staff: Joan Jackson (administrator), Jacob Clark, Doris Parker, and Lutricia Perry.

Gladys Topkis, our senior editor at Yale, gave us the courage to demand the best from ourselves and our contributors. Her remarkable skill and tact as an editor enabled us to bear the pain of cutting and reworking to find our best.

We thank our families for their patience with us and their support.

Robert A. Glick, M.D.
Stanley Bone, M.D.

Introduction

ROBERT A. GLICK, M.D.
STANLEY BONE, M.D.

> What is alone of value in mental life is rather the feelings. No mental forces
> are significant unless they possess the characteristic of arousing feelings.
> —Freud, "Jensen's Gradiva"

Clinical psychoanalysis deals with conflicted pleasures and disavowed emotions. They are aspects of the psychodynamic models we use in our daily work to foster our patients' self-understanding and growth. However, the links between our clinical work and our theories are often obscure and incomplete. There are important and challenging gaps between these experience-near clinical phenomena and current general psychoanalytic theories of pleasure and of the emotions. New knowledge from outside psychoanalysis and new conceptual frames of reference from within psychoanalysis need to be integrated into modern psychoanalytic thinking.

Comprehensive and consistent definitions of affect and pleasure are elusive and often unsatisfying because the underlying theoretical assumptions and fields of observation vary greatly. In what follows, we shall consider affects (or emotions) as having essentially three dimensions: (1) the physiological-activational, (2) the expressive-communicative, and (3) the subjective-experiential. With pleasure, however, definitions become more problematic and abstract. Pleasure means, in the dictionary sense, a state of gratification or a feeling of delight or enjoyment; beyond this self-evident level, explications fail because pleasure is not an affect per se but rather the hedonic quality in emotional experience. This quality has complex relations to the biological, expressive, and subjective dimensions of affect. As such, it is open to many levels of meaning and interpretation that arise from a potentially wide range of implicit and explicit assumptions, beliefs, and values.

Pleasure is clearly a feature of human biology as well as psychological life. It is an in-built capacity that serves as a potent motivator and organizer of wishes and behaviors. It is a component of our adaptation to our selves and our environment. Pleasure guides our actions and gives meaning to our experiences. Of

1

course, pleasure is in part sensual and sexual, but its nature also encompasses the symbolic, the abstract, and the intensely individual and personal. We find pleasure in an extraordinary range of activities; we know the pleasures that come from the gratification of our appetites, from mastery and achievement, the pleasures of attachments and relationships, the pleasures of knowledge, and aesthetic and transcendental pleasures. Tempests of passion and the power of painful pleasures in masochism and sadism demonstrate that pleasure and pain are not poles of a single continuum, where more of one means less of the other, but are separate dimensions of experience, admixtures of which are evident in thrills, challenges, anticipations, and in falling in love (Person 1988).

Freud did not, of course, offer the last word on affect and pleasure. Clinical experience has pointed out the limited applicability of early theoretical models. Our contributors pay great attention to Freud's explorations and formulations, but they also take account of important work on the relation of pleasure and emotion by later psychoanalysts, academic psychologists, developmentalists, neurobiologists, and others. Psychoanalytic theory must have a rich enough conception of pleasure to encompass complex meanings and mechanisms of motivation in psychological life. It must also move "beyond the pleasure principle" and the naive reductionism of our theoretical past. Crucial questions have evolved from neuroscience that challenge established notions of the nature and organization of pleasure; questions have evolved from observational studies of mothers and infants that stress the importance of communication and the exchange of pleasures in the development of self and object representations. Extensions of psychoanalytic thought into philosophy and other humanistic disciplines have produced critical examinations of our fundamental assumptions and methodologies.

Efforts to understand pleasure as the motive and organizer in human existence are ancient. Aristotle believed that "desire is an impulse towards what is pleasant, happiness [pleasure] is the End at which all actions aim." Plato introduced a dynamic concept of pleasure: "when the harmony in the organism is disturbed, this is at once a dissolution of the normal condition and simultaneously an origination of pain. On the other hand, when it is reconstituted and reverted to its normal conditions, pleasure is originated" (in Berlyne and Madsen 1973). This definition of pleasure as the restoration of harmony or return to equilibrium became the metaphysical basis for Freud's pleasure principle and his affect theory.

Freud's creative transcendence of the physicalistic-physiologic brain science of his laboratory mentors grew out of his consulting room experience with hysterics and their forbidden and forgotten pleasures. With Josef Breuer, he observed that hysterics got "sick" to ward off (and express) painful, unacceptable feelings. Their hysteria was "cured" when these defensively dissociated affects and ideas were reunited. Childhood sexual trauma (pleasures), reawakened after puberty, produced memories that were morally repugnant, necessitating psychic censorship and repression. These pleasures could not be experienced directly.

Conversion hysteria was the discharge through somatic symptoms of the accumulated excitation left by the traumatic memories and was therefore a disguised pursuit of (sexual) pleasure.

Freud was a committed evolutionist. With Darwin, he believed that our emotions were the symbolic traces of archaic forms of expression and that their meanings and mechanisms came from their role in the prehistoric past. Instead of following this idea of innate affects and hedonics further, he applied his energic hypothesis and the principle of constancy (equilibrium) in an important but unsuccessful attempt to explain affect and pleasure. Freud tried to integrate quality (wish, desire, and meaning) and quantity (mechanisms and energy). (The hypothesis of core affects and hedonics is elaborated by Nathanson in chapter 5.)

One of his earliest statements on affect (*The Neuropsychoses of Defence*, [1894] 1962) was that "in mental functions something is to be distinguished—a quota of affect or sum of excitation—which possesses all the characteristics of a quantity . . . which is capable of increase, diminution, displacement and discharge, and which is spread over the memory-traces of ideas somewhat as an electric charge is spread over the surface of the body" (60). Thus, at this early point, Freud believed that "mental apparatus" functioned as an elaborate reflex arc. Stimuli impinged on the afferent end, either from within the organism or from the environment, and this accumulated excitation was discharged at the efferent end as motor activity or affect.

We know that Freud associated affects and sexuality when he began his theoretical investigations of mental life. Psychic energy arose from the somatic sexual processes, the instincts. As displaceable and transformable forms of this energy, affects became discharge processes, and pleasure became successful discharge. These ideas ultimately led Freud to his theories of infantile sexuality, libido theory, and drive-based conflict theory. Only much later, with the formulation of the structural hypothesis, did affect (in the form of anxiety) and affective meanings and mechanisms recapture his theoretical attention and take a central position in his thinking.

Freud's self-analysis and its reliance on dreams drew him toward the formulation of the topographic hypothesis and the instinctual drives. In a major conceptual leap, he perceived the drives, our biologically derived appetites, arising as wishes in the unconscious, to be the motivators of behavior, and he relegated affects to the status of epiphenomena. In *The Interpretation of Dreams* ([1900] 1953), he wrote that "[affect] is regarded as a motor or secretory function, the key to the enervation of which is to be found in the ideas of the unconscious." This was a nascent "arousal" theory of emotion; internal disequilibrium of the drives would give off signals as feelings.

The problems in Freud's subsequent formulations on pleasure arose from his attempts to reconcile them within his energic, topographic, and ultimately libido theories. As forms of instinctual expression—tamed, attenuated, disguised, or displaced—all pleasures parallel orgasm (as release phenomena). In this phase of his mental model building, Freud envisioned instinctual drives as having been represented in the mind as separable ideas and affects, each undergoing its own complex vicissitudes. Ultimately, all pleasures were explainable as the result of the successful sublimation (modification) of the ideas within the instinctual drives. In his review of psychoanalytic affect theory, Rapaport (1953) notes: "The affect theory of the second phase of the development of psychoanalysis is . . . a dynamic theory . . . [with] discharge as a safety valve function when discharge of drive cathexes by drive action meets opposition (conflict). . . . This theory remains an id-theory of affects." Freud's unitary concept of excitation-discharge led to the reductionistic and clinically barren notion that pleasure and unpleasure could be seen as points on a continuum, an increase in one essentially equating with a decrease in the other. We now know that this unitary concept of pleasure-unpleasure is contradicted by modern neurobiology, which suggests that pleasures and pains are organized in separate and distinct neurophysiological and neuroanatomical systems. (See Doidge, chapter 7.)

When Freud formulated the structural theory in *The Ego and the Id* ([1923] 1961) and *Inhibitions, Symptoms, and Anxiety* ([1926] 1959), he made the affect of anxiety central in the appraisal of the internal state of the mind. Freud retained his basic instinctual / energic hypothesis but enhanced the importance of the ego; one of its functions was to protect the psychic apparatus from excessive unbound stimulation. The ego monitors for "situations of danger" engendered by the pressure of the infantile drives for satisfaction; it then initiates the necessary protective defenses. Freud the evolutionist retained his view of affects as "incorporated in the mind as precipitates of primeval traumatic experiences . . . when a danger situation occurs, they are revived like mnemic symbols" (Freud [1926] 1959). In this way, we do not have to learn anew to adapt to danger. Our mind-brain has a prehistory from our ancestral past; we are born preadapted with an inherited memory. Freud was thus able to weave together threads of Darwinian adaptational positivism, Lamarckian inheritability of acquired traits, and phylogenetic recapitulation for his speculations on the history of man's sexual and emotional development.

With this step Freud no longer considered affects simply as passive expressions of drive or energy but recognized them as appraisal and motivation capacities that involve memory and symbolization. With an ability to monitor itself, a signal-affect capacity, the mind can appraise the internal and external environments; it can gather and adapt to information from many sources over the course of development. This was a crucial theoretical step. There is now a place in the theory where it is possible to learn and make judgments about past, present, and future pleasures. In this way, we gain a significant adaptive advantage and can give meaning to experience.

The problem of masochism, both in perversion and in character, presented important challenges to Freud's ideas on the nature of pleasure. He conceptualized masochistic pleasure ([1924] 1961) as based, first, on the physiological mammalian origins and important observational studies on how mother rats influence biological regulating functions in the postnatal life of their infants. In his chapter, Myron Hofer poses the question, Where do affects come from? Using concepts from behavioral biology—state organization, symbiosis, and biphasic-approach withdrawal theory—he suggests some potential answers. Early affect states seem conducted with proximity to mother and are reflected in various physiological responses. Hofer is attempting to establish bridging concepts between the biologic and psychologic to further our understanding of affective development.

In part II, the authors pose provocative challenges to traditional assumptions of psychoanalytic affect theory. Recognizing the limitations and the strengths of Freud's profound insights, contributors insist that modern affect theory must consider knowledge gained from beyond the customary borders of psychoanalysis. Freud certainly hoped to explain emotions as phenomena of the evolving brain, but he did not have the benefit of what we have learned about the nature of in-built emotional expression and the neurobiological bases of pleasure and pain. While integrative attempts have been made, questions about the nature of affect, hedonic motivation, and the organization of memory and representation continue to intrigue and perplex us.

Charting a course between the dangers of radical materialism, "the mindless brain," and the impoverished abstraction and subjectivism of "pure mind," contributors point to the directions in which psychoanalysis must go in developing a clinically relevant and theoretically fruitful modern affect theory. Boldly drawing on computer metaphors, Donald Nathanson invites us to imagine a "device" to study emotion, capable of including everything from the biological subsystems involved in the production and maintenance of affects to the experience of meaningfully felt emotion. With respect to the intellectual forces that shape Freud's thinking, Nathanson explodes the concept of the primacy of the drives as the source of affect, suggesting that drives are subordinate to affects and motivation and that we should expunge terms like "drive derivatives" from our literature. A student of Silvan Tomkins, he insists that we come into this world, like our mammalian cousins, "hard-wired for innate affects," that "the face is the display board of the affects system," and "that we gradually become ourselves and what is interestingly human about us through the modulation of these affects."

On the basis of considerable evidence from modern neurobiology, Andrew Schwartz offers a challenging examination of narcissism. He recasts important questions about self-representation and self-esteem regulation within the framework of a complex learning model that departs strikingly from "classical" conflict theory. Using Freud as his subject, Schwartz suggests that self-esteem can be "deconstructed" into its neurobiological elements of affects, associated processes, and self-representation. He reconsiders affects or "feelings as neural appraisals, warnings, and goals." Euphoric affect, generated by circuitry independent of that responsible for sexual excitement and orgasm, constitutes perhaps the prime factor in the self-esteem fluctuations that Freud so clearly described. These euphoric affects serve as anodynes to such intense dysphoric affects as anxiety, depression, shame, embarrassment, and disgust, which are fostered by the unconditional stimuli of parental spoken and nonverbal communications, especially signs of anger and discontent, such as Freud's father saying, "The boy will amount to nothing." Schwartz goes on to suggest that "narcissistic disorders and related defenses may represent an instance of evolution gone awry," the affected individual provoked from both the environment and within himself by those very reactions to which he is most exquisitely vulnerable. Looking ahead to the future of psychoanalysis, Schwartz urges a re-anchoring of Freudian thought in the hard sciences, a rejoining of psychoanalysis and basic biology that could advance theory, interpretative understanding, and technique.

Norman Doidge addresses the possible connections between brain chemistry, self-esteem regulation and self- and object-regulation, and self- and object-representation. Drawing on the work of Donald Klein and reminding us of cocaine's place in psychoanalytic history, he outlines the psychopharmacology of appetitive and consummatory pleasures. Using a dual track method, considering simultaneously the pharmacological and the psychological, he offers a complex look at pleasure, enthusiasm, moods, and defenses. Contrasting stimulants and narcotics, he suggests how appetitive and consummatory pleasures can be seen as "feed-forward" and "feedback" systems, having powerful motivating and organizing roles in mental life.

The clinical situation is the focus of part III, involving the patient and the analyst and the importance of pleasure.

The traditional data-base of psychoanalysis has been the psychoanalytic situation. In this complex dialogue, the analyst, with his theories as guides, endeavors to help the patient free himself from neurotic suffering. These theories of emotion and motivation, of memory and fantasy, are the challenges in our work and are in constant need of reappraisal.

In part III Otto Kernberg explores the clinical manifestations in the experience and expression of hatred derived from primitive rage. Arguing against the artificial separation of affects, cognition, behavior, and object relations as developing psychic structures, Kernberg focuses on the connection of internal object relations and reactivated affects. His interest is in the theories of aggression. Using the clinical situation, he describes the complex relations of aggression and pleasure. He focuses on those difficult and dauntingly painful analyses in which the analyst is confronted frequently with the countertransference reactions of hatred and the need to find escape routes to deal with shared intolerable situations—that is, to mobilize defenses against sadistic pleasures.

For Charles Brenner, the data of psychoanalysis come from the clinical situation. The analyst as scientist gains insights from the introspective experience of conducting analysis. Reminding us that analysis explores how people "deceive themselves about their most important thoughts and feelings," Brenner describes the role of unpleasurable affects as signals in psychic conflict. He suggests that we consider broadening our view of the signal function in conflicts to include a wide range of affects. Reviewing the history of psychoanalytic affect theory, he stresses that affect and idea are inseparable and that affect development depends upon ego and superego development. Pleasure, in Brenner's model, remains closely linked to drive tension and drive discharge.

Freud's "project" attempted to build a "mind" from the prevailing models of the brain. In chapter 10 Michael Stone suggests that we reappraise our current view of mind in light of modern neurobiological data. By looking at anhedonia as an aspect of severe psychiatric disorders that are beyond the influence of psychoanalytic treatment, Stone offers a comprehensive clinical view of hedonic capacity. With illustrations from a spectrum of clinical presentations, he takes us through a systems analytic approach, from the molecular to the clinical level.

Part IV seems a fitting complement to the preceding developmental, theoretical, and clinical sections. In it the contributors explore the nature of the pleasurable in human experience from aesthetic and philosophic points of view. Here, once again, psychoanalysis is both tool and specimen, and again the questions raised pose intriguing multidisciplinary challenges.

Ellen Handler Spitz, in chapter 11, applies psychoanalysis to the aesthetic experience. Using the Talmud, the visual arts (particularly the paintings of Manet and Magritte), and a story by Edgar Allan Poe, Spitz introduces us to a central debate in aesthetics. "Is the aesthetically pleasurable to be found in the properties of the object or in the subject?" Taking the position supported by psychoanalytic understanding that "the nature of aesthetic pleasure is pleasure in desiring," she offers a fascinating exploration of the dynamic tensions, the "longing look, the unsettled seeking for the spice or taste," that makes for aesthetic pleasure: "Psychoanalysis has to do with the perception of significance—with the restoring of links to the chains of meaning."

Our two final chapters both start with the same charge—a critical examination of Freud's *Beyond the Pleasure Principle*. As much as Freud throughout his life tried to build a scientific model of the mind, he was from the beginning caught up in the major philosophic questions of human experience. While attempting to be a scientist, he drew on crucial philosophic assumptions that were not always consistent, often not reconcilable, but nonetheless potent in his thinking. We include in this volume two thoughtful readings of what is perhaps Freud's most problematic and intriguing philosophic text. These look at the question of human motivation and human emotion from the perspective of their philosophic foundations. Edward Casey literally takes Freud at his word and begins a systematic deconstruction (or, in a sense, follows Freud's autodeconstruction) of the pleasure principle as dominant in human life and human existence. He takes us not beyond the pleasure principle but (as he says) out in front of it or behind it. Casey traces Freud's attempt to wrestle with the quantity–quality dialectic and places Freud's effort in the history of efforts by other philosophers, including Plato and Kant.

Starting from the text as well, Judith Butler explores the meanings of repetition, and the notions of temporality and intentionality in human motivation for her critical examination of Freud's reevaluation of the pleasure principle. Butler suggests that we should not discount the death instinct as a purely speculative notion but should rather examine it for its explanatory power in an effort to understand more clearly the nature of experiences that are both pleasurable and repetitious. Here, she draws on sadism. She seeks to demonstrate how sadism as pleasurable repetition will challenge the death instinct; in so doing, she brings up points of connection between the phenomenologic doctrine of intentionality and psychoanalytic object relations theory. Butler suggests, "Pleasure is not a substance or a state that has any meaning outside the context in which it is related to an object."

REFERENCES

Berlyne, D. E., and Madsen, R. B., eds. 1973. *Pleasure, reward, preference: Their nature, determinants, and role in behavior.* New York: Academic Press.

Freud, S. [1894] 1962. The neuropsychoses of defence. In *Standard edition*, 3.

———. [1900] 1953. The interpretation of dreams. In *Standard edition*, 5.

———. [1923] 1961. The ego and the id. In *Standard edition*, 18.

———. [1924] 1961. The economic problem of masochism. In *Standard edition*, 19.

———. [1926] 1959. Inhibitions, symptoms, and anxiety. In *Standard edition*, 20.

Person, E. 1988. *Dreams of love and fateful encounters.* New York: Norton.

Rapaport, D. 1953. On the psychoanalytic theory of affects. *International Journal of Psychoanalysis* 34:177–98.

I
Developmental
Considerations:
An Infant's Pleasures

1

Joy and Satisfaction in Infancy

DANIEL N. STERN, M.D.

In this chapter we examine various positive affective experiences in infancy. We focus on pleasure—specifically on joy and satisfaction—in the hope that it may cast some light on considerations (developmental ones at least) of the pleasure principle and affect theory in general. Pleasure early in life will be approached from several points of view: (1) the conceptualization of different forms of pleasure, (2) a descriptive view of pleasures in everyday life, (3) pleasure and self-regulation, and (4) the representation of different pleasurable experiences.

Conceptualizing Different Pleasurable Experiences

There are two main routes to be taken. One leads from Freud and libido theory, the other from Darwin and object relations theory. Starting with Freud, the psychoanalytic literature has considered pleasure early in life within the conceptual framework of the pleasure principle. In this view, pleasure results from the gratification of a drive state. More exactly, pleasure is the experience of a fall in internal excitement (consequent to a discharge of energy) and a return to a state of minimal internal activation (hereafter *activation* alone). I will call pleasure, conceptualized in this way, "satisfaction." Pleasure at the mother's breast (satisfaction of hunger) has always been the prototypic situation and key metaphor for this form of pleasure in early life, just as sexual orgasm has been the key metaphor for the pleasure of satisfaction within this conceptual framework for adults.

The importance of satisfaction is clear both in observing infants and in theorizing about their subjective experiences. However, I will have the least to say about the pleasure of satisfaction, because it has been so fully treated in psychoanalytic writings and because the findings of the past two decades of

13

research on infancy have been more revealing about the presence and importance of another form of pleasure, namely "joy." Here we rejoin the Darwinian
and object relations tradition.

There are several important differences between satisfaction and joy as concepts of pleasurable experience. Satisfaction requires the buildup, then falloff,
of activation. Joy may occur with only the buildup of patterned activation. The
difference is great because the breadth of the explanatory power of the pleasure
principle is at stake. (The crux here is similar to the old question of how both
the excitation of foreplay and the discharge of orgasm can be pleasurable in the
context of the pleasure principle, when activation is climbing in one situation
and falling in the other. This was a question Freud wrestled with (1924) when
he attempted to reconcile the "constancy principle" with the pleasure principle.
Observations of infants rekindle this question because it is so widely recognized
that infants seek stimulation which arouses, excites, and activates them. And
they find this state of heightened activation pleasurable. They will, in fact,
expend much time, energy, and ingenuity to create and maintain heightened
states of delight and joy. The buildup of certain patterns of activation, then, is
experienced as pleasurable; the deactivation of these patterns is experienced as
unpleasurable and not satisfying.

The situation is not quite as neatly dichotomous as drawn here. Many have
commented on the "discharge" aspects of laughter and the cathartic features
of comedy. Indeed, certain well-articulated explanations of humor (for example,
Berlyne 1966) speak of an "arousal jag" as the crucial element—that is, a
relatively rapid buildup, then an even more rapid falloff, of activation. This
explanation works well to explain certain aspects of pleasure in infancy outside
the context that would involve the satisfaction of psychophysiological drive states.
For instance, the smile of recognition that infants manifest when confronted
with a difficult perceptual problem (which activates cognitive processes) is
thought to emerge at the moment when the infant solves the problem and his
or her cognitive "tension" is resolved and solution seeking is suddenly deacti-
vated. (The same mechanism operates in those awaiting and then hearing the
punchline of a joke.) However, this explanation of an arousal jag—which is a
good microexample of the pleasure principle—does not explain the majority of
situations in which joy is seen in infants. Even if one considers the expressions
of joy (smiles, laughter) as discharge phenomena, they seem to serve to push
the system to higher and higher levels of activation, rather than to send it to
lower and lower levels.

A second important difference between joy and satisfaction concerns their
specificity. Joy is usually conceptualized as a discrete organization of patterned
activation accompanied by specific qualities of subjective experience and manifested by specific patterns of behavior (particularly facial expression) and even
by specific patterns of autonomous nervous system activation. This discrete
organization called joy is conceived as only one among many (at least six or
seven) other discrete patterns of activation that define the classical affect states

in the Darwinian tradition. Satisfaction, on the other hand, is seen as dividing the hedonic world in two, and it is conceptualized not as a specific organization but rather as the dissolution of patterned organizations seeking discharge and relaxation. (There is, of course, specific patterning of the particular behaviors that permits the discharge of different need states, but the activation involved in that patterning is far less discussed, especially in the energic model.)

A third difference concerns the social contexts in which joy and satisfaction occur. Joy in the beginning (after about six weeks of life) occurs only in a social context. It is a totally social event. (Infants do not smile and laugh at inanimate objects or situations until well after five or six months.) Joy is an affect generated between individuals and therefore situated within the context of an object relationship. Satisfaction is an event that occurs within an individual, where the social context is secondary and the object is related to the satisfaction only by association. It is in this sense that joy is more a pleasure of primary object relations, while satisfaction is more a pleasure of libido theory.

Pleasures in Everyday Life—A Descriptive View

What are the relative frequencies, seeming intensities, and apparent motivational forces of the different forms of pleasure as observed? Theoretically, the pleasure principle is in constant operation, and strictly speaking, all manifestations of affective, cognitive, or behavioral life are plotted on this hedonic gradient. In the realm of observable behavior, however, the principle is manifest in infants only when major psychobiological motivational systems, such as hunger, curiosity or sleep, are activated. The more physiologically based motivational systems (hunger or sleep) are cyclical, and their manifestation reaches sufficient strength to activate characteristic behavioral patterns cyclically. Joy, as a product of social interaction, will arise only when these other satisfaction-producing situations are not at full activation (from the point of view of amount of time spent in joy or satisfaction). In an average ("good-enough") parenting situation, joy is probably the more frequent event, emerging from the many mutual chains of smiling between parent and infant, the many delightful exchanges, and the exciting games and rituals that punctuate a day.

But is joy not a less potent event? Yes and no. The psychophysiological need states, when at full activation, usually override object-related need states. However, in daily life, before the hunger becomes truly preemptory, or when the edge has just been taken off—only a third or half of the bottle has been drunk—the infant would rather play socially, seeking stimulation and joy rather than satisfy a not-yet-maximal or a waning hunger. (Many mothers must be careful not to present enticing social invitations to joyful exchange during meals—even a small eyebrow raised and the suggestion of a smile may be too much, causing the infant to stop eating and start to play.) So in daily experience sometimes satisfaction seeking will override joy seeking and sometimes the reverse will occur. The two states alternate roles as the predominating tendency.

But is not the strength or intensity of satisfaction more than that of joy? A too-frequent opinion on this question is that in relative magnitude, joys are like small waves that play upon the great tides of hunger buildup and satisfaction, an opinion not borne out by observation. First, a distinction must be made between the observable intensity of hunger distress, which is high, and that of hunger satisfaction, which is low and largely assumed. In energic theory, discharge and its pleasure is assumed to be roughly as great as the preceding buildup and its displeasure. In other models this need not be so. In purely descriptive terms this relationship is not evident. Simply, going to sleep after a meal is not observational evidence of profound pleasure.

Second, the level of intensity, in terms of activation, reached during joyful states in infancy is often underestimated. In descriptive, observational terms the excited, ebullient, joyful infant can be at very high levels of activation—almost maximally tolerable by the nervous system, so that if one more drop of excitement is added, he or she will disorganize in distress. So much of the art of delighting an infant requires exactly this regulation of excitation just below the break-point. That is what games like "I'm gonna getcha," or "itsy-bitsy spider," and some bouts of peekaboo are all about. So even from the point of view of intensity, it is not always the case, and not even usually the case, that joy is the less intense form of pleasure.

This comparison of joy and satisfaction may seem artificial, but it is necessary for the discussion to follow. Theories of what comes to be remembered and represented are largely based on such issues as the relative frequency, intensity, and salience of experiences.

Which form of pleasure is more vital for establishing social bonds of attachment in the infant? This has of course been the basic point of departure between object relations theory (including attachment theory) and the more classical libido theory. This dialogue will not be reviewed here, except to note that while people say, referring to classical theory, that "the stomach is the way to a man's heart," they also say that "fear is the lock, but laughter is the key to your heart," referring to attachment theory.

Pleasure and Self-Regulation

There is another, perhaps an important, difference between satisfaction and joy. The infant's capacity for self-regulating his or her own level of activation is different for each. Joy is the product of a mutual regulation of social exchange by both partners. Smiling back and forth is the prototypic example; it usually begins at a relatively low level of intensity. Each partner then progressively escalates—kicking the other into higher orbit, so to speak. The exchange occurs in overlapping waves, where the mother's smile elicits the infant's, which crescendoes just as hers is fading, reanimating her next smile at an even higher level, and so on. These overlapping waves build in intensity until, most often, simultaneous mutual hilarity breaks forth. (See Stern 1977, 1985, for greater detail on these dyadic regulations.) The point is that the infant has equal control over the regulation of the buildup of activation. Further, it is generally the infant who is given (by the parent) major control over the deactivation of the state of joy. This is accomplished with a simple maneuver on the infant's part—usually a gaze aversion with or without a turning away of the head. This maneuver achieves two things at the same time. First, it is a signal to the mother to lower the level of intensity. Second, more important and more immediately effective, it takes the infant out of the field of the exciting stimulation. When infants feel the level of joyful excitation mounting too high, pushing their limits, they will turn away to bring the level of internal activation back down. Once it has fallen, they will turn back and reenter the interaction and reinitiate the excitement. This auto-regulation of internal states can also be evaluated by following the infant's heart rate, which slows dramatically when he or she turns away, starts to climb back when the infant returns to the interaction, and accelerates further as the infant's observable level of activation rises. (A mother can, of course, break the infant's auto-regulation. This is largely what we mean by intrusive maternal behavior at this early age.)

The importance of the auto-regulation of joy lies in the fact that the baby is learning a self-regulatory function, a coping mechanism, and a more inte-grated sense of self at the same time (Stern 1985).

The self-regulatory aspects of satisfaction are less clear. Generally, the infant has less-fine control over the activation and even deactivation, and he or she stands to learn less about self-regulation and what the various functions are that belong to and are controlled by himself or herself. Joy and satisfaction each preside over different aspects of experience.

The Representation of Joyful and of Satisfying Experiences

In the clinical situation, after the infant has grown up, the following ontogenetic question arises: which pleasurable infantile experiences were of sufficient im-portance, salience, or cathexis to be encoded and retrievable and ultimately organized into representations that guide thought and action? The answers in-volve an exploration of the original affect experience and an examination of the likely nature of memory and representation of affective experience.

We will be considering, then, three different forms or domains of experience: (1) the lived experience, (2) the memory of that experience and similar others, and (3) the representation of those experiences.

The first problem encountered is the conceptualization of a lived affective experience for an infant. What are the units of such experiences? How long do they last? What are their boundaries? After all, these units are likely to be the building blocks of representations. Their existence as a heuristic problem seems unavoidable.

Indivisible lived affective experiences come in various forms and sizes. At the shortest end, there are flashbulb experiences which occur instantaneously, that is, essentially having no duration beyond shutter speed. At the other extreme, there are events that might last many minutes, even an hour, which have at least one unchanging, essential feature. Accordingly, they are experienced as a single indivisible unit. Take, for example, what Sunday evenings at home were like when you were a child. Many different things may have happened, but they will exist as subjective units, as certain enduring moments that capture a single indivisible feeling, tone, or state.

As far as joy and satisfaction are concerned, how long might a discrete lived experience be during infancy and of what would it consist? One might imagine that a discrete lived moment of satisfaction would take its duration and form in large part from the hedonic shift from hunger to satisfaction. The perceptual and motor features of the experience would appear to be less marked. In a discrete lived moment of joy the absolute level and minute-by-minute rapid shifts in activation would be highly salient, but so would be the infant's motor behavior and that of the partner and the partner's role as agent and regulator. The two discrete lived moments, as imagined above, would be of different duration and composed of different elements.

Before addressing the question of the potential importance of these differences, I will summarize in an outline a model of the progression from lived affective experiences, to memories of them, to representations.

Think of any kind of lived experience that is affectively loaded. If you are a baby, you may be experiencing it for the first time. We will assume for theoretical reasons that the baby is having a lived affective experience for the first time. This experience is somehow encoded in memory. It is a *specific memory* of something that has actually happened (subjectively). Then the baby has a similar lived experience again. It becomes the second specific memory of that kind of lived event. By the time the baby has registered the second or third similar specific memory, his or her mind will start to operate on those two recalled affective experiences and will do the things that we now expect human minds to do, beginning very early in life. They will identify patterns to try to see what was the same in each of those recalled experiences or memories. That is, they will search for the features common to each memory; these are the invariant features. Other features that change from one memory to the next are the variant features and can be discarded from the composite memory that starts to form. This composite memory of invariant features is thus a prototypic memory.

An example of this process of prototype formation may be seen clearly in an experiment performed on ten-month-old babies (Strauss 1979). The baby is shown a series of schematic drawings of a face. Each drawing differs from the others, in the size of the eyes, length of the nose, or the placement of the ears, and so forth. At the end of the series the baby is "asked" (using a visual preference-habituation paradigm) which drawing of those about to be presented best represents (is seen as most familiar, relative to) the series of drawings already seen. The baby will choose as the most familiar, or most representative, a picture of a face that has, in fact, never been shown, but one that is the mathematical average of all of the positions of the features that have been shown. This is what is meant by forming a prototype of a series of specific memories. The prototype has, in fact, never been experienced; it is a construction from reality—but it represents reality as multiply experienced. In order to avoid having our minds cluttered with specific memories, we merge (and lose) most specific memories by subsuming or integrating them into prototypic memories, so that we are left with fewer specific memories and more generally useful prototypic memories or representations. This example seems to be generally applicable, even though it concerns an experimentally manipulated visual perception and we are interested here in lived affective experience.

Suppose instead that we took a series of pictures of something far more complicated and affectively laden, such as a playful event with laughter between a caregiver and a baby—that enormously common event that occurs many times a day, seven days a week. Accordingly, the baby is in the position of having many instances of this positive affective experience and accordingly, many opportunities to abstract prototypes of what it is like to be in the situation of laughing with somebody who in this case is the mother. Similarly, an infant on a feeding schedule will experience the buildup and satisfaction of hunger four to six times a day, every day.

These examples, "laughing with mother" or "getting hungry and feeding," are lived affective events that contain affects, motives, cognitions, actions, and perceptions. From the point of view so far outlined, a central issue will concern which invariants (affect, motor actions, perceptions, and so on) of the lived experience the infant is capable of registering, or likely to notice and identify. Which of these invariants are privileged because of the infant's constitution or maturational age? Which, if any, invariants have a dominating salience so as to play a more central role in the formation of prototypes and representations? Depending on the answers to these questions, the very nature of the lived experience (as a subjective event) as well as its specific memory, and moreover the nature of the prototypic memory and representation that could result, will all be different.

Let us consider three different points of view and see what differences they will make in our conception of lived experiences and the representations of these affective events.

Centrality of Excitation

This first view holds that the buildup and discharge of excitation, among all the attributes of infant experience, occupies a privileged position as the preemptive feature in defining the subjective unit of a lived event and, therefore, plays the core role in determining the overall nature of representations. This position adheres most closely to Freud's in placing the pleasure principle (in terms of shifts in excitations) in the forefront of consideration. In essence, this position holds that among the welter of features in any lived experience, the organism's first task is to evaluate and react to the internal state of excitation buildup or discharge, so as to keep internal nervous excitation at a minimum. We can call this position that of the *centrality of excitation.* The problems with this position are twofold.

First, it specifies that the infant's primary (and even exclusive) focus and sensibility is directed toward his or her internal state of excitation or subjective hedonic tone. This internal focus has often been assumed to be so preemptive that it does not allow the infant the liberty even to be attentive to the external events that may or may not be related to his internal state. In its extreme, in this view one finds "normally autistic" infants. Given such a state of affairs, all lived experiences will be confined to internal states or gradations of pleasure to unpleasure and the other possible invariants of lived experience (action, perception, and so on) initially go unnoticed.

As the infant becomes more mature, and the "stimulus barrier" less operant, the infant will be in a position to take more notice of the external events that may be invariant features of certain lived events, along with an identifiable gradient of excitation. The door seems to have been opened to a new kind of lived experience and representation, but only partially. The privileged place of the level of excitation and the hedonic tone is never given up—all other attributes of experience (such as perceptions of external events) become part of the representational world as associated (learned) satellites to the level of excitation and the hedonic tone which remains at the center—and remains the sole criteria by which such episodes can be categorized. This was Freud's position in much of his early writings and that of most psychoanalysts when describing the very young infant. It clearly defines and limits the nature of lived experience, and thereby of memory and representation, to global experiences of internal states; these gradually include small, associated pieces of "external" events or even of other internal events.

This position is not only the product of psychoanalytic thinking. Biologists such as Schneila (1959) began a tradition of research which indicated that the organism's first task was to evaluate the strength of stimulation of any event and to determine whether to approach or withdraw based on the evaluation. Survival favored the avoidance of strong stimulation, the approach to mild or moderate stimulation, and the ignoring of very weak stimulation. This is a different version of the pleasure principle, since it seems to require an evaluation of the external milieu rather than of the internal state (although this is not always clear, nor necessary). This version changes the dial setting, so to speak, for pleasure; approach is reset at moderate stimulation (excitation) not at a falling or zero excitation, where Freud had placed it. Nonetheless, the centrality of hedonic tone (that is, excitation or stimulation) remains undiluted as the most basic and salient attribute of experience.

In a different vein, Emde (1980) has shown that as the baby gets older, mothers show a growing confidence in judging different aspects of the baby's internal state. In the youngest babies, the mothers were more confident about judging hedonic tone; as the infants got older, the mothers felt they could judge states of consciousness, and then discrete affect states. Emde suggests that this progression in maternal attribution may parallel an actual progression in the infant. This is a widely held belief, whose conclusion would be that the infant's earliest lived experiences, memories, and representations have hedonic tones that are limited, bounded, or defined. The "stimulus barrier" has been reintroduced, but for different reasons; it is also conceptualized differently.

From this point of view, experiences of satisfaction will form the most important memories and thus the most influential representations, because satisfaction involves the highest levels of excitation and the greatest swings in excitation compared to joy.

The Centrality of the Subjective Qualities of Experiences

This second view assumes that it is the quality of subjective experience, not the shifts in excitation per se, that are the salient elements of experience. Energic shifts and affective quality of experience are unlinked; separate patterns of subjective experience can prevail unrelated to shifts in general excitation. This view permits a variety of affects to occupy center stage as the privileged elements for the formation of lived moments, memories, and representations. Angry representations, joyful ones, and sad ones are all now possible. Here, satisfaction and joy would be equally privileged but would result in quite different experiences, memories, and representations, because they are sufficiently distinct as subjective qualities of experience. This seems reasonable.

A position midway between the centrality of excitation and different subjective qualities of experience is also possible. Pleasure and unpleasure as subjective qualities of experience predominate in such a view, rather than excitation levels and shifts. For instance, one can take the position of the centrality of hedonic tone and then add to it the mechanism of splitting, as did Melanie Klein (1952). The result is two separate and impenetrable types of lived experience—pleasurable and unpleasurable conditions are sufficiently distinct that the organism needs to make dichotomous action decisions, such as whether to approach or withdraw. One could also consider here the weight of cultural evidence suggesting the commonality of good-bad dichotomous categories concerning objects, persons, and events. There is also an accumulating body of evidence suggesting that the nervous system is equipped with a system for the rapid and independent (from cognition or energy shifts) evaluation of the hedonic value of a stimulus (Zajonc 1980) and that such a system should operate very early in infancy.

There are some experiments that bear on the issue of the independence of positive and negative experiences, as far as memory is concerned. Manic patients given a list of items to remember will recall more of them when they have returned to the manic state than when they were in an intervening depressive state. The same is true for manic-depressives taught a list while in the depressive state—they remember more of the items when again in a depressive state (Bower 1981). This controversial research lends some support to the idea of affect state-dependent learning (or recalling). However, what is just as striking as the affect state dependence is the seeming absence of it: the depressed patient will also remember items he or she has learned when manic (and vice-versa, although not as many). In brief, while there may be some affect state–dependent features of memory organization, it is equally clear that attributes of experience encountered under (or encoded during) one hedonic state are readily accessible, or retrievable, in another hedonic state. Certain adult patients (see Kernberg 1980) certainly experience this kind of splitting; however, the distinction between splitting as a defensive event and state-dependent memory as an encoding or recall event needs to be maintained, especially in considering the young infant.

From this variation of the second point of view, joy and satisfaction would be equally pleasurable. Once pleasure and excitation are severed, it is hard to argue that satisfaction is more pleasurable than joy; however, it seems unlikely that they would lose their distinctness.

Any Attribute of Experience as Central

The third view would state that affects are not necessarily privileged attributes of experience so far as memory and representation are concerned. There are two variations of this point of view. First, affects really are privileged attributes, but some of life is encountered under conditions of low or neutral affect. Such conditions are usually obtained in laboratory experiments. The experimenter tries expressly to minimize affective and hedonic variables so as best to study cognition or memory or perception under conditions of relatively neutral affect. The major experimental corpus in developmental psychology results from work under these conditions. Most of what we know about infant memory, affect, categorization, and representation comes from this approach, which makes it abundantly clear that the perceptual, cognitive, motor, and sensory attributes of lived experience will be memorialized and represented even when affect—as one of the attributes—of the lived experience is not very marked. (For example, see the experiment of Strauss described above.)

It is exactly on this point that many psychoanalysts contend that such controlled experiments (affective attributes minimized) are irrelevant for the lived moments of clinical interest, which generally are those occurring when the affective attributes of the experience are assumed to be quite considerable.

Such criticisms are important correctives for reminding us that more experimentation must be done wherein marked affect or hedonic tone is one of the salient attributes of the experimental situation. The number of such attempts is now increasing.

Nonetheless, the following points need to be made: (1) the majority of clinically relevant moments in a developing person's life need not occur under conditions of marked affect (at the time). Such moments are rather the daily and ordinary events of what life is like, and what can be expected in a relationship with self and others (Stern 1985). Such events account for a considerable part of clinical material that during formation did not necessarily contain affect as a striking attribute, only as one of many. (2) While some affect may be a necessary ingredient in any memory—at least in the form of interest so that attention is appropriately distributed—there is no reason to believe that affect plays a special role in the organization of memories, that is, that affect acts like the glue, the core, or the organizing theme, that holds together the other attributes of perception, action, and so forth, in order to create the memorial event. Such a notion is often, as a metaphor, behind our imagined picture of how affect works to create lived moments, their memories, and their representations. There is no evidence for such a view.

A recent experiment in the laboratory tested whether babies would remember a puppet better one week later if the experience with the puppet was accompanied by positive rather than neutral affect. The infants remembered equally well in either case. The presence of positive affect as one of the attributes of the experience did not make remembering any easier (Nachman, Stern, and Best 1986).

A second variation of the position that affects are not necessarily privileged attributes of experience suggests that during a lived experience any one of the attributes of the subjective event may have the central role during that particular lived moment. Thus, for some kinds of experience, the central attribute could be the motive, or the perception, or the motor act, or the state of consciousness. This viewpoint shares much with the idea of Pine (1981) that the infant occupies in the course of a day many different moments of experience that are best considered as organized by different prevailing influences. Pine's argument is directed largely to the conception of a child as being in only one developmental stage and working on only one life issue, such as anality or autonomy as against independence, rather than on the rapid shifts from moment to moment in the prevailing attribute. However, his argument is readily usable in this context as well. The solution makes eminent clinical sense, as most memories seem to be dominated by one attribute that acts as the key to the moment—in the sense of creating, delineating, and organizing the moment in memory. In such a system, affect per se need not have the privileged role for any given lived moment, memory, or representation, but it could—or it could give over such a role to another attribute. In either event one of the attributes is fulfilling this assumed central role of organizer of the lived moment and core of the memory.

No Attribute is Ever Central

Suppose, for an additional point of view, that there is no need for one or another attribute to assume a central role. That is, lived moments do not necessarily organize around a central and privileged attribute, even momentarily. Rather, all attributes are equal as far as memory is concerned. This viewpoint represents the most extreme version of the assumption that affects are not privileged attributes of experience, as far as the creation of a clinically relevant representational world is concerned. The separate attributes are given equal status in this moment and equal structural roles in the organization of the moment. This is the model used in the memory research when considering episodic memories. This model allows for the greatest flexibility and for a greater range of interconnections between representational elements; in this sense, it is closest to what is clinically evident.

This last point of view and the previous one would give joy certain advantages over satisfaction as an event to be encoded in memory, retrieved, and represented. Namely, the infant is more likely in a joyful experience to be attentive to many more elements of the lived moment: what he or she is doing as well as feeling, what mother is doing, his or her role as agent, his or her role as self regulator. Accordingly, the network of elements in the lived moment will be richer, the representation can be accessed more readily from many different points, and will also be applicable to a wider variety of life experiences.

I have gone into some detail and speculation here because the different weight and role we give to different attributes of an infant's lived experience will ultimately determine how we conceptualize the nature of his or her subjective experience and representations of pleasure. It will also define the very unit of experience that makes up our subjectivity, the general rules whereby memories have access to other memories, and the structure and integrability of some of our representations. Finally, the differential consideration of the various attributes of lived experience will open up different paths for distortion on the infant's part and for different kinds of fantasy formation. The different weights given to the various attributes of experience will determine which kinds of personal subjective constructions of reality are most likely to emerge.

REFERENCES

Berlyne, D. E. 1966. Curiosity and exploration. *Science* 153:25–33.

Bower, G. 1981. Mood and memory. *American Psychologist* 36:129–48.

Emde, R. N. 1980. Levels of meaning for infant emotions: A biosocial view. In *Development of cognition, affect, and social relations*, ed. W. A. Collins. Hillsdale, N.J.: Erlbaum.

Kernberg, O. F. 1980. *Internal world and external reality: Object relations theory applied.* New York: Aronson.

Klein, M. 1952. *Developments in psychoanalysis*, ed. J. Rivere. London: Hogarth Press.

Nachman, P.; Stern, D. N.; and Best, C. 1986. Affective reactions to stimuli and infants' preference for novelty and familiarity. *Journal of the American Academy of Child Psychiatry* 6(25): 801–4.

Pine, J. F. 1981. In the beginning: Contributions to a psychoanalytic developmental psychology. *International Review of Psychoanalysis* 8:15–33.

Schneila, T. C. 1959. On evolutionary and developmental theory of biphasic processes underlying approach and withdrawal. In *Nebraska Symposium on Motivation*, ed. M. R. Jones. Lincoln: University of Nebraska Press.

Stern, D. N. 1977. *The first relationship: Infant and mother.* Cambridge: Harvard University Press.

Stern, D. N. 1985. *The Interpersonal World of the Infant: A View from Psychoanalysis and Developmental Psychology.* New York: Basic Books.

Strauss, M. S. 1979. Abstraction of proto-typical information by adults and ten-month-old infants. *Journal of Experimental Psychology: Human Learning and Memory* 5:618–32.

Zajonc, R. B. 1980. Feeling and thinking: Preferences need no inferences. *American Psychologist* 35(2): 151–75.

2

Play, Pleasure, Reality

EUGENE MAHON, M.D.

A man should be able to play the flute but not too well.
—Aristotle

The relationship between affect, the principal topic of this volume, and play may not seem immediately obvious. And yet if one takes an old definition of affect as the discharge phenomena of the instincts, a definition antiquated to ears that have become more attuned to ego psychology and object relations theory than to the atavistic hydraulics of early Freudian theory, one gets the impression that an organism laden with affects that press for discharge will need "intermediaries" if chaos and caprice are ever to be transformed into law and order. The ego is by definition a warehouse of intermediaries, but developmentally play may be without equal in its role as conductor of the affective orchestra.

If thought is trial action—the psyche mulling over its strategies before action is taken—then play is trial action, whereby the mind uses action itself to modify action and to titrate affect. A child cannot manage the complexity of affect and conflict as a whole: it approaches the issue piecemeal, breaking large psychic phenomena into components that can be managed discretely in play. In a sense, play is a dress rehearsal for the theaters of reality that the child faces every day. If Winnicott is correct, this theater opens its doors very early in the child's development indeed. Already, in the first year of life, the infant invests the blanket with the feel and smell of mother and begins to rely on this "illusion" to survive the first experiences of separation, the first affects of loss, and the first aesthetic attempts at separation. Winnicott calls this "transitional" object the first *not-me* possession, suggesting one of the ironies of the human condition: our possessions establish a sense of self, to be sure, but they also inevitably signal the existence of the other. This is nowhere more poignantly obvious than in infancy, when the mind confronted with the first subjectivity of loss creates a comforting illusion out of a piece of cloth! For Winnicott, reality always inhabits this space between illusion and disillusionment, with play the great psychic organizer that straddles both. If the mind is forever pulled and pushed by vectors of pleasure and dictates of reality, play is one of the early developmental jugglers that keeps these principles aloft; the principles are psychic spheres, so to speak, that must learn to be equally at home grounded or up in the air.

In *Beyond the Pleasure Principle* (1920), Freud asserted that although play may seem at times to be beyond the pleasure principle, it actually is not. In fact Freud used the example of his grandson's manipulation of the pull toy to show that play conforms to the dictates of the pleasure principle, whereas transference and the death instinct yearn to repeat past traumas and thus to disobey the pleasure principle, marching to the beat of a very different psychic drummer.

My argument, if I can get beyond the intimidation principle and disagree with Freud, will suggest that play is both within and beyond the pleasure principle all at once: mind is the sum of its principles, and play—like any other mental product—will reflect all the coordinates of psychic determinism, not just two or more principles of mental functioning but all the imaginable principles of psychic life.

The evolution of Freud's ideas is the best confirmation of what I have just said: Freud invented principles and discarded them. His mind was as restless as the restless topic he sought to explore. His heroic imagination, if I can steal a phrase from Frederic Ewen, could be pictured as a series of beyond the beyonds. Beyond the neurology of Jean Charcot, he discovered, side by side with Charcot, the psychic correlatives of what until then had been a neurology of hysteria. But beyond neurology lay the psychic principle; it was still, however, embedded in a cultural, environmental principle at this stage of Freud's development in the 1890s. Seduction was still an adult perversion, not yet a corrupt motivation of the innocent. But suddenly, beyond the seduction hypothesis, Freud discovered the corrupt imagination of children. Beyond the principle of unconscious imagination he discovered the tripartite structures of the oedipal mind. Beyond the classical Greek of the Oedipus complex he discovered the Minoan-Mycenaean fossils of a preoedipal life. Beyond the pleasure principle he discovered death. And beyond death he discovered analysis terminable and interminable, which might have been subtitled "beyond therapeutic optimism."

Let us focus for a moment on Freud the child observer. Here are some excerpts from the celebrated passage in *Beyond the Pleasure Principle* in which he describes his grandson's reaction to brief separations from the mother.

> This good little boy, however, had an occasional disturbing habit of taking any small objects he could get hold of and throwing them away from him into a corner, under the bed, and so on, so that hunting for his toys and picking them up was often quite a business. As he did this he gave vent to a loud, long-drawn-out "o-o-o-o," accompanied by an expression of interest and satisfaction. His mother and the writer of the present account were agreed in thinking that this was not a mere interjection but repre-

sented the German word "*fort*" ["gone"]. I eventually realized that it was a game and that the only use he made of any of his toys was to play "gone" with them. One day I made an observation which confirmed my view. The child had a wooden reel with a piece of string tied round it. It never occurred to him to pull it along the floor behind him, for instance, and play at its being a carriage. What he did was to hold the reel by the string and very skillfully throw it over the edge of his curtained cot, so that it disappeared into it, at the same time uttering his expressive "o-o-o-o." He then pulled the reel out of the cot again by the string and hailed its reappearance with a joyful "*da*" ["there"]. This, then, was the complete game—disappearance and return. As a rule one only witnessed its first act, which was repeated untiringly as a game in itself, though there is no doubt that the greater pleasure was attached to the second act.

The interpretation of the game then became obvious. It was related to the child's great cultural achievement—the instinctual renunciation (that is, the renunciation of instinctual satisfaction) which he had made in allowing his mother to go away without protesting. He compensated himself for this, as it were, by himself staging the disappearance and return of the objects within his reach. (Standard Edition 18, 14–15)

Freud makes it clear that the child was using rudimentary play and language to master the affects that each human being must struggle with as the reality of physical and psychic separateness sinks in.

What does all this have to do with the topic of affect? What light can the introduction of child's play and the endlessly playful mind of Sigmund Freud shed on such a serious topic? It is my belief that the ability to express affects in words and to communicate these words affectively to another human being is the hallmark of the human condition at its most superlative. Some people never reach this state of affairs. Others do mature into it with or without psychoanalytic help, depending on their constitutions and on their experiences. My argument suggests that children are born expressing affects mindlessly and wordlessly. Gradually they discover their minds and their words. Play is one of the grand intermediary steps. Time and again in child analysis we can see examples of children struggling to tell us about a complicated affect but first mulling over the components of it in play. In adult analysis one sees a similar struggle, of course, but the adult analysand does not reach concretely for the building blocks to make an architectural statement of his or her needs and frustrations as children do. He or she reaches, to be sure, for transference, resistance, and defense before stumbling on insight and genuine communication of affect. A stretch of the imagination could gather all these adult reachings into a general definition of play, but this overinclusiveness blurs rather than defines, rendering definition itself a verbal utensil that has lost its usefulness.

If affect is mostly action—initially the kickings and thrashings, the smiles and nonverbal whispers, the colics and frolics, the fussiness of immediate post-umbilical life—it should come as little surprise perhaps that Homo sapiens (as a fledgling) might use a product half action, half symbol, to intermediate between the unrememberable action-affects that mark the shaky dawn of life and the unforgettable verbal attempts of the imagination to hold on to the unholdable. One is reminded of Freud's definition of instinct as half mental, half physical; in that context play could be seen as the ego's aesthetic response to the instinctual life of the id.

If as Freud insisted instinct is half physical, half mental, is it not neat and contrapuntal that play would seem to be half symbol and half action? In fact, for Jean Piaget it is an incremental series of sensorimotor actions that eventually creates the symbol. Fingers in motion create numbers, not vice versa. Abstraction is born in a concrete cradle of flesh.

I realize that I have been talking about play without defining it. Allow me to introduce my own idiosyncratic definition.

Whereas the modern definition of play as "games, diversion" captures the "ludic" nature of the activity, the Anglo-Saxon meaning of play (*plega*) implied less sportive intent, that is, to strike a blow (*asc–plega* = playing with spears, that is, fighting with spears, or *sword–plega*, fighting with swords [Skeat 1976]). How etymology shifts the meaning of a deadly earnest word describing warlike activity to a totally new sense that implies action as "only playing," is one of the ironies of the history of language. Even the notion of playing the cymbals or the piano owes its meaning to violence in the sense that one *strikes* the instrument. Perhaps the history of the concept of sublimation lies hidden in these shifting meanings, in the psychological journey from swordplay to the bloodless percussion of musical instruments.

If we follow these etymological leads, play would seem to have begun with actions that were anything but "playful" in the modern use of the word. Action, however, would seem to be the hallmark of play in ancient or modern usage, certainly common to swordplay or child's play. But action of a unique kind. *Action*, for a psychoanalyst, is a complicated, intriguing word. If we borrow one of Freud's early insights about source, aim, impetus, and object, new light will fall on this discussion. Freud, as we know, said that human psychological events could be broken into components that would allow a dissection of the phenomena that might otherwise escape attention. Human motivation has a source (in erogenous zones), an aim (in the actions that bring about satisfaction), an impetus (the quantitative factor), and an object (the least stable of the variables, according to Freud). The subject matter of play would seem to be primarily *aims* and their vicissitudes. This is not to say that play and action are synonymous. Sucking, one of the aims of the mouth, is not an example of playing. And yet an infant can "play" with food, much to the exasperation of mothers who overvalue nutrition and undervalue exploration. The difference between eating, sucking, swallowing, and activities of the mouth that might be called playful (such as blowing bubbles or whistling) surely lies in the aim and its vicissitudes. The adage that "you can't whistle and chew gum" captures the conflict between aims of instant gratification, and aims in which postponement, delay, experimentation, detour, and compromise lead to other horizons of pleasure.

While we can speak of play according to its multiple functions, developmental aspects (presymbolic, symbolic, and so on), or its contacts with other mental activities (fantasy, drives), the essential and required ingredient in the definition from a formal point of view would seem to be action—not all action, but discrete types of action in which immediate gratification of instinct is not the goal, and exploration and even the creation of reality above and beyond immediate gratification take precedence over desire. Thus, ironically, play that is not supposed to be "for real" is the greatest ally of the reality principle in its struggle with the pleasure principle.

A working definition of play, therefore, would suggest perhaps that play consists of actions in humans or animals that do not seek immediate gratification of desire or the obvious solution of a problem, but seem rather to explore alternate or multiple possibilities of experience. If reflex is the shortest distance between the two points of stimulus and response, play would seem to be the opposite of reflex, a protean defiance of the reflex arc in favor of expanded horizons, in which new meanings, new experiences can be explored. In humans, as opposed to animals, in play one can explore options with the assistance of thought and fantasy. It is this cooperation between the actions of play and the other psychic realms of thought and fantasy that makes play the great window into the psyche that the child analyst can exploit so profitably. In the strictest sense, however, play should not be confused with thought or fantasy even when it is inextricably bound up with them. A psychoanalytic definition of play would narrow the meaning to the realm of aims and their vicissitudes. Even the concept of playing with words, or playing with ideas (the hallmark of formal thought, according to Piaget) should not intimidate us or force us to relinquish the core of the definition, since these examples imply internalized *actions*—thought itself is compared by Freud to trial action. If action has a complicated history from its birth in the reflex arc to maturity in decisive behavior, becoming a slave of the unconscious all too often in periods of acting out, it nevertheless has a creative workshop called play where the future can be worked on before it happens. To confine the definition in this manner need not restrict it: if play is neither acting out nor fully realized action, it is nevertheless the crucible in which make-believe reaches toward belief, and doubt advances toward conviction.

My thesis gets support from developmental facts: when the adolescent mind develops the more sophisticated hypothetico-deductive reasoning or, as Piaget would put it, when preoperational and operational cognition yield to the higher level formal operations, play recedes also, and playful thought takes over. Play has become internalized as the action-oriented childish mind grows up.

In *Play, Dreams and Imitation in Childhood* (1962) Piaget gave his most elaborate description of the process of play, comparing it to imitation. For Piaget two principles characterize the adaptive struggles of the human mind: each person comes in contact with the phenomenal world and either accommodates or assimilates it (or, most likely, uses a combination of both strategies). An example will illustrate these processes more graphically than terms alone: when one grasps an orange one *accommodates* one's hand to the shape of the orange, the better to hold it; when one peels the orange or squeezes the juice out of it, one has *assimilated* the orange to one's own desires, the better to acquire its nourishment.

Comparing and contrasting play and imitation, Piaget asserted that in play assimilation triumphs whereas in imitation accommodation seems to be the goal. These insights have obvious implications from a psychiatric point of view, although I doubt that Piaget ever spelled them out as such. The as-if character would seem to have a disease of accommodation, a false self that can mold itself slavishly to the needs of others rather than staking out some autonomous psychological territory for itself alone. Pathological narcissism of the Napoleonic variety could be characterized as a malady of assimilation, in which tyranny of self-aggrandizement attempts to subject the rest of the world to its own monopoly of desire. These disorders of "play" and "imitation," the Napoleons or Zeligs of our world, could of course be defined also as diseases of affect: the as-if cannot tolerate the anxiety of opposing his self against another's, and the pathological narcissist cannot tolerate the emotional interplay with anyone else's needs. These are the grossest of oversimplifications, to be sure; the crucial point being stressed here is that play and imitation as reflected in character styles are only the visible phenomenological counterparts of affective processes that are decidedly more hidden.

If these definitions of play are correct, a pathology of the process is definable from yet another standpoint. Irving Steingart has described pathological play in his remarkable book, *Pathological Play in the Borderline and Narcissistic Personalities* (1985). Compressing Steingart's complex ideas into a sentence or two will do violence to the scope of his thesis; nonetheless, here is the gist of his argument. Play like other mental activities strives to create meaning. If a healthy mind is the sum of its meanings—consensually validatable meanings—then a meaning disturbance can exist as an expression of pathology. Pathological play as opposed to normal play will express such meaning disturbances. A patient who refuses to lie on the couch but needs to sit on the analyst's desk and look down at him, the way adults once looked down at her in childhood, is in the grip of pathological play that relies on concrete preconceptual imagery rather than on higher level imagery in the Piagetian sense. Steingart implies that play that can be idealized as purely aesthetic, and therefore a quality of Homo sapiens at his or her most sapient, can also however be seen as ludicrous—etymological pun intended. If illusion means *in ludens,* the willing suspension of ourselves in play, then the word *ludicrous* seems to remind us that fool-acting is also an inevitable aspect of man that defines his worst and limits his best.

So far I have suggested that play is the ego's adaptive aesthetic mode of dealing with the pressures of the id, helping the developing mind to harness affect and language, to play the great ambassador, the resourceful go-between, "the tireless explorer," as Chukovsky might have put it. I have also said that play is both beyond and within the pleasure principle, and I would like to illustrate this seeming contradiction with a couple of examples of child's play.

Case 1 is Freud's grandson from *Beyond the Pleasure Principle.* The details as quoted earlier are well known: missing his mother, the child invented a game of loss and retrieval, which at first seemed to be preoedipal in nature but later took on oedipal significance when father was away. Later when the mother died, the child showed no signs of grief. Freud seems to be implying that the triumph of aggression in the game of good riddance allowed the child a griefless victory when the mother actually died. I doubt that anyone would read this material similarly today. Freud, grief stricken at the death of his daughter, was probably astonished at the seeming callousness of the little boy. One is reminded here of the film *Jeux interdits* (Forbidden Games), in which the children suddenly bereaved show no emotion; instead, they involve themselves in cemetery games. They bury things and place crosses over them. When their forbidden games are discovered by the elders, they are chastised, stripped of their defenses, and the unsheddable tears begin to flow. I have argued elsewhere (Mahon 1977) that these forbidden games are the grief of the child framed by the proscenium arch of play. An adult may misread this play as callous, but this is merely a confusion of tongues, as Sándor Ferenczi would have put it. Freud does not give us a follow-up report on his grandson, but we can assume that his hidden grief found expression beyond the pleasure principle in repetition compulsions of resurrection and loss.

Case 2 is somewhat similar to Freud's. A child whose mother did not die but was in many ways emotionally unavailable to him from his birth onward had relied on a warm, primitive housekeeper to fulfill his needs. This surrogate was extremely important since the father's oedipal rivalry with his son did not allow him to be maternal and fill in for the emotionally disturbed mother. When the surrogate left suddenly, this boy went wild. The reason for his wildness was poorly understood until his grief emerged a year into his analysis at age five and a half: like that of the children in *Jeux interdits*, his unspeakable grief could not emerge in word or affect until play built a proscenium to hold the drama in place, in person, in time.

Let me describe his play before and after he told me of his grief. For the first six months of his analysis, his play was a grand theater of transference resistance: he built huge towers of blocks and knocked them down as if to show me he could build a universe, destroy it and make it rise again pheonixlike no matter what I said. There was no question that the play had to do with every component of preoedipal life and oedipal life; loss of the object, loss of the love of the object, and castration all merged in a symphonic statement. The elegant power of his defenses was all that could be interpreted at this stage, or else, like Berta Bornstein's King Booboo (1949), he would have panicked at the least stripping of his defensive camouflage. But it was clear that while he was keeping his analyst at a distance by insisting on his own phallic autonomy, he was also dying to get close. This emerged in the eighth month of the analysis in a crucial piece of play. He was playing with a boat being buffeted by giant waves. He brought the boat home safely to port (the "terminal," as he called it) and then turned to the analyst and said genuinely, "Maybe you can become a person-terminal for me?" This was a crucial therapeutic moment. The child was compressing many metaphors into one epiphany of insight. The displacement of his plight in the play boat and terminal was suddenly available to him in a less displaced form. The diminutive analysand seemed to be saying: "I can explore the typhoons and shipwrecks that toss the fragile vessel of my mind but return from the seas of transference to the safe port of the analytic situation in which the analyst as person will moor the transference safely back in the harbor of reality." The analyst could be a person terminal, a safe human refuge for the patient. Person-terminal does suggest a darker motif, of course—the image of people terminating their relationships—but the available affect at this therapeutic moment seemed to be trust and reaching out toward the analyst, and this was the affective connection that was negotiated. The analyst said, "Yes. When you're afraid like a ship at sea with so many feelings, I will try to help you understand what you feel and get over your fears." The darker side of his communication was analyzed later. The images contained in this piece of play continued to generate new therapeutic moments. When his parents would try to appease him by shoving a toy in his face, he would complain to his analyst, "Don't they know I need the person feelings?" In terms of the boat, as the analysis proceeded, he carved boats out of wood, calling one the "Catch-up," a multidetermined vessel that was meant to catch up with losses of mother, housekeeper, father, and so on. When termination was an issue, when his person-terminal was about to leave him, he made a boat with his own initials and mine carved into it, making a covenant between us that would survive the separation, a child's version of Horace's *Exegi monumentum aere perennius* ("I have built a monument more lasting than bronze").

I think you may agree with me that this play and its vicissitudes throughout the analysis suggest that my patient was both within and beyond the pleasure principle, depending on the shifting meteorology of transference. Let me explain. "Maybe you can be a person-terminal for me" could have two—at least two—meanings, one within and the other beyond the pleasure principle: (1) I hope you will help me when the going gets rough with my affects; and (2) I hope you will disappoint me also and permit me to wallow in the death instincts of despair and depression and masochism.

I want to leave the world of children briefly and make a few comments about the relevance of play in adult analysis.

If play is the sine qua non of child analysis, why is it that so little play and so few memories of play seem to present themselves for scrutiny in adult analysis? Is the playground really condemned, as Cyril Connolly suggested in another context? Memories of play in adult analysis seem to be unusual, swept away it would seem by infantile amnesia and developmental progressions. In comparing borderline patients to neurotics, it has been suggested that persistence of imaginary companions into adult life in borderlines contrasts strikingly with their disappearance under normal developmental circumstances, in which they are discarded after they have outlived their usefulness. Could we entertain a similar hypothesis in regard to memories of play? Let me try to be clearer. I am suggesting that memory usually relies on infantile amnesia and a handful of screen memories, or a recurrent dream perhaps, to organize the past, to synthesize a personal myth, to rehistoricize the historical truth with the fiction and nonfiction of narrative. Memories of play and the day-to-day existentials of life seem to get short shrift in revisionist histories of memory. When a patient tells us that he remembers his play, our ears are alerted. A hypothesis begins to germinate. Do certain patients need to remember play experience for dynamic reasons? Why was screen memory and dream not enough for them? Did they need to remember an action-packed drama, as depicted in play, rather than a still life of memory as depicted in the usual icons that memory preserves as fossils under the glass of infantile amnesia?

A clinical vignette is required to highlight this issue. An adult patient in analysis remembers recurrent playing with cutout dolls and the clothes they would wear. She assembles the dolls. She prepares their wardrobes. This takes so long the dolls never interact. If my hypothesis is correct, this patient needed to block certain holes in her infantile amnesia with memories of play in which she assembled, and clothed, and rehearsed the protagonists but never let them interact in any real drama. In the transference she bent over backward not to interact with me. She continuously clothed herself and me in defensive narratives, but she rarely let the curtain rise on the affects in the transference that she perceived as overwhelming.

Eventually, cannibalism, jealousy, and ambition (preoedipal and oedipal) rocked the transference and made clear what unconscious activities were being screened by unconscious passivities. But the key point being stressed here is that if the mind in general is a delicate balance between active and passive aims, certain individuals with active-passive imbalances may want to remember the action language of play rather than the inert still lifes of screen memory. Just as the stillness of the wolves in the Wolf Man's dreams alerted Freud to the activities they were hiding, might memories of play not conceal the *passivities* of psychic life, which need to be disavowed?

Discussion

Affect defies definition. Freud circumvented the problem of definition somewhat when he invented the mythology of instincts and tried to picture the mind as force and counterforce, using the cybernetics of energy and energy regulation. His much-criticized hydraulic metaphors have not been replaced by metaphors that sparkle with avant-garde clarity; the whole topic of affect is far from a psychological explication that is comprehensive, coherent, or in any way convincing. Affect seems to invite definition from within and without, but it seems nonetheless mercurial regardless of one's approach. If one approaches from "without," describing the behavioral equivalents of affects, one ends up describing actions, as Darwin does in *The Expression of the Emotions in Man and Animals* or as Emde, Harmon, and Gaensbauer do in *Emotional Expression in Infancy* (1976). This is not a criticism; it is merely a recognition of the limits of the mode of research. Darwin was attempting to describe the muscular pathways of affect in man and animals, the synergisms and antagonisms of actions beneath the skin that culminated in the sneer or the smile, the facial architecture of contempt or fear, the loss of face in shame, and so on. Similarly, the infant researchers without language to guide them use inference and observation to pursue the genetic choreography of affect in gesture and body language. The mystery of affective origins can pull poetry from the stones of the most hardheaded research: Spitz (1972), for instance, argues that the birth cry is "an experience when affect and percept meet for the first time and also as the first experience of *time* in the form of duration of unpleasure. The factor of duration moves in a direction opposite to the Nirvana principle of immediate discharge. The addition of the time dimension promotes an active preference for percepts with survival value. Affects, thereby, direct and quicken perception." The psychoanalyst approaching affect from within is not to be envied by ethologists or infant researchers, because his intrapsychic vantage point at times seems to offer no more illumination than a window opening on the night. If making unconscious affects conscious is the analyst's therapeutic mandate and daily labor, this does not imply that guilt, envy, pride, hatred, and joy can be desynthesized like chemicals in a solvent. At the risk of being tautological, one can still assert that mind is a mystery. If scientists still argue as to its location (there is no absolute proof that it is housed in the brain or that such metaphors as house or brain can even begin to define it), its component affects will hardly yield their secrets to a psychoanalytic paint-by-numbers technique. This is not scientific nihilism, merely a sober description of the art in the final decades of the twentieth century. In fact, I believe that the humble product, play, can approach the mystery of affect and at times speak more eloquently than verbal language itself. I have argued that play's unique intermediary location between gesture and symbol may afford it an unusual perspective on the journey of affect from inception to execution. If "the play's the thing to catch the conscience of the king," it seems to be able to catch not merely the affects of the superego, but the emotional derivatives of the ego and id as well. If transference is the adult equivalent of play, one comes away with the impression that these two play-modes of childhood and adulthood are the theaters par excellence in which affects can come out of hiding and rehearse and perform before the curtain rises on post childhood, on postanalytic experience. To paraphrase Montaigne, then, while play is not "real," it may be very "serious" indeed!

Conclusion

1. I have suggested that play is within the confines of the pleasure principle but also beyond it.

2. I have attempted to provide a tentative psychoanalytic definition of play, suggesting that the hallmark of play has to do with aims and their vicissitudes. If reflex is action at its most primitive, and mature decision making is action at its most developed, then play holds an intermediate position between these poles.

3. I have suggested that affect expression in words portrays the human mind at the pinnacle of its development. The immature mind is afraid of affect and relies initially on play to dramatize the components of the theater of affect before all the pieces can be assembled in words.

4. I have suggested that if instinct is half mental, half physical, in a contrapuntal corollary play is half action, half symbol. Play is the ego's response to the challenges of the id. If in a Newtonian sense every action is met with an equal counter reaction, play is the ego's reaction to the actions of the id.

5. I have argued that if play can be described as normal, there is nonetheless a pathology of the process.

6. I have suggested that play seems to be remembered little in adult analysis. When play *is* described by the adult analysand, it may mean that screen memory and the infantile amnesia were not reconciled enough to hold the personal myth in place. Memories of action-in-play were required to maintain the balance between active and passive aims in the delicate balancing act of the mind.

7. I am perhaps now ready to explain Aristotle's cryptic comment: "A man should be able to play the flute but not too well." I feel that Aristotle is saying that the play of aesthetics is part of a well-rounded mind but is not all of it. Play, as D. W. Winnicott (1971) put it, is inherently exciting but also inherently precarious. One senses that Aristotle, if asked to comment on play, would have said, "Play? Yes. Play is a phenomenon like pleasure and reality. Let's not idealize it. Let's study it."

REFERENCES

Bornstein, Berta. 1949. "The Analysis of a Phobic Child." *Psychoanalytic Study of the Child*, vols. 3, 4. New York: International Universities Press.

Chukovsky, Kornei. 1971. *From Two to Five*. Berkeley: University of California Press.

Emde, R. N.; Gaensbauer, T.; and Harmon, R. 1976. Emotional Expression in Infancy: A Biobehavioral Study. *Psychological Issues*, Monograph 37. New York: International Universities Press.

Ewen, Frederic. 1984. *Heroic Imagination*. Secaucus, N.J.: Citadel Press.

Freud, Sigmund. [1920] 1971. *Beyond the Pleasure Principle. Standard edition*, 18.

Mahon, Eugene. 1977. "The Painted Guinea Pig." *Psychoanalytic Study of the Chid*, vol. 32.

Piaget, Jean. 1962. *Play, Dreams and Imitation in Childhood.* New York: W. W. Norton.

Skeat, Walter W. 1976. *An Etymological Dictionary of the English Language.* London: Oxford University Press.

Spitz, R. A. 1972. "Bridges: On Anticipation, Duration and Meaning." *Journal of the American Psychoanalytic Association* 20:727–28.

Steingart, Irving. 1983. *Pathological Play in Borderline and Narcissistic Personalities.* New York: Spectrum Publications.

Winnicott, D. W. 1971. *Playing and Reality.* New York: Basic Books.

3

A Developmental Approach to Pleasure and Sexuality

STANLEY I. GREENSPAN, M.D.

The role of pleasure and sexuality in human development and personality functioning has long been recognized, from Freud's early work, including his *Three Essays on the Theory of Sexuality* (1905), to more recent studies relating emotional, neurophysiologic, and anatomic dimensions of sexuality. To understand pleasure and sexuality in the context of more recent clinical observations of infants and young children, I will trace its development from infancy in the context of a new model of development, a developmental structuralist model (Greenspan 1979, 1981, 1987), which postulates a series of substages to account for the unique way in which individuals organize their experiential world.

The Developmental Structuralist Approach

We developed an approach that focuses on the organizational level of personality along multiple dimensions and on mediating processes or "structures." People working in many fields of medicine had long ago learned enough about pathologic and adaptive pathways to understand the organizational and intervening pathophysiologic processes between etiological factors and response patterns. For example, an understanding of allergic mechanisms suggests that individuals regardless of their different symptom complexes may be having a common allergic reaction.

With regard to our approach to adaptive and pathologic personality configurations, there was a need for a classification system that would focus on the organism's individual way of processing, organizing, integrating, and differentiating multiple dimensions of experience—that is, the pathways that lead to certain behavioral outcomes. This "final common pathway" connects the influence of multiple etiological factors with varying outcomes and suggests something fundamental about the organism's manner of organizing its experience of its world, internal and external, animate and inanimate. At each developmental stage the characteristics that define the experiential organization may be viewed as a structure (Piaget 1962, 1970). Piaget (1970) provided a detailed review of structuralism in both its larger context and as applied to understanding psychological process. Piaget, as Cicchetti and Hesse (1983) have recently pointed out, had an affective as well as an impersonal cognitive theory, described most fully in his 1954 lectures at the Sorbonne (Piaget 1954). For a variety of reasons, however, Piaget did not attempt to integrate the notions of the drive, wish, and dynamic unconscious into his formulations (Greenspan 1979). The developmental structuralist approach defines these experiential organizations (structures) at each stage for depth psychological-emotional as well as cognitive experience (Greenspan 1979).

There are two assumptions related to this approach. One is that the capacity to organize experience is present very early in life and progresses to higher levels as the individual matures. This implies an ability to organize in stable patterns an ever-widening and more complex range of experience. For example, it is now well documented that the infant is capable, even at birth or shortly thereafter, of organizing experience in an adaptive fashion. He or she can respond to pleasure and displeasure (Lipsitt 1966); change behavior as a function of its consequences (Gewirtz 1965, 1969); form intimate bonds and make visual discriminations (Klaus and Kennell 1976; Meltzoff and Moore 1977); organize cycles and rhythms—for example, sleep-wake, alertness states (Sander 1962); evidence a variety of affects or affect proclivities (Tomkins 1963; Izard 1978; Ekman 1972); and demonstrate organized social responses in conjunction with increasing neurophysiologic organization (Emde, Gaensbauer, and Harmon 1976). It is interesting that this empirically documented view of the infant is consistent with Freud's early hypotheses (1911) and Hartmann's postulation (1939) of an early undifferentiated organizational matrix. That the organization of experience broadens during the early months of life to reflect increases in the capacity to experience and tolerate a range of stimuli, including responding in social interaction in stable and personal configurations, is also consistent with recent empirical data (Emde et al. 1976; Stroufe, Waters, and Matas 1974; Escalona 1968; Stern 1974a, 1974b; Sander 1962; Brazelton, Koslowski, and Main 1974; Murphy and Moriarty 1976). That increasingly complex patterns continue to emerge as the infant further develops is indicated by complex emotional responses such as surprise (Charlesworth 1969), affiliation, and wariness and fear (Ainsworth, Bell, and Stayton 1974; Bowlby 1969; Sroufe and Waters 1977) observed between seven and twelve months; exploration and "refueling" patterns (Mahler, Pine, and Bergman 1975); behavior suggesting functional understanding of objects (Werner and Kaplan 1963) observed in the middle to latter part of the second year of life; and the eventual emergence of symbolic capacities (Piaget 1962; Gouin-Decarie 1965; Bell 1970).

The interplay between age-appropriate experience and maturation of the central nervous system ultimately determines the characteristics of this organizational capacity at each phase. The active and experiencing child uses his maturational capacities to engage the world in ever-changing and more complex ways. In addition to a characteristic organizational level, a second assumption is that for each phase of development there are also certain characteristic types of experience (for example, interests, wishes, fears, curiosities) that play themselves out, so to speak, within this organizational structure.

The organizational level of experience may be delineated along a number of parameters, including age or phase *appropriateness* (see table 3.1 for a description of expected capacities), *range* and *depth* (animate and inanimate, full range of affects and themes), *stability* (response to stress), and *personal uniqueness*.

The other component of an individual's experiential world relates to the *type* of experience organized. Here one looks at the specific affects and behavioral patterns or later, at thoughts, concerns, inclinations, wishes, fears, and so on. The type of experience is, in a sense, the drama the youngster is experiencing, whereas the organizational level might be viewed metaphorically as the stage upon which this drama is being played out. To carry this metaphor a step further, it is possible to imagine some stages that are large and stable and can therefore support a complex and intense drama. In contrast, other stages may be narrow or small, able to contain only a very restricted drama. Still other stages may have cracks in them and crumble easily under the pressure of an intensely rich and varied drama.

According to the developmental structuralist approach, at each phase of development, certain characteristics define the experiential organizational capacity, that is, the stability and contour of the stage. At the same time, there are certain age-expectable dramas, themes characterized by their complexity, richness, depth, and content.

The degree to which an individual experiences the full range of stage- and age-appropriate experience in stable, stress-resilient, personal configurations may be viewed as an indicator of the involvement in a particular stage of development and readiness for progressing into those experiential realms that emerge from these earlier ones and constitute part of the next developmental stage. In this sense, the most optimally adaptive structure at each developmental stage facilitates further development.

The developmental structuralist approach is unique in an important respect. In focusing on levels and organizations of experience, it alerts the clinician to look not only for what the infant or toddler is *evidencing* (for example, psychopathology) but for what he or she is *not evidencing*. For example, the eight-month-old who is calm, alert, and enjoyable but has no capacity for discrimination or reciprocal social interchanges may be of vastly more concern than an irritable, negativistic, food-refusing, night-awakening eight-month-old with age-appropriate capacities for differentiation and reciprocal social interchanges. In other words, each stage of development may be characterized according to "expected" organizational characteristics. Specific symptoms or behaviors in this

Table 3.1. Developmental Structuralist Approaches to Development Stages

Stage-Specific Tasks and Capacities	Capacities		Environment (Care Giver)	
	Adaptive	Maladaptive (Pathologic)	Adaptive	Maladaptive
Homeostasis (0–3 months)	Internal regulation (harmony) and balanced interest in world	Unregulated (e.g., hyperexcitable), withdrawn (apathetic)	Invested, dedicated, protective, comforting, predictable, engaging, and interesting	Unavailable, chaotic, dangerous, abusive, hypostimulating or hyperstimulating; dull
Attachment (2–7 months)	Rich, deep, multisensory emotional investment in animate world (especially with primary care givers)	Total lack of, or nonaffective, shallow, impersonal, involvement (e.g., autistic patterns) in animate world	In love and woos infant to "fall in love"; affective multimodality pleasurable involvement	Emotionally distant, aloof, and/or impersonal (highly ambivalent)
Somatopsychological differentiation (3–10 months)	Flexible, wide-ranging affective multisystem contingent (reciprocal) interactions (especially with primary care givers)	Behavior and affects random and/or chaotic, or narrow, rigid, and stereotyped	Reads and responds contingently to infant's communications across multiple sensory and affective systems	Ignores infant's communications (e.g., overly intrusive, preoccupied, or depressed) or misreads infant's communication (e.g., projection)
Behavioral organization, initiative, and internalization (9–24 months)	Complex, organized, assertive, innovative, integrated behavioral and emotional patterns	Fragmented, stereotyped, and polarized behavior and emotions (e.g., withdrawn, compliant, hyperaggressive, or disorganized toddler)	Admiring of toddler's initiative and autonomy, yet available, tolerant, and firm; follows toddler's lead and helps him organize diverse behavioral and affective elements	Overly intrusive, controlling; fragmented, fearful (especially of toddler's autonomy); abruptly and prematurely "separates"

NOTE. From Greenspan 1981.

Table 3.1 (Continued)

Stage-Specific Tasks and Capacities	Capacities		Environment (Care Giver)	
	Adaptive	Maladaptive (Pathologic)	Adaptive	Maladaptive
Representational capacity, differentiation, and consolidation (1½–4 years)	Formation and elaboration of internal representations (imagery) Organization and differentiation of imagery pertaining to self and nonself; emergence of cognitive insight Stabilization of mood and gradual emergence of basic personality functions	No representational (symbolic) elaboration; behavior and affect concrete, shallow, and polarized; sense of self and other fragmented and undifferentiated or narrow and rigid; reality testing, impulse regulation, mood stabilization compromised or vulnerable (e.g., borderline psychotic and severe character problems)	Emotionally available to phase-appropriate regressions and dependency needs; reads, responds to, and encourages symbolic elaboration across emotional behavioral domains (e.g, love, pleasure, assertion) while fostering gradual reality orientation and internalization of limits	Fearful of or denies phase-appropriate needs; engages child only in concrete (nonsymbolic) modes generally or in certain realms (e.g., around pleasure) and/or responds noncontingently or nonrealistically to emerging communications (i.e., undermines reality orientation); overly permissive or punitive
Capacity for limited extended representational systems and multiple extended representational systems (middle childhood through adolescence)	Enhanced and eventually optimal flexibility to conserve and transform complex and organized representations of experience in the context of expanded relationship patterns and phase-expected developmental tasks	Derivative representational capacities limited or defective, as are latency and adolescent relationships and coping capacities	Supports complex, phase- and age-appropriate experiential and interpersonal development (i.e., into triangular and post-triangular patterns)	Conflicted over child's age-appropriate propensities (e.g., competitiveness, pleasure orientation, growing competence, assertiveness, and self-sufficiency); becomes aloof or maintains symbiotic tie; withdraws from or overengages in competitive or pleasurable strivings

approach are viewed not in isolation but in the context of the overall phase-specific experiential organization expected or achieved. The potential to observe continuity or stability of either normal or disordered behavior should be enhanced by this approach, which focuses on the level of integration rather than specific symptoms or behaviors.

Developmental Structuralist Approach

In table 3.1 (see Greenspan 1981 for detailed discussion) the organizational tasks and adaptive and maladaptive infant and care-giver patterns have been summarized for each level in the developmental structuralist framework. The support for this model has been discussed elsewhere (Greenspan 1979).

As indicated above, the developmental structuralist approach focuses attention on the way in which the infant and young child organize experience. Two ways of considering how the infant organizes experience involve the interrelated dimensions of sensory and affective-thematic experience. To facilitate this observation of thematic experience, we have formulated a number of categories that we have found to be clinically relevant. With these categories it is possible to look at the degree to which all or only some affective-thematic areas are organized in the context of phase-specific tasks. Conversely, it is possible to see how certain affective-thematic proclivities when not present may hinder the full attainment of an expected level of organization.

The categories we found clinically useful include (1) interest and attentiveness; (2) relaxation or calmness; (3) dependency (including holding or comforting type behaviors, and so on); (4) pleasure or joy (including enthusiasm); (5) assertiveness—explorativeness and curiosity; (6) protest or other distinct forms of unpleasure including anger; (7) negativism or stubbornness; (8) self-limit setting (often not seen until children are in the middle of the second year of life); and (9) after the age of three, empathy and more stable feelings of love.

Each affective-thematic area may have many distinct contents. One two-and-a-half-year-old will evidence assertiveness or anger by shooting guns, another by "beating up" his father, and another by winning a car race. Similarly, pleasure may be reflected in the excitement of feeding and undressing dolls or in the joy of building a huge tower. The contributions of psychoanalytic observers and psychosexual theory toward understanding the phase-specific organizing fantasies or "dramas" are of inestimable importance in the study of what contributes to distinctly human experience.

It is interesting that whereas in the first month or two it is difficult to observe all these affective-thematic areas, by four months of age, it is possible to observe clinically each of them in a series of free exchanges between mother and baby. A healthy four-month-old, for example, often has no difficulty showing focused attentiveness (particularly to the mother's face and voice); using this focused attentiveness to be relaxed or calm; contributing to dependency by holding and finding comfortable positions (the infant holds mother's neck and even begins directing her toward the type of rhythmic movements or sensory experiences that are most comforting); evidencing pleasure and joy by smiling in synchrony with mother's smile or vocalizations; showing assertiveness and curiosity by somewhat chaotically but purposely moving his arms to grasp an object; evidencing anger, frustration, or protest with a distinct cry, angry look, and a flailing of arms and legs when a desired object is taken away; and evidencing negativism and even belligerency by refusing to open his mouth or by spitting up what he does not like.

This conceptualization helps us understand how the autonomous functions of the ego (sensory and motor functioning) and drive-affect patterns (thematic elements) work together in the early organization of experience. The way in which the infant organizes experience can be characterized as a critical factor of early ego development (the stages in early ego development are more fully described in Greenspan 1989).

Before outlining how the infant experiences sexuality and pleasure at each stage of development in the context of the developmental structuralist model described above, I will consider some theoretical issues concerning drives in relation to the types of learning involved in the model of ego development. The model integrates aspects of classical psychoanalytic theory with more recent clinical work and observations of infants and young children.

Drives and Developmental Theory

Freud's (1915) theory of instincts was an important contribution toward delineating the relation between somatic or biologic processes and psychological processes. By postulating psychic energy that could be transformed into drives and become attached to wishes and ideas, he advanced a relationship between physiologic and psychological phenomena. The use of these energic concepts from early psychoanalytic theory has been seriously questioned, however, and psychoanalytic ego psychology has attempted to resolve these questions by placing emphasis on the formation of ego substructures that evolve through early object relations. Psychic structure, rather than being seen as evolving from the transformation of drive energies, is viewed as existing from the beginning as part of an "undifferentiated matrix," whereas drive-affect dispositions are acquired through maturation and the accumulation of human experience (Hartmann 1939). In a sense this approach begs the issue of transformation of drive energy by taking as its starting point mental representations with drive-affect dispositions accruing to them (Kernberg 1975). Neither early instinct theory nor the more recent developments in ego psychology and object relations theory have accounted for the clinical phenomena Freud was attempting to explain. How does one account for the intensity of excitation or degree of pleasure? How does one account for zonal preferences?

Early in his theorizing, Freud postulated hypercathexis, investments of larger amounts of energy, as a way of explaining intensity of sensation as well as "awareness." He also postulated that different zones of the body or different modalities could become hypercathected. The skin can become "libidinized," for example. He postulated that at different stages of development different zones become cathected (the oral zone, the anal zone, the phallic zone). Although Freud's theory of instincts cannot be recapitulated here, models that have attempted to ignore Freud's theory of instincts have had difficulty in accounting for the phenomena he was trying to understand. For example, Klein (1976) proposed a model involving cognitive schemes, but in so doing, he did not deal with precognitive somatic levels of excitation and other neurophysiologic events. A theoretical model that posits representational or symbolic form overlooks the issue of mind-body relations that Freud was struggling with as well as much of development in the first year of life.

The model of three levels of learning (Greenspan 1979) offers an alternative. With this model we can understand the observations relating to intensity and awareness, and those relating to zonal or modal preference in the following manner. Early on, *somatically based schemata* stemming from the earliest experiences with the environment may establish both intensity and zonal specificity. Each baby has his own individual maturational pattern, and these innate givens in part account for intensity of sensation and zonal preferences. There may, for example, be individual differences in the number of nerve fiber endings in different zones. It is maturation, together with environmental experience in the earliest states, however, that establishes these early somatically based schemata. A mother who sensitively and pleasurably breast-feeds her baby may help to consolidate the baby's already pleasurable experiences around the oral zone. One can envision repeated stimulation of certain zones at pleasurable levels, leading to a schema that represents this early experience. This does not postulate that psychic energy is disposed at a location in the body; it merely postulates that certain repetitive patterns of experience become organized into a somatic schema (see Piaget's early sensorimotor schema formed through repetition in the cognitive realm). The repetition itself sets up the consolidation of an organization of early experience. To the degree that this early experience is highly pleasurable, the schema consolidates the physiologic and emerging affective components.

At the level of *consequence learning*, the second level, further differentiation of these schemata may occur. For example, a mother may selectively reinforce pleasurable experience around certain parts of the body. These body parts may become experienced not only as zones of pleasure but as zones of attachment and contact with the nurturing object.

As experience begins to shift to the third level of learning through the organization of imitative and identificatory processes seen in the last half of the first year and second year of life, we may observe another process that accounts for the phenomena of intensity and zonal specificity. As discussed earlier, during this period experience is becoming internalized and takes on meanings. The interaction that was recorded initially purely at the somatic level of learning (a mother strokes her infant's body and the infant begins to organize schemata of pleasure around bodily stroking) now becomes an experience with memory traces of social interactions. Both the emotional experience and the cognitive schema of how this experience occurs become part of an organized system of memories. Eventually, an organization of experience emerges that becomes identified as the "self," perhaps initially a "body self." The self that becomes organized is *the self that has been experienced.* This self-representation need not be an accurate perception of the way the person actually is; it is the self of perceptions and sensations. Thus, if a bodily zone has been an intense focus of experience (either of pleasure or of pain), it may assume a relatively prominent place in the initial self-representation. At the level of meanings, therefore, we may see special emphasis or zonal specificity, or both. With continued maturation, the development of the central nervous system (for example, sphincter control) in interaction with environmental experience further determines zonal configurations.

But once the mental representational system is formed, how are variations in intensity (for example, excitement) explained? How does one account for the relation between changing somatic experience and representational experience without using a concept such as the transformation of energy? We can postulate that *the representational system, just as it organizes itself in order to perceive the external world, organizes itself to perceive sensation from the interior of the body.* How and what it perceives depend on earlier learning as well as on constitutional and maturational patterns.

Sensations in the somatic sphere of the body are experienced and organized into somatic schemata. The representational-structural level of learning then perceives these experiences, and depending on its dynamic relation to earlier somatic levels of learning, may perceive accurately or may perceive inaccurately, downplay, hyperreact, or in other ways distort what is going on. For example, one youngster may deny pleasure because mother withdraws when she is feeling excited. Once this pattern becomes internalized at the level of representation, it may foster a tendency to ignore certain kinds of sensations from the interior of the body. Another toddler, whose interpersonal relationships are minimal, may develop relationships mostly to the inanimate environment. In this instance, interpersonal, emotion-laden somatic schemata and representations are barely formed. Or, if a youngster's explorative and assertive behavior is undermined by a mother who is overly controlling and belittling, he may turn toward the inanimate world, which he can control and over which he can feel a sense of mastery. In another situation, a youngster's discomfort may generate exaggerated responses that facilitate the internalization of experience to the point that she feels every minimally uncomfortable sensation from within to be of major significance (internal sensation is exaggerated). In yet another situation, a youngster may, for defensive purposes, begin to split and change certain feelings into others, such as hate and love (for example, ego splitting and later, reaction formations).

The intensity of the somatic patterns themselves also determines the resulting experience. The importance of somatic dispositions, as illustrated by the different drive proclivities that are related to constitutional, maturational, and developmental factors, is well known.

Thus, the issues of intensity and specificity can be accounted for under the rubric of the three levels of learning. They are related to the vicissitudes of the initial somatic schemata that are laid down, the experiences that lead up to internalization, the structure and character of the representational system itself, and the later somatic shifts and transformations that representations can undergo.

With the above theoretical constructs in mind, the organization of human pleasurable and sexual experience can be viewed according to a number of substages in the organization of experience (that is, the development of the ego), which will be described below.

Developmental Stages

Homeostasis

As the infant negotiates the first substage of *homeostasis* (birth to three months), the primary tasks are to become interested in the world and to feel regulated, comforted, and soothed. Both the initial interest in the world and the initial feeling of comfort and being soothed can be thought of in a global sense as the first pleasurable experiences. If a sense of balance is lacking, the infant is hyperirritable, withdrawn, or apathetic (not interested in the world), and pleasurable experiences are reduced. Tactile sensitivities as well as hypo- or hyperreactivity in any sensory mode will obviously make the earliest challenges of achieving pleasure and comfort more difficult. These constitutional-maturational differences are seen in many children and often confuse parents and later on, therapists. It is through pleasurable experiences (for example, rhythmic rocking, soft vocalizations, the presentation of novel stimuli) that regulation and engagement are attained.

Attachment

From this undifferentiated state of regulation and interest in the world evolves differentiated interest in the primary caretaker, and the stage of *attachment* (one to four months) is negotiated. Here we may observe rich affective dyadic expressions (for example, from gleeful pleasure to protest and assertiveness), or in contrast we may observe no human intimacy or shallow, mechanical attachments that are relatively devoid of bodily pleasure. Here we observe how the infant's constitutional-maturational differences and emerging somatic preferences—for example, firm holding rather than light touch, low-pitched sounds rather than high-pitched sounds—become part of a synchronous relationship pattern. Again we see how the essential experiences of the body become organized in the infant's fundamental involvement in the human world.

Somatopsychological Differentiation

Following the stage of attachment, we notice infants and their primary care-takers beginning to communicate, responding to each other's signals in a con-tingent fashion. The infant has embarked upon the process of *somatopsychological differentiation* (three to ten months). He or she begins to differentiate not only the primary caretakers from others (stranger anxiety) but means-end relation-ships—that is, the impact of his own actions on the world. As part of this process the infant also differentiates internal states, physical hunger from emotional hunger, and pleasure of one sort from pleasure of another. Here we begin to see, under favorable circumstances, the differentiation of pleasurable pursuits. Although all the senses and the whole body operate as sources of pleasure, we begin to note preferred modes that characterize the dyadic communication sys-tem such as certain parts of the body (hair, genitals, and so on), sensory mo-dalities (vision, hearing), and sensorimotor patterns. We also observe with this increased intentionality preferred modes of self-stimulation. Parents describe infants holding different parts of their bodies, including their genitals, and often wonder if this is the beginning of masturbation. It is here that somatic states and meanings in terms of differentiated part-object patterns become related (for example, drive-part self-object patterns).

Behavioral Organization, Initiative, and Internalization

As development proceeds we see the emergence of higher levels of orga-nization in the behavioral, emotional, and cognitive spheres. We find compli-cated emotional reactions such as fear and wariness, affiliation, and love—for example, the child runs up to the parent and gives a big welcoming hug. This organized behavioral emotional reaction is characteristic of the stage of *behav-ioral organization, initiative, and internalization* (ten to twenty months). During this stage we see much greater imitative capacities and emerging identifications as toddlers copy complex behavioral and emotional patterns from their parents and others. Out of this greater behavioral organization, initiative, and internal-ization emerge the building blocks for internal representational life. Especially important at this time is that we observe the toddler exploring his or her body and indicating a special interest in sexual differences. It is the first sign, perhaps still prerepresentational, of a capacity for discrimination of the genitals and the beginning of a sense of gender. Now pleasure is tied to a complex sense of self and a conceptual (presymbolic) understanding of the body. We begin seeing, for example, the first sign of anxieties related to sexuality (for example, ambiv-alent feelings toward the genitals) in part because of this new conceptual ability.

Organized Mental Representations

Although there are always fragments of internal imagery and sensation avail-able to the growing infant and toddler, toward the end of the second year the *capacity for forming organized mental representations* (sixteen to twenty-eight months) reaches an important level. At this time, experience is organized through the now well-developed capacities for forming internal symbols. The capacity for forming mental representations, which over time delineates a representation of the self and a representation of the significant other, relies heavily on early experiences of all the sensory modalities and in particular the experiences of early rhythmic rocking, holding, feeding, action, and pleasure patterns.

It could be said that at the most basic level, the first representation of the self is a body self; the self that is experienced physically and somatically is the self that is organized representationally. Thus, at this pivotal point, the *sensual self* is at the very foundation of the representational system. Therefore, the self that has been experienced becomes a self that can be perceived at a mental representational (symbolic) level. Here somatic proclivities (drive-affect patterns) are experienced in terms of self-object representations and become part of the structure of the self-object representational system.

Now the awareness of sexual differences, the intensity of various pleasures, preferred modes, and related patterns of relationships all become established at a mental representational level. For example, if experiencing pleasure is associated with closeness, warmth, and security with the primary caretaker, this constellation may become organized at a representational level (which not unimportantly is the foundation for formation of psychic structure). On the other hand, sensual experiences associated with parental withdrawal or aggressive, intrusive, or undermining behavior may also become organized as mental representations and form the foundation of evolving psychic structure.

As development proceeds into the latter stages of the second and third years, we see an elaboration of the representational capacity—for example, greater use of words, memory for emotional events, and an ever-increasing capacity for symbolic play and communication. It is interesting that before there can be "primary process thinking proper," a primary process language must first be learned; that is, symbols must be developed, enlarged, and permitted to coalesce into associative continuity with other representations or symbols. Whether or not the environment supports this capacity for mental imagery plays a role in the degree to which the capacity to use fantasy adaptively is developed.

Consolidated and Differentiated Representational Capacity
Pleasure at the symbolic level may be a decisive force supporting curiosity and an expanding representational world. Under favorable circumstances, this representational capacity exists initially in a relatively undifferentiated form. As the youngster moves from the second year to the fourth, a greater capacity to appreciate reality emerges. Differentiation now occurs at the mental representational level. The attainment of object constancy, well described by Mahler and colleagues (1975) leads to a constant delineated representation of self and others, resilient to both separations and upsurges of drive and affect—the postulated state of *consolidated and differentiated representational capacity*. This differentiation of self and other is the cornerstone of such basic ego functions as

reality testing (distinguishing inner from outer), organization of thought, stabilization of mood, and regulation of impulse.

The role of sexuality in achieving differentiated self-representation and object-representation—a milestone in the line of development of object and human relationships, and psychic structure—is both important and complex.

The youngster's feelings toward her body and in particular her emerging differentiation of sexual self play a pivotal role in the overall organization and differentiation of her self-representation and object-representation. This is based in part on the centrality of phallic body attitudes at this time (object constancy) in both boys and girls and the shifts that are seen during the later phallic and oedipal phases of development. The early phallic phase of development, the dyadic-phallic phase, brings with it a special focus on the child's own body and a special investment in the self. Two factors intensify this. Maturationally the drive organization leads to increased focus on the genital area as representative of the new phallic organization. At the same time, from the point of view of internalized self-representation and object-representation, object constancy is not yet fully consolidated but is on the way toward consolidation. Ego functioning in such basic areas as reality testing, regulation of impulses, integration of thought and affect, and integration of self-representation and object-representation is on its way to a stabilized organization but is not yet there. Thus the investment in the representation of the self, which at this time because of drive development is in part a *phallic* self in an overly intense way, serves the developmental need for differentiation and consolidation of one's personality. The focus on the representation of the self and sexual differences is necessary in part to fight off the regressive pulls back into less-differentiated states. This phallic self-focus becomes the alternative to an undifferentiated self-object focus.*

Where there are already developmental limitations and excessive fragility in the self-organization, some youngsters, in order to achieve a consolidated representational system (basic ego functions), may compromise the integrity of their emerging picture of themselves as sexual beings. Various perversions and other alterations in the developmental pattern of sexual functioning may be used in the service of maintaining basic ego functions. For example, a passive attitude may sometimes have to be adopted because assertion and aggression may threaten a fragile ego organization. An extensive focus on pregenital body parts and their related pleasure may be used to avoid the hazards of further development into a full oedipal triangle, because the complex and intense wishes and feelings associated with this higher phase (competition, lust) would also threaten a fragile preexisting ego structure. Phallic narcissistic orientations are common, but specific "perverse" inclinations and even gender confusion may be a way to preserve a distorted but cohesive sense of self and the world. Derivatives of

---

*This may be why we observe both increased narcissism (the self-focus) in the early phallic phase in almost all normal healthy children and why the interest in body parts is so intense.

early bodily attitudes may be seen in every aspect of ego structure and character. We are not suggesting here that the process is directed only from the sexual to the interpersonal and psychic structural; rather, it is an interactive process. What is emphasized, however, is that because of the special interest in one's body at this stage of development, the body plays a pivotal role in overall organization of psychic structure.

Limited and Multiple Extended Representational Systems

The next substage of development involves development of the opportunity for *limited extended representational systems* (ages four to ten), consistent with the oedipal and latency stages of development. Here we see the young child's internal emotional world enlarge in the context of expanded relationship patterns (triangular) and the capacity to develop derivative (transformed) representations that are tied to and related to the earlier representations—for example, the capacity for reaction formations, sublimations, or rationalizations.

We have observed that sexual issues during latency are not so latent. In the early stage of latency we see the youngster still struggling with oedipal and preoedipal issues, but now in the context of constraining and controlling them rather than elaborating on them, as he pursues school work, peer relationships, and the development of higher-order cognitive functioning. Toward the end of the latency stage, if the primitive wish and affective components of oedipal and preoedipal derivatives have been sufficiently repressed to afford the youngster appropriate freedom to look ahead, we see the anticipation of puberty. The youngster now shows direct interest in differences between boys and girls and raises questions of genital and pregenital sexuality from what often seems like a precocious adolescent perspective (using prohibited language with accompanying embarrassed giggles, looking at pictures of scantily dressed or naked men and women in magazines, and so on). This has the quality of anticipated excitement about what is to come in the future as well as a quality of preparation. Frequently the pregenital, anal attitudes are more prominent than the phallic, genital ones during this stage of development (calling friends "shit-head" and "asshole" in comparison to adolescence where such a term as "prick" tends to be used more).

Where the ego structure is not flexible and has not advanced to extended representational levels, these concerns are too frightening to the youngster, and preparation for adolescence does not occur in the same way. We may then encounter overobsessive concerns with cleanliness and rules, apprehension, anxiety, and even disorganization or withdrawal when sexual issues arise—for example, in the peer group or in the therapeutic setting.

In adolescence we observe an emerging capacity for a higher level of psychic organization, the level of *multiple extended representational systems*. The maturation of the central nervous system permits the adolescent to integrate an infinite number of variables into an organized system. In the emotional sphere this capacity for combinatorial thinking makes possible a *self*—or more appropriately now, an emerging *identity*—which can synthesize various experiences, even discordant ones, into an interconnected system. Thus, during adolescence we find the higher-level sublimatory processes and, under favorable circumstances, the relinquishment of primitive defenses such as denial, projection, ego splitting, and so on.

These new mental capacities are especially important because the demands on the personality structure are now much greater. Somatically, it is a new ball game. Not only are earlier preoedipal and oedipal bodily attitudes reworked, but the body has now grown and is capable of adult sexual relationships. The physical sensations in the body are of a different quality than in earlier development. The adolescent is now preparing not just for a symbolic psychological separation from the parents but for a real separation and entry into adulthood.

In adolescence, just as in the early phallic or dyadic-phallic phase, one's attitude toward the body and its developing sexuality can take the initiative and become the focal point for the relatively flexible, rich organization of a psychic structure that is capable of organizing an identity in the context of multiple extended representational capacities (an identity that has incorporated past and present in anticipation of the future in a flexible human manner). In contrast, it can be the basis for various limitations, constrictions, or even defects in the personality. The body becomes the focus for the sense of self. It once again becomes the foundation upon which the now highly transformed derivatives that may bear little resemblance to bodily and sexual attitudes rest—for example, concerns with values, abstract thoughts and ideas, and a high capacity for problem solving. Just as earlier the interest in the phallus helped organize a sense of self (in contrast to an undifferentiated self-object organization), in adolescence the emerging actual genital sexual inclinations and bodily changes may lead the way for the emerging adolescent separation-individuation process and final crystallization of psychic structure.

Where progression is not favorable because of earlier experience or experience during the adolescent phase proper, we may see compromises in terms of relinquishment of certain sexual inclinations, alterations in sexual patterns, or in contrast, preservation of certain aspects of adolescent and adult sexuality but at the expense of severe modification and alterations in overall psychic structure. For example, we may see somewhat polymorphous or impulsive sexual behavior (or other patterns such as addiction to substances, and so on) as a way to try to maintain a rather fragile ego organization. Such patterns may serve multiple functions at once and may involve regressive feelings toward parental figures, a precarious, nonetheless *existent* sense of individualized self, a way to deny deeper and earlier dependent yearnings, and a type of "pseudomaturity" or fantasized resolution of the separation from parental figures.

At the other extreme we may see a totally asexual teenager, where sexuality and, to some degree, an overall sense of bodily pleasure is relinquished because it would threaten an otherwise fragile ego organization. This asexuality, however, does not lead the way to a differentiation of ego structure. In contrast, it results in a pseudomaturity, as with rigid obsessive character patterns.

Conclusion

I have presented the outline of a developmental approach to pleasure and sexuality and discussed how traditional drive theory may fit into this model. Observational and clinical work with infants and young children, combined with reconstructive work for the analysis of older children and adults, will continue to refine our understanding of both the motivating and the structural factors in human functioning.

REFERENCES

Ainsworth, M.; Bell, S. M.; and Stayton, D. 1974. Infant-mother attachment and social development: Socialization as a product of reciprocal responsiveness to signals. In M. Richards, ed., *The integration of the child into a social world.* Cambridge: Cambridge University Press.

Bell, S. 1970. The development of the concept of object as related to infant-mother attachment. *Child Development* 41:219–311.

Bowlby, J. 1969. *Attachment and loss.* Vol. 1, *Attachment.* London: Hogarth Press.

Brazelton, T.; Koslowski, B.; and Main, N. 1974. The origins of reciprocity: The early mother-infant interaction. In M. Lewis and L. Rosenblum, eds., *The effect of the infant on its caregiver.* New York: Wiley.

Charlesworth, W. R. 1969. The role of surprise in cognitive development. In D. Elkind and J. Flavell, eds., *Studies in cognitive development.* Oxford: Oxford University Press.

Cicchetti, D., and Hesse, P. 1983. Affect and intellect: Piaget's contributions to the study of infant emotional development. In R. Plutchik and H. Kellerman, eds., *Emotion: Theory and research.* Vol. 2. New York: Academic Press.

Ekman, P. 1972. Universals and cultural differences in facial expressions of emotion. In *Nebraska Symposium on Motivation.* Lincoln: University of Nebraska Press.

Emde, R. N.; Gaensbauer, T. J.; and Harmon, R. J. 1976. *Emotional expression in infancy: A biobehavioral study.* Psychological Issues, monograph 37. New York: International Universities Press.

Escalona, S. 1968. *The roots of individuality.* Chicago: Aldine.

Freud, S. 1905. Three essays on the theory of sexuality. In *Standard edition,* 7:135–243. London: Hogarth Press, 1953.

———. 1911. Formulations on the two principles of mental functioning. In *Standard edition,* 12:218–26. London: Hogarth Press, 1958.

———. 1915. Instincts and their vicissitudes. In *Standard edition,* 14:109–40. London: Hogarth Press, 1953.

Gewirtz, J. L. 1965. The course of infant smiling in four child rearing environments in Israel. In B. M. Foss, ed., *Determinants of infants' behaviors.* Vol. 3. London: Methuen.

———. 1969. Levels of conceptual analysis in environment-infant interaction research. *Merrill-Palmer Quarterly* 15:9–47.

Gouin-Decarie, T. 1965. *Intelligence and affectivity in early childhood: An experimental study* of Jean Piaget's object concept and object relations. New York: International Universities Press.

Greenspan, S. I. 1979. *Intelligence and adaptation: An integration of psychoanalytic Piagetian developmental psychology.* Psychological Issues, monograph 47 / 48. New York: International Universities Press.

————. 1981. *Psychopathology and adaptation in infancy and early childhood: Principles of clinical diagnosis and preventive intervention.* Clinical Infant Reports, no. 1. New York: International Universities Press.

————. 1989. *The development of the ego: Implications for personality theory, psychopathology, and the psychotherapeutic process.* Madison, Conn.: International Universities Press.

Hartmann, H. 1939. *Ego psychology and the problem of adaptation.* New York: International Universities Press, 1958.

Izard, C. 1978. On the development of emotions and emotion-cognition relationships in infancy. In M. Lewis and L. Rosenblum, eds., *The development of affect.* New York: Plenum.

Kernberg, O. F. 1975. *Borderline conditions and pathological narcissism.* New York: Aronson.

Klaus, M., and J. H. Kennell. 1976. *Maternal-infant bonding: The impact of early separation or loss on family development.* St. Louis: Mosby.

Klein, G. S. 1976. Freud's two theories of sexuality. In M. Gill and P. Holzman, eds., *Psychology versus metapsychology: Psychoanalytic essays in memory of George S. Klein.* New York: International Universities Press.

Lipsitt, L. 1966. Learning processes of newborns. *Merrill-Palmer Quarterly 12*:45–71.

Mahler, M. S.; Pine, F.; and Bergman, A. 1975. *The psychological birth of the human infant.* New York: Basic Books.

Meltzoff, A., and Moore, K. 1977. Imitation of facial and manual gestures by human neonates. *Science 198*:75–78.

Murphy, L. B., and Moriarty, A. 1976. *Vulnerability, coping, and growth.* New Haven: Yale University Press.

Piaget, J. 1954. *Les relations entre l'affectivité et l'intelligence dans le développement mental de l'enfant.* Paris: Centre de Documentation Universitaire.

————. 1962. The stages of the intellectual development of the child. In S. Harrison and J. McDermott, eds., Childhood psychopathology. New York: International Universities Press, 1972.

————. 1969. *The psychology of the child.* New York: Basic Books.

————. 1970. *Structuralism.* New York: Basic Books.

Sander, L. 1962. Issues in early mother-child interaction. *Journal of the American Academy of Child Psychiatry 1*:141–66.

Sroufe, L. A., and Waters, E. 1977. Attachment as an organizational construct. *Child Development 48*:1184–99.

Sroufe, L. A.; Waters, E.; and Matas, L. 1974. Contextual determinants of infant affective response. In M. Lewis and L. Rosenblum, eds., *The origins of fear.* New York: Wiley.

Stern, D. 1974a. Mother and infant at play: The dyadic interaction involving facial, vocal and gaze behaviors. In M. Lewis and L. Rosenblum, eds., *The effect of the infant on its caregiver.* New York: Wiley.

————. 1974b. The goal and structure of mother-infant play. *Journal of the American Academy of Child Psychiatry 13*:402–21.

Tomkins, S. 1963. *Affect, imagery, consciousness.* Vols. 1 and 2. New York: Springer.

Werner, H., and Kaplan, B. 1963. *Symbol formation.* New York: Wiley.

4

Early Symbiotic Processes:
Hard Evidence from a Soft Place

MYRON A. HOFER, M.D.

> When I was born, all I knew was how to suck, and how to lie still when my body sensed
> comfort or cry when it felt pain. Later on I began to smile as well, first in my sleep, and
> then when I was awake. Others told me this about myself, and I believe what they said,
> because we see other babies do the same. But I cannot remember it myself. Little by little I
> began to realize where I was and to want to make my wishes known to others, who might
> satisfy them. But this I could not do, because my wishes were inside me, while other people
> were outside, and they had no faculty which could penetrate my mind. . . . And if my wishes
> were not carried out . . . I would get cross with my elders, . . . simply because they did not
> attend to my wishes; and I would take my revenge by bursting into tears. By watching babies
> I have learnt that this is how they behave, and they, quite unconsciously, have done more
> than those who brought me up to convince me that I behaved in just the same way myself.
> —St. Augustine, Confessions, AD 397

Psychoanalytic Theory and Modern Biology

While preparing for this talk, I had a fantasy. In it, Freud's birth had been
delayed one hundred years and now, in April 1987, there was no psychoanalysis.
But I imagined the young Freud having just completed his medical training,
with an M.D., Ph.D. in neuroscience. But his grant proposals have been given
too low a score for funding at the National Institute of Health; his ideas were
judged to be too innovative and overly ambitious. So he has turned to his
practice, where he is now treating patients with affective disorders, puzzling over
the nature of affect while he prescribes various pharmacologic agents. In 1992,
instead of 1892, he will publish his first theory of affect. Could his "Project for

An abridged version of this paper was presented at a symposium sponsored by the Columbia University Center for Psychoanalytic Training and Research in collaboration with the
Association for Psychoanalytic Medicine; "Pleasure Beyond the Pleasure Principle: Developmental and Psychoanalytic Concepts of Affect"; New York City, 4 April 1987.

a Scientific Psychology" be successful in 1995 instead of the failure he felt it had been a hundred years before?

In this paper, I would like to explore the possibilities of looking at the early development of affect, and of pleasure in particular, from an evolutionary and a biological perspective. What are the concepts and research advances that Freud would draw on, were he just beginning today to derive from neurobiology and from his patients the beginnings of psychoanalytic theory? Sociobiology, systems theory, and cognitive science immediately come to mind in addition to the neurosciences. We can easily imagine Freud's delight today in discovering ethology, cybernetics, and kin selection theory in addition to the dazzling world of modern neurobiology. And he might revise his harsh opinion of "Project for a Scientific Psychology" (Freud 1895, 281–397), when he realized how accurately it anticipated the development of these fields during the twentieth century and their central role in our current understanding of behavior. Think of the satisfaction he would take in having correctly built his first theory of the mind out of a network of neurones, in having identified the central role of feedback of neural information in operating a self-regulating "psychic apparatus" (Pribram and Gill 1976), an approach now used in the analysis of neural circuit diagrams by neurobiologists. In addition, many of the advances in modern cognitive science (Gardner 1985) have proceeded from a systems approach he began to use to deal with perception and memory in "The Project." Finally, Freud could easily build on his own evolutionary perspective in order to incorporate current theories on the evolutionary basis for motives in social behavior (Wilson 1975). Indeed, "The Project" anticipated the development of new scientific fields to a degree that gives it an air of uncanny prescience when read today.

Unfortunately, several of the basic attributes of Freud's psychic apparatus, drawn as they were from physiological views of the late nineteenth century, have proved to be wrong. Some of these particularly concern the role of affect. First, the concept that all brain (and thus mental) activity derives from sensory stimulation, originating either from outside or within the body (instinctual drives), has been conclusively disproved. Turn-of-the-century physiologists did not know of the chemical processes underlying the intrinsic activity of nerve cells. The crucial experiments could not be done at that time to show that neurones actually develop characteristic patterns of activity while being kept isolated from sensory stimulation. Freud, along with his colleagues, were prisoners of a powerful contemporary intellectual revolt against the vitalism of their predecessors who had postulated mysterious unverifiable inner sources of energy within the brain (Holt 1965, 93–125; Sulloway 1979). Thus, Freud built the operating principles of his conceptual model firmly around an "objectifiable" source of energy, delivered to sensory nerve endings, and was convinced that without such stimulation the brain would be inert. He and other early neurophysiologists interpreted their observations to indicate that the function of nerve cells was to rid themselves of excitation. This inference was built by Freud into the *constancy principle* of his first affect theory (Freud 1895) and survived in a somewhat different form in the later *pleasure principle* (Freud 1920). In this he deduced from his principle of the sensory source of mental energy that the mind is an *apparatus* for the discharge, control, and regulation of this sensory-based energy and is organized in such a way as to tend to seek out the pleasure of energy discharge and to avoid the unpleasure of accumulated excitation. Freud, and other students of human behavior, have had great difficulties in reconciling this pleasure principle with the many apparent exceptions to its predictions.

Ironically, some psychoanalysts cling to a theory based on a supposedly objectifiable source for mental activity while being widely criticized for *not* devising an objectifiable theory and while ignoring potential rescue from the dilemma by the new understanding of brain and behavior coming from neurophysiologists and developmental biologists. Psychoanalytic concepts of the psychic apparatus (for example, Brenner, chapter 9) are protected from evidence against them by the assertion that they are meant to apply to *mental* activity rather than to brain activity. But why cling to a set of principles of mental functioning that is so incongruent with what is now known about brain function? This would be somewhat understandable if the new principles of brain function were incompatible with the main body of clinically useful theory, but they are not. Indeed, it appears possible to carry out an updating of psychoanalytic theory that could eventually provide a description of the mental apparatus that has retained its clinical validity and usefulness while being compatible with current understanding of brain function.

But we are in an era of diminished interest in broad new theories of the mind. Psychoanalysts do not attempt to re-derive the principles of their theory from new biological knowledge, and biological psychiatrists show no interest in developing theories that can deal with how patients come to think and feel in the particular way they do. Systems theorists and sociobiologists are too far from clinical cases. Thus it will come as no surprise that these fields have not developed a systematic approach to pleasure in early development. Within the new field of developmental psychobiology, however, I have found three concepts that I believe provide the basis for considering how pleasurable affects evolved, how they can be conceptualized within a biological framework, and finally how psychoanalytic and biological thinking about early parent-infant interaction may share common ground.

Three Bridging Concepts

First, we must ask how a concept like affect, which sounds distinctly psychological, can possibly be conceptualized in a way that allows us to relate it to biological processes. The concept of *state organization* (Hobson 1977, 1–15; Wegman 1985) is a great help in this task, as it bridges the gap between structure and function, and ultimately between biology and psychology. In animals with simple nervous systems, we now can specify the neuronal elements of the systems involved in a particular state and measure various indices of their function as states change (see figure 4.2). In each state, the elements are organized into a particular functional pattern. A change in the state of the system alters the way in which information is processed: things are perceived differently, perceptions are differently integrated, and the nature and intensity of the behaviors likely to result are altered during a state change. The cycles of sleep-wake states (for example, REM sleep, waking) are everyday examples of these changes of state. But animals and humans also have motivational and emotional states, and it is here that affects enter the picture.

The inner experience of an affect derives from the characteristic functional organization of the central neural state and the communicative aspect of affect derives from special characteristics of behavioral output. One of the great remaining scientific mysteries is how a functional brain state translates into inner experience, a gap we cannot yet bridge. However, the features, the tone of voice, the posture, and above all the nuances of facial expression communicate affect among people and allow us to identify and even to empathize with the affect of others. In this way, we are given clues as to precisely what state they are in and to predict what kind of behavior we are likely to encounter in our relations with them. This is clearly an important capacity, one that is likely to have had great adaptive usefulness and that should be built into social species of animals, including humans, by powerful genetic and developmental processes. But what processes are these? And where do affects first arise, in evolutionary terms as well as in the developmental time span?

In mammals, the answer to the second part of this question is fairly straightforward: affects must arise in the early parent-infant relationship, for this is the environment encountered by all mammals from birth to the beginnings of independent living. Thus we must ask what there is about the nature of this relationship that is likely to underlie the beginnings of positive affects. Here a second concept is available that is used by both biologists and psychoanalysts, *symbiosis*. Anton de Bary, a botanist, first used this word in 1879 to describe the close association of two different organisms that contribute in some ways to each other's support (de Bary 1879). In 1983, the proceedings of a conference were published by researchers in the biology of behavior development called *Symbiosis in Early Parent-Offspring Interactions* (Rosenblum and Moltz 1983). *Symbiosis* was generally understood to refer to a complex of processes, hidden within early mammalian social relationships, with diverse functions such as mutual regulation and resource exchange that serve developmental purposes and maintain attachment between the partners.

The psychoanalytic concept of symbiosis used by Margaret Mahler has a central core that shares much with the biological concept. This is the characterization of the early mother-infant relationship as "a dual unity within one common boundary" (Mahler, Pine, and Bergman 1975, 74). Regardless of the question of whether experiences of merging and loss of ego boundaries in older children and adults derive from experiences during this phase of life (Pine 1986, 546–69), the special characteristics of dual unity are worth exploring. For this is the context in which affects develop and the distinguishing qualities of positive affects are likely to derive from the nature of symbiotic processes. Evidence that mutual regulation, synchrony, and reciprocity are built into mammalian mother-infant interactions at a deep biological level will be presented in the final section of this chapter along with speculations as to how this occurrence may determine some of the qualities of positive affects and even of internal object representations.

Finally, there is a theory formulated by T. C. Schneirla, one of the first American ethologists, that helps us to deal with the question of how affects evolved and to identify the precursors of affects in simple forms of life, both early in evolution and early in development. Schneirla has noted, from his studies of the behavior of a wide variety of species and developmental stages, that "approaches toward the source of stimulation occur to effectively weak stimulation, whereas withdrawals occur to effectively intense stimulation" (Schneirla 1939, 501–2). The diagram I have drawn (figure 4.1) summarizes the main features of this deceptively simple model, with the additional insight contributed by one of Schneirla's colleagues, Ethel Tobach, that positive and negative emotions are likely to have evolved from these simple approach and withdrawal responses. Schneirla and Tobach use the phrase "effective stimulus intensity"

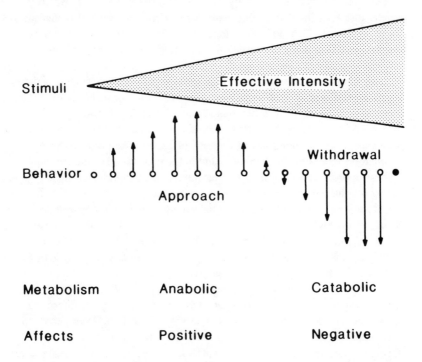

Figure 4.1 Schema based on T. C. Schneirla's approach-withdrawal theory for origin of emotions in simple forms of life

to indicate their appreciation of the need to account for the qualitative features of stimuli, the existing state of the organism, and indeed the prior history of experience with similar stimuli and settings. Schneirla additionally observed that internal physiological adjustments accompanied the approach behaviors and that these were typically of the sort required to build tissues, anabolic processes (for example, absorption, digestion, protein synthesis), whereas the physiological adjustments accompanying withdrawal responses were energy-mobilizing, tissue destructive, catabolic processes. These accompanying physiological adjustments may be considered to contribute to the states out of which affects subsequently emerge. Tobach pointed out that "the modulation of the processes bringing about approach or withdrawal *is* the emotional process . . . Emotion modulates, filters, amplifies and attenuates approach-withdrawal responses" (Tobach 1970, 238–50).

A system does not have to be very complex to "modulate" simple locomotor responses. Indeed, Daniel Koshland has described a chemical system involving two enzymes that appear to accomplish this in a single-celled organism, the typhoid bacillus (Koshland 1980, 43–75). Cell membrane receptors for specific nutrients and fine, whiplike flagella allow for sensory and motor functions, including appropriate approach and withdrawal responses to changes in its fluid environment. Interestingly, this organism has an organized state in which its five flagella lose coordination so that instead of swimming gracefully, the bacillus "tumbles" in place, happily absorbing molecules of nutrient, a state induced when it senses optimal concentrations of a preferred nutrient. This may be the simplest example of pleasure yet discovered!

The simplicity and short duration of the typhoid bacillus's chemical memory (a half second) and the mechanical, stereotyped nature of its behavior make the simplest invertebrate with a nervous system appear highly intelligent by comparison. As animals evolved with increasingly complex nervous systems, they were able to devote neurones to the task of communicating and storing some information about ongoing behaviors and to the registration of the consequences of these approach and withdrawal behaviors. Thus, memories of the action, the setting in which it occurred, and its consequences could be elaborated, maintained for long periods of time, and finally made available in response to certain signals in the environment. Through the action of modulating nerve cells that influence receptive as well as motor pathways, such signals can alter the state of the organism so that information is-processed differently and actions are modified. Such a state may be considered a prototype affect in the sense described for state organization. The sea snail, *Aplysia californica*, has a feeding arousal response with the above characteristics which Irving Kupfermann and his colleagues have been able to analyze at the cellular level (Weiss et al. 1982). The neuronal circuit diagram underlying this state, portrayed in figure 4.2, illustrates how simple neuronal systems can be organized to mediate central states that have the behavioral characteristics of affects.

To summarize, I have approached the development of affect by asking the

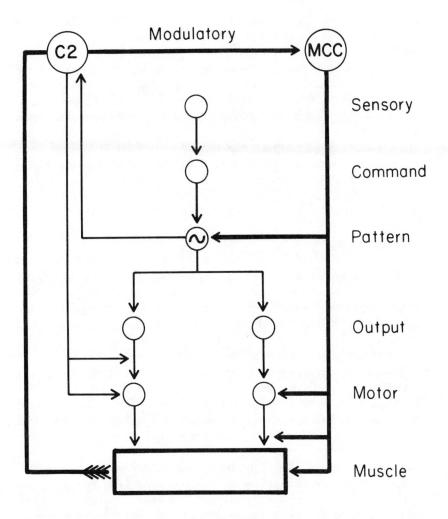

Figure 4.2 Schematic diagram of hypothetical levels of control of neurons controlling consummatory feeding responses in *aplysia*. Types of neurons for which there is evidence in *aplysia* and other mollusks include the following: sensory cells or sensory neurons, which excite command neurons or systems of command neurons. Command neurons drive central pattern generators, whose output to motor neurons either can be direct or, as indicated, can be mediated by way of output neurons. Various levels of control are influenced by at least 2 types of modulatory neurons: C2 and the MCC. Feedback loop involving C2 and the MCC is indicated by dark lines. (Source: Weiss, Chiel, Koch, and Kupfermann 1986. Reprinted by permission of the *Journal of Neuroscience*.)

question, Where do affects come from? I have described three concepts from behavior biology that are useful in thinking about the events and processes, in simple or very young organisms, that provide the elements from which affects develop: state organization, symbiosis, and the biphasic approach-withdrawal theory. By outlining the minimal conditions, I have shown that from very early in postnatal life, the neural substrates for simple affective states are likely to be present and that the experiences for the building of specific pleasurable states are likewise built into the symbiotic nature of the earliest mother-infant interaction. In the next section, I will explore what is beginning to be known about the actual functioning of such processes in relatively simple subprimate laboratory mammals where the experimental approach can be used to gain hard evidence on how simple affective states develop.

The Formation of Affect

I will discuss now the processes that take place within the individual infant that lead to the acquisition of a brain state that we can identify as a pleasurable affect. Then I will describe recent new evidence on processes within the relations between the individual infant and mother that influence the development of affects.

Infant mammals are highly adapted to finding their way about the ventrum of their mothers, an environment filled with soft tactile, thermal, and olfactory stimulation. This is the soft place of this chapter's title, the place where affect originates. Infant mammals' first responses are simple reflex actions in response to tactile and thermal stimuli; these responses have been known for a long time. Once referred to as *tropisms* (Crozier and Pincus 1928, 789–802), these simple, directed motility responses are guided by the relative intensity of stimulation on either side of the animal (see figure 4.3), which allows it to navigate effectively in its inherited environment of the mother's body. These responses are analogous to the head turning, rooting, and simple reaching responses of newborn humans at the breast and are examples of the simple approach responses to low effective levels of stimuli described by Schneirla.

There is another major response that occurs in the first week of life in rat pups, a diffuse behavioral arousal response that has been described by W. G. Hall (figure 4.4). Hall found that in an isolated infant rat, a pulse of milk, delivered to the mouth by a tiny catheter, elicits a panoply of behaviors: mouthing and probing are accompanied by vigorous twisting, curling, and rolling (Hall 1979, 206–9). Even specialized postures such as the lordosis position typical of the female sexual response would occasionally appear. This diffuse and global mobilization of behavior patterns does not occur in infants older than a week of age and is much subdued in nondeprived pups. When pups are on the teat, the activation is expressed as a single response, the arched extension of the "stretch" response to milk let down by the dam. Older pups respond with

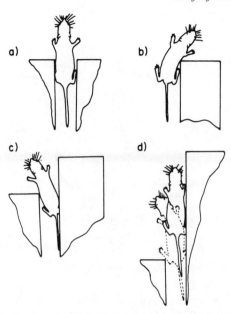

Figure 4.3 Rat pups crawling between two walls, stimulated equally, continue to crawl straight ahead (a); stimulated unequally, they turn first to the side at which the wall ends (c); then back to the wall that continues (d); when stimulated on one side they turn to that side when the wall ends (b). (Source: Crozier and Pincus 1928, reprinted by copyright permission of the Rockefeller University Press.)

exclusively ingestive responses, such as licking and mouthing, to the same pulse of milk when off the teat.

The responses of the week-old infant seem to represent a primitive activation capacity that is potentially connected to a variety of behavioral components. Although it embodies an arousal component, it does not provide the organized information-processing capability nor the specific communicative capacity that are typical of affect states. The eliciting stimulus, milk in the mouth, does occur in a particular, predictable relation to the approach responses that culminate in suckling, however. Furthermore, we have learned that this kind of activational response can be induced by other aspects of the mother-pup interaction, such as the mother's licking and treading on pups that are also likely to occur in association with the pup's approach responses (Sullivan, Hofer, and Brake 1986, 615–23).

Mother rats often stimulate pups both in response to certain pup behaviors and in association with certain scents that are secreted by glands on her ventrum or may be carried on her fur from the outside world. The olfactory system of infant rats is highly functional at birth. After the first few days of life, pups become so dependent on this sense that when deprived of it, they show no apparent interest in their mother, treating her like an inanimate object. They

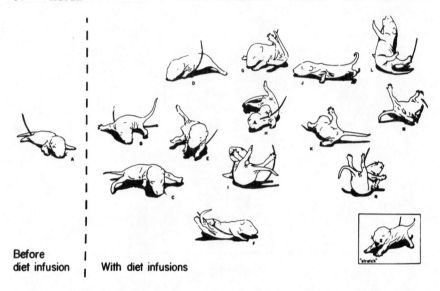

Before
diet infusion | **With diet infusions**

Figure 4.4 Diagram of some behaviors shown by three-day-old pups in response to milk infusions. The individual drawings do not portray an actual sequence but do give examples of the pups' initial responses to infusion with mouthing and probing of the floor (B, C) that becomes more vigorous and is extended to twisting and locomotion (D, E, F, G). Pups then often roll and curl (H, I) and exhibit forms of locomotion, probing, reaching, and posturing (J–N). Some of the positions are also suggestive of righting attempts, but more often than not these movements are initiated from an upright position and result in the pup rolling. The insert depicts the "stretch" response as it appears when it occurs away from the mother's nipple. (Source: Hall 1979, reprinted by permission of the American Association for the Advancement of Science.)

ultimately die of inanition despite her continued presence with them (Singh, Tucker, and Hofer 1976, 373–82). Loss of olfaction immediately after birth has far less severe effects, apparently because it has not yet been built into the infant's motivational and emotional systems (Teicher et al. 1978, 553–61). Olfaction is a highly sensitive system, capable of forming specific discriminations at an early age. Indeed, human infants can distinguish their own mothers from other nursing mothers within the first ten days of life, using only their sense of smell (MacFarlane 1977). Thus, as Jay Rosenblatt has pointed out, olfaction is a sensory modality capable of a high level of specificity and naturally suited to the role of mediating the transition from responding to stimuli in terms of simple intensity to responding in terms of their meaning in the life of the infant (Rosenblatt 1983, 347–75).

What experiences give olfaction its special place in the infant rat's life? Could this sense come to mediate the earliest affect states of pleasure, without which the young rat perishes? Experiments on the systematic association of odor with activating stimulation in infant rats provide us with some clues to the processes involved. It had been found that a novel odor could be used to elicit nipple attachment in one-day-old pups, provided that the pup had previously been stroked with a brush in its presence, mimicking maternal licking (Pederson and Blass 1982, 349–55). Subsequently, my colleagues and I found that associating a novel odor with activating stimuli similar to those presented by the mother gave that odor the capacity to attract the infant rat, to enhance olfactory-guided orientation in a novel environment, and to increase huddling with its littermates (Sullivan et al. 1986, 625–35). After the first week of life, such associations no longer had these effects.

Here, in this series of contrived experiences, we could abstract from the welter of exchanges in the maternal situation certain associative processes that established a special role for a particular odor. Such a signal thereafter acted to arouse a state in the pup that altered its information processing so that other cues in the environment were responded to in a new way. It would appear that the odor had come to induce a simple form of pleasure in the young rat.

What might such a pleasurable state look like in the brain? One of the exciting aspects of modern neurobiology is that we can actually begin to answer such a question. Michael Leon and co-workers used a brain-imaging technique to investigate changes produced in the olfactory brains of infant rats by associative experiences such as those described earlier (Leon 1987). Infant rats were allowed to experience a novel odor (peppermint) in association with stroking stimulation for ten minutes every day during the first two weeks of life. Later, as young adults, they were exposed to the odor for forty-five minutes, just before sacrifice. Slices of their brains from the olfactory bulb region were then compared with slices from rats that had experienced the odor without the associated stroking during infancy. Three regions of the olfactory bulb showed increased metabolic activity in both kinds of animals, a specific pattern associated with the odor of peppermint. But the rats with the brief infantile associative experience showed far higher levels of metabolic activity extending over a greater area (figure 4.5). Using this mapping as a guide, microscopic anatomical and neurophysiological studies revealed altered patterns of neural activity in mitral and tufted nerve cells leading to and from these areas of increased metabolic activity. There were even microscopic anatomical differences suggesting that the early associative experience caused certain neuronal structures to survive, which in control animals succumbed to a natural process of cell death. This work gives us the closest look we have yet had at an affective memory trace in the brain.

Taken together, these studies allow us to trace the formation of a pleasurable brain state out of experiences known to occur during the infant's daily life (figure 4.6). Other activating stimuli, such as isolation or poisoning in association with odor, have none of the affects just described. The communicative aspect of the acquired affect state should also be pointed out. Behaviors such as huddling and nosing into the fur of the mother's ventrum elicit care-giving responses from the mother. Pups that do not show these behaviors—for example those that are experimentally deprived of their olfactory sense—do not communicate

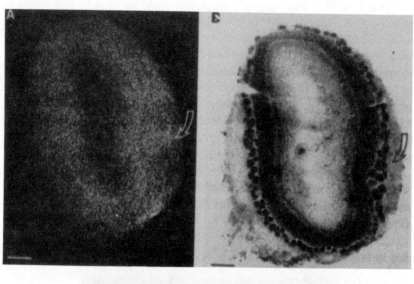

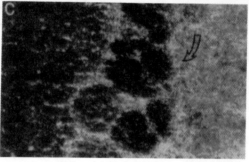

Figure 4.5 (A) Brain imaging autoradiograph of peppermint-familiar pups exposed later in life to peppermint, with an arrow showing an area of heightened activity in the olfactory bulb. (B) Adjacent section stained for a metabolic enzyme with the arrow in the corresponding area. (C) Magnified view of this area, showing the modified cellular clusters shown in B. Scale bars: A and B = 400 μm; C = 100 μm. (Source: Leon 1987, reprinted by permission of Academic Press.)

to the mother and do not elicit those caregiving responses. The reciprocal feedback between mother and infant will be discussed in the next section.

Biological Symbiosis and Its Consequences for Affect Development

Hidden within the observable interactions between a mother and her infant are a number of biological processes that have important implications for the nature

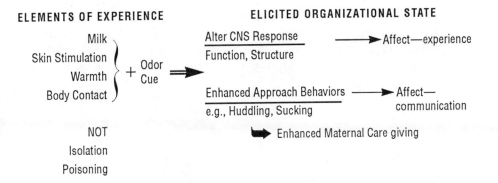

ELEMENTS OF EXPERIENCE   ELICITED ORGANIZATIONAL STATE

Figure 4.6 Summary of events and contingencies underlying acquisition of pleasurable affective state in very early life, based on recent research with infant rats

of early affect formation. Neither traditional biologists nor developmental psychologists have been interested in looking for biological processes in early social relationships, so that their extent and importance have generally been underestimated. There are different experimental approaches that can be used, but one that I have found particularly useful is to separate infant animals from their mothers and then to substitute different components of the interaction while measuring biological and behavioral responses of the infants (Hofer 1987, 251–74).

After an infant rat is separated from its mother, at two weeks of age when it can survive on its own, its responses can be characterized by the three different curves in figure 4.7. The general features of this pattern are similar for all social mammals studied to date. First, there are acute responses of increased vocalization and searching behavior, with accompanying increases in cardiac and respiratory rates and other signs of acute arousal. The ultrasonic vocalizations (USV) of the infant rat constitute a prototype of this class of response in figure 4.7. This acute phase has been termed "protest" by Bowlby; it declines in intensity at the time a second phase of more slowly developing responses are beginning to be evident. These slow changes in the levels of various functions may be either in an upward or downward direction. Heart rate and activity response to a novel environment are illustrated as prototypes in the figure. The number of systems known to be so affected after separation is large and growing. Nutritive and nonnutritive sucking, adrenocortical secretion, spontaneous arousals from sleep, autonomic arterial constrictor tone, and endogenous opioid release are responses that tend to follow behavioral reactivity levels in an upward direction after separation, while respiratory rate, oxygen consumption, central catecholamine levels, rapid-eye-movement (REM) sleep, growth hormone, and the enzyme it induces (ornithine decarboxylase) follow cardiac rate in a downward direction after separation.

When I first observed the slow decreases in cardiac and respiratory rates, I concluded that they were part of an integrated emotional response to the separation. Bowlby had characterized the slower developing changes in humans and certain primates as a second stage in the emotional response and termed it "despair" because of characteristic postures, facial expressions, and reductions

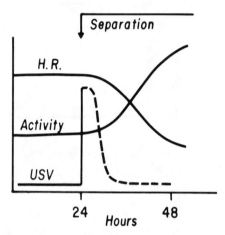

Figure 4.7 Schematic representation of typical responses to separation of a two-week-old rat from social companions. USV = ultrasonic vocalizations

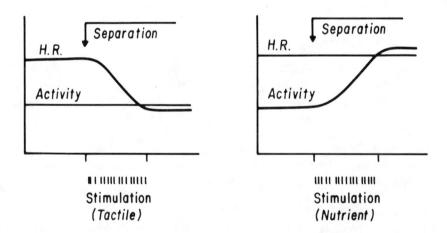

Figure 4.8 Schematic representation of the effects on separation responses of replacing specific elements of mother-infant interaction. Note how tactile stimulation prevents activity level changes but not heart rate changes while the provision of nutrient has opposite effects.

in spontaneous activity levels observed in these species (Bowlby 1969). But when Harry Shair and I replaced different elements of the maternal interaction singly or in selective combination, we found that the three classes of response were independent of each other (Hofer and Shair 1982). For example, the acute response (USV) could be prevented by a furry, warm object with nest odors on it, but the slow developing responses continued unabated (figure 4.8). Next we found that heart rate and activity levels could be maintained at normal levels by providing other aspects of the mother-infant interaction, selectively. For example, patterns of tactile and olfactory stimulation maintained activity at a normal level while heart rate continued to fall by 40 percent (see figure 4.8).

Apparently the mother provides several different *regulators* of infant biological and behavioral control systems in the form of her many interactions with them. The reason the characteristic pattern of changes shown in figure 4.7 was produced each time we removed the mother from the cage was that the response pattern is in fact an assemblage of independent processes. Withdrawal of all of these interactions at once released the infants' systems from the influences of all these regulators, some maintaining systems at high functional levels (up-regulation) and others down-regulating them. For example, the perioral stimulation of having a teat in the mouth and the nonnutritive sucking it elicits, normally down-regulates the level of nonnutritive sucking in the infant. But this element of experience does not influence the functional level of *nutritive* sucking,

Table 4.1 Regulators Hidden within the Mother-Infant Interaction

Infant Systems	Direction	Maternal Regulators
Behavioral		
Activity level	Increased	Body warmth
	Decreased	Tactile and olfactory
Sucking		
Nutritive	Decreased	Milk (distention)
Nonnutritive	Decreased	Tactile (perioral)
Neurochemical (central nervous system)		
NE, DA	Increased	Body warmth
ODC	Increased	Tactile (dorsal)
Metabolic		
Oxygen consumption	Increased	Milk (sugar)
Sleep–wake states		
REM sleep	Increased	Periodicity, milk, and tactile
Arousals	Decreased	Periodicity, milk, and tactile
Cardiovascular		
Heart rate (β-adrenergic)	Increased	Milk (interoreceptors)
Resistance (α-adrenergic)	Decreased	Milk (interoreceptors)
Endocrine		
Growth hormone	Increased	Tactile (dorsal)

SOURCE: Hofer 1984.

NOTE: NE = norepinephrine; DA = dopamine; ODC = ornithine decarboxylase, a rate-limiting enzyme important in growth of brain and most other tissues; resistance = arterial resistance, the constriction of peripheral blood vessels; REM = rapid-eye-movement sleep.

which rises slowly after separation, despite this oral experience. Nutritive sucking, in contrast, is down-regulated by feedback from distention of the stomach
caused by the milk normally provided by the mother. Other regulators are given
in table 4.1, involving warmth, olfactory and tactile stimulation, and milk acting
in different ways on the infant's gut. We went on to find that more complex
qualities of stimulation were necessary for regulation of some systems, such as
those controlling the pattern of sleep-wake state organization. Here the element
of periodicity or the rhythm of stimulation was almost as important as the modality (Hofer and Shair 1982, 229–44). Each of these regulatory systems within
the mother-infant interaction has its own dynamics and its own physiological
mechanisms, which we are beginning to explore.

The discovery of these regulators tells us something new about the nature
of symbiosis in young mammals. Apparently the infant, even at an age when it
can survive on its own, delegates a portion of the control of its internal environment to processes within its relationship with its mother. In this way the
individual homeostatic organization of an infant old enough to survive on its
own is still partially subordinated to the organization of the symbiosis that characterizes the early postnatal development of mammals.

These characteristics of symbiosis have implications for affects relating to
attachment and loss (Hofer 1984, 183–97). First, it is clear that the simple affect
state that grows out of approach responses in the infant is from the beginning
associated with processes of regulation of internal biological systems by the
mother. It seems possible that this experience gives a depth of internal sensation
and a dimension of external control at the biological level that may account for
the overwhelming quality of positive affects experienced by humans in connection with attachment and dependency, especially those deriving from the earliest
of life stages. Second, we may speculate that the presence of multiple independent processes of altered regulatory control during separation may supply, at
the biological level, a basis for the quality of fragmentation and loss of control
that characterizes the experience of object loss and the affects of grief in humans,
as outlined in the next section of this chapter. Third, these processes provide
us with a way to understand responses to separation in human infants prior to
seven to eight months of age, before the classical attachment system develops.
We can now take a new view of the nature of the "preattached" infant's relationship with its mother.

Finally, I think these findings tell us something about the evolution of attachment systems and the pleasurable affect associated with them. Because
infant attachment is so widely distributed among species, there has been considerable speculation as to its survival advantage. Current theories usually favor
protection from predators as the crucial issue (for example, Bowlby 1969). However, since environmental regulators of physiological systems clearly evolved
before attachment systems, might it not be that the potential for the regulation
of developmental processes by the mother conveyed a selective advantage to
animals that maintained close attachment between mothers and their infant

offspring? For the mother would thus be capable of inducing modifications in her offspring (through her regulatory effects) that would preadapt them to the environment that had shaped her own behavior—a kind of biological analog to cultural evolution. Such vertical transmission of the effects of experience to subsequent generations has been described for several kinds of environmental influences such as early separation, early handling, and shock avoidance (Hofer 1981a, 77–115). This formulation places the affects of pleasure and security in attachment at the center of crucial developmental and evolutionary processes.

But thus far I have described only one side of the symbiotic relationship. Do we have evidence that infants regulate their mother's biological and behavioral systems? In fact, the infant is crucial in eliciting and maintaining parental behavior, even in a simple laboratory mammal such as the rat. Although the hormonal priming of late gestation accounts for the immediate onset of maternal behavior after parturition, inexperienced females and males can be induced to show maternal behavior simply by the experience of several days proximity to neonates (Rosenblatt 1987). The maintenance of normal maternal behavior after parturition is dependent upon continued interaction with pups; if pups are taken away from dams for three to four days after birth, the mothers will show little or no maternal behavior when reunited with them. Pups also regulate the endocrine levels that support the maternal milk delivery system (for example, high levels of the hormone prolactin) and the increased appetite of the lactating dam (Leon 1983, 945–57). Through their sucking stimulation, pups regulate the periodic release of the hormone oxytocin, which produces milk letdown (Lincoln 1983, 77–112). The pups' sucking induces the slow-wave sleep state in the dam that is necessary for the burst-firing of the hypothalamic neurones that release oxytocin into the circulation where it can act on the contractile mammary gland tissue to produce milk letdown at the teat. Finally, the activity and heat generated by the litter regulate the maternal brain temperature, which in turn triggers the termination of each nursing bout (Woodside, Pelchat, and Leon 1980, 61–68).

The picture that emerges (figure 4.9) is of two individual homeostatic systems linked in a superordinate organization that merits the term symbiosis. The guiding principle of this dual unity appears to be to integrate the developmental changes that the relationship must pass through in its course toward eventual independence of both partners. This integration involves mutual regulation of vital endocrine, autonomic, and central neural systems of both mother and infant by elements of their interaction with each other. Pleasurable affects arising within this context are going to be strongly influenced by the elements of synchrony, mutuality, and reciprocity inherent in the relationship at a deep biological level. This may account for these elements being so much a part of the inner experience of affects of pleasure in our relationships with people we love.

Implications for Internal Object Representation

The multiple pathways we have discovered by which the infant is regulated in its early symbiotic relationship with its mother, and the associative experiences

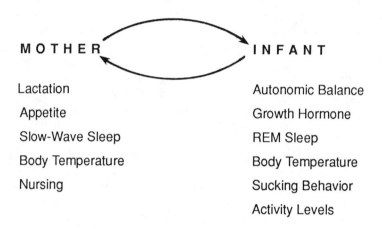

Figure 4.9 Summary of interdependent systems found within mother-infant interaction that constitute a "dual unity" in physiological and behavioral regulation in a simple animal model system

described for the formation of affect, provide us with a close look at some of the pathways by which internal object representations are formed in early life. As soon as associative memories begin, infants start to conduct their lives at a symbolic level of meanings as well as at a sensorimotor level. In infants of species with sufficient cognitive capacity, complex maternal representations are gradually formed, enabling them, for example, to endure temporary separations without full-scale separation responses. These mental structures appear to be laid down in memory during early social interactions. Individual units of experience are gradually integrated into something like a network of attributes that are imbued with the affects associated with the individual experiences. Ordinarily, in older children and adults, the whole network is reexperienced as a unified entity when elicited by some associative cue. But the constituent units can be revealed under certain conditions. For example, in bereavement, once the reality of the loss is accepted, the network begins to loosen and individual representational units recover their separate existence in the minds of the survivors. As Freud described it, "the work of mourning is carried out piecemeal" (Freud 1917). In psychoanalysis also, constituent units of early experience underlying internal object representations gradually become evident as treatment progresses.

It seems possible that as internal object representations are laid down, with their characteristic affective components, these organized mental structures act like states (as described in the first section of this chapter) to regulate biological systems, gradually supplanting the sensorimotor regulators found in younger infants. This would link biologic systems with internal object representations so that the biological health-sustaining action of human relationships (Cobb 1976, 300–314) in older children and adults may be transduced not only by the sensorimotor and temporal patterning of the actual interactions, but also by the internal (largely unconscious) experience of the relationship as it is carried out in the mind of the person involved. And it provides us with a new view of how a *psychological* event, like hearing of a parent's death, may set in motion the *biologic* upheaval of bereavement (Hofer 1984, 183–97).

Conclusion

Biological Evidence for a New Theory of Affect

In this paper, I have tried to describe how recent developments in the biology of early behavior provide some intriguing clues that may be of use to psychoanalysts in building a new theoretical basis for the origin and development of affect and of motivation. Because we do not understand how consciousness is derived from the workings of the brain, there are many possible starting points for a theory of mind. But knowledge about the biology of the brain, of evolutionary processes and development in experimental animals, can provide an interesting place to begin and a rich source of ideas that are particularly likely to be relevant to the workings of the mind as revealed to us by inner experience. Thus, in the following I have referred consistently to *brain* or *nervous system* activity, function or organization rather than to *mental* functioning. Our best understanding is that inner experience and self-awareness are emergent properties of highly complex brain organization as this takes place in our species (Sperry 1969, 532–636; Humphrey 1986), but it is clear that most of the vast extent of nervous activity is not available to our consciousness. Until we know a great deal more about how some of this brain activity is translated into our awareness, biology will have little to contribute to our understanding of the principles by which, for example, memories are made available to inner experience or how accurate our inner perceptions of our own judgments, plans, and motivations may be. Here, psychoanalytic experience is our best guide. The workings of complex unconscious processes are now being incorporated into current cognitive science research, and collaboration between this field and psychoanalysis has exciting potential (Wegman 1985). Until we have a Rosetta stone to help us resolve this ultimate psychobiological mystery, we must struggle to make the translation, to the best of our abilities, between the properties of the brain and of the mind.

My own version of the current biological view of the human brain is arranged to provide a comparison with the late nineteenth-century views used by Freud as a basis for the properties of his psychic apparatus (for example, Freud 1895; Freud, with Breuer 1895; Freud 1920) and persisting today in current psychoanalytic theory (for example, Brenner, chapter 9). We now have ample evidence that the origin of brain activity lies in the electrochemical processes intrinsic to neurones, and those neurones act to influence the activity of other neurones by chemical signals. In this sense the function of the brain is to communicate. The evolution of specialized sensory organs and of motor systems consisting of muscles and bones allows the nervous system to communicate with its environment as well as within itself. The brain is thus an information-processing system as well as the engine of behavior and the source of our inner experience. The specific ways by which the brain is predisposed to process information and predisposed to act has been determined by evolution through natural selection. From our present understanding of evolutionary processes, this means that the forms of brain organization that underlie these predispositions have been selected because they contribute in some way to a single ultimate goal—the perpetuation of the individual's genes and those of close relatives. In this sense, there is only one goal of brain activity, but achieving this goal requires that the organism is predisposed to accomplish a number of subsidiary or intermediate goals. These, in turn, have been organized in a roughly hierarchical order with the most urgent and comprehensive being survival, with sex, feeding, parenting, attachment, sleep, and play being examples of subsidiary predispositions. It is convenient to refer to the organized modes of function that underlie these predispositions as motivational systems. Naturally, the relative priorities of the subsidiary goals change with development as do the capacities of the organism and the characteristics and demands of its environment.

To accomplish various age-specific tasks, the brain must be able to shift from one state of functional organization to another and thus from one mode of information processing to others within an essentially modular structure. These organized states constitute an important component of motivational systems, and they can be considered to provide the neural substrates for affect—both the internal experience of affect and the communicative aspects that are embedded in the form and patterning of the behavior that is produced during these states.

In general, pleasure is experienced during the carrying out of activities related to the goals determined by our evolution, and unpleasure is felt when the attainment of these goals appears to be threatened, when we fail, or when we are prevented from attaining them. In general, the inner experience of affect is congruent with the behavioral expression communicated to others; but one of the most interesting questions confronting psychoanalysts has to do with explaining clinical examples of the various ways in which affect regulation fails to develop normally, or becomes dissociated from adaptive behavior, from inner experience, and from communicative behavior. It is beginning to be possible to study these aberrant developmental paths experimentally in genetically specified animal models, and their neural substrates can now be approached with the biological techniques available today.

The functional organization of the brain underlying motivational systems and affects develops as cellular connections are formed during the fetal period and as interactions exert their influence on this organization from the fetal period onward (Hofer 1981b). Of course, in the beginning, the available sensory, motor, and integrative capacities are relatively limited. During the early fetal period, mammals first begin to show spontaneous neuromuscular movements and sub-sequently become responsive to tactile sensation in the mouth and nose area. Then simple approach and avoidance reflex movements appear and the pat-terning of spontaneous and elicited movements becomes subject to cyclic fluc-tuations as state organization becomes sufficiently advanced. Finally, in the last one-third to one-fourth of the fetal period, associative learning becomes pos-sible, as demonstrated by Smotherman and Robinson in the rat fetus (1987). Work by Fifer and others in our laboratory has indicated that human infants probably acquire the ability to recognize their own mother's voice *before* birth (Fifer 1987).

Affect appears to be involved in some of the earliest transactions of the newborn mammal with its natural environment, its mother's breast. In following the development of affect, we are helped by the concept of state organization, a bridging concept between physiology and psychology, together with our grow-ing understanding of biological processes underlying learning and other forms of neural plasticity. I have suggested that the first affective states come into being during the elicitation of simple approach responses by newborns to low levels of effective stimulation and of simple withdrawal responses to more in-tense stimulation, according to the theory put forward by T. C. Schneirla and Ethel Tobach. Feedback from these behaviors and their consequences, when repeated, establishes anticipatory states in which simple affects of pleasure and unpleasure appear to operate. An example of how this may happen was pre-sented in a series of experimental observations on infant rats involving associative experiences likely to occur in interaction with the mother and culminating in the demonstration of altered brain neurophysiology likely to underlie a simple form of pleasure.

Since affect appears to develop coincidentally with the acquisition of the infant's earliest flexible behavior repertoire, it can be thought of as a fundamental driving and shaping force for behavior from the newborn period on. To the extent that inner experience develops together with behavioral states, affective experience in some form is likely to be a critical component of our earliest mental life. Thus, to understand early affect development, we need to know a great deal more about the nature of the infant's primary environment, the par-ent-infant interaction. Knowledge about the biological processes hidden within first relationships will be fundamental in making inferences about early affects and their development, since it is the experience the infant has in this environ-ment that will have a major influence on the characteristics of later affective life.

Finally, I have described the biological concept of symbiosis and some of the biological and behavioral processes we have discovered within the mother-infant interaction of the rat that support the use of such a concept denoting, in Mahler's words, "a dual unity with one common boundary" (Mahler, Pine, and Bergman 1975). Inferences and speculations derived from this concept help bridge the gap between biological studies in experimental animals and clinical observations on attachment, responses to loss, and the psychology of grief.

REFERENCES

Barlow, G. W., and Silverberg, J., eds. 1965. *Sociobiology: Beyond Nature/Nurture.* AAAS Symposium, no. 35. Boulder, Colo.: Westview Press.

Bowlby, J. 1969. *Attachment and Loss.* Vol. 1, *Attachment.* New York: Basic Books.

Cobb, S. 1976. Social support as a moderator of life stress. *Psychosomatic Medicine* 38:300–14.

Crozier, W. J., and Pincus, G. 1928. On the geotropic orientation of young mammals. *Journal of General Physiology* 11:789–802.

de Bary, H. A. 1879. *Die Erscheinung der Symbiose.* Strasbourg: Karl J. Trubner.

Fifer, W. 1987. Neonatal preference for mother's voice. In *Perinatal Development: A Psychobiological Perspective,* ed. N. Krasnegor, E. Blass, M. Hofer, and W. Smotherman. New York: Academic Press.

Freud, S. 1895. Project for a scientific psychology. *Standard edition,* 1:281–397, 1966.

———. 1917. *Mourning and Melancholia. Standard edition,* 14.

———. 1920. *Beyond the Pleasure Principle. Standard edition,* 18, 1955.

Freud, S., with Breuer, J. 1895. *Studies on Hysteria. Standard edition,* 2, 1955.

Gardner, H. 1985. *The Mind's New Science: A History of the Cognitive Revolution.* New York: Basic Books.

Hall, W. G. 1979. Feeding and behavioral activation in infant rats. *Science* 205:206–09.

Hobson, J. A. 1977. What is a behavioral state? In *Society for Neuroscience Symposia.* Vol. 3, *Aspects of Behavioral Neurobiology,* ed. J. A. Ferrendelli, 1–15. Bethesda: Society for Neuroscience.

Hofer, M. A. 1981a. Parental contributions to the development of their offspring. In *Parental Care in Mammals,* ed. D. J. Gubernick and P. H. Kloper, 77–115. New York: Plenum Press.

———. 1981b. *The Roots of Human Behavior: An Introduction to the Psychobiology of Early Development.* New York: W. H. Freeman.

———. 1984. Relationships as regulators: A psychobiologic perspective on bereavement. *Psychosomatic Medicine* 48:183–97.

———. 1987. Shaping forces in early social relationships. In *Perinatal Development: A Psychobiological Perspective,* ed. N. Krasnegor, E. Blass, M. Hofer, and W. Smotherman, 251–74. New York: Academic Press.

Hofer, M. A., and Shair, H. 1982. Control of sleep-wake states in the infant rat by features of the mother-infant relationship. *Development Psychobiology* 15:229–44.

Holt, R. H. 1965. A review of some of Freud's biological assumptions and their influence on his theories. In *Psychoanalysis and Current Biological Thought,* ed. N. S. Greenfield and W. C. Lewis, 93–125. Madison: University of Wisconsin Press.

Humphrey, N. 1986. *The Inner Eye.* Cambridge: Cambridge University Press.

Koshland, D. E. 1980. Bacterial chemotaxis in relation to neurobiology. *Annual Review of Neuroscience* 3:43–75.

Leon, M. 1987. Neural and behavioral plasticity induced by early olfactory experience. In *Perinatal Development: A Psychobiological Perspective,* ed. N. Krasnegor, E. Blass, M. Hofer, and W. Smotherman. New York: Academic Press.

Leon, M., and Woodside, B. 1983. Energetic limits on reproduction: Maternal food intake. *Physiology and Behavior* 30:945–57.

Lincoln, D. W. 1983. Physiological mechanisms governing the transfer of milk from mother to young. In *Symbiosis in Parent-Offspring Interactions,* ed. L. A. Rosenblum and A. Moltz, 77–120. New York: Plenum Press.

MacFarlane, A. 1977. *The Psychology of Childbirth.* Cambridge: Harvard University Press.

Mahler, M. S.; Pine, F.; and Bergman, A. 1975. *The Psychological Birth of the Human Infant.* New York: Basic Books, 44.

Pederson, P. E., and Blass, E. M. 1982. Prenatal and postnatal determinants of the first suckling episode in albino rats. *Developmental Psychobiology* 15:349–55.

Pine, F. 1986. The "symbiotic phase" in light of current infancy research. *Bulletin of the Menninger Clinic* 50:546–69.

Pribram, K. H., and Gill, M. M. 1976. *Freud's "Project" Re-assessed.* New York: Basic Books.

Rosenblatt, J. S. 1983. Olfaction mediates developmental transition in the altricial newborn of selected species of mammals. *Developmental Psychobiology* 16:347–75.

———. 1987. Factors underlying the mother's participation in the mother-young relationship in the rat. In *Perinatal Development: A Psychobiological Perspective,* ed. N. Krasnegor, E. Blass, M. Hofer, and W. Smotherman. New York: Academic Press.

Rosenblum, L. A., and Moltz, A. 1983. *Symbiosis in Parent-Offspring Interactions.* New York: Plenum Press.

Schneirla, T. C. 1939. A theoretical consideration of the basis for approach-withdrawal adjustments in behavior. *Psychological Bulletin* 37:501–02.

Singh, P.; Tucker, A. M.; and Hofer, M. A. 1976. Effects of nasal $ZnSo_4$ irrigation and olfactory bulbectomy on rat pups. *Physiology and Behavior* 174:373–82.

Smotherman, W. P., and Robinson, S. R. 1987. Psychobiology of the fetus. In *Perinatal Development: A Psychobiological Perspective,* ed. N. Krasnegor, E. Blass, M. Hofer, and W. Smotherman. New York: Academic Press.

Sperry, R. W. 1969. A modified concept of consciousness. *Psychological Reviews* 76:532–636.

Sullivan, R. M.; Hofer, M. A.; and Brake, S. C. 1986. Olfactory-guided orientation in neonatal rats is enhanced by a conditioned change in behavioral state. *Developmental Psychobiology* 19:615–23.

Sullivan, R. M.; Brake, S. C.; Williams, C. L; and Hofer, M. A. 1986. Huddling and independent feeding of neonatal rats can be facilitated by a conditioned change in behavioral state. *Developmental Psychobiology* 19:625–35.

Sulloway, F. J. 1979. *Freud, Biologist of the Mind: Beyond the Psychoanalytic Legend.* New York: Basic Books.

Teicher, M. H.; Flamm, L. E.; Williams, M.; Eckhert, S. J.; and Lumia, A. R. 1978. Survival, growth and suckling behavior of neonatally bulbectomized rats. *Physiology and Behavior* 21:553–61.

Tobach, E. 1970. Some guidelines to the study of the evolution and development of emotion. In *Development and Evolution of Behavior: Essays in Memory of T. C. Schneirla,* ed. L. R. Aronson, E. Tobach, D. S. Lehrman, and J. S. Rosenblatt, 238–50. San Francisco: W. H. Freeman.

Wegman, C. 1985. *Psychoanalysis and Cognitive Psychology.* New York: Academic Press.

Weiss, K. R.; Chiel, H. J.; Koch, U.; and Kupfermann, I. 1986. Activity of an unidentified histaminergic neuron, and its possible role in arousal of feeding behavior in semi-intact *Aplysia. Journal of Neuroscience* 6(8): 2403–15.

Weiss, K. R.; Koch, U. T.; Koester, J.; Rosen, S. C.; and Kupfermann, I. 1982. The role of arousal in modulating feeding behavior of *Aplysia*: Neural and behavioral studies. In *The Neural Basis of Feeding and Reward,* ed. B. G. Hoebel and D. Novin. Brunswick, Maine: Haer Institute.

Wilson, E. O. 1975. *Sociobiology.* Cambridge: Harvard University Press.

Woodside, B.; Pelchat, R.; and Leon, M. 1980. Acute elevation of the heat load of mother rats curtails maternal nest bouts. *Journal of Comparative and Physiological Psychology* 94:61–68.

II

The Theoretical Frontier:
Mind-Brain Questions of
the Pleasurable

5

Project for the Study of Emotion

DONALD L. NATHANSON, M.D.

What is pleasure for one may be pain for another, and what is pain at the moment it occurs may be described as pleasure in retrospect. A word with too many meanings ceases to have utility when it no longer symbolizes that which can be validated consensually. When used in common parlance, "pleasure" and "anxiety" remain acceptable (and properly vague) referents for emotions or ideoaffective complexes that suggest a wide range of experiences and associated positive or negative affective tonality. The very title of this volume suggests that psychoanalysis has gone so far beyond Freud's (1911, 1920) use of those words that it is time for a thorough overhaul of the language of emotion.

I will outline here the data described by such a language, offering the vocabulary and syntax that facilitate its use. The concept of pleasure will be defined in terms of the innate affects *interest-excitement* and *enjoyment-joy* and the dynamic interplay of the innate affects as introduced by Tomkins (1962), and placed in equilibrium with a wide range of information from the disciplines of infant observation, neurophysiology, psychopharmacology, sociology, and psychoanalysis.

Classical Psychoanalytic Theory

Using the language of traditional psychoanalysis, let us start with the most cursory of explanations of emotion as presented by Brenner (1955): Powered by the paired drives called libido and aggression, the forces of the id motivate the organism to gratify instinctual wishes. The ego, unable to hold such wishes in abeyance, is overwhelmed by an influx of stimuli. Psychic energy, unable to

Portions of this paper were presented to the Vienna Psychoanalytic Society, 13 October 1987.

accomplish its aim and incapable of restraint by the ego, courses through genetically determined drainage channels and subsequently is experienced by the ego as the affect of anxiety. The experience of emotion depends on the presence of the ego, for it is within the ego that drive energy is converted to affect. Other, variously named, unpleasant emotions are considered to be forms of anxiety, renamed by the ego for further defensive purposes. The gratification of drive-based wishes causes a reduction in anxiety and the experience of pleasure. Other, variously named, pleasant emotions are considered to be forms of anxiety reduction or drive gratification, renamed by the ego for further defensive purposes. Wherever in our clinical work we encounter an emotion, it can be shown to be derivative of a drive; the emotions are therefore referred to as *drive derivatives.*

I doubt that there exists today one practicing psychoanalyst who continues to accept the schema outlined above in its entirety. Many would argue that no single statement in that paragraph remains acceptable, for solid evidence exists to refute it in every aspect. Yet in order to replace this neat theoretical construct with one not only conforming to the available data but one that incorporates *all* known data, we must look beyond psychoanalysis. It is helpful to examine the soil from which Freud's ideas about emotion grew.

The Scientific Milieu of Freudian Theory

Central to the science of Freud's era was a belief that beneath complex phenomena lay simple, discrete mechanisms. Sir William Osler, who influenced medicine much as did Freud psychiatry (and who was but seven years his senior), pioneered a philosophical approach in which the diagnostician attempted to reduce to a single disease entity a patient's symptomatology, no matter how perplexing and intricate. Syphilis was called "the great imitator," because it could mimic any other disease. Students were admonished "Know syphilis and you know medicine." Where no discrete mechanism could be identified, frequently recurring symptom patterns were grouped to form syndromes, which were named and then accorded the status of distinct entities. After Osler, it became unfashionable to suggest that a patient might have two or more illnesses at the same time. Einstein's hope for a "unified field theory" that would draw together all the known physical forces as subsets of energy itself represents another outgrowth of this philosophical ideal. It was in such a scientific environment that Freud attempted to describe all mental phenomena in terms of their relation to the drives.

Steeped in the science of hydraulics, Freud understood the drives both as some sort of fluid transmitted through invisible pipes and a force akin to electricity. The "energy" that traveled along these conduits was called psychic energy, and those thoughts and memories touched by the drives were said to be "invested" with this energy. In keeping with the physics of his day, Freud postulated further that the amount of psychic energy available to the organism was limited and was parceled out to various subsystems of the mind according to the degree to which they were cathected.

Theories emanate from whatever is chosen as data. The patient population initially amenable to psychoanalysis was canted in favor of that having hysterical illness. Prevailing social custom had defined sexuality as inappropriate material for study or discussion. When Freud opened the door to disclosure of what previously had been kept hidden, he released a flood of information about sexual mores and their influence on the development of the personality. As he watched the symptom complexes of neurotic patients improve during his analytic work, Freud could not help but be impressed about the importance of sexuality in the development of their illnesses.

Earlier (1891), in his neurological work with aphasic patients, he had noted that certain types of brain damage left people unable to name objects placed in their hands, despite their being able to use the objects correctly. As Basch (1983) has pointed out, "Freud concluded that such pathologic phenomena were decompositions that reversed the process of normal development. That is, if perception and speech can be separated by disease, that indicates that originally these two were discrete functions synthesized during development. In other words, pathology reverses ontogeny. This assumption may explain why Freud never found it necessary to study the development of infants and children in any systematic way. He was always convinced that insight into normal development could be obtained by extrapolating from pathology" (16). Thus Freud was prepared to assign to sexuality a critical role in the development of the entire personality—those mental functions that could be disturbed or distorted by interference with sexuality were seen by him as facilitated or developed in the context of sexuality.

Discovered only a few years before his death, abjured by him, and unpublished during his lifetime, was a work now called the "Project for a Scientific Psychology" ([1895] 1966), which helped to link Freud's understanding of aphasia to his later work on the psychoneuroses. In the "Project," Freud suggested that "the process of thought is essentially a two-step operation. First, a stimulus in the form of an image is received and registered by the brain; this is perception. Then, if the percept is significant enough and there is no obstacle, this pictorial image becomes connected with verbal imagery, with language. Once a picture and the words describing it unite, the perception can be further manipulated logically by the brain—i.e., associated with other picture-word complexes in the interest of arriving at some goal" (Basch 1983, 16). So Freud had moved from an explanation of aphasia in terms of images linked with words to a concept that all thought involved the link between images and words. Throughout his career he behaved as if the role of psychoanalysis was to reunite structures that had been separated by trauma much in the way a neurologist might seek to repair the rift between words and images created by physical trauma as found in aphasia. Although he recognized that this idea could not be substantiated (there is plenty of evidence that nonverbal animals, including the preverbal human infant, manipulate thoughts and images), clearly derivative ideas related to composition and decomposition, to the dualistic theories he called his "metapsychology," remained active throughout his career.

Here, then, are the key elements in the puzzle of Freud's attitude toward emotion: (1) a culturally determined desire to find a force that unifies all mental phenomena; (2) a belief that psychopathology, like neuropathology, was the result of the decomposition of links forged during normal development; (3) clinical evidence that disturbances in the development of sexuality led to psychiatric illness; (4) the decision that libido, a basic life force driving the human toward sexual congress and therefore continuation of the species, was the unifying force he sought. Later, recognizing that certain actions of the organism could not be explained in terms of a life-*maintaining* force, he added the drive called *aggression* to explain those situations in which we attack ourselves or others; and (5) the hypothesized structure of the unconscious, assigning to the id all the power of the drives, to the ego all the executive abilities of the mind, and to the superego all the qualities of morality associated with the child's growing understanding of society. Whereas most of the emotions could be located within the ego, guilt, shame, and pride were products of the superego (even though the emotions themselves were still experienced by the ego).

One of the little-discussed characteristics or attributes of genius is tenacity, the ability to maintain a cognitive construct in the face of overwhelming opposition. Freud knew better than anyone else of his era how important was the link between sexuality and neurosis. He knew, too, that the intrapsychic mechanisms of repression and denial might turn professional and societal attention away from what he saw as the centrality of sexual issues were he to allow any rift in the seamless web within which he interwove drive theory, his concept of emotion, and the structure of the unconscious. Furthermore, he was quite correct to deduce that the science of his era was inadequate to test his theories. While the patient lived, the brain (although by definition the repository of the "mind") was considered to be a mysterious organ shielded within its "black box," bearing little relation to what was studied by the neuropathologist with fixatives, microtomes, stains, slides, and microscope. There simply was no way to alter brain function and to test the effect on intrapsychic development of such alterations. If Freud was to study the relation between variations in libidinal development and the variety of neurotic experience, it could be accomplished only through the analysis of neurosis as the product of decomposition caused by psychic trauma.

Freud never gave up his search for a truly scientific explanation of unconscious function, yet time after time his forward progress hit the unbreachable wall created by the inadequacy of the science of his day. The tenacity and genius that had made him the dominant figure in psychoanalysis and that had led him to reject or exclude from his circle of intimates (and indeed, from the status of respectability within the psychoanalytic movement) any theoretician who disagreed with him, forced his followers to take the position that any other new science leading to any other new theory must similarly be disavowed. Just as Brenner (1955) excused the inability of mid-twentieth-century biology to explain the human situation any better than Freud had ("As yet it does not seem possible to accomplish this satisfactorily, though some interesting attempts are being made in this direction. When such attempts will be successful, no one can say, and in the meantime the formal or theoretical links between psychoanalysis and other branches of biology are few" [25–26]), so psychoanalysis today tends to reel away from any suggestion that there is good scientific evidence requiring that we shift our focus from that assumed by its founder. As Radó (1962) insisted, "psychoanalysis must seek to win its logical place in the system of medical sciences or else . . . float in mid-air."

In a sense, psychoanalysis can cling to Freud's theoretical structure only if it maintains the position that not enough is known about the brain and its relation to the mind to allow major alterations in psychoanalytic theory. It is as if the evolutionary level of the cortical and neocortical development that fosters the kind of learning called "ego function" removes man too far from the ranks of the "lower" animals to permit the use of data from animal experimentation. So deeply entrenched is this mind-set that those who attempt to forge links between the new data about brain function (and much of it, being more than a quarter-century old, is no longer new), our understanding of human development, and the relation of these bodies of knowledge to the understanding and treatment of human emotional illness, are treated as the enemies of psychoanalysis much as were those contemporaries of Freud who rejected libido theory for reasons unconnected to such streams of scientific data.

As I will demonstrate, it is the growing awareness that human emotion is not derivative of the drives and that it represents another, discrete system of cerebral function that forced such thinkers as Radó, Tomkins, and Kohut into this position and that makes the conclusions drawn from infant observation problematic for classical psychoanalysis. It is time to link modern neurobiology, psychopharmacology, infant observation, and psychoanalysis to make a solid theory for emotion that will carry us into the next century.

How to Study Emotion

Imagine, for the moment, a device operating in more than the conventional three dimensions, one that allows us to study human emotion from every conceivable vantage point at the same time. An adult in the moment of emotion will exhibit certain characteristic behaviors—when angry, one may yell; when embarrassed, turn away; when frightened, flee. Alterations in internal biological function accompany these outward displays of emotion; the heart, for example, beats faster during the moment of fear or anger. For these large-scale events to occur, a host of events must take place at the microscopic and submicroscopic level; electrochemical messages must travel along pathways within the central nervous system. Yet nothing recorded so far by our hypothetical device quite resembles the experience of emotion—what this emotion *feels like* to the individual being observed.

Emotions, which themselves are events in the life of an individual, are triggered by events. Whatever resides in our memory is stored with its accompanying emotion. Thus each of us has a highly personal information bank of emotion-related data. This information, held mostly as preconscious or unconscious memory, makes for the coloration of an event, that which is personal for each of us. Our machine must be able to detect, sample, and sort each and every life experience as held in memory and to determine the influence of memory on our perception of the emotion of the moment.

Built into this device must be some method for the assessment of veracity, for the display of emotion can be mimed so precisely as to fool most observers. Whereas one might guess that some mimesis might involve only an "outward" display without any of the inner, neurohumoral manifestations (one can dissemble by smiling when unhappy or sobbing when covertly pleased), actors trained in the Stanislavsky method are clearly "living" the emotions they display. Nevertheless, some people can seem to have an emotion when they do not feel that emotion.

Infants and children scream when they are enraged; an adult is capable of expressing rage over a continuum of displays ranging from an apparently identical mode of screaming to the most minimal and economic of gestures, including the quiet clenching of jaw muscles or drumming fingers on the table. Intuitively we know that the modulation of emotion expression is tied up with maturity. Our machine must be able to detect and correlate data from the entire emotion system no matter what its level of expression or visibility. It would be helpful were our machine to offer some judgment as to the maturational level of the individual under investigation.

If the reader finds daunting the mere description of the amount and complexity of the data outlined above, imagine the plight of the investigator faced with the task of correlating it. We are, however, assisted by tools like the computer, which may enable us to handle such vast amounts of information. For this chapter I will sketch the direction of my thinking, which reflects, in essence, the questions posed by Tomkins in his monumental treatise *Affect/Imagery/Consciousness* (1962–63). Not all of them have been answered, but enough is now known that we may approach them in a scientific fashion.

Components of the Affect System

At this point I will introduce some of the language used by the modern student of emotion. Basch (1976) has suggested that we reserve the term *affect* for strictly biological events, *feeling* to indicate that the organism is aware of an affect, and *emotion* for the coassembly of an affect with our associations to previous experience of that affect. This definitional system allows us to place the human on a continuum within the animal kingdom, rather than in a special category unrelated to our brethren. It suggests that the life forms from which we evolved are capable of affect, that feeling depends on whatever central neurological systems are necessary for the development of awareness, and that the degree and sophistication of emotion will be directly correlated to the organism's capacity for information storage and retrieval and to its ability to make links between realms of information.

This section, then, is about the nature of the biological subsystems involved in the production and maintenance of affect and will describe what may be called *sites of action, effectors, mediators,* and *organizers.* Each of these can be dealt with far better at book length but will be described here only in enough detail to allow discussion of the concept of emotion for this volume.

Sites of Action
By site of action I mean to imply all the places within the body that an individual can sense as being affected during affect. Sites of action are where affect can become feeling. By mechanisms I have yet to discuss, in fear the *erector pili* muscles contract, making the hair stand on end. In distress, we cry; the lacrimal apparatus is another end organ of the affect system. Affect can alter patterns of secretion and motility in the gut, for in fear some people are cotton-mouthed while others have diarrhea or nausea. Secretion by other exocrine systems, like the sweat glands, can be observed to change under the influence of affect. Clearly, the primary function of tearing is protection of the eyes from dryness or noxious chemical stimuli. Of course, gastrointestinal secretion, under the control of the autonomic nervous system, varies in response to the needs of digestion. Nonetheless, these preexisting mechanisms *can* be triggered during affect.

Crying is more than tearing, for sobbing involves a vocal expression of distress. The voice, independent of its use in the production of words, is a major instrument of the affect system. Whereas the preverbal child can communicate only by affect, using such wordless expressions as cooing, laughing, screaming, and grunting, the adult can add affect-loaded tonality to verbal symbolic expression and produce exquisite shades of meaning. Tomkins (1962) suggests that the voice evolved primarily because the additional power it gave affect expression increased the organism's ability to survive. The growls, barks, and whines of nonverbal animals seem to represent varying forms of affective expression used for both intentional and unintentional communication. Notwithstanding the reason a dog barks or growls, our actions relative to that dog are informed by those sounds. Our lifetime of experience with pet dogs suggests that other dogs may derive even more information from dog sounds than we do, just as a human mother can sense the needs of her baby from its affective nonverbal utterances.

The circulatory system is intimately involved in the experience of affect. Variations in heart rate accompany fear and excitement. Peripheral vascular manifestations of affect include the cold, sweaty hands of fear and the blush of shame. Differential sites of variation in skin temperature accompany the anger of the redneck and the flush of sexual excitement. Similarly, the respiratory apparatus may act as an end organ for affect expression when we breathe faster in excitement, suspend our breathing in fear, or make the sudden intake of breath associated with surprise.

Observing an organism during the experience of emotion, one notes many alterations in posture. We may stand erect when proud, droop in shame, adopt a fighting stance, jut the head forward in anger or disgust, or cringe in fear.

But by far the most important realm of affect display is the face. Most likely, there is no site of action for affect that is not also used by the organism for another purpose, save for the facial muscles of expression. Whereas the other somatic sites of action seem to have primary functions unrelated to affect, as in the case of the lacrimal apparatus, the muscles of the face (except for those involved in chewing, which contract and bulge during the expression of anger) appear to serve no *primary* function other than their work within the affect system.

Working from the standpoint of his predominant interest in evolution, Darwin ([1872] 1979) was the first to note that most animals show facial expressions indistinguishable from those of man and that the closer a life form to us in phylogeny, the better the match of facial expressions both in form and range. Nowhere else in the body can the anatomist demonstrate so many perfectly developed muscle groups packed together so well, each group served by its own specific nerve trunk. Additionally, as Darwin pointed out, facial expression remains the same throughout life, from birth through adulthood. There is a great deal more to say about the face (which Tomkins considers the display board for the affect system), but for the moment I wish only to include it among the bodily sites capable of displaying affect. The face can provide data from which the organism can derive whatever complex of information is needed to determine the existence of a feeling.

Effectors

Each end organ of affect expression must be served by discrete nerve trunks carrying a message acceptable to that organ or triggered directly by chemicals brought through circulation. I regard as *effectors* those anatomical structures that carry such messages, and *mediators* those chemicals that are capable of specific action on affect-related structures. What follows is a cursory survey of effectors.

Best-known among the many central nervous system structures impinging on affect behavior is the reticular activating system, which seems to be responsible for varying levels of arousal. Various hypothalamic nuclei have been implicated in the production of anger, "sexual aggression," fear, and pleasure. In the presence of bilateral temporal lobe lesions, an organism develops the Kluver-Bucy syndrome, with blunted affect and inappropriate affective responses. Bilateral ablation of the amygdala can cause dramatic reductions in both fear and anger, while stimulation of this portion of the limbic system can evoke ragelike attack and fearlike defensive behaviors. Facial expression can be triggered by stimulation of the brain stem through the bulbofacial tracts or by pyramidal fibers coursing from the neocortex. Pseudobulbar palsy is considered to be a neurologic disorder of affective expression in which interruption of corticobulbar tracts lying between the internal capsule and the pons can cause unrestrained outbursts of laughing and crying with no associated emotional meaning. The autonomic nervous system, with its paired sympathetic and parasympathetic trunks (including the vagus nerve), controls gut function and mediates affect-related changes in motility and secretion.

I have listed these inherently complicated neurological structures and syndromes without references and in no particular order. The point is that a myriad of brain structures is involved in the production of affect-related behaviors, behaviors over a wide range from arousal to quiescence, and that much confusion exists about the relation between these structures and the pathways for normal emotion.

Mediators

The brain is more than a large ganglion acting to handle electrical impulses like a telephone switching office. It is also an endocrine organ, and some investigators believe that fully a third of its bulk subserves this function. Some of the chemicals known to have an impact on the affect system include, but are by no means limited to, the following:

Variations in the amount of circulating epinephrine can affect heart rate; the degree of such excitation will be proportional to the amount of thyroid hormone available. When epinephrine acts directly on cardiac muscle we may say that, in terms of whatever emotional experience might follow that increase in pulse rate, it is a direct mediator of affect. Often a chemical substance does not act directly on the muscle, gland, or other structure operating as the actual site of affective display but on a subsystem higher in the chain of events that leads to the eventual effect on a site of action. Here I would classify it as an indirect mediator of affect.

We know of a host of neurotransmitter substances, notably norepinephrine and serotonin, responsible for the maintenance of mood. Studies of the action of the tricyclic and monoamine oxidase inhibitor antidepressants suggest that a deficiency of these neurotransmitters in the fluid bathing the interface between adjacent neurons may be implicated in the etiology of some forms of depression. Few if any investigators differentiate among the highly specific negative affects seen in the conditions lumped under such rubrics as "depression" or "affective illness." Yet people who are treated with antidepressants complain not just of "blue moods," but of feelings of guilt and shame unassociated with actual experience. As I have noted elsewhere (Nathanson 1987a), the oral ingestion of reserpine can produce profound feelings of guilt. Studies of macaque monkeys given alpha-methylparatyrosine suggest that this chemical interferes with neurotransmitter function to produce shame-related behaviors incorrectly called depression.

Too much thyroxin can produce a syndrome indistinguishable from anxiety, possibly from its ability to potentiate the effect of epinephrine; too little can be implicated in depression. High doses of other hormones, like the corticosteroids, can cause mania, with its stigmata of excitement and hyperactivity. Ingestion of simple medications taken for the common cold, like nasal sprays or pills containing adrenergic compounds, will stimulate anxiety. Agents that release neurotransmitters from their storage granules in brain cells, like cocaine and amphetamine, can cause affective responses over a wide range—from euphoria to profound dysphorias like terror. The very fact that the profound guilt or shame seen in morbid depression (and which seem unaffected by any form of therapy based either on uncovering prior experience or the modification of behavior) can be altered by the use of medication, suggests that chemical mediators play a large role in the experience of affect.

Two additional hormone systems bear an as yet undetermined relation to human emotional behavior. Endogenous morphinelike substances, called *endorphins* or *enkephalins,* act to produce a wide range of positive affective states. Although endorphin release is postulated as the internal reward accompanying such prolonged tasks as long-distance running, the role of such compounds in normal development is unknown. Known for some years, but poorly linked to human physiology, is a group of compounds called *pheromones,* hormonelike chemicals released by exocrine glands into the envelope of air that surrounds each animal. Pheromones are detected by chemoreceptors located in the nose and may be responsible for some portion of sexual arousal.

Organizers

Any recurrent, patterned display of affective expression may be described as organized. Tomkins (1962, 1963) has described nine such patterns of expression, giving for each the probable configuration of neural events acting as its stimulus; the consistent grouping of bodily sites in which this expression may be noted; the effect on psychological function of that pattern of expression; and the range of feelings and emotions associated with that affect. He has also suggested the role of that innate affect both in child development and adult interpersonal relations. Affective responses are mediated by the autonomic nervous system. Although the innate affects cause demonstrable alterations of function throughout the body, they are named, as suggested by Darwin, on the basis of the way they are displayed on the skin and muscles of the face.

This attention to the face takes into account what actually seems to be going on between mother and infant during the earliest postnatal period. The eyes of the nursling are focused neither on breast nor bottle but on the face of the caregiving other. Indeed, the normal distance between the eyes of the feeding infant and the face of the mother is approximately fourteen inches, the focal length of the neonatal lens. Before the emergence of speech and the ability to use words as a vehicle for symbolic communication at perhaps eighteen months, it is through the observation of each other's facial affect display that mother and child communicate.

In general, each innate affect is given a two-word group name, covering the range over which that affective state may be expressed, from the mildest to the most intense form of expression. The first six of these "hardwired" mechanisms are triggered by alterations in the intensity of neural stimulation or variations in stimulus gradients. All information entering the brain is equally weighted with respect to the affect system. Thus, affect can be triggered by neural stimulation emanating from the digestive tract, from proprioception, or any other sensory system, including sound, light, and temperature, as well as from dreams and drives and later from memory and any form of neocortical cognition.

When stimulus density is rising at a slow, optimal level, as when we are confronted by novelty, a subcortical affect center triggers the affect called *interest-excitement,* in which the eyes stare at or track the object of interest and the brows are furrowed. Too many data entering the system at too rapid a rate trigger *fear-terror,* in which the eyes are held open in a fixed stare or alternatively look to the side. When data enter the system very rapidly, as when we hear the sound of a pistol shot (in mathematics this would be called a "square wave"), the autonomic nervous system responds with the affect *surprise-startle,* with the eyebrows raised and the eyes blinking. Each affect is recursive. Interest, which is a response to an optimal rise in stimulus density, itself motivates the organism by increasing our attention to stimuli in an optimal fashion. Fear makes us fearful by increasing further the rate of data accumulation to an uncomfortable level, while when we are startled the entire neuropsychological system is cleared for a moment, in direct analogy to the square wave that triggered it, preparing us to assess whatever attracted our attention and produced the affect of surprise.

Any decrease in stimulus density triggers the affect of contentment, the smiling response that Tomkins calls *enjoyment-joy,* the continuum between a slight smile and joyous laughter depending on both the intensity of the stimulus that has been decreased and the rapidity with which it has been decreased. At the level of innate affect, enjoyment implies relaxation and a generalized reduction in the internal level of stimulus density. There are a myriad of situations in which the organism is bombarded by stimuli at a relatively constant but higher than optimal level of intensity. A very high level of such stimulation is capable of triggering the equally high density affect *anger-rage,* with a frown, clenched jaw, and reddened face; a lower level of constant but higher than optimal stimulation triggers the affect *distress-anguish,* the crying response. It seems likely that these six innate affects (interest, fear, surprise, enjoyment, anger, and distress), thought to be triggered by sets of stimulus gradients and densities, are phylogenetically the earliest organized affective programs present in the human. Three others seem to have evolved to the status of innate affects as auxiliaries to other forms of cerebral function, two as drive auxiliaries and one as an auxiliary limiting other affects.

The drive hunger is assisted by a group of chemoreceptors capable of de-

tecting possible foodstuffs and making decisions about their suitability for ingestion before they have gained entry to the gastrointestinal system. The sense of
smell allows us to evaluate substances on the basis of their emitted odor. Should
a possibly noxious substance get to the mouth, we are protected by the sense
of taste. Directly proportional to the importance of these sensory modalities as
auxiliaries to hunger is their importance in the development of emotion, for the
organism's responses to noxious taste and smell seem to be evolving in such a
way that they now also function as affects.

Tomkins differentiates between *dissmell*, in which the infant wrinkles its
upper lip, turns up the nose and withdraws, and *disgust*, in which the lower lip
is protruded as if to spit out the offending substance, while the head juts forward.
Dissmell may be seen as the origin of the force with which one person will
reject another on the basis of personal odor—leading on the one hand to the
power of such epithets as "stinker" and on the other to our immense societal
expenditure on soaps and perfumes. Much of the "hatred" or "anger" that
characterizes the enmity between previously intimate adults may be derivative
of the affect disgust. What we have taken into ourselves as nourishing, on the
symbolic level, has now become alien.

Tomkins suggests that the adult emotion called *contempt* represents a developmental fusion of the affects dissmell and anger. A person exhibiting contempt will express anger with the head held back and the upper lip curled as if
rejecting an odor. The highly refined and modulated gesture known as the sneer
of contempt, with one side of the mouth curled up and the other twisted down,
may be seen as a miniaturization of the affects dissmell and disgust combined.
Although many people express anger with the head jutted forward and the lower
lip protruded as in disgust, our vocabulary does not contain a specific word for
this particular blend of affects. *Horror* seems to contain varying amounts of both
disgust and dissmell merged with fear to produce an adult emotion qualitatively
different from its component affects. The face of horror often demonstrates
both the eyes of fear and the mouth of dissmell and disgust.

Are there situations in which an affect, once triggered, maintains itself in a
way that can be dangerous for the organism, much as the drive hunger, if
unchecked, might allow us to ingest something toxic? Dissmell and disgust differ
from the first six affects discussed above in that, although they are exhibited
primarily as facial displays, they are triggered by mechanisms related to a drive
rather than to levels and gradients of neural stimulation. Using the analogy of
these two affects as drive auxiliaries, Tomkins suggests that *shame-humiliation*
has evolved as a program auxiliary to the positive affects interest-excitement and
enjoyment-joy, much as dissmell and disgust have evolved as auxiliaries to hunger. Shame will be triggered in situations where there is a perceived barrier to
positive affect (as, for instance, with another person), the innate patterned response including lowering of the eyelids, turning the head, loss of tonus in the
facial muscles and the head producing the characteristic slump of shame, and
a blush. Shame affect functions to reduce the affects interest and enjoyment

when the organism seems unable or unwilling to do so voluntarily. Elsewhere (Nathanson 1987a) I have suggested that pure shame affect is mediated by a humoral vasodilator substance transmitted upward (both physically and phylogenetically) from its subcortical program center to cortical and neocortical structures, causing both the surface manifestations seen throughout life and the cognitive shock associated with the adult experience of shame. I have presented therein a timetable for shame, demonstrating how this simple physiological mechanism may become intertwined with the growing sense of self, with sexuality, and with all the manifestations of shame as an adult emotion. Nevertheless, the consequence (the initial action) of shame affect is to reduce enjoyment or excitement, no matter what the level of neocortical cognition with which the affect is coassembled.

These, then, are the nine innate affects described by Tomkins and functioning as the core vocabulary of human emotion. The passages above contain an extraordinary amount of information. Affect theory does not simplify the task of the developmental theorist. Instead of a paired system of vaguely defined drives from which any psychic function could be derived by metapsychological manipulation, we have an extremely complex system of small, tightly defined mechanisms, each carrying highly specific forms of information and affecting the organism in highly specific ways. Not all emotional experience devolves from the action of these innate affect programs, for there is a host of situations in which affect is triggered by electrochemical or mechanical stimulation of the subunits normally organized by these programs. Furthermore, with maturity comes the ability to trigger affect by learned as well as innate stimuli. What the reader should learn from this description of the innate affects is that the myriad of cerebral structures that I have called effectors and the enormous number of chemical mediator substances that are all capable of producing discernible effects on the various sites of action can be organized into discrete patterns by a group of subcortical programs.

Each era of science is dominated by some major theoretical system that gained ascendance because it explained two realms of data: that which was known and understood within previous systems and that which had been excluded from consideration because it could not fit into that system. The true test of a new system of thought is its ability to stimulate further research and to interpret the data emerging from such research. That the biology of the brain no longer fits into drive theory as elaborated by Freud is the compelling reason for a volume such as this. Computer technology can allow us to interpret the vast amount of biological and observational data accumulated in the century since Freud offered the lens of his genius to explain what was available then. Although the brain is not a computer, certain aspects of cerebral function may be studied as if they were analogous to computer function. For our particular interest, the *logic* of computer science may provide analogues from which particular aspects of emotion may be understood.

The Drives

Acceptance of Tomkins's schema for the innate affects forces a reappraisal of the nature of the drives, for with emotion and motivation removed from the psychoanalytic understanding of the drives, what remains must be considerably reduced in its significance within psychoanalytic theory. If the affects are made more biological, so must the drives be capable of description in line with other phenomena found in the sciences. Rather than present in detail all of the information that suggests such a complete revision of the concept of the drives— one that removes the artificial and definitional difference between the hypothetical psychoanalytic drives and the well-established biological drives—I will sketch briefly some of this new understanding.

Freud's idea of a drive called aggression not only can no longer be sustained but is unnecessary. Everything previously assigned to aggression can be explained better by the affects anger, excitement, shame, and distress alone or coassembled with other drives, cognitions, and affects as ideoaffective complexes.

Libido is downgraded from the status of a master drive providing all the excitement of life, the major source of intrapsychic conflict, and that for which most of the mental mechanisms evolved, to a biological drive of relatively minor proportions. This conforms to our experience as humans in society for many reasons. None of the legion of those actually observing infants can substantiate the existence of oral, anal, and phallic phases of libidinal development. It now appears that libido is sexual from birth and perhaps before. I have begun to collect data from ultrasound scans of fetuses in utero, showing them manipulating their genitals! In a session recently, the mother of a seven-month-old described him looking up at her with a grin (as she paused while changing his diaper) and *then* developing an erection. Tabin (1985) presents compelling evidence that gender identity develops in the toddler as the result of genital excitement. Only if we close our eyes to the mountains of evidence informing us that libido is never anything but sexual can we maintain the fiction that to be sexual the human infant must emerge from oral and anal phases of development into a phallic stage allowing coalescence of such developmental gains only when the toddler discovers the opposite gender parent in the context of the libidinal urge.

To me, the great mystery of libido is neither the circuitry of its structural neuronal connections within the brain, nor the intricate programming that results in patterns of sexual response, but rather the search for the trigger to these programs. No one has ever shown the nature of the stimulus for sexual response. We have no idea what makes most boy babies respond sexually only to women, and most girl babies respond sexually only to men. If, as I believe, homosexuality is not an "illness" caused by failures in parenting but is more likely one of the variants in fetal development caused by hypothalamic neuroectodermal migration patterns, it still does not help us to understand why little boys heading for a homosexual orientation are sexually aroused when they look at men. It is time for us to study libido as a biological phenomenon.

More to the point here, only by disavowing the information available on the face of the infant can we continue to maintain that the drive libido is the source of the affect excitement. Whatever interests us is not interesting because it has captured some of the psychic energy left over when libido is desexualized but because the affect interest has been coassembled with the subject of our attention. Terms like drive derivative must be expunged from the literature.

Certainly in contemporary Western society the phenomenology of adult sexuality bears little relation to libido as a drive. Until the latest group of venereal diseases threatened the population into a new morality, one could observe easily the comedy of sexual pursuit and how poorly it seemed connected to our theories. The frequency of sexual intercourse is far greater in coupling singles than in married couples. (There is an old folk legend to the effect that if a couple drops a coin in a container each time they have intercourse during the first year of marriage, and removes a coin each time they have intercourse during the remainder of their marriage, they will never empty the container.) Why should a drive like libido be stilled or quieted when allowed free exercise of its urge, in a situation where wish means yes? Shorn of the affective amplification conferred upon sexuality by novelty, sex can become boring. It is difficult to conceptualize a Freudian drive, with its supposed concomitant of psychic energy, becoming bored. Some portion of sexual appetite may be drive-related but much of it derives from such matters as tension around issues of self-esteem, which I have described as part of the shame-pride axis (Nathanson 1987a, 1987b).

What, then, is a drive? Tomkins (1962) suggests that all drives inform us about a specific bodily need with a specific site of consummation. He points out that we are hungry or thirsty in the mouth, sexually aroused in the genital, or need air in the respiratory tree. "An infant who experienced the hunger signal in his hand instead of his mouth would starve to death before he discovered the correct consummatory response" (35). Further, the drive supplies information which is motivating: information which "drives" and a drive which "informs," at once. Without such motivating information the human being could not live. The basic nature of this information is of *time*, of *place*, and of *response—where* and *when* to do *what*—when the body does not know otherwise how to help itself" (30–31, emphasis in original). "Air, water, food and sex, in man, constitute a series of diminishing temporal urgency. Just when any of these drives must be attended to is vital information which has been built into each separate drive signal system" (37). But despite their supplying information for motives, they do not supply the motivation itself.

That the drives are subordinate to the affects in the matter of motivation may be seen easily by looking at some of the coassemblies of drives and affects in everyday life. Assembled with interest or excitement, sexuality is vibrant; assembled with fear or shame, sexuality becomes impotence or perhaps masochism; with anger, sadism. Shorn of the usual or "proper" amplifying affect, any drive can be ignored in favor of whatever has garnered affective amplification and entered consciousness. Soldiers in battle can continue to fight despite wounds that will cause debilitating pain when they can be afforded attention; we are rarely hungry when excited about the activity under way, but are "famished" when it is over. "Affect either makes good things better or bad things worse" (Tomkins 1980, 148). The affects can be intensely rewarding, as in the case of the positive affects, or intensely punishing, "but the biological effect of this amplification is to make the organism care about quite different kinds of events in different ways" (Demos 1988, 32). Although the drives remain the major biological system that promotes the maintenance of individual life and the integrity of a species, they are incapable of achieving their goal without amplification by affect.

The Central Assembly System

Clearly, far too much is going on in the body at any one time for all of it to garner the form of attention we call awareness. Tomkins postulates the existence of a central assembly system where all information from the brain is being processed constantly. When any operation achieves more than a critical amount of affective amplification, it takes over the central assembly and enters consciousness. What we call consciousness is a product of the central assembly, for nothing is conscious unless it has significant affective amplification. We can pay attention to anything amplified by any affect, whether interest, fear, distress, or anger. What happens when we are startled is that the central assembly is cleared, preparing us to pay attention to whatever happens next, with whatever affect will be triggered by that stimulus.

When memory achieves such amplification, we are focused on our past, as often happens naturally in neurosis and by our artifice in the uncovering forms of therapy. When libido achieves amplification by excitement, we are sexually aroused. Yet whatever competing stimulus achieves a higher level of affective amplification will supersede and replace the previously current focus of attention.

Growing Up with Affects

One of the major contrasts between the drive system and the affect system is the matter of information specificity. Whereas the drives inform the organism as to the nature of the substance to be transported, as well as the site of its disposition, the affects are entirely neutral with respect to their triggering stimulus. The drives are complex programs called into operation by some form of bodily need (usually involving a substance), while the innate affects represent an autonomic response to stimulus intensity and gradients of intensity unrelated to whatever has created this neural electrochemical environment. How, then, does a human personality emerge from this complex system of reaction patterns?

Earlier I noted that one of the major features of the innate affects is their visibility. Although one of the tasks of childhood is the mastery of emotionality—leading to whatever style of display is considered normative in a particular society—in infancy the innate affects appear on the face with remarkable clarity. Recall how we smile at an infant whose face is wreathed in smiles, contorted with pure distress, or reddened and scowling in anger. Our adult reaction to the "purity" of this display is the "secret smile" of one who is suddenly privy to that which normally (in the adult) is kept hidden. If, as Tomkins suggests, the face is the display board for the affect system, by the time we have reached maturity that display is partially conscious and only partially innate. It is what happens in infancy around the locus of the face that must occupy our attention at this moment.

By the unfortunate accident of history, Freud stumbled into the world of developmental theory from his work with aphasic adults, using the heuristic model that decomposition caused by trauma revealed the true path along which the infant had traveled on the way to adulthood. Listening to the *verbal* reports of adult patients with severe emotional illness, he could accumulate data no further back in time than the beginning of verbal, symbolic communication, near the end of the period when affective communication dominates the relationship between child and mother. As Freud, moving behind the patient, withdrew farther and farther from the face of the speaker, he became locked into the world of verbal symbology.

Doing so, he was able neither to draw inferences about adult interaffectivity, nor to draw a line backward in time to study the rapt attention with which mother and infant each study the face of the other, nor how the mother mirrors the affective display of her child, nor the powerful relationship emerging during this period of affective communication (Stern 1985). Primary narcissism (the theory that the entirely self-involved child sees the mother only as a satisfier of drive-initiated needs until those drives awaken a sense of relatedness in the context of sexual hunger) works only if one ignores the face of the infant. It represents another piece of our heritage from the classical era in psychoanalysis that must be relegated to museum status if we are to integrate psychoanalysis with modern biology.

It is useful to understand that affect-related information goes in two directions after it is expressed on the display board of the face (and, of course, by vocal mechanisms and any number of odors, postures, and behaviors). Affect display is broadcast outward where it is witnessed by the caregiver, usually the mother; and affect information is fed inward to higher cerebral structures where it is named. Infantile displays of affect are of the all-or-none variety, for the manner in which the subcortical affect programs co-opt the operation of structures remote from the brain is completely unmodulated. The infant must learn to control its display of affect, and this learning is a matter of cortical and neocortical function. Basch (personal communication, May 1987) has suggested that the evolutionary function of both cortex and neocortex was the modulation of innate affect; cognitive development is partly the story of learned affect modulation. That these neocortical structures are capable of other functions, like calculation and varying levels of abstruse cognition, is as much a coincidence as the fact that television, seen by its inventor as possibly useful to check products coming off an assembly line, turned into a medium for entertainment (personal communication, Vladimir Zworykin, July 1957). Good evidence exists to suggest that among the earliest cognitive concerns of the child are those related to affect modulation.

As the growing child becomes more and more aware of his or her affective states and learns to link them to their precipitating causes, a library of emotional responses is formed. Affect is biology, but emotion is biography. The developmental paths along which we travel from infancy to maturity turn the biology that is brain into the biography that is called mind.

But affect behaviors are visible to the caregiver, the mother who spends much of her time watching the infant. Videotape studies of the mother-infant dyad confirm that both mother and infant spend a great deal of time imitating each other's facial expressions. Mimicry of the facial affect display of another person is still the facial display of affect. When I arrange my facial musculature so that my face looks like yours, I can feel whatever affect you are feeling (Ekman, Friesen, and Levinson 1983—confirmation, incidentally, of a suggestion made by Freud 1921). By the language system we call interaffectivity (Stern 1985), the mother learns to tune in on the inner environment of her infant, and as the cognitive skills of the infant improve, the infant learns about the inner state of mother. Such interaffectivity is central to the development of empathy, which begins with this sharing of physiological affect mechanisms but which becomes a highly sophisticated source of interpersonal information (Basch 1983a).

Although Spitz accepted without challenge Freud's belief that "affects are the perceived end results of discharge processes" (1965, 144), he was the first experimental observer to recognize the importance of affective interchanges between mother and newborn, introducing (1947) the term "*affective climate* to designate the totality of the forces which influence development in the infant" (1965, 139, emphasis in original). Further, he stated that "it is of special interest for our research that the unfolding of affective perception and affective exchanges precedes all other psychic function; the latter will subsequently develop on the foundations provided by affective exchange. The affects appear to maintain this lead over the rest of development at least until the end of the first year of life. It is my personal opinion that they will maintain it a good deal longer" (140).

So sensitive, at this early period, are mother and child to each other's affective display that one wonders how the adult can be relatively immune to such interaffectivity. Part of maturity seems to include a reduced sensitivity to the emotions of others, so much so that the empathic ability of artists and therapists is considered special rather than ordinary. Rather than ask how or why such people have gained empathic sensitivity, it is instructive to inquire how others lost it. In an earlier paper (Nathanson 1986), I introduced the concept of an ego mechanism called the *empathic wall*, a group of functions allowing the child to sense whether the affect experienced at the moment derives from resonance with broadcast maternal affect or from innate mechanisms generated from within. Attendance at an entertainment presupposes willingness to relinquish this empathic wall and experience the feelings of the protagonists, as in a play or motion picture, as well as those of the rest of the audience. In an expansion of that contribution (Nathanson 1989) I have delineated a few of the many clinical syndromes in which lesions of the empathic wall mechanism may figure significantly.

Other types of clinical syndromes may be capable of study around the locus of affect expression and affective resonance. Sacks (1985) offers his observations of a woman with Tourette's syndrome who had become the center of much attention on a New York street. He describes her remarkable ability to mimic the facial display of affect of each person encountered, altering only the temporal contour. "Every mirroring was also a parody, a mocking, an exaggeration of salient gestures and expressions, but an exaggeration in itself no less convulsive than intentional—a consequence of the violent acceleration and distortion of all her motions. Thus a slow smile, monstrously accelerated, would become a violent, milliseconds-long grimace; an ample gesture, accelerated, would become a farcical convulsive movement" (117). People literally ran from the unpleasant mirror so presented.

Asking us to consider the inner experience of a person able to mimic or afflicted with the need to mimic and distort such affective display, Sacks wondered "how it must be for *her* in this whirlwind of identities. . . . The answer came soon . . . for the build up of pressures, both hers and others', was fast approaching the point of explosion. Suddenly, desperately, the old woman turned aside, into an alley-way which led off the main street. And there, with all the appearances of a woman violently sick, she expelled, tremendously accelerated and abbreviated, all the gestures, the postures, the expressions, the demeanours, the entire behavioural repertoires, of the past forty or fifty people she had passed. She delivered one vast, pantomimic egurgitation, in which the engorged identities of the last fifty people who had possessed her were spewed out. And if the taking in had lasted two minutes, the throwing-out was a single exhalation—fifty people in ten seconds, a fifth of a second or less for the time-foreshortened repertoire of each person" (118, emphasis in original).

It would be difficult to imagine a better description of the facial manifestations of innate affect, the normal contour of innate affect as compared to the extremely brief temporal profile described here for Tourette's syndrome; of innate affect as opposed to consciously mimed affective display; of the ability of innate affect to act as a communication system; the tendency of adults to experience unexpected affective resonance as an uncomfortable personal emotion because of a temporary lapse in the empathic wall; and the relation between affect modulation and the sense of self. (Like Sacks, I watch the "Touretters" who walk around my city, squawking and screaming, frightening passers-by; they look for all the world like people whose affects explode rather than unfold. If this is a fit, it is an affect fit.) Perhaps Tourette's syndrome involves a lesion at the level of the mechanisms that trigger innate affect.

The normal range of affect expression, allowing the process of affective attunement, allows mother to do more than communicate with her infant. By tuning in on the infant's distress, rage, laughter, or any other affective display, the mother can provide her child with a means of affect modulation. Thus, by cooing, stroking, chanting, singing, rocking, or distracting to an outside focus of attention, the mother can teach relaxation and move the child from the earliest form of all-or-none affect display to more modulated displays of affect. In short, one of the jobs of mothering is this operation of the mother as an external modulator of infantile affect display.

Elsewhere (Nathanson 1988) I have noted that all of the techniques by which the mother acts as an external modulator of neonatal affect are used by the hypnotist as techniques of hypnotic induction. What I believe happens in the hypnotic situation is that an operator uses the techniques of affective attunement (Emde, Gaensbauer, and Harmon 1976) to enter the central assembly of another person and thus can allow any cerebral function to be taken over in a manner agreeable to both operator and subjects. Although the affect system remains unchanged throughout life, growth and development produce tremendous changes in the structure and function of neocortical cognition, so that although similar, fusion between adults is not identical to fusion between caregiver and neonate. Trance can be induced by purely verbal means not possible during early infancy, and trance states can involve images well beyond the capability of the infant. Yet I am certain that hypnotic induction is a system of affect mutualization allowing intentional alteration of what Tomkins calls the central assembly system, and that trance logic and trance behavior involve variations in neocortical cognition called upon by intentional alteration of this central assembly.

Observing the process of hypnosis, watching hypnotist and subject, I am impressed by the rapt attention paid to the face of the subject by the hypnotic operator. (See Gelman 1986, 74–76 for a good example of this phenomenon.) It seems likely that hypnotists watch the face because they are looking for data about the inner affective disposition of their subjects. This observation deserves more study within the world of hypnosis research. If my theory of the nature of hypnosis is correct, no study of hypnotic mechanisms can be considered valid unless accompanied by a film or videotape study of facial affect display.

To summarize this section, I have explained how a group of highly communicable unmodulated physiologic mechanisms triggered by nonspecific stimuli slowly becomes a system of private emotions and gestural language held partially under conscious control. Continuing the analogy between the language of computers and the world of human emotion, I suggest that we understand the structural effectors, chemical mediators, and sites of action through which the affects are expressed as the *hardware* of the emotion system, the innate genetically transmitted programs for affect as the *firmware* (programs built into the machine), and the way we are reared in a particular family and culture as the *software* of this now complete system. Psychoanalysis is a way of debugging software, of retrieving from memory the group of interactions through which we learned to modulate our affects and answer the call of the drives, altering them in terms of the therapeutic relationship. Psychopharmacology involves the detection and repair of problems in firmware and hardware. Depression can be caused by neocortical software mechanisms as when loss triggers distress that in turn triggers more distress experienced as sadness, or by interference with chemical mediators of affect. Pleasure can attend the successful completion of a difficult task or the ingestion of a chemical mediator of a positive innate affect.

Pleasure and Innate Affect

Now that we have discussed the nature of affect, feeling, and emotion, and placed affective attunement, affect mutualization, interaffectivity, intersubjectivity, empathy, hypnosis (including its implied relation to the pleasure called relaxation), and a variety of disturbances of mood within the framework of the innate affects, we can turn our attention to the group of experiences termed pleasurable and unpleasurable. By definition, the positive affects are pleasurable and the negative affects are unpleasant. Thus pleasure would operate at the locus of interest-excitement and enjoyment-joy, while unpleasure would involve the full range of negative affects.

Note the apparent disparity between our adult experience of "fun" or "a good time" and the innate affect Tomkins calls enjoyment-joy. Most people are puzzled by the idea that enjoyment-joy, the smiling response, is triggered by *reductions* in stimulus density and produces further reduction in activity—contentment and calm, rather than excitement. Few of us would find much fun in an event offering only calm. Consider, however, our experience of any entertainment, whether a sporting or theatrical event, experienced actively or passively. Viewed at the level of pure cerebral activity, we would see frequent oscillations between increases in stimulus density—as when we become involved (interested, frightened, embarrassed, distressed, startled, and so on) in the event—and decreases, as "tension" is relieved.

Notwithstanding the associational meaning of the images brought to mind (its ideoaffective content), a joke by its structure involves a relatively slow recruitment of interest followed by a rapid decrease in interest and consequent laughter as the punch line draws us away from the initial focus of attention. (To say that jokes are about hostility as a derivative of the drive aggression ignores the affect dynamics central to their function; in any event, jokes are much more about shame than anger.) Any activity that provides sequences of increased and decreased levels of stimulus density will be experienced as entertaining. In addition, both interest-excitement and enjoyment-joy are positive affects that can be mutualized in an interpersonal interaction to produce a pleasant encounter, lending an additional dimension to our understanding of fun.

Is pleasure dependent on the reduction of tension? Notwithstanding the fact that we humans are "wired" so that certain stimuli intrinsically feel good and other stimuli feel bad, one must look far beyond the pleasure principle to understand pleasure. Unless we understand the pleasure of excitement, the thrill of overcoming chronic shame through the experience of competence in the face of danger, and the camaraderie produced by the contagion of affect mutualization, it would be difficult to explain the claim of a motorcycle gang member describing the rout and victimization of a small town and the subsequent escape from law enforcement officials that such activity constituted fun. Furthermore, we can enjoy our own interest-excitement or enjoyment-joy, we can enjoy that of another person through the mechanism of affective resonance, or we can identify with a fictional character and experience our own version of his or her affective experience.

Tomkins (1962) addressed many of these issues in his chapter "Affect Dynamics," offering nineteen hypotheses about the interrelations between specific affects. In view of the current unavailability of this seminal volume, I will summarize those premises most applicable to the subject of pleasure. The first concerns the relation between negative affect and no affect. Tomkins states that "the reduction of any negative affect is rewarding whether or not it instigates positive affect. Such a reward is sufficient to motivate future attempts to reduce the same negative affect. The basis of this reward is the contrast between the experienced quality of the negative affect and the experienced quality of no affect. . . . Not to feel afraid any more, not to feel distressed, not to feel ashamed is innately preferred to feeling afraid, distressed or ashamed" (283). The second hypothesis, a corollary of the first, states that "the reduction of any positive affect is 'punishing' whether or not it instigates negative affect" (284).

Tomkins continues: "Third, the instigation of negative affect is generally more punishing than the sequence positive affect followed by neutral affect [hypothesis two, above]. . . . Fourth, the instigation of positive affect is generally more rewarding than the sequence negative affect followed by neutral affect [hypothesis one, above]. . . . Fifth, the reduction of negative affect is a specific activator of the positive affect of joy, the intensity and duration of which is proportional to the duration of the prior negative affect, to the absolute magnitude of intensity change and the time over which this change is made. Thus, the intensity and duration of joy produced by the reduction of fear (or any other negative affect) depends on how long that fear has been experienced, how intense it was and how suddenly it was reduced" (284). Conversely, "Sixth, the sudden interruption of positive affect is a specific activator of negative affect, of distress or (anger), the intensity and duration of which is proportional to the duration, intensity and gradient of interruption of the prior positive affect" (286).

"Seventh, the interruption and attenuation of excitement and or joy by virtue of inner or outer constraints activate the shame responses, the lowering of the eyelid, the lowering of the eyes, or the hanging of the head" (287–88). Hypothesis number eight is that the sudden reduction in anger is a powerful activator of joy. Tomkins's ninth hypothesis states that the temporal profile of the affect surprise-startle is so brief that it evokes a neutral state of no affect. The tenth hypothesis states that "the sudden reduction of intense, enduring fear, if complete, releases joy, but if incomplete releases excitement. . . . The lure of the death-defying sports such as automobile racing and bull fighting . . . represents the positive affect of excitement released by the partially reduced fear. . . . On the other hand, when intense enduring fear is completely reduced suddenly we commonly observe the smile of joy on the face of both children and adults" (290–92).

Hypothesis eleven states that "the sudden reduction of intense enduring distress produces joy" (292–93), as in the case when pain is reduced suddenly. Twelfth, "The complete, sudden reduction of intense, enduring shame activates joy; the incomplete sudden reduction of intense, enduring shame activates excitement. . . . Achievement motivation which is powered by shame is enormously strengthened by the incremental rewards of joy which are released by the sudden reduction of shame when success attends protracted effort toward the solution of a problem or the attainment of a goal" (293).

In hypothesis fifteen, Tomkins states that each affect is capable of activating itself, the principle of affective contagion. Fear is frightening, joy is enjoyable, shame is embarrassing. Just as each innate affect is capable of activating itself by internal resonance and extending its temporal contour to produce an affective state or mood, each innate affect can by external affective resonance activate a similar response in one who forms an empathic relationship with the primary broadcaster of that affect. "The self-reproducing characteristic of the affective response is one of the primary supports of moods. A mood of sadness is a distress response which feeds upon itself without further stimulation. It is as saddening to feel sad as it is to hear bad news. The characteristic of contagion is critical for the social responsiveness of any organism. It is only when the joy of the other activates joy in the self, fear of the other activates fear within, distress of the other activates distress within, anger of the other activates anger within, excitement of the other activates one's own excitement that we may speak of an animal as a social animal" (296–97).

Pleasure redefined in terms of innate affect takes into account many of the situations that have so interested the therapist and the developmental theorist. Play contains elements of novelty as an activator of interest, sequences of negative affect (fear, distress, anger) relieved suddenly to produce excitement or joy, and experiences of affect mutualization with peers and supervising adults, and constitutes one of the models available for the study of affect dynamics. Elsewhere (Nathanson 1987b) I have discussed pride as the coassembly of either positive affect with an efficacy experience—the pleasure of competence. When the environment joins with the child's pleasure in efficacy, there is created a psychic structure favoring the development of creativity. To the extent that the environment reacts to creativity with scorn, distress, contempt, anger, fear, or disgust, creativity will not bring pleasure.

Families and cultures differ in their expectations of children. Some, like the Philadelphia Quakers, eschew anger; others applaud the demonstration of rage. Systems of religion may encourage behavioral control through attention to guilt and shame (Judaism and Christianity); release from shame through ecstatic dancing or the use of drugs (various indigenous tribes in the United States and South America); reverence for elders with consequent reduction in excitement through identification with their style of affect modulation (Presbyterian or Shinto worship); or release from such reverence and enhancement of spontaneity (Zen Buddhism). Tomkins (1979) has described human growth, development, and maturation within family and cultural groupings as involving the differential magnification of innate affect.

The Temporal Contour of Innate Affect

Affects do far more than merely appear on the display board of the face. They are recursive, as I mentioned above, in that each affect continues to trigger more affect of the same sort, and also recursive in their manner of operation. *Each affect is by definition an analogic amplifier of its own triggering stimulus.* The variations in stimulus gradient capable of triggering an innate affect, such as rising or falling stimulus density, will be amplified in precisely the direction and manner that allowed them to function as triggers of affect. This, of course, is why each affect can evoke contagion within the organism or with the empathic other. It is why interest and excitement provoke greater attention and enjoyment produces calm. Including surprise-startle, with its remarkably brief (square-wave) duration of action, each affect has its own characteristic temporal contour; it occurs over time, beginning and ending in a form analogous to its triggering stimulus. What happens if we ignore the face and investigate affect from a point immediately after its facial display as a classical innate affect?

Stern (1985) introduces the concept of *vitality affects* (51) to describe situations in which feelings "do not fit into our existing lexicon or taxonomy of affects. These elusive qualities are better captured by dynamic, kinetic terms, such as 'surging,' 'fading away,' 'fleeting,' 'explosive,' 'crescendo,' 'decrescendo," 'bursting,' 'drawn out,' and so on" (54). I believe that by this colorful language, he has described the vital characteristics of innate affect—the contour of an affect described after its facial component has been triggered—rather than a separate form of affect. Any description of an affect that leaves out its facial characteristics, or at least demonstrates unequivocally that it has no facial characteristics, must be considered incomplete. Significant as well for our study of pleasure is the possibility that some of what Stern describes as the range of vitality can be interpreted as varying degrees of the affect interest and its coassembly with other affects.

One aspect of affect theory that seems most difficult for psychoanalysts is the affect interest-excitement. Classical analytic training is so imbued with the idea that all excitement comes from libido and that all realms of interest represent desexualized libido as a drive derivative, that it blocks appreciation of this particular affect. Demos discusses what some infant observers describe as the "cyclical states along the sleep-wake continuum, regular sleep, irregular sleep, drowsiness, alert inactivity, waking activity, alert activity and crying" (1988, 36), pointing out that the inspection of the face of the infant reveals the interplay of a number of affects, including interest-excitement.

She continues "the initial states of the neonate are affective states. ... In the state of alert inactivity the limbs and trunk are at rest, the face is relaxed, the eyes are open, and have a 'bright, shining appearance.' The eyes move together and are coordinated with head movements in order to maintain visual contact with an object." (Descriptions are taken from Wolff 1973.) Please note the similarities between the relaxed face and open, bright shining eyes of alert inactivity and Izard's (1979) description of the facial indicators of the affect interest: "brows raised or knit, eyes widened and rounded, cheeks raised, mouth relaxed or may be opened. ... I would therefore maintain that what has been called alert inactivity or infant attention is in fact the affective state of interest" (37). Drawing parallels between such description of "states" and the Facial Affect Coding System devised by Ekman and Friesen (1978) on the basis of the prior work of Tomkins, she presents what I believe to be adequate evidence that much of "vitality" is interest-excitement.

The entire literature of the attachment theorists, from the initial contribution of Bowlby (1958, 1982) to the work of Ainsworth and coworkers (1978), Sroufe (1984) and many others, suggests that robust conclusions about the future development of an individual may be made by observing the behavior of a year-old infant placed in a standard setting. Children are said to be securely attached, insecurely attached, or avoidantly attached to their mothers, depending on the way they behave when in her presence and in her acute absence. It would seem only natural, in terms of the material presented in the body of this chapter, to expect that such broad generalizations about the most basic forms of interaction between mother and child would include data about facial affect mechanisms. Yet save for the mention of crying and smiling as built-in signals that promote physical closeness and bonding between them, attachment theorists ignore the face.

In a recent interview, Bowlby (ACP 1987) commented that he had been powerfully influenced by the work of Tinbergen (1951), immersing himself in the literature of ethology for a number of years before venturing forth with his own theories about imprinting in the human. Unfortunately, Tinbergen studied the attachment behavior of newly hatched aquatic birds, life forms nearly devoid of facial affect. It would seem only reasonable to replicate the experiments of Bowlby and his followers using videotape or ultra-high-speed motion picture photography allowing slow motion study of facial affect display in both infant and mother. Many of the vocal and large-muscle data reported by these observers seem to represent the affects interest-excitement, distress, anger, shame, and enjoyment-joy. Yet without competent data about the face it is impossible to state with any certainty what is going on between infant and caregiver in the situations described. I cannot believe that the absence of such data is insignificant.

Emotion in Illness and Health

The term "normal development," of course, is a misnomer. More accurately we should speak of a range of possible pathways toward maturity. For a moment, scan the number of ways the system can go wrong. (It would be helpful to have the assistance of the magic computer described earlier as necessary for our study of emotion.) Much can be learned about the full range of possible health and illness if we vary independently each of the moieties described above and (at least) consider the problem of varying them in combination. Optimal emotional health can be defined in terms of one's ability to use one's equipment (hardware and firmware) when raised in a family that permits understanding of our gifts and integration of our personality with the surrounding culture. Too much difference between the family within which we are taught affect modulation and the clusters of families that make up the local culture will make us "healthy" in one setting but "strange" within another. A chronically depressed mother will foster a style and range of affect modulation quite different from a chronically angry or a chronically embarrassed mother. In such situations, psychotherapy assists by increasing the range of options for an individual. There is, then, a wide range of possible emotional illnesses caused by relatively "pure" alteration of developmental software.

Now consider what happens when we alter another variable, like one of the built-in packages of programs, the firmware as described by Tomkins. Might there be illnesses characterized by genetically determined variation in the programs for the interpretation of stimulus gradients (the trigger to innate affect) or for the execution of specific affects? Children born with such firmware would interpret many life situations differently from their peers, would communicate differently, and would experience life considerably differently from those with normative affect programs. I suspect that the condition called alexithymia involves some form of physiological blunting of affect experience around this locus.

For many years I have been fascinated by the emotion shame (Nathanson 1987a). The nature of shame is to impel hiding, and so successful has been this hiding that, for the overwhelming majority of therapists (despite their persuasion or discipline) shame has remained out of sight in our clinical work. Our patients deal more with shame outside our offices by attending to the comedy of embarrassment and the drama of blackmail in the world of entertainment and the banter of the street. The study of shame led me to consider its appearance in clinical syndromes not known primarily for embarrassment but for what Lewis

(1971) called *humiliation fury*, the anger that defends against the reduction of self-esteem. It has been traditional to describe such anger as part of the range of "narcissistic disorders," in which narcissism is considered the central focus of attention. I would agree with Lewis (1987) that the work of both Kernberg (1975) and Kohut (1971), establishing the modern concept of narcissism, ignores the range, extent, and sources of shame. The healthy person uses shame as an indication that some part of his or her self-image needs adjustment. Healthy pride bears little relation to narcissism, which is always pathological and results from the disavowal of shame.

Nowhere is this to be studied as easily as in the syndrome of manic depressive illness. The tendency to bristle at imagined slight or rage when thwarted is part of the classical description of bipolar affective illness. But is shame the only affect involved in this "affective" illness? Hardly. As I have suggested (Nathanson 1987a, 50–58) mania is an amplification expression of the affect interest-excitement—there is no feature of mania that cannot be so explained—just as depression may be thought of as a diminishment lesion of the affect interest. And is this not the language of the patient, who says when depressed that he or she is interested in nothing, but that when manic the entire world is fascinating? Is not innate shame the physiological reducer of inappropriate innate interest? If we are to make emotion our project, we must contemplate the effect on normal development and on adult function of excesses and deficits of each innate affect. Excessive fear can be studied at many levels of the system I have described and still be called phobia.

So the positive affects by themselves do not immutably bring with them the experience of pleasure. Too much interest-excitement does not make for a happy person. To the extent that manic-depressive illness can be seen as an aberration in the positive affect interest, it will be understood that the healthy mind may not be able to handle too much "positive" affect unless it is modulated by the type of affect dynamics described by Tomkins and summarized above. Optimal health does not mean a life of pleasure. It demands a psychological structure that can modulate all of the innate affects.

What if we alter the amount of circulating thyroid hormone, or corticosteroid, or epinephrine? What if, instead of increasing or decreasing the amount of such substances throughout the body as carried in the circulation, we postulate local intracerebral alterations in the concentration of these chemical mediators of affect? Most important of all, we must study the differences between such variations from the norm on a longitudinal basis. An infant born with alterations in mediator function will be affected differently from an adult for whom these alterations are but the momentary climate of his or her emotional life. When emotion is triggered by an interpersonal or intrapsychic event, some combination of innate affect and memorialized affect experiences is experienced. When the brain is suffused with too much thyroid hormone we are fearful; when there is too little thyroid hormone we experience guilt or shame and say we are depressed; when fed alpha-methylparatyrosine we exhibit the stigmata of shame.

In each of these situations some chemical mediator has initiated the sequence we recognize as belonging to an affect. We scroll through memory in order to assign a rational explanation for that affect, which we then call an emotion. The psychopharmacologist must recognize that some emotion is caused by intrapsychic events, and the psychoanalyst must accept that some emotion is caused by biology.

Conclusion

Any method of therapy aimed at the relief of human distress must be based on a sound theory for the nature of that distress and for the nature of all emotion. Ours is an era in which the amount of data available to the clinician-scientist mounts daily and has already reached proportions beyond our grasp. It is unlikely that any one mind will ever again be able to assemble into a coherent pattern all of the information available unless aided by some device that reduces complexity. By virtue of its ability to make complexity accessible to analysis through the repetition of innumerable small, simple tasks, the computer may allow the modern scientist of emotion to establish a circuit diagram for the affect system and to foster the evolution of theories as well as therapies based on that new understanding.

The scientific data available to the founders of psychoanalysis suggested that the search for pleasure represented one of the most important themes around which the growing child might coalesce a personality. Work done in the succeeding century has not only confirmed but amplified the accuracy of that intuition. The human is built to seek pleasure and avoid discomfort. It is the specific nature of the circuitry involved that has turned out to be vastly different from that envisioned by Freud and his circle, for rather than a psychology based on drive theory, our science is turning toward a system based on a solid understanding of the nature of all affect.

This contribution may be viewed as an early attempt to group information from the laboratories of neurology, neurophysiology, psychopharmacology, psychology, infant observation, and psychoanalysis so that programs for its analysis may be determined. By organizing the biological mechanisms related to emotion into the categories that I have called sites of action, effectors, mediators, and organizers of innate affect, and grouping the variety of clinical syndromes that can be explained by altering variables within each of these categories, it is possible to generate new theory that may carry us into the next era of research on the nature of emotion. Only with such an integration can our theories be based on fact and our attempts at therapy based on a solid understanding of the human being.

REFERENCES

Ainsworth, M.; Blehar, M.; Waters, E.; and Wall, S. 1978. *Patterns of Attachment*. Hillsdale, N.J.: Erlbaum.

American College of Psychiatrists (ACP). 1987. Attachment theory: New directions. *ACP Psychiatric Update* 7(2). Interview of J. Bowlby by J. Anthony.

Basch, M. F. 1976. The concept of affect: A reexamination. *Journal of the American Psychoanalytic Association* 24:759–78.

―――. 1983a. Empathic understanding: Review of the concept and some theoretical considerations. *Journal of the American Psychoanalytic Association* 31:101–26.

―――. 1983b. The concept of "self": An operational definition. In *Developmental Approaches to the Self*, ed. B. Lee and G. G. Noam. New York: Plenum Press.

Bowlby, J. 1958. The nature of the child's tie to his mother. *International Journal of Psycho-Analysis* 39:350–73.

―――. 1982. *Attachment and Loss*. Vol. 1, *Attachment*, 2d ed. New York: Basic Books.

Brenner, C. 1955. *An Elementary Textbook of Psychoanalysis*. New York: International Universities Press.

Darwin, C. [1872] 1979. *The Expression of the Emotions in Man and Animals*. London: Julian Friedmann.

Demos, E. V. 1988. Affect and the development of the self. In *Frontiers in Self Psychology: Progress in Self Psychology*. Vol. 3, ed. A. Goldberg. Hillsdale, N.J.: Analytic Press.

Ekman, P., and Friesen, W. 1978. *Manual for the Facial Affect Coding System*. Palo Alto, Calif.: Consulting Psychologists Press.

Ekman, P.; Friesen, W. V.; and Levinson, R. W. 1983. Evidence for autonomic activity in specific emotions. *Science* 221:1208–10.

Emde, R. N.; Gaensbauer, T.; and Harmon, R. 1976. Emotional expression in infancy: A biobehavioral study. *Psychological Issues*. Monograph 37. New York: International Universities Press.

Freud, S. [1891] 1953. *On aphasia*. Trans. E. Stengel. New York: International Universities Press.

―――. [1895] 1966. Project for a scientific psychology. *Standard edition*, 1:281–397.

―――. 1911. Formulations on the two principles in mental functioning. *Standard edition*, 12.

―――. 1920. Beyond the pleasure principle. *Standard edition*, 18.

―――. 1921. Group psychology and the analysis of the ego. *Standard edition*, 18.

Gelman, D., with Abramson, P., and Risinger, B. 1986. Illusions that heal. *Newsweek*, 17 November, 74–76.

Izard, C. E. 1979. *The Maximally Discriminative Facial Movement Coding System (Max)*. New York: Plenum Press.

Kernberg, O. 1975. *Borderline Conditions and Pathological Narcissism*. New York: Jason Aronson.

Kohut, H. 1971. *The Analysis of the Self*. New York: International Universities Press.

Lewis, H. B. 1971. *Shame and Guilt in Neurosis*. New York: International Universities Press.

―――. 1987. Shame and the narcissistic personality. In *The Many Faces of Shame*, ed. D. L. Nathanson. New York: Guilford Press.

Nathanson, D. L. 1989. Denial, projection and the empathic wall. In *Denial: A Theoretical Clarification of Concepts and Research*, ed. E. Edelstein, D. L. Nathanson, and A. M. Stone. New York: Plenum Press.

―――. 1988. Affect, affective resonance and a new theory for hypnosis. *Psychopathology* 21:126–37.

———. 1986. The empathic wall and the ecology of affect. *The Psychoanalytic Study of the Child* 41:171–87.

———. 1987a. A timetable for shame. In *The Many Faces of Shame*, ed. D. L. Nathanson. New York: Guilford Press.

———. 1987b. The shame/pride axis. In *The Role of Shame in Symptom Formation*, ed. H. B. Lewis. Hillsdale, N.J.: Lawrence Erlbaum Associates.

Radó, S. 1962. *Psychoanalysis of Behavior*. Vol. 2, *Collected Papers*, 1956–61. New York: Grune and Stratton.

Sacks, O. 1985. *The Man Who Mistook His Wife for a Hat*. New York: Summit Books.

Spitz, R. 1947. *Grief: A Peril in Infancy*. New York University Film Library. Film.

———. 1965. *The First Year of Life*. New York: International Universities Press.

Stern, D. N. 1985. *The Interpersonal World of the Infant*. New York: Basic Books.

Sroufe, L. A. 1984. The organization of emotional development. In *Approaches to Emotion*, ed. K. R. Scherer and P. Ekman, 109–28. Hillsdale, N.J.: Erlbaum.

Tabin, J. K. 1985. *On the Way to Self: Ego and Early Oedipal Development*. New York: Columbia University Press.

Tinbergen, N. 1951. *The Study of Instinct*. London: Oxford University Press.

Tomkins, S. S. 1962. *Affect / Imagery / Consciousness*. Vol. 1, *The Positive Affects*. New York: Springer.

———. 1963. *Affect / Imagery / Consciousness*. Vol. 2, *The Negative Affects*. New York: Springer.

———. 1979. Script theory: Differential magnification of affects. In *1978 Nebraska Symposium on Motivation*, ed. H. E. Howe, Jr., and R. Dienstbiener, 201–36. Lincoln: University of Nebraska Press.

———. 1980. Affect as amplification: Some modifications of theory. In *Emotion: Theory, Research and Experience*. Vol. 1, *Theories of Emotion*, ed. R. Plutchik and H. Kellerman. New York: Academic Press.

Wolff, P. 1973. Organization of behavior in the first three months of life. *Early Development* 51:132–53.

6

On Narcissism:
An(other) Introduction

ANDREW SCHWARTZ, M.D.

Prelude to a New Model

One of course begins with Freud. In his analysis of the "Count Thun" dream, Freud (1900) wrote the following deceptively simple paragraph, one that well merits reproduction here not only because of the many crucial clinical insights it offers but also because of the implicit conceptual propositions it quietly announces, ideas quite relevant to the prime concern of the present chapter: the explication of narcissistic phenomena in neuroscientific terms.

> When I was seven or eight years old there was another domestic scene, which I can remember very clearly. One evening before going to sleep I disregarded the rules which modesty lays down and obeyed the calls of nature in my parents' bedroom while they were present. In the course of his reprimand, my father let fall the words: "The boy will come to nothing." This must have been a frightful blow to my ambition, for references to this scene are still constantly recurring in my dreams and are always linked with an enumeration of my achievements and successes, as though I wanted to say: "You see, I *have* come to something." This scene, then, provided the material for the final episode of the dream, in which—in revenge, of course—the roles were interchanged. The older man (clearly my father, since his blindness in one eye referred to his unilateral glaucoma) was now micturating in front of me, just as I had in front of him in my childhood. In the reference to his glaucoma I was reminding him of the cocaine, which had helped him in the operation, as though I had in that way kept my promise. Moreover, I was making fun of him; I had to hand him the urinal because he was blind, and I revelled in allusions to my

Presented as a precirculated paper at the annual meeting of the American Psychoanalytic Association, Montreal, 6 May 1988.

111

discoveries in connection with the theory of hysteria, of which I felt so proud. (216–217)

Examining carefully the passage above, one quickly encounters a number of intriguing conclusions and assumptions. First and most broadly, Freud emphasized the lasting power of the scornful "the boy will come to nothing" remark, the globally depreciatory meaning of which no doubt helped give that phrase its considerable salience even against the background of an angry rebuke. However, Freud's paragraph suggests that he had an awareness of and interest in more than the verbal denotations of speech. Although Freud obviously did not describe how his father's voice had sounded while enunciating the painful judgment in question, the cadence and implications of the comment certainly convey the snarling quality of contempt, and one can thus conclude that Freud's childhood memory illustrates and underscores the potency of prosodic and other nonverbal features of human communication, the clinical importance of which he had stressed even earlier (Breuer and Freud 1895, 281).

Freud, moreover, not only implicitly attributed considerable impact to verbal and nonverbal expressions of contempt, he also, with the phrase "frightful blow to my ambition," suggested that scorn takes as its target the victim's self-esteem. Given the enduring effect on Freud of the boy-will-come-to-nothing remark, one can infer the operation here of a pathogenic "mechanism" described more fully in other writings early and late (Freud 1895, 317–321; 1926). Aversive experience, Freud in effect argued, can link painful feelings powerfully and lastingly to one's sense of oneself—it can, in other words, forge rather permanent associations between such dysphoric affects as depression, anxiety, and humiliation and aspects of self-representation (see Schwartz 1987, 1988). Throughout *The Interpretation of Dreams*, Freud recorded his recognition of his own and others' vulnerability to ridicule and devaluation: he noted with interest his intense reaction to the story of his father's encounter with the anti-Semite (1900, 197), and, of course, the epochal "Irma dream" (Freud 1900) itself represented in part a response to Freud's professional and personal self-doubts and insecurities.

Alongside Freud's early thoughts about the psychogenesis of self-esteem disturbances, and carrying implications of perhaps equal clinical and conceptual interest, are Freud's insights into his ways of reacting to and compensating for— or "defending against"—narcissistic hurts. When speaking of his dreams' "enumeration of my achievements and successes" (1900, 216) and of having "revelled in allusions to my discoveries . . . of which I felt so proud" (217), Freud both clearly recognized the self-protective and analgesic function of his exhibitionistic desires and also hinted at further, if less explicit, ideas of central significance for the arguments to follow: first, that an excited, elated affective state—a "high"—is possibly the most readily available and effective anodyne for "self"-related depression, anxiety, and humiliation; and second, that a wounded individual may expend considerable effort and may even mold his entire life toward inducing within himself this emotional painkiller.

What Freud thus implies—this chapter will attempt more explicitly to argue—is that there exists "pleasure" independent of the classically formulated pair of "instinctual drives," separate in ways even from sexuality, and unrelated fundamentally to the "discharge" of "energies." In other words, Freud himself hinted at a concept very different from the generally acknowledged thrust of metapsychology, at an idea that is one focus of the present essay: gratifying affect may derive principally not from "release" and "quiescence" but rather from specific forms of "activation," which can themselves become goals of thought and behavior.

Certainly, the theme of achievement-as-analgesia appears in Freud's writings of all periods, and he offered a further personal example in a letter to Fleiss, where he referred to the "marble tablet" that might eventually grace the house in which he had analyzed the "Irma dream" (Freud 1900, 121, editor's footnote). One can infer that the same idea ultimately underlay Freud's conclusion (1925) that a woman seeks a man, his penis, and a baby to compensate for "the wound to her narcissism" and "sense of inferiority" (253) that follow her perception of the "anatomical distinction between the sexes" (248). Freud (1925) saw the female Oedipus complex as a reaction to antecedent narcissistic devastation: for him "castration" fundamentally implied injured self-esteem—not simply concrete "anomalous anatomy" or urological surgery (compare Freud 1909; Grossman and Stewart 1976).

At this point one might suggest that the long-established if lamentable tendency to reify Freud's ideas and illustrative metaphors has accompanied—and conceivably may have helped produce—the obfuscation of the important position that narcissism has from the outset occupied in his thinking. Even in recent years, one periodically hears clinical discussions in which practitioners speak of women who "want the penis," as if that organ were literally a flesh-and-blood goal of behavior independent of either sexual longings or self-esteem needs—as if this anatomic feature were almost a missing material element essential for complete assembly of some affectless mechanical apparatus. Technical terms occasionally lose the "shorthand" quality that Brenner (1982; 1987, 101), for example, keeps crisply in focus. Similarly, as numerous critics of metapsychology have stated or implied (Gill 1976; Klein 1976a, 1976b; Peterfreund 1971, 1975; Schafer 1975, 1976), the "ego" also seems often to attain the status of a "thing" quite different from the sentient, experiencing "I" that Freud's "Ich" evokes. Moreover, this particular instance of reification appears to originate in sources beyond those of a less-than-optimal German-to-English translation. As Grossman (1986) notes, "ego" was, in Freud's time and in Strachey's, an acceptable equivalent of "Ich," but contemporary definitions of ego—"The *I*; the conscious, thinking subject.... Also ... the 'self'" (Oxford 1944, 587)—have unaccountably succumbed, perhaps to collective professional insecurity and resultant attempts to concoct mentalistic substitutes for hard neuroscience, and given way to more abstract conceptualizations which fail to retain the "self-ish" nature of Freud's original choice of noun. With some scholarly justification, then, one could propose that "ego psychology" was from its beginnings a "self psychology." Inarguably, such a key hypothesis as the assertion that the "ego" is at first a "body ego" (Freud 1923) becomes truly meaningful only if one thinks of a "self-awareness" that derives from "bodily" information generated by the infant's somatosensory and proprioceptive pathways.

At any rate, to return to the paragraph quoted above, one may note hints of a nascent theory of "aggression." In addition to responding with a search for "highs," Freud suggests, the narcissistically wounded person seeks also to gain revenge against the tormentor and attempts, for example, to exchange positions and become the one making fun of the source of hurt. What emerges from Freud's 1900 discussion, then, is a view of "aggression" as a *defensive reaction* to "self"-involved injury or threat, and this idea endures in later publications (Freud 1916, 1925) despite the concurrent development of the "death instinct" speculations (Freud 1920) and derivative notions of an almost appetitive "aggressive instinctual drive."

One can conclude that Freud from the start of his career accorded considerable significance to self-esteem disturbances and developed a number of interesting but quite variably explicit hypotheses about the nature of, psychogenesis of, and defensive response to this important variety of psychological difficulty. First, as the "boy will come to nothing" excerpt illustrates, Freud implicitly suggested that narcissistic "conflict" fundamentally consists of painful emotion that has become persistently linked to—associated with—some aspect of self-image or "self-representation." Furthermore, Freud believed, this associative process could apparently begin both with aversive interpersonal experience of the kind he himself recalled and with traumatic cognitive-affective perception to which he attributed the origin of penis envy. Freud recognized that tone of voice, such as that of contempt, exerts powerful effects; moreover, Freud obviously held that intensely painful incidents can generate a lasting impact seemingly far out of proportion to the events' frequency or duration. Finally, Freud noted two significant responses to, or "defenses against," threat or injury to self-regard—"getting high" and "getting even"—and one might to this pair of reactions append a third, the withdrawal and hiding that can accompany anxiety, depression, and mortification.

The examination here of a sample of early Freudian thought does not have as a goal any implication that by 1900 Freud had written the last word on the subject of narcissism: an enormous mass of relevant literature, the review of which obviously extends far beyond the intent and scope of this chapter, has appeared in the past eighty-plus years. Similarly, the reference to Freud's 1925 paper on female sexuality and character should suggest no endorsement of those early conclusions about the origins of gender-related envy and inferiority feelings, notions that even in eminently classical circles have recently undergone extensive reappraisal (see Grossman and Stewart 1976; Silverman 1981; Brenner 1982). Rather, the foregoing discussion has aimed both to document in

1900 Freud an intense and perhaps surprisingly sophisticated interest in self-esteem difficulties and to sculpt from Freud's beguilingly simple paragraph the key constituents of narcissistic disturbance: *self-representation, dysphoric affect, associative mechanisms* both sensitive to and triggered by afferent information, getting high, and getting even—all of which not only remain germane to clinical understanding but also relate easily enough to current neurobiologic concepts to serve as components of a somewhat updated model (see Freud 1914) of self-regard and its vicissitudes, a revised hypothesis rooted in data from neuroscience, experimental psychology, and ethology.

Fundamentally, this proposed model rests on one quite, perhaps alarmingly, simple idea: that self-esteem ultimately resides in the nature and intensity of feelings associated with aspects of self-image and thus derives from the interaction of three of the essentially neurobiologic elements just listed—*affect, associative processes,* and *self-representation.* Furthermore, in these terms, narcissistic difficulty or conflict therefore consists primarily of dysphoric emotions persistently linked to registrations of one or more features of one's "self." Moreover, should an individual develop self-regard disturbance, characteristic biologically based defensive reactions might well emerge—snarling efforts at revenge, appetitive seeking of "highs," frightened or mortified hiding—but the relative overt strength of these responses could in turn depend on the degree to which these self-protective behaviors themselves become "conflicted," once again through association with various forms of emotional pain.

Obviously, the conclusion that conflict depends fundamentally on *association* is the core element of the model offered here, and this formulation, as argued in more detail elsewhere (Schwartz 1988), can encompass not only both narcissistic and "instinctual drive"–related phenomena (Brenner 1982), but may also work to erase the appearance of conceptual distance between these ostensibly distinct classes of psychological difficulty. The difference, after all, lies merely in the *content*—"drive derivative" or "self-image"—whose registration has become linked to dysphoric affect. Moreover, drive-focused problems logically form just a subset of self-related issues: clearly, any awareness of one's own erotic or vengeful wishes constitutes nothing but one species of self-perception and representation; additionally, the fears that one's impulses engender frequently grow from real or imagined dangers posed to—what else?—one's *self.*

Of course, the very meaning of the term self could well become a topic for debate, but perhaps for present purposes one might allow a loose definition that comprises the innumerable and varied registrations a person makes of the concrete physical and more abstract qualities of body and mind. Thus Freud's 1923 suggestion that self-awareness begins with sensory data is a particularly good point of transition toward the neurobiological, after pausing to note the small irony in enlisting a passage from the "dream book" to reunite psychoanalysis and basic biology. By the time he wrote the paragraph quoted, of course, Freud had decided that his earlier integrative speculations (1895) were grossly premature. But we have reached now the end of a later century, and neuroscience has started to close the gap between the *Project* and the laboratory.

Registration and Representation: Neurobiologic Pick-ups and Recorders*

Although one must at the start acknowledge, and in fact stress, that modern neuroscience has so far provided, even in arenas in which most successful, only preliminary sketches of the operation of any single neural module, contemporary neurobiology has nevertheless progressed enough to furnish valuable first impressions of how the brain notes, processes, and registers information both from the outside world and from the internal milieu. Very broadly, the neuronal systems subserving vision, hearing, taste, smell, and somatic sensation transduce physical and chemical stimuli into electrophysiologic signals—receptor and action potentials—which transmit centrally survival-essential data that, in turn, subcortical relays and cortex receive and handle in highly organized fashion (Martin 1985; Kandel 1985b; Kelly 1985; Castellucci 1985).

For example, as Hubel and Wiesel (1970) helped to demonstrate (Hubel 1982; Kandel 1985b), neurons of the primary visual or "striate" cortex have, as do cells in the retina and lateral geniculate, limited and definable "receptive fields"—slices of the total visible area to which they are sensitive—and moreover they respond preferentially to bars of light of specific spatial orientation, direction of movement, and, in some cases, length.

Every striate-cortical neuron, then, appears to serve as a compact detector of specific form and motion within a particular segment of the field of vision, and the quite organized and structured groups of these cells, which constitute the visual cortices, seem in sum to possess the further ability to register and record cortically complex shapes and movements. Although full understanding of this "cognitive assembly" process must await results of future exploration, a crucial conclusion that has already emerged is that the cortex comprises several "maps" of the retina's arena of observation and thus represents cellularly what the eye perceives.

While shape, movement, and color provide the input to the neural equipment underlying vision, the detection, processing, and registration of waveforms and pressure changes in the ambient air form the task of the auditory system. More precisely, both because of biophysical characteristics of the cochlea's basilar membrane and because of cell-to-cell differences in ionic conductance that endow individual receptor neurons in the organ of Corti with particular responsiveness to specific frequencies of vibration, the inner ear can subject incoming sound to Fourier analysis and decompose complex wave patterns into their constituent constant-wavelength sine waves (Kelly 1985). In addition, sin-

---

*The following three sections draw on material from an earlier paper (Schwartz 1988) used by permission of the *Journal of the American Psychoanalytic Association*.

gle cells in the cochlear nuclei, medial geniculate, superior colliculus (Allon and Wollberg 1978), and other relays exhibit well-defined tonal "preferences"; thus show greatest electrophysiologic sensitivity to relatively restricted frequency band-widths; and have, moreover, anatomic grouping that reflects these acoustic predilections.

In the examples provided, both visual and auditory components systematically reduce complex afferent information to small bits processed by neural elements most highly responsive to input of specific configuration, and from these microdata—in a fashion still incompletely understood—the brain then reassembles a representation of the total stimulus. Despite the extent of what remains unknown, one can extract from contemporary sensory physiology a further conclusion—one that Kandel (1983; 1985d) has emphasized—that has notable relevance to psychoanalysis in general and to this chapter in particular: neuroscience has begun to demonstrate that "mental representation" has a biologic and, in fact, a cellular basis.

Moreover, current research findings strongly suggest that the CNS enregisters everything, including activation of its constituent modules, in one fundamental language—that of cellular and synaptic activity. This principle, if extrapolated with due circumspection, would imply that the brain encodes and records— "represents"—affects and appetites in ways basically little different from those in which it processes sight and sound. Thus, all "psychological" phenomena— emotions, "impulses," images of self and others—reside ultimately in the physiological function of neural components which in turn, under the influence of incoming data from life experience, can combine to yield the loves and loathings, tastes and terrors of human character.

Implicit in the very idea of mental representation are two significant assumptions: that such registrations persist, and that if they did not endure, they would have decidedly less usefulness for the organism. More specifically, the power to inscribe and maintain records of sensory and affective impressions has essential adaptive and survival value—learning from experience clearly depends on this ability—and documentation of a complex "conditioned fear" reaction in the primitive invertebrate *Aplysia* (Walters et al. 1981; Carew et al. 1981a; Kandel 1983, 1985d) suggests that the very earliest life forms evolved neurophysiologic apparatus able to enregister and store "internally" information about critical environmental conditions and changes—including, most crucially, those announcing threat and danger.

Obviously, then, the concept of mental representation implies memory and thus introduces the topic of *neural plasticity*—the modification by afferent information of neurobiologic function and even structure (Schwartz 1987, 1988). Although the investigation of learning and data-storage mechanisms remains a frontier area of research, Kandel and associates' elegant studies of neural sensitization in *Aplysia* have elucidated not only the neurophysiologic and biochemical processes involved (Kandel 1976, 1978; Kandel and Schwartz 1982) but have also demonstrated ultrastructural synaptic changes in the neurons affected (Bailey and Chen 1983)—anatomic alterations which necessarily implicate the power of an experience-triggered neurochemical cascade to influence a cell's genetic apparatus and to induce the derepression of inactive genes and the synthesis of new proteins (Kandel 1983, 1985d, 1986).

Although because of their obviously greater size and intricacy mammalian brains and their learning processes are still much more of a mystery than are those of invertebrates like *Aplysia*, recent primate research has documented an example of input-dependent alteration of cortical somatosensory maps that is in principle highly relevant to a first understanding of how mental representations might change to reflect shifting circumstance and evolving data. Employing single-unit recording techniques, Merzenich, Kaas, and collaborators (Merzenich and Kaas 1982; Merzenich et al. 1983a, 1983b) reported that following median nerve transsection in owl and squirrel monkeys, the cortex that originally served the severed fibers was not electrophysiologically inactive but was instead unexpectedly and progressively responsive to afferent stimuli carried by other, intact sensory pathways—findings suggesting gradually reorganizing patterns of synaptic connections.

While the above examples illustrate physiologic and structural plasticity in mature animals, the now-classic researches of Hubel and Wiesel (1970; Wiesel 1982) have demonstrated that skewed informational input during critical postnatal periods can produce profound and permanent distortion of brain function and anatomy. Using unilateral translucent eye occluders or eyelid suture to effect pattern—but not light-dark—deprivation in young kittens and monkeys, Hubel and Wiesel observed lasting electrophysiologic and histologic visual system abnormalities—experimental results which may, as Kandel has noted (1979; 1985c), point also toward mechanisms underlying such experience-dependent developmental syndromes as hospitalism. In fact, in his 1981 Nobel lecture Wiesel himself suggested that "other aspects of brain function, such as language, complex perceptual tasks, learning, memory, and personality" may when studied show comparable "sensitivity to the effects of experience . . ." (1982, 591).

Affects Reconsidered: Feelings as Neural Appraisals, Warnings, and Goals

From a general survey of the neurobiology of sensory systems and of representation, one moves easily to a reevaluation of the nature of affects, the second class of phenomena essential to the model of narcissism sketched earlier. Far from being simple "drive-discharge" accompaniments (Freud 1915), "ego signals" (Freud 1926), or some mélange of the two (Rapaport 1953), emotions in light of present knowledge seem as basically biologic as do sensations.

Actually, from several perspectives—functional, adaptive, evolutionary, and neurophysiologic—emotions closely resemble certain of the classic sensations and share with them some fundamental properties. More precisely, although the sensory pathways of vision, hearing, touch, and proprioception generate phenomenologic data that have a more simply representational and value-neutral nature—these channels can let us know, for instance, if in fact our son did leave the gold pen on the brown table, whether the person on the phone is asking for us or, more usually, for our teenaged daughter, or where our fingers might be vis-à-vis the shoulder blade we hope to scratch—the senses of pain, temperature, taste, and smell respond to physical and chemical stimuli in our inner and outer milieux and deliver *appraisals* of our circumstances experienced as sweetness or acidity, caress or cramp, bouquet or stench, and which can in addition elicit stereotyped but helpful reflexes such as flexor-withdrawal, vomiting, or sneezing (Kupfermann 1985c). In sum, these neurobiologic "scales" *weigh* the "quality" (Freud 1895)—for example, the olfactory or gustatory allure—of our environments; thus provide survival-essential information; and therefore earn a basic definition which, from a biologic standpoint, one may easily apply also to feelings—they are *neural processes which allow us to judge, gauge, and confront the dangers and desirabilities that surround us.*

Affects thus in part appear to be highly evolved sensationlike signals with an *appraisal* function (Rosenblatt and Thickstun 1977a, 1977b; Rosenblatt 1985), but these phenomena originate not in structures of the classic senses but rather in elements of the limbic system and related regions of the hypothalamus, upper midbrain, and frontal and temporal cortices (MacLean 1952, 1967, 1969, 1972, 1977, 1978; Kandel 1985a; Kupfermann 1985a, 1985b). Although attempts to localize precisely the neuroanatomic substrates of individual feelings have so far generated only preliminary and occasionally confusing and controversial findings (Kandel, pers. com., 1983), current data do indicate, for example, that septal, lateral hypothalamic, nucleus accumbens, and ventral tegmental areas contain circuits subserving apparent pleasure or "reward" (Olds 1976; Rolls 1976; Stellar and Stellar 1985; Wise and Bozarth 1985). The amygdala and medial hypothalamic loci seem comparably implicated in unpleasure experiences and in defensive affectomotor responses (Olds 1976; Adamec 1975).

More central to a psychoanalytically focused discussion than current anatomic uncertainty, though, is one basic conclusion which now seems reasonable even in the face of very incomplete basic data: just as have motor activity and classic senses, so should feelings also prove to have their individual neurobiologic substrates (Kandel 1985a; Kupfermann 1985a, 1985b). Although one cannot as yet predict whether the "labeled line" principle—the carrying of a given kind of sensation by a particular specialized pathway (Martin 1985)—will apply to the physiology of, for instance, anxiety or shame as it does to that of cold and light, recent neuropharmacologic findings (Snyder 1980; Wise and Bozarth 1985) both suggest that affect-specific circuitry may indeed exist and raise the further possibility that a chemical vocabulary of emotions will emerge from future research.

Supporting such inferences are data of particular relevance to the proposed psychobiologic model of narcissism. More specifically, the finding within limbic system circuitry of dopamine-containing and opioid-peptidergic neurons (Snyder 1980) *and* the recognized phenomenologic effects of such corresponding neurotransmitter agonists as cocaine, amphetamine, and heroin together suggest a distinct neurobiology of euphoria that may centrally involve the mesolimbic dopaminergic pathway that originates in ventral tegmental cell bodies and terminates in synapses within the nucleus accumbens (Wise and Bozarth 1985). Furthermore, the relationship of substance addiction and the "subjectively experienced drug euphoria" (Wise and Bozarth 1985, 122) that the abused chemicals induce points toward an additional and significant inference—that enjoyable affects serve not only as "appraisals" but as the most compelling goals of behavior (Schwartz 1987, 1988). Laboratory studies of intracranial self-stimulation (Olds 1976; Rolls 1976; Stellar and Stellar 1985) and of the self-administration of drugs (Wise and Bozarth 1985) accord with this idea and with a more general hypothesis, developed elsewhere but crucial to the present argument—that appetitively sought pleasant emotions or sensations and aversive dysphoric feelings function respectively as the ultimate, "brain-synthesized" positive and negative reinforcers of emotional learning (Schwartz 1987, 1988).

Affective manifestations comprise elements beyond subjective "signals," however, and as Darwin (1872) and other investigators have observed (such as MacLean 1952, 1967, 1969, 1978; Tomkins 1970; Ekman and Friesen 1975; Ekman et al. 1983), each affect tends to trigger complex motor and hypothalamic-autonomic stereotypies which (1) represent "genetically installed" and relatively "hard-wired" fixed-action patterns originally of evolutionary significance and adaptive value (see Breuer and Freud 1895, 180–181); which (2) generate sensations via proprioceptive and enteroceptive feedback loop pathways that in turn foster our learning to distinguish, identify, and label our own feelings; and which (3) finally, through facial expression and tone of voice, for example, transmit the eminently *physical* data that underlie empathy and emotional communication (Schwartz 1987, 1988). Although the above concepts certainly apply to any emotion regardless of its place on the pleasure-pain spectrum, these ideas in particular offer a perspective of the unpleasure that contributes usefully to the model of narcissistic conflict: *anxiety / fear, sadness / depression, embarrassment / shame, disgust,* and *anger / contempt* all constitute intricate psychobiological alarm reactions that, by instituting specific motor, cardiovascular, respiratory, exocrinologic, endocrinologic, and other sympathetic / parasympathetic responses, ready the organism for emergency and crisis, "fight or flight" (Schwartz 1988).

To anticipate somewhat the argument to follow, one might suggest that when in a given individual one or more dysphoric affects have become significantly associated with self-representations, this person's "character" and actions will at least in part reflect the behavioral stereotypies which the feelings in question elicit. Thus, for instance, since anxiety tends to foster flight (Schwartz 1987), "freezing," or some combination of the two, the student with ingrained fears about intellectual adequacy is likely to "put off until later" the equation-laden chapters on membrane biophysics that stir self-doubt. Comparably, because the snarling defensive anger that we call contempt often represents a response to narcissistic threat, patients who suffer from intense and chronic insecurities and envy not infrequently display varyingly obvious signs of the facial sneer and vocal scorn that we have come to consider integral elements of superciliousness.

If, therefore, character reflects affect, personality traits must rest also on biological foundations, and the complex, emotion-elicited stereotypies discussed above have at least preliminarily identified anatomic substrates. In animals, electrophysiologic stimulation of numerous limbic system and brainstem loci can trigger the motor and hypothalamic responses that combine to write the visible and audible "signatures" of individual feelings (for reviews, see MacLean 1952, 1969; Kupfermann 1985a; Schwartz 1987), and in humankind, moreover, the capacity to generate and decode the patterned gestures, inflections, and timbres that constitute *prosody* and endow speech with its emotional overtones apparently requires the integrity and participation of frontal and temporal cortical tissue contralateral to and possibly homologous to the areas of Broca and Wernicke requisite to verbal expression and comprehension (Ross 1984; Heilman et al. 1975; Kandel 1985a).

Although sensations and feelings share a variety of biologic, functional, and adaptive characteristics, in one significant anatomic and physiologic respect the wiring of the neurobiologic generators of affect does differ from that of the classic sensory circuits. For instance, although receptor neurons in the retina and cochlea respond directly to physical stimuli in the environment and thus provide raw data to visual and auditory pathways, the circuitry subserving emotion has no comparable capacity to sample input from outside the CNS and instead receives information through shunts, as in the olfactory system (Castellucci 1985), from the primary senses.

All afferent data, therefore, submit to the *parallel processing* of both sensory and affect-generating modules, and the acoustic startle-response illustrates nicely not only this principle of two channel assessment but also its notable relevance to a full understanding of emotional communication. When we jump and spin around on hearing a sudden, usually unanticipated noise, our auditory system offers us refined information about the direction, source, loudness, and other sonic properties of the stimulus; but the surge of anxiety and tachycardia that we might well observe result from the participation of limbic and hypothalamic components in the "evaluation" of the sound. At this point, then, if one takes into account the sophistication of our neural audio-analyzers and of the prosody-sensitive circuitry of the right temporal lobe, one can only conclude that the evocative—and potentially pathogenic—power of tone of voice resides ultimately in our genetically funded neuronal endowment. This last idea introduces, and hints at answers to, the questions that now logically follow: what mechanism combines self-representations and emotions to yield the feeling-charged images of narcissism—and how does this *associative* linking commence?

Association: Brain Syntax of Learning and Linchpin of Narcissism

Obviously, *association*, the functional knotting of representation and affect, is a core component of the model of narcissism here proposed, and current evidence makes ineluctable the conclusion that the processes underlying such associative phenomena as classical or Pavlovian conditioning are as basically biological as are sensation and movement. In studies of beasts that range from *Aplysia* to rhesus monkey, numerous investigators (Carew et al. 1981a, 1981b, 1983; Hawkins et al. 1983; Hawkins and Kandel 1984; Kandel 1983, 1985d; Kandel and Spencer 1968; Mora et al. 1976; Walters et al. 1981; Walters and Byrne 1983; Thompson 1986) have accumulated data demonstrating that the capacity to link, for example, a memory of one's face with a feeling pleasant or otherwise in all probability derives from "genetically diagrammed" and "hard-wired" circuitry that can, once facilitated, tie neural registration of image to emotion. Moreover, because of the considerable electrophysiologic and biochemical overlap between mechanisms of associative learning and of sensitization (Kandel 1983, 1985d; Hawkins et al. 1983) one might predict that future work will reveal in a Pavlovian paradigm anatomic synaptic modifications comparable to those already observed in sensitized neurons (Bailey and Chen 1983).

Illustrating both the principles and mechanisms of the associative model is Thompson's (1986) example of a classically conditioned eye-blink in the rabbit. When an innocuous and thus behaviorally neutral audible tone repeatedly and thus *predictably* precedes a puff of air to the eye—the latter functioning as the *unconditioned stimulus* that reliably elicits the hard-wired reaction or *unconditioned response* of reflex eyelid closure—after a number of trials the sound will become the conditioned stimulus and will alone, in advance of the air puff, trigger the blinking or *conditioned response*. Mediating this learned linkage, experiments suggest (Thompson 1986), are facilitations within climbing and mossy fiber tracts, Purkinje cells, the nucleus interpositus, and other components of cerebellar circuits—neurophysiologic changes that illuminate the ways in which experience can powerfully influence the operation and efficacy of preexisting pathways.

Despite the frontier status of research into memory mechanisms, associative conditioning and its cellular correlates have, significantly, proved demonstrable in species of all levels of evolutionary sophistication (Carew et al. 1981a, 1981b, 1983; Kandel 1983, 1985d; Mora et al. 1976; Thompson 1986), and this apparently universal form of learning endows any organism with an invaluable adaptive advantage—the *capacity to inscribe and retain neurobiologic records of survival-essential predictive relationships*. Thus, just as Thompson's rabbits "internalize" the likelihood that an air puff to the eye will follow an innocuous tone, so can a young boy find that to disregard "the rules which modesty lays down" may evoke "a frightful blow to [his] ambition" (Freud 1900, 216) which will in turn leave a persistent emotional scar and will therefore continue to shape behavior.

To ascribe considerable impact to single noxious events may seem jarringly simplistic and may appear also to ignore the contribution of motivational states to one's vulnerability, for instance, to contemptuous remarks. Obviously, a scornful brush-off from a long-idealized teacher, respected colleague, or over-valued lover will have particular power, but one must consider too the common observation that disdainful attitudes and contumelious behavior can themselves paradoxically evoke forms of admiration, can spark in others strong desires to befriend, affiliate with, or resemble the "aggressor," and can, in sum, potently shape appetites and desires. Thus the following quip has always met large and receptive audiences: "I wouldn't join any club that would stoop to have me as a member." Furthermore, as is argued in greater detail elsewhere (Schwartz 1988), both laboratory data (for discussions see Olds 1976; Castellucci 1985; Kupfermann 1985d) and clinical observations of the analytic process (such as Stein 1973; Brenner, pers. com., 1983; Silverman 1985; Jacobs 1986) attest to the remarkable speed, durability, and tenacity of one-trial aversive associative learning. Even when uttered just once, words at times do "break bones."

Current data indicate, therefore, that classical associative conditioning represents a basic *neurobiologic syntax of learning* intrinsic to neural circuitry of invertebrate and higher primate alike, and in humans, one can additionally infer, our hard-wired and remarkable sensitivity to prosodic properties of speech makes nonverbal communications enormously effective unconditioned stimuli in those commonplace, ostensibly educative or disciplinary, but potentially path-ogenic encounters in which parental tones of displeasure follow a forbidden behavior of the child. The snarling anger we label "contempt" seems, moreover, a particularly potent conditioning stimulus and psychopathogen; it readily stirs such powerful "brain-synthesized" reinforcers as anxiety, depression, embarrassment, and shame; and it appears, not unexpectedly, to contribute notably to the psychogenesis of at least some instances of severe neurotic character disorder (Abend et al. 1983; Willick, pers. com., 1985; Schwartz 1988).

While classical conditioning generally depends on *repeated* presentations of paired stimuli—the tone must precede the air puff numerous times before the former acquires the ability to elicit the eye-blink—Freud's boy-will-come-to-nothing anecdote implied in 1900 what laboratory data have now established: that relatively few aversive experiences can have an impact far greater than their frequency and duration might lead one to predict. Furthermore, experiments with one-trial conditioned food avoidance (for discussions, see Olds 1976; Kupfermann 1985d) not only document an innate capacity for essentially permanent single-exposure learning but also suggest the evolutionary and adaptive value of such vulnerability to environmental contingencies: some survival-critical lessons demand immediate mastery. How these research findings relate to clinical phenomena becomes clearer if one considers, for example, the implications of recent articles on countertransference (such as Blum 1986a, 1986b; Jacobs 1986; Silverman 1985). Jacob's vignettes in particular demonstrate the unsettling ease with which a solitary technical lapse may engender months of impasse and even induce formation of new transference-neurotic symptoms.

Classical conditioning, on the other hand, is probably not the sole type of cellularly based learning contributing to symptom psychogenesis, and *neural sensitization,* the progressive increase of a circuit's response to a repeated but unvarying afferent stimulus and a behaviorally important form of nonassociative plasticity extensively investigated in both invertebrates (Kandel 1978) and mammals (Groves et al. 1972; Parker et al. 1974) could well underlie the emotional hyperreactivity and volatility characteristic of serious personality disorders. In a detailed study of "borderlines," Abend, Porder, and Willick (1983) argue that unusual *intensity*—not *content*—marked their patients' conflicts, and noxious, hyperstimulating childhood and adolescent experiences of the sort these authors report would certainly tend to activate associative *and* sensitizing processes and produce precisely what Abend and collaborators describe—neurotic constellations of common composition and extraordinary affective strength.

A last variety of learning now deserves consideration, and "operant" or "instrumental" conditioning, which promotes motor acts *associated with* securing rewarding or avoiding aversive stimulation, shares with the Pavlovian paradigm not only widespread phylogenetic distribution but also, possibly, basic cellular mechanisms (Hawkins et al. 1983). When, in A. Freud's words (1965, 86) an "infant seems to concentrate on the development along those lines which call forth . . . the mother's love and approval . . . and to neglect others where such approval is not given," the baby's activity illustrates these operant principles, underscores the power of interpersonally evoked feeling states to shape and reinforce emotional and behavioral proclivities, and provides, finally, an example of the phenomenon of the appetitive seeking of pleasant affects—most importantly euphoria.

Brain-Generated Euphoria: Nature's Ultimate "High"—and Reward

Among the more interesting and impelling neuroscientific developments of the past third of a century has been the gradual delineation of a specific neurobiology of reward or "pleasure" (Olds 1976; Rolls 1976; Wise and Bozarth 1985; Kupfermann 1985b; Stellar and Stellar 1985). As noted earlier, current data suggest strongly that both electrophysiologic intracranial self-stimulation and such abused drugs as cocaine, amphetamine, and opiates share a common general locus of action, the key elements of which appear to be the mesolimbic dopaminergic system and the structures on which its terminals synapse. Thus, we today have at hand the beginnings of a behavioral biology of euphoria or high, and some well-established findings from this field seem now of considerable conceptual and clinical relevance to psychoanalysis. Specifically, and as numerous studies demonstrate, animals will readily learn to perform "addictively" an operant task that triggers self-administration of reinforcing electrical pulses or chemicals. Most significantly, experimental subjects will in this paradigm work to obtain these kinds of gratification in preference to all others, *food, drink, and sex included*—results indicating that *euphoric states are perhaps the most appetitively compelling experiences available to life forms as so far evolved.*

If, then, experimental evidence and clinical observations of drug abuse and "risk addiction" combine to suggest that high feelings may of all brain-synthesized reinforcers have the greatest potency, the question next confronted is, of course, that of the evolutionary value of such a powerful intrinsic reward system. While the thoughts in this section are speculative and likely, for a time at least, to remain so, one might expand the data and inferences of Wise and Bozarth (1985), MacLean (1952, 1969, 1977, 1978), and Noshpitz (1984), and propose that the generation of euphoric states may represent the brain's signaling the attainment of a wide variety of survival-valuable or essential goals: the acquisition of power and territory; the finding of attractive, interested, and receptive mates; the identification of impressive and protective leaders; and the mastery of threat and complexity.

While one could probably extend the foregoing list of high-related behaviors and achievements, success with any of the activities and goals already cited can elicit a euphoria that is not only a delicious condition in and of itself but that is also an effective anodyne to the depression, anxiety, and humiliation that loss, failure, defeat, and rejection may engender and link to stored images of oneself and one's condition. If one feels "up," no challenge appears insuperable, and no danger seems truly to threaten: one knows only an optimism that shrinks terror—and that even, as this paper will suggest, vitiates the realistic perception of genuine risk.

Obviously, the sorts of euphoria-inducing behavior mentioned earlier often appear, sometimes to the point of caricature, in the repertoires of "narcissistic personalities." On the other hand, to the degree that almost everyone suffers from some feelings of relative inadequacy and defectiveness, these affect-seeking activities form part of us all. If one defines "the idealized" as a *representation associated with euphoric emotion,* one can infer that we hold on to "highly" invested "superego" values, remembered heroes, current leaders, and intellectual systems, because the sense of closeness to our ideals lifts our moods and diminishes our fears (see Freud 1914, 1923). Thus, for instance, extending the observations of Blum (1983) and Kernberg (1987) about our profession's tendency toward idealization of teacher and theory, one might suggest that this proclivity has as its aim protecting us against anxieties growing from a perceived lack of the hard science concepts and experimentally derived and tested therapeutic tools of other biomedical disciplines. Similarly, although they are ostensibly from another world of meaning, spectator sports perhaps serve a function comparable to that of the cherished ideology. If the fans' team takes the championship, they taste exultation; however vicariously, they have "won" an often frankly territorial contest—football, for example—and enjoy the elation of conquest.

How the brain transduces, for instance, achievement of power or success in seduction into sensations of high remains a neurobiologic mystery, but one can offer a few hypotheses, which may not only fit grossly observable data but may also lend themselves ultimately to psychophysiologic examination. If one views operationally these examples, one can suggest that common to the acquisition of influence and to the winning of mates is the eliciting from others of nonverbal signs of admiration, respect, and desire for physical proximity and even contact. The politician or lover hopes to feel looked up to and wanted and tastes a rush on reaching these goals. Furthermore, we applaud and cheer our leaders and artists in part because our cultural forebears discovered the intoxicating hard-wired response one experiences when one finds oneself the trigger and object of such noise. In other words, just as our preprinted circuits decode "electron-ically" the facial expression and sound of contempt, so also do we perhaps comprehend automatically homologous indices of positive regard.

From an adaptive viewpoint, the ability to gain territory, power, or receptive mates confers on its possessor a variety of practical advantages—among them, land to guarantee a food supply, followers to aid and protect one, mothers or fathers for one's offspring—and thus it appears that organisms have evolved brains so wired that what is biologically useful also feels good. Again, neuro-science has yet to elucidate the mechanisms by which the CNS generates eu-phoric states in response to information, for example, about extensive real estate holdings and great physical size, but simple observations do suggest some po-tentially testable hypotheses.

Specifically, optic and vestibular input may participate in the above sorts of data processing and affect generation, and one can propose, for instance, that focusing visually on points at infinity helps to trigger euphorialike emotion. People enjoy looking at distant sunsets and gazing over ocean or mountain-top scenes—viewing such panoramas seems to engender a kind of rush—and one might thus deduce that country-house designers often put large state rooms *enfilade*—in a row—with mirrors at the ends because they knew that peering down some hundred or more feet of mansion tends to evoke in the beholder a comparable feeling of awe clearly including an element of high. In different terms, architects may have operantly, if unwittingly, learned to exploit hard-wired circuitry to stimulate in their audiences the euphoric roots of idealiza-tion—and, of course, to elicit such responses was in the first place a principal purpose of these buildings and a primary goal of their owners (Girouard 1980).

Again, the principle implied is that evolution has equipped us with the neural capacity to receive information potentially of adaptive value and to respond to these data with a signal of intensely rewarding properties. Subsequently, among other affect-seeking skills, humans developed "aesthetic" abilities, the operantly acquired arts and crafts that produce stimuli capable of evoking gratifying feel-ings. Thus, one can deduce possible relationships between vestibular stimula-tion, generation of high, architectural and decorative forms, and an evolutionary advantage. Children love spinning and rolling games—such activities bring a giddy sort of elation—and perhaps also, by inducing us to tilt our heads upward and thereby to activate the hair-cell receptors of the utricle, saccule, and semi-circular ducts, the imposing vaults of gothic cathedrals and the lofty, elaborately plastered and gilded ceilings of country house halls and state rooms similarly use intrinsic circuitry to stir in us the euphoria, awe, and resultant idealization that, to the builders, seemed appropriate to guests of deities and noblemen.

Once more, this mechanism might originally have conferred an adaptive advantage: so wired, we would in the presence of large people and objects note a salient sensation that could, for example, function to alert us to the presence of a potential protector. Similarly, if one considers the hypothesis that the perception of congruities and symmetries may help trigger the high gained both from visual beauty and from problem solving, one can then propose, extending suggestions of Wilson (1975), that visible regularities and smooth contours perhaps served, in our prehistory, as the most obvious and reliable indices of the physical health, strength, and intactness of prospective mates.

Although evaluation and substantiation of these hypotheses would demand considerable research, one can emphasize that available data demonstrate impressively the behavioral importance of intrinsic, euphoria-related reward systems. Therefore, under the influence both of laboratory findings and of clinical observations, one might today propose the following modifications of traditional psychoanalytic views of sexuality and narcissism. While Freud (1914) obviously believed that "libido" is the form of "psychic energy" fueling such phenomena as idealization and grandiosity, current knowledge suggests instead that *euphoric affect*, generated by circuitry independent of that responsible for sexual excitement and orgasm, constitutes perhaps *the prime factor in the self-esteem fluctuations* that Freud so clearly described. Erotic arousal and the high of elation may, in other words, represent *neurobiologically distinct processes*, often activated separately.

Often, but not always. Laboratory and clinical observations (compare Fenichel 1941; Holt 1976) combine to suggest that euphoria-related affects and more purely erotic excitement may both contribute to the complexities of human sexuality. As Fenichel (1941) noted, narcissistic needs, not orgastic gratifications, clearly predominate in some ostensibly seductive and copulatory behaviors. Furthermore, perceptions of a potential partner's aesthetic, personal, political, or socioeconomic "specialness," traits all of which obviously appeal principally to self-esteem appetites, frequently precede and spark frankly sexual desires.

The hypothesis is therefore that human sexual behavior derives its appetitive urgency from the synergistic influence and participation of at least *two neurophysiologically distinct reward systems*—one generating a high and triggered by afferent data conveying the interest and desire of an appealing mate, the other producing the separate but also intensely pleasurable sensations of erotic arousal and orgasm. From an evolutionary viewpoint, moreover, one could further conclude that species survival may demand a dual-reinforcement process: one can gratify orgastic hungers without a partner, but to do so will fertilize no ova. Conception—and the euphoria of feeling loved, wanted, and admired—requires another being.

As suggested above, more than two reward processes may contribute to sexual activity. Sandler and Joffe (1968, 1969) and Rosenblatt (pers. com., 1987) stress the importance to humans of the low intensity, comfortable, and warm emotion that Sandler and Joffe (1968) have labeled "the safety feeling." At any rate, clear to all observers is the enormous evocative power which one person can exert over another, and, one might parenthetically add, this factor may set an intrinsic limit to the efficacy of self-analysis: perhaps one actually does need the real presence of an attuned and unshakably benign other to help convince one that childhood dreads have become genuinely negligible.

Proposals and Pathology:
Applications and Implications of the Model Offered

Having surveyed from a neurobiological perspective topics including representation, affect, associative and sensitizing forms of learning, and euphoria as reward and anodyne, subjects which all had forerunners even in Freud's nineteenth-century clinical observations and conceptual speculations (Schwartz 1987, 1988), one can attempt to summarize how a model comprising these elements might account for features of narcissistic disturbance. Fundamentally, this chapter proposes that *parental spoken and nonverbal communications,* especially signs of anger and contempt, *serve as the unconditioned stimuli in a classical conditioning/sensitization paradigm* and thus foster the child's forming tight links between self-representations and such intense dysphoric emotions as anxiety, depression, shame, embarrassment, and disgust. In reaction to these initial hurts, then, the young person's first lines of defense would likely reflect closely the motor stereotypies triggered by the dominant painful feelings—for example, behavioral tendencies toward avoidance, hiding, or withdrawal—reactions very possibly augmented by hard-wired vengeful rage and operantly shaped elation-seeking grandiosity.

Secondarily, however, infelicitous responses by parents to their offspring's defensive reactions could potentially, again through classical associative learning, pile one painful emotion on another. Specifically, for instance, a father who mocks scornfully his little boy's shrinking from a wading pool might well evoke in his son not only anxiety and humiliation over timidity but also a consequent, high-seeking, counterphobic diathesis. Furthermore, through similar conditioning mechanisms, the mother who explodes at a child's hurt-triggered rage may comparably induce acquired fears around feeling or venting anger. The possible permutations of conflict appear almost limitless.

At any rate, however, by "soliciting" and using the combined contributions of the classical conditioning, operant learning, and sensitizing mechanisms, parent-child interactions initiate the complex processes, generally labeled "identification," through which the young seem to assimilate the character structure and traits of their elders. However, adults are probably as much active participants in this conveyance of personality as are offspring. For example, a deeply insecure father who needs his sons' successes to bolster his own sense of self-worth, and who reacts to his boys' failures with anger, contempt, and withdrawal will with his scorn and rejection infect members of the new generation with his illness and reproduce in them his own narcissistic lesions. Once wounded, the children can, as A. Freud (1965) sketched, follow nonverbal cues from parents and learn operantly both to avoid further injury and to secure some affective balm and reward—in so doing inevitably copying and thus internalizing those parental values, tastes, and mannerisms whose adoption seems likely to appease or propitiate displeased grownups.

Clearly, classical associative conditioning is a key component of the proposed models of pathogenesis and of identification. Features of this same learning process additionally suggest a revised conceptualization of the fearfulness, suspiciousness, and expectation of humiliation so often observed in narcissistic disorders and frequently attributed to projective mechanisms, which, standard theory holds, assign to other people elements of an individual's own "conflicted inner contents." This conventional explication can, however, lead to clinical interpretations befuddling to a patient who does not, for example, find it "easier" or "more comfortable to think of a conflict between" herself and her analyst "than to consider a conflict within oneself": analysands commonly feel genuinely worried about potential criticism or shaming and see nothing remotely reassuring in such anxieties. Underlying such troubling if rather ordinary misunderstandings might be this possibility: projection may have little to do with the particular phenomena described.

As experiments have long demonstrated, classical conditioning frequently shows *generalization*—fear one snake, dread them all, so to speak—and this fundamental and evolutionarily useful property of a basic form of learning, a characteristic possibly deriving from intrinsic, hard-wired circuitry (Hawkins and Kandel 1984), may account for a considerable portion of the externalization clinically encountered. Certainly, projection does occur: When, if teased about his naked crush on the cute blonde classmate sitting two desks away, an eight-year-old boy insists, "I don't like her. Jimmy does," he denies emotions that he fears could, if acknowledged, bring him further humiliation; and he instead attributes his feelings to another person. In conventional psychoanalytic language, he "projects" "conflicted drive derivatives." Again, however, this mechanism differs profoundly from the tendency of patients to distrust, for example, all adults who share features with, and thus have associative links to, stored representations of a sadistic parent. Moreover, technical approaches appropriate to the former defensive reaction may provoke only confusion and complication if imposed on the latter association-related phenomenon.

Still another facet of severe character disorder to which associative mechanisms may contribute is the tendency to perseverative behaviors which persist regardless of their ineffectiveness and lack of adaptive value—activities that perhaps persuade some observers to pause before relinquishing fully even such a fundamentally tautological concept as the "repetition compulsion." When, however, one considers the durability of aversive conditioning, one can predict that operantly learned efforts to avoid and compensate for the acquired pain will similarly continue as long as the hurt does. If, for example, a patient suffers from "castration depressive affect" (Brenner 1982), a conviction of inferiority and defectiveness growing from childhood trauma, he or she may repeatedly search for elation-evoking, if risky, experiences which ease or temporarily cancel underlying unhappiness and humiliation.

Furthermore, high-seeking behaviors may possibly derive their compulsive quality from factors other than independently persisting pain. While speculative and in need of basic neuropharmacologic support, the hypothesis proposed elsewhere (Schwartz 1987) of "auto-addiction" to one's own opioid peptides seems a tenable idea to some workers in the field (Rothman, pers. com., 1984; M. Herkenham, pers. com., 1987). Such an inference certainly accords with clinical observations of depressed, anxious, and almost frantic feelings in narcissistic patients who for various reasons must for a time survive without their accustomed sources of euphoria. Thus perseverative appetitive activities, actions fitting notions both of "compulsion to repeat" and of "resistance from the id" (Freud 1937, 242), might in part derive their considerable urgency from patients' striving to avoid an "endogenous withdrawal syndrome."

The latter hypothesis introduces a final topic: the possibility that narcissistic disorders and related defenses represent an instance of *evolution gone awry* and constitute a set of connected but mutually interactive phenomena in which relatively hard-wired protective reactions and derivative learned behaviors frequently—and paradoxically—tend to evoke from environment and self the *very responses to which the afflicted individual is most exquisitely vulnerable.* Specifically, for example, a basically depressed and insecure patient auto-addicted to the euphoria he or she obtains from serial extra-marital liaisons may continue to act in ways regarded as risky, shameful, and immoral simply because the underlying dysphoria and attempted withdrawal feel worse. In addition, the high from the "next" seduction perhaps seems always the most potent available antidote to the anxiety, embarrassment, and guilt stirred by the last affair. An "auto-reinforcing" but potentially self-destructive pattern thus easily consolidates, and, moreover, "masochistic pain" here resolves fundamentally into "a small price to pay" to escape even more excruciating emotions (compare Brenner 1959).

In addition, euphoria-seeking exposes its practitioner to still other hazards. Feeling truly high can foster tendencies to overestimate one's own powers and to minimize genuine external risks, and this auto-intoxication may thus contribute significantly to the self-defeating outcomes that not infrequently await ambitious behaviors. Furthermore, exhibitionism, which aims to kindle positive emotion by eliciting the affect-inducing admiration of others, has also the potential to invite dangers capable of reopening basic wounds and reinforcing characterologically central aversive learning. Showing off will at times incite envy, embarrassment, and anger and will therefore provoke only further rejection and hurt.

Quite apart from euphoria, other defense-related affects (Schwartz 1987, 1988) and their accompanying stereotypies may, once again, elicit environmental responses likely to strike patients at their most vulnerable points. Anxiety, depression, and humiliation, for example, tend to trigger reactions of avoidance, inactivity, withdrawal, and hiding, and these behaviors in turn do not generally foster successful adaptive efforts. The academic too frightened, demoralized, and ashamed to write and submit to journals the scholarly articles she must publish to gain promotion will probably earn only bad news from her university's tenure committee. Comparably, a socially uneasy and self-conscious teenager may make peers so uncomfortable that he generally returns home from dances and parties feeling even more snubbed, wounded, and insecure than he does at the start of these evenings.

Last and obviously, the contempt frequently prominent in narcissistic characters often hurts, humiliates, and angers others and provokes them to retaliate scornfully in a fashion that such patients find particularly excruciating. Thus in many ways, self-esteem disorders can initiate a variety of vicious cycles, and while the arguments offered here in no way suggest insignificant roles for guilty "fear of success" and "need for punishment" in the intricacies of self-destructive syndromes, one should perhaps remain alert to the many additional contributions that self-regard disturbances can make to self-defeating and masochistic behaviors (compare Brenner 1959).

Equally obviously, psychoanalysis and derivative interpretive psychotherapies aim to avoid, clarify, and indeed break these vicious cycles. But of course, analysts and therapists at times succumb to the same provocations that affect other people in the patient's world and may thus, through the untoward responses we label "countertransference enactments" (Jacobs 1986), exacerbate the very wounds they intend to treat. As humans and as animals, we always face in ourselves this dangerous and significantly hard-wired potential for retaliation against those who come to us for help; as trained and diligent professionals, however, we acquire and polish the skills of self-observation and discipline that can keep us out of the traps (Stein 1973).

Conclusion

Possessing both remarkable psychological acuity and for his time sophisticated neuroscientific knowledge (McCarley and Hobson 1977), Freud at the start of his psychoanalytic career not only developed striking clinical insights into self-esteem and its disorders (Freud 1900) but also formulated similarly intriguing speculations about associative learning, its neuronal basis, and its psychopathological significance (Freud 1895)—early ideas that have received perhaps more neglect than attention from the analytic community. In response to a *perceived* undervaluation of narcissistic issues in classical analysis, a competing and possibly incompatible theoretical and technical paradigm began to emerge some sixteen years ago (Kohut 1971). Concepts of Pavlovian and operant conditioning, moreover, have found their way into our literatures (see French 1933; Pribram 1965; Sandler and Joffe 1968; Greenspan 1975) about as infrequently as observers have recognized Freud's own interest in the underlying phenomena and principles (McCarley and Hobson 1977; Kandel 1983, 1985d; Reiser 1984, 1985; Schwartz 1987, 1988).

Now, however, as psychoanalysis nears the end of its first hundred years, new neurobiologic understanding and careful reexaminations of Freud's first writings may together allow development and synthesis of the interesting notions about learning and narcissism that surfaced early in Freud's thinking but that perhaps never received the notice they merited. With current knowledge of basic science, affect in general, euphoria in particular, representation, emotional communication, and associative conditioning—phenomena all at least implicitly recognized in Freud's initial works—become more deeply and completely comprehensible and can serve as components of the preliminary psychobiological model proposed here for self-esteem and its disturbances.

As suggested elsewhere (Schwartz 1987, 1988), reanchoring Freudian thought in the hard sciences may solidify the analytic field's epistemologic and intellectual foundations and meet contemporary political exigencies, but one can here express a further hope: that the addition and interplay of ideas from neurobiology, experimental psychology, and ethology might ultimately help to clarify and explain such *clinical* complexities as the intricacies of narcissism and its vicissitudes. Should this latter end prove attainable, the rejoining of psychoanalysis and basic biology could potentially advance three of our discipline's prime concerns—theory, interpretive understanding, and technique—and would therefore represent a useful step along the approach to the entry into our second century.

REFERENCES

Abend, S. M.; Porder, M. S.; and Willick, M. S. 1983. *Borderline Patients: Psychoanalytic Perspectives.* New York: International Universities Press.

Adamec, R. 1975. Behavioral and epileptic determinants of predatory attack behavior in the cat. *Canadian Journal of Neurological Sciences* 1975:457–66.

Allon, N., and Wollberg, Z. 1978. Responses of cells in the superior colliculus of the squirrel monkey to auditory stimuli. *Brain Research* 159:321–30.

Bailey, C. H., and Chen, M. 1983. Morphological basis of long-term habituation and sensitization in *Aplysia. Science* 220:91–93.

Blum, H. P. 1983. The position and value of extratransference interpretation. *Journal of the American Psychoanalytic Association* 31:587–617.

———. 1986a. Countertransference and the theory of technique: Discussion. *Journal of the American Psychoanalytic Association* 34:309–28.

———. 1986b. Countertransference: Concepts and controversies. In *Psychoanalysis, The Science of Mental Conflict: Essays in Honor of Charles Brenner,* ed. A. D. Richards and M. S. Willick, 229–43. Hillsdale, N.J.: Analytic Press.

Brenner, C. 1959. The masochistic character: Genesis and treatment. *Journal of the American Psychoanalytic Association* 7:197–226.

———. 1982. *The Mind in Conflict*. New York: International Universities Press.

———. 1987. Working through: 1914–1984. *Psychoanalytic Quarterly* 56:88–108.

Breuer, J., and Freud. S. 1895. *Studies on Hysteria*. Standard edition, 2, 1962.

Carew, T. J.; Walters, E. T.; and Kandel, E. R. 1981a. Associative learning in *Aplysia*: Cellular correlates supporting a conditioned fear hypothesis. *Science* 211:501–4.

———. 1981b. Classical conditioning in a simple withdrawal reflex in *Aplysia californica*. *Journal of Neuroscience* 1:1426–37.

Carew, T. J.; Hawkins, R. D.; and Kandel, E. R. 1983. Differential classical conditioning of a defensive withdrawal reflex in *Aplysia californica*. *Science* 219:397–400.

Castellucci, V. F. 1985. The chemical senses: Taste and smell. In *Principles of Neural Science*, 2d ed., ed. E. R. Kandel and J. H. Schwartz, 407–25. New York: Elsevier.

Darwin, C. [1872] 1965. *The Expression of the Emotions in Man and Animals*. Chicago: University of Chicago Press.

Ekman, P., and Friesen, W. V. 1975. *Unmasking the Face*. Englewood Cliffs, N.J.: Prentice-Hall.

Ekman, P.; Levenson, R. W.; and Friesen, W. V. 1983. Autonomic nervous system activity distinguishes among emotions. *Science* 221:1208–10.

Fenichel, O. 1941. *Problems of Psychoanalytic Technique*. New York: Psychoanalytic Quarterly.

French, T. M. 1933. Interrelations between psychoanalysis and the experimental work of Pavlov. *American Journal of Psychiatry* 12:1165–1203.

Freud, A. 1965. *Normality and Pathology in Childhood*. New York: International Universities Press.

Freud, S. 1895. Project for a scientific psychology. *Standard edition*, 1, 1967.

———. 1900. *The Interpretation of Dreams*. Standard edition, 4, 5, 1962.

———. 1909. Analysis of a phobia in a five-year-old boy. *Standard edition*, 10, 1962.

———. 1914. On narcissism: An introduction. *Standard edition*, 14, 1962.

———. 1915. Instincts and their vicissitudes. *Standard edition*, 14, 1962.

———. 1916. Some character-types met with in psychoanalytic work. *Standard edition*, 14, 1962.

———. 1920. *Beyond the Pleasure Principle*. Standard edition, 18, 1962.

———. 1923. *The Ego and the Id*. Standard edition, 19, 1962.

———. 1925. Some psychical consequences of the anatomical distinction between the sexes. *Standard edition*, 19, 1962.

———. 1926. *Inhibitions, Symptoms, and Anxiety*. Standard edition, 20, 1962.

———. 1937. Analysis terminable and interminable. *Standard edition*, 23, 1969.

Gill, M. M. 1975. Metapsychology is not psychology. In *Psychology Versus Metapsychology: Psychoanalytic Essays in Memory of George S. Klein*, ed. M. M. Gill and P. S. Holtzman, 71–105. *Psychological Issues*, Monograph 36. New York: International Universities Press.

Girouard, M. 1980. *Life in the English Country House*. New York: Penguin.

Greenspan, S. I. 1975. *A Consideration of Some Learning Variables in the Context of Psychoanalytic Theory*. *Psychological Issues*, Monograph 33. New York: International Universities Press.

Grossman, W. I. 1986. Before the pleasure principle: Translation and its vicissitudes. *Journal of the American Psychoanalytic Association* 34:488–89.

Grossman, W. I., and Stewart, W. A. 1976. Penis envy: From childhood wish to developmental metaphor. *Journal of the American Psychoanalytic Association* 24 (Suppl.):193–212.

Groves, P. M.; Miller, S. W.; and Parker, M. V. 1972. Habituation and sensitization of neuronal activity in the reticular formation of the rat. *Physiology and Behavior* 8:589–93.

Hawkins, R. D.; Abrams, T. W.; Carew, T. J.; and Kandel, E. R. 1983. A cellular mechanism of classical conditioning in *Aplysia*: Activity-dependent amplification of presynaptic facilitation. *Science* 219:400–405.

Hawkins, R. D., and Kandel, E. R. 1984. Is there a cell-biological alphabet for simple forms of learning? *Psychological Review* 91(3): 375–91.

Heilman, K. M.; Scholes, R.; and Wilson, R. T. 1975. Auditory affective agnosia. *Journal of Neurology, Neurosurgery, and Psychiatry* 38:69–72.

Holt, R. R. 1976. Drive or wish? A reconsideration of the psychoanalytic theory of motivation. In *Psychology Versus Metapsychology: Psychoanalytic Essays in Memory of George S. Klein*, ed. M. M. Gill and P. S. Holtzman, 158–97. *Psychological Issues*, Monograph 36. New York: International Universities Press.

Hubel, D. H. 1982. Exploration of the primary visual cortex, 1955–1978. *Nature* 299:515–24.

Hubel, D. H., and Wiesel, T. N. 1970. The period of susceptibility to the physiological effects of unilateral eye closure in kittens. *Journal of Physiology* (London) 206:419–36.

Jacobs, T. 1986. On countertransference enactments. *Journal of the American Psychoanalytic Association* 34:289–307.

Kandel, E. R. 1976. *Cellular Basis of Behavior*. San Francisco: W. H. Freeman.

———. 1978. *A Cell-Biological Approach to Learning*. Bethesda: Society for Neuroscience.

———. 1979. Psychotherapy and the single synapse. *New England Journal of Medicine* 301(19): 1029–37.

———. 1983. From metapsychology to molecular biology: Explorations into the nature of anxiety. *American Journal of Psychiatry* 140(10): 1277–93.

———. 1985a. Brain and behavior. In *Principles of Neural Science*, 2d ed., ed. E. R. Kandel and J. H. Schwartz, 3–12. New York: Elsevier.

———. 1985b. Processing of form and movement in the visual system. In *Principles of Neural Science*, 2d ed., ed. E. R. Kandel and J. H. Schwartz, 366–83. New York: Elsevier.

———. 1985c. Early experience, critical periods, and developmental fine tuning of brain architecture. In *Principles of Neural Science*, 2d ed., ed. E. R. Kandel and J. H. Schwartz, 757–770. New York: Elsevier.

———. 1985d. Cellular mechanisms of learning and the biologic basis of individuality. In *Principles of Neural Science*, 2d ed., ed. E. R. Kandel and J. H. Schwartz, 816–33. New York: Elsevier.

———. 1986. Presentation to symposium "Mind, Brain, and Body," Yale University School of Medicine, New Haven, Conn., 24 May 1986.

Kandel, E. R., and Schwartz, J. H. 1982. Molecular biology of learning: Modulation of transmitter release. *Science* 218:433–43.

Kandel, E. R., and Spencer, W. A. 1968. Cellular neurophysiological approaches in the study of learning. *Physiological Reviews* 48(1): 65–134.

Kelly, J. P. 1985. Auditory system. In *Principles of Neural Science*, 2d ed., ed. E. R. Kandel and J. H. Schwartz, 396–408. New York: Elsevier.

Kernberg, O. F. 1987. Institutional problems of psychoanalytic education. *Journal of the American Psychoanalytic Association* 34:799–834.

Klein, G. S. 1976a. Freud's two theories of sexuality. In *Psychology Versus Metapsychology:*

Psychoanalytic Essays in Memory of George S. Klein, ed. M. M. Gill and P. S. Holtzman, 14–70. *Psychological Issues,* Monograph 36. New York: International Universities Press.

———. 1976b. Two theories or one? In *Psychoanalytic Theory: An Exploration of Essentials,* 41–71. New York: International Universities Press.

Kohut, H. 1971. *The Analysis of the Self.* New York: International Universities Press.

Kupfermann, I. 1985a. Hypothalamus and limbic system I: Peptidergic neurons, homeostasis, and emotional behavior. In *Principles of Neural Science,* 2d ed., ed. E. R. Kandel and J. H. Schwartz, 611–25. New York: Elsevier.

———. 1985b. Hypothalamus and limbic system II: Motivation. In *Principles of Neural Science,* 2d ed., ed. E. R. Kandel and J. H. Schwartz, 626–35. New York: Elsevier.

———. 1985c. Genetic determinants of behavior. In *Principles of Neural Science,* 2d ed., ed. E. R. Kandel and J. H. Schwartz, 795–804. New York: Elsevier.

———. 1985d. Learning. In *Principles of Neural Science,* 2d ed., ed. E. R. Kandel and J. H. Schwartz, 805–15. New York: Elsevier.

MacLean, P. D. 1952. Some psychiatric implications of physiological studies on frontotemporal portion of limbic system (visceral brain). *Electroenceph. Clinical Neurophysiology* 4:407–18.

———. 1967. The brain in relation to empathy and medical education. *Journal of Nervous and Mental Diseases* 144:374–82.

———. 1969. The hypothalamus and emotional behavior. In *The Hypothalamus,* ed. W. Haymaker, E. Anderson, and W. J. H. Nauta, 659–78. Springfield, Ill.: Charles C. Thomas.

———. 1972. Cerebral evolution and emotional processes: New findings on the striatal complex. *Annual of the New York Academy of Science* 193:137–49.

———. 1977. On the evolution of three mentalities. In *New Dimensions in Psychiatry: A World View.* Vol. 2. Ed. S. Arieti and G. Chrzanowski, 306–27. New York: John Wiley.

———. 1978. A mind of three minds: Educating the triune brain. In *Seventy-Seventh Yearbook of the National Society for the Study of Education,* 308–42. Chicago: University of Chicago Press.

McCarley, R. W., and Hobson, J. A. 1977. The neurobiological origins of psychoanalytic dream theory. *American Journal of Psychiatry* 134(11): 1211–21.

Martin, J. H. 1985. Receptor physiology and submodality coding in the somatic sensory system. In *Principles of Neural Science,* 2d ed., ed. E. R. Kandel and J. H. Schwartz, 287–300. New York: Elsevier.

Merzenich, M. M., and Kaas, J. H. 1982. Reorganization of mammalian somatosensory cortex following peripheral nerve injury. *Trends in Neuroscience* 5:434–36.

Merzenich, M. M.; Kaas, J. H.; Wall, J.; Nelson, R. J.; Sur, M.; and Felleman, D. 1983. Topographic reorganization of somatosensory cortical areas 3B and 1 in adult monkeys following restricted deafferentation. *Neuroscience* 8:33–55.

Merzenich, M. M.; Kaas, J. H.; Wall, J.; Sur, M.; Nelson, R. J.; and Felleman, D. 1983. Progression of change following median nerve section in the cortical representation of the hand in areas 3b and 1 in adult owl and squirrel monkeys. *Neuroscience* 10:639–65.

Mora, F.; Rolls, E. T.; and Burton, M. J. 1976. Modulation during learning of the responses of neurons in the lateral hypothalamus to the sight of food. *Experimental Neurology* 53:508–19.

Noshpitz, J. D. 1984. Narcissism and aggression. *American Journal of Psychotherapy* 38:17–34.

Olds, J. 1976. Reward and drive neurons: 1975. In *Brain-Stimulation Reward*, ed. A. Wauquier and E. T. Rolls, 1–27. Oxford and New York: North-Holland/American Elsevier.

Oxford University. 1944. *The Shorter Oxford English Dictionary*. London: Oxford University Press.

Parker, M. V.; Miller, S. W.; and Groves, P. M. 1974. Neuronal habituation and sensitization in the reticular formation of the rat. *Physiological Psychology* 2:464–70.

Peterfreund, E. 1971. *Information, Systems, and Psychoanalysis. Psychological Issues*, Monograph 25 / 26. New York: International Universities Press.

———. 1975. The need for a new general theoretical frame of reference for psychoanalysis. *Psychoanalytic Quarterly* 44:534–49.

Pribram, K. 1965. Freud's project: An open, biologically based model for psychoanalysis. In *Psychoanalysis and Current Biological Thought*, ed. N. S. Greenfield and W. C. Lewis, 81–92. Madison: University of Wisconsin Press.

Rapaport, D. 1953. On the psychoanalytic theory of affects. *International Journal of Psycho-Analysis* 34:177–98.

Reiser, M. F. 1984. *Mind, Brain, Body*. New York: Basic Books.

———. 1985. Converging sectors of psychoanalysis and neurobiology: Mutual challenges and opportunity. *Journal of the American Psychoanalytic Association* 33:11–34.

Rolls, E. T. 1976. The neurophysiological basis of brain-stimulation reward. In *Brain-Stimulation Reward*, ed. A. Wauquier and E. T. Rolls, 65–87. Oxford and New York: North-Holland/American Elsevier.

Rosenblatt, A. D. 1985. The role of affect in cognitive psychology and psychoanalysis. *Psychoanalytic Psychology* 2:85–97.

Rosenblatt, A. D., and Thickstun, J. T. 1977a. Energy, information, and motivation: A revision of psychoanalytic theory. *Journal of the American Psychoanalytic Association* 25:537–58.

———. 1977b. *Modern Psychoanalytic Concepts in a General Psychology. Psychological Issues*, Monograph 42 / 43. New York: International Universities Press.

Ross, E. D. 1984. Right hemisphere's role in language, affective behavior and emotion. *Trends in Neuroscience* 7(9): 342–46.

Sandler, J., and Joffe, W. G. 1968. Psychoanalytic psychology and learning theory. In *The Role of Learning in Psychotherapy*, 274–87. CIBA Symposium. Boston: Little, Brown.

———. 1969. Towards a basic psychoanalytic model. *International Journal of Psycho-Analysis* 50:79–90.

Schafer, R. 1975. Psychoanalysis without psychodynamics. *International Journal of Psycho-Analysis* 56:41–55.

———. 1976. Emotion in the language of action. In *Psychology Versus Metapsychology: Psychoanalytic Essays in Memory of George S. Klein*, ed. M. M. Gill and P. S. Holtzman, 105–33. *Psychological Issues*, Monograph 36. New York: International Universities Press.

Schwartz, A. 1987. Drives, affects, behavior – and learning: Approaches to a psychobiology of emotion and to an integration of psychoanalytic and neurobiologic thought. *Journal of the American Psychoanalytic Association* 35:467–506.

———. 1988. Reification revisited: Some neurobiologically filtered views of "psychic structure" and "conflict." *Journal of the American Psychoanalytic Association* 36(Supp.): 359–85.

Silverman, M. A. 1981. Cognitive development and female psychology. *Journal of the American Psychoanalytic Association* 29:581–605.

———. 1985. Countertransference and the myth of the perfectly analyzed analyst. *Psychoanalytic Quarterly* 54:175–99.

Snyder, S. H. 1980. Brain peptides as neurotransmitters. *Science* 209:976–83.

Stein, M. H. 1973. Acting out as a character trait. *Psychoanalytic Study of the Child* 23:347–64.

Stellar, J. R., and Stellar, E. 1985. *The Neurobiology of Motivation and Reward.* New York: Springer-Verlag.

Thompson, R. F. 1986. The neurobiology of learning and memory. *Science* 233:941–47.

Tomkins, S. S. 1970. Affect as the primary motivational system. In *Feelings and Emotions: The Loyola Symposium,* ed. M. B. Arnold, 101–10. New York: Academic Press.

Walters, E. T.; Carew, T. J.; and Kandel, E. R. 1981. Associative learning in *Aplysia*: Evidence for conditioned fear in an invertebrate. *Science* 211:504–6.

Walters, E. T., and Byrne, J. H. 1983. Associative conditioning of single sensory neurons suggests a cellular mechanism for learning. *Science* 219:405–8.

Wiesel, T. N. 1982. Postnatal development of the visual cortex and the influence of environment. *Nature* 299:583–91.

Wilson, E. O. 1975. *Sociobiology.* Cambridge: Harvard University Press, Belknap Press.

Wise, R. A., and Bozarth, M. A. 1985. Actions of abused drugs on reward systems in the brain. In *Neurotoxicology,* ed. K. Blum and L. Manzo, 111–33. New York: Marcel Dekker.

7

Appetitive Pleasure States:
A Biopsychoanalytic Model of
the Pleasure Threshold, Mental
Representation, and Defense

NORMAN DOIDGE, M.D.

Foreign substances cause us pleasurable sensations; and they also alter the conditions governing our sensibility so that we become incapable of receiving unpleasurable impulses. The two effects not only occur simultaneously, but seem to be intimately bound up with each other. But there must be substances in the chemistry of our own bodies which have similar effects, for we know at least one pathological state, mania, in which a condition similar to intoxication arises without the administration of any intoxicating drug. Besides this, our normal mental life exhibits oscillations between a comparatively easy liberation of pleasure and a comparatively difficult one, parallel with which there goes a diminished or increased receptivity to unpleasure. It is greatly to be regretted that this toxic side of mental processes has so far escaped scientific examination.
—Freud, 1930

Introduction

There are many ways of slicing the pie of pleasure. One time-honored way is to divide pleasure into two large portions, as first described in Plato's *Philebus* (1945, 31c, 32c). There Socrates speaks of those pleasures associated with anticipation and those that attend the restoration of a lost harmony, as occurs

Many thanks are due to Stanley Bone, M.D., Karen Lipton Doidge, Abby Fyer, M.D., Robert Glick, M.D., Jack Gorman, M.D., William Honer, M.D., Bari Katz, Eric Marcus, M.D., Edward Nunes, M.D., and Barry Simon, M.D., all of whom made helpful comments. Catherine Buttinger, M.D., assisted in translation. Special thanks are due to Roger MacKinnon, M.D., for his encouragement for such a synthetic project; to Merrill Rotter, M.D., and Meriamne Singer, M.D., who helped organize these thoughts; and to Donald Klein, M.D., for his constructive review.

This work was supported in part by NIMH Research Training Grant MH15144 in connection with work with John Oldham, M.D., and Andrew Skodol, M.D.

in such consummatory acts as eating. In recent years the ethologists (Lorenz 1957; Hinde 1966) have begun to speak of a division of pleasurable activities, which surely owes much to the ancient one. They divide animal activities into the *appetitive* ones that have to do with anticipation and the pleasures of the chase, and the *consummatory* activities, which include the pleasures of the feast. Following the ethologists, Donald Klein (see Klein and Davis 1969; Klein 1974, 1987; Klein et al. 1980) hypothesizes that these differing activities correlate with underlying appetitive and consummatory pleasure systems, each of which has a different underlying neurochemistry. In an attempt to integrate these views with psychoanalytic thought, the first part of this chapter will take up the general problem that exciting, appetitive pleasure states pose for psychoanalytic theory. Reiser's (1984) methodology for integrating neurobiology and psychoanalysis will be outlined. In the second part, Klein's theory and other biological work on the neurochemistry of the appetitive and consummatory pleasure systems, the pleasure centers, and most importantly, the pleasure threshold, will be reviewed. In the third part, psychoanalytic clinical material on enthusiasm and related exciting pleasure states will be integrated with the neurobiological theories. A speculative "dual track" or biopsychoanalytic model will be proposed for synthesizing a sequence in which specific fantasies trigger the appetitive system and pleasure threshold changes, which in turn trigger new psychological modifications. The general implications of this model for understanding the effects of medication, substance abuse, hypomanic defenses, moods, and mood disorders on intrapsychic life will be examined.

Specifically, I propose a sequence in which certain thoughts trigger the appetitive pleasure system and lead to changes in the pleasure threshold (Klein and Davis 1969; Kornetsky 1985) that have a global influence upon consciousness. Under the influence of this process, which I will call *globalization,* particular cognitive affective units or states of mind (Kernberg 1976; Horowitz 1987) can flow into consciousness or preconsciousness, while others are reciprocally inhibited from doing so, in a process similar to that described by Freud in the above epigraph. Reciprocal inhibition of some cognitive affective states by other cognitive affective states will be discussed in connection with defensive activity, especially the hypomanic defenses. The link between changes in energy regulation and self-esteem will also be discussed. I argue that the appetitive system fills a gap in early psychoanalytic theorizing that was often filled awkwardly by the psychic energy model. This model, if found useful, will be of most obvious importance to clinicians who are treating patients with mood disorders and who use both psychotherapy and mood medications. But a model integrating mood change and defense has a broader application as well.

Several developments make a model, which integrates these aspects of psychoanalysis, psychopharmacology, and neurobiology, propitious at this time. First, Reiser (1984) and others have, through much struggle, provided a satisfactory methodology for approaching the sequential integration of sectors of neurobiology and psychoanalysis. Second, the understanding of semiotics, and of self and other schemata (Horowitz 1987) has provided a now-familiar language for discussing mental states that is scientifically sophisticated. Third, Klein's theory, which presents one of the first overarching psychopharmacological attempts to deal explicitly with pleasure states and their regulation, has important affinities with Freud's later formulations, which go beyond the tension-reduction model which sees pleasure as a lessening of excitement. All of this work is part of the shift that Freud began when he moved from emphasizing the quantitative aspects of anxiety and began to focus on its semiotic or signal aspects. However, some important aspects of experience were addressed by the earlier energic models which are not addressed by the current semiotic (or narrative) ones. Only a synthesis of both energic and semiotic views can open the way for understanding the two-way street between thought and energy regulation in mood states without recourse to the psychic energy model.[1]

The intimate link that exists between changes in self-esteem and energy regulation (Kohut 1971) has at times been obscured by the separation of psychoanalytic and biological thought about depression. Psychopharmacologists have often been concerned with the obvious vegetative changes in sleep, appetite, energy regulation, and so on, that go with abnormal mood states while being incurious about the psychological changes. However, Klein and others are increasingly turning their interest to areas that are often explained psychologically—such as the changes seen in self-esteem and the subjective experience of pleasure. In a number of mood states, energy, euphoria, and self-esteem rise and fall together. All rise in enthusiastic states (Greenson [1962] 1977; Liebowitz 1983) such as love, appetitive pursuit, hypomania, and mania (Lewin 1950). All appear to fall together in disappointment reactions and in depression (Abraham 1911; Freud [1917] 1957). It is these parallel crescendos and de-

---

1. The many critiques of the concept of psychic energy and the tension reduction model (Holt 1965; Rubenstein 1967; Schafer 1976, 1983; Peterfreund 1971; Modell 1963; Pribram and Gill 1976; Applegarth 1977; Greenberg and Mitchell 1983) point out that the psychic energy concept postulates a single homogenized energy to explain diverse categories of phenomena, including (1) mobile versus bound energy, (2) cathexis in the sense of attention cathexis, (3) directional energy associated with the drives, wishes, or affects, (4) neutralized energies, (5) the dynamic forces of opposition between structural agencies—or countercathexis, (6) the energy of external stimuli, or (7) the energy that we consciously feel in invigorated states or in elevated moods and which we assert has left us in depression, illness or fatigue. Krystal (1978) argues that Freud originally formed this comprehensive theory of psychic energy to explain the pathogenic effects of trauma. If external physical stimuli are transformable into the quantities of excitation that govern internal psychological regulation, one can argue the "outside" influences the "inside" through the passage of energy or excitation. Freud describes the psychic apparatus as a passive reflex arc that cannot discharge excess amounts of excitation. These quantities are conserved, according to the laws of thermodynamics, and this build-up leads to psychopathology. However, as Holt (1965) points out, the nervous system is perpetually active—not passive—and the effect of external stimulation is primarily to modulate the energic activity of the nervous system. The tiny energies of the nerves bear encoded information that is quantitatively negligible and bears no proportional relation to the motivational state of the person.

crescendos of energy, euphoria, and esteem that were explained with the psychic energy concept (Freud 253–54; Ostow 1965), as will be reviewed below. Though that concept is no longer so passionately embraced, the problems it addresses and the relation between energy, euphoria, and self-esteem still demand explanation.[2]

The Economic Problem of Exciting Pleasure

As long as Freud held the tension reduction model of the psychic apparatus, pleasure was theoretically equated with the discharge of an inherently noxious excitation or psychic energy and the lowering of tension. From his clinical work, however, Freud recognized that there were subjectively experienced "pleasurable tensions," which implied that rises in excitation or tension or psychic energy could be pleasurable. So Freud moved toward a modification of his model. He relegated the tendency of the organism to reduce sums of excitation to the Nirvana principle and called for a new pleasure principle that would distinguish between pleasure and pain qualitatively and allow for exciting or "tension" pleasure. He wrote:

> It cannot be doubted that there are pleasurable tensions and unpleasurable relaxations of tension. The state of sexual excitation is the most striking example of a pleasurable increase of stimulus of this sort, but it is certainly not the only one. Pleasure and unpleasure, therefore, cannot be referred to an increase or decrease of a quantity (which we describe as "tension due to stimulus"), although they obviously have a great deal to do with that factor. It appears that they depend, not on this quantitative factor but on some characteristic of it which we can only describe as a qualitative one. . . . Perhaps it is the rhythm, the temporal sequence of changes, rises and falls in quantity of stimulus. We do not know. ([1924] 1961, 160)

Jacobson (1953a, 1957, 1964, 1971) following Freud, describes the building of tension as pleasurable and suggests that tension and discharge are not opposites but in a dynamic relationship, and that both can be pleasurable. Prolonged relaxation, though initially pleasant, can lead us to seek a change—a new sort of pleasure in excitement.

> Tension pleasure may induce the urge for more intense excitement; climactic pleasure, the urge for relief; and relief pleasure, the longing for again experiencing pleasurable tension. . . . When Goethe states that "nothing is harder to bear than a series of good days," he evidently means that in a prolonged specific pleasure experience we become gradually

2. For this discussion, energy will be defined as the capacity to do physical or mental work that can be measured in terms of the speed, force, and intensity of all activities (Krystal 1982). Authors in the psychoanalytic literature tend to use terms like *tension, excitation* and *build-up of psychic energy* interchangeably, which often leads to confusion.

aware of unpleasure feelings indicating the "urge for a change" of the situation. The wish to supplant one kind of pleasurable experience with another certainly affects the pleasure qualities of the original experience. . . . We very rarely gain sheer, unmixed pleasure from one special experience for a prolonged period of time. (1971, 26–27)

Jacobson thus tries to modify the pleasure principle by saying that it directs "the course of the biological swings" (1971) between pleasurable excitement and pleasurable relief. Jacobson's formulation as to how this might occur remains vague, and like Freud, she uses the psychic energy concept to explain the quantitative factors in mood regulation and refers to "psychophysiological energy" (1964, 14), which seems to have characteristics of both Freud's psychic energy concept and physical energy.

Rubenstein (1967) points out that the early Freud (and we might add, Jacobson at times) assumed that the energy of the motivational structures (wishes or drives) passes somehow into effector structures (the central nervous structures concerned with planning, integration, and execution of activities and consummatory acts). The implicit assumption is that the "tension" that we subjectively experience when excited is a manifestation of the energy associated with a particular wish. Rubenstein, however, criticizes this speculative jump by Freud, saying that little explanatory power is gained by assuming that such a passage of energy occurs. This lumping together of effector and motivational energy is also seen in the work of Ostow, who has made a concerted effort to develop a psychoanalytic theory of medication effects.[3]

The Unit of Investigation: Protracted States of Mind or Moods

Any psychological study must choose an appropriate unit to investigate. The original psychiatric phenomenologists, with roots in the philosophical movement

3. Following Freud ([1917] 1957, [1927], 165) Ostow describes a model of depression and mania in which large shifts of psychic energy between the ego and superego are said to occur in mania and melancholia (1962, 1965, 1966, 1975). Ostow treats psychic energy as having an organic substrate, or being based upon a system of organic substrates. Small quantities of psychic energy are available to the ego in melancholia (or states of ego depletion) and high amounts are available in mania. This may be termed a bipolar rheostat model (Klein et al. 1980) in which too little psychic energy in the ego leads to depression, too much to mania. Ostow, following this model, proposes that monoamine oxidase inhibitors (MAOIs) work by increasing "the ego's content of libidinal energy," whereas major tranquilizers lower it. Interestingly, Ostow (1962) formulated this hypothesis at a time when psychopharmacologists were also using a rheostat model—the early catecholamine hypothesis—which saw depression as a deficiency and mania as an excess of catecholamines. However, psychopharmacologic evidence (Klein 1969, 1980) appears to contradict this rheostat model. Treatments such as lithium, electroconvulsive therapy (ECT), and chlorpromazine all have well-documented antidepressant and antimanic effects. Alternative biological models include the cybernetic model (Klein et al. 1980), which sees depression and mania at a biological level as involving the dysregulation of complex neurotransmitter systems and makes use of positive and negative feedback loops. (See also Siever and Davis 1985.) Ostow made several interesting clinical observations—in some cases, anticipating some of Klein's clinical observations about hysteroid dysphoria and MAOIs.

bearing that name (Spiegelberg 1972), the field theory of Lewin, the configurational analysis of Horowitz (1987), and the cognitive affective units of Kernberg, all view states of mind as key units of psychological investigation. For all the above authors, the state of mind includes self- and other representations or schemata and associated affects and attitudes. Though this is not always explicitly stated by the authors, a change in one component of the state of mind necessarily gives rise to a change in all the other components, giving rise to a new state of mind. A change in self-representation is associated with a new affect and a new object representation.

Protracted states of mind are called moods. Moods have been well described psychoanalytically and psychopharmacologically by Jacobson (1971) and Wender and Klein (1981), respectively. There is much agreement about the phenomenology of moods—a necessary prerequisite for a dual track investigation. Both writers identify biological and psychological factors as contributing to mood formation. Klein emphasizes that moods can be changed by biological processes but does not rule out the role of psychological processes leading to mood change (Wender and Klein 1981, 40). Jacobson, on the other hand, emphasizes how moods are regulated psychologically but accepts that biological influences can also exert a direct influence upon them (see 1953b, 51–52). Both writers are at least theoretically open to the contributions of the other.

Phenomenologically, moods are global states—affecting all of one's "here-and-now" experience. Insofar as they exist over a period of time, they can be said to be resistant to change. A person in a good mood will tend to stay that way for a while and interpret experiences in an optimistic light. As Jacobson (1971, 73) observes, "We know that in depressed and elated states the whole self is felt to be 'different,' either bad and inferior or good and superior, and the entire object world correspondingly appears unpleasantly or pleasantly transformed." Moods, for both Jacobson and Klein, can influence or regulate not only behavior but self-evaluation; as well, self-evaluation can influence or regulate moods. (See Wender and Klein, 1981, 40.)

A difference between the two writers is that Jacobson emphasizes that moods are temporarily fixed affect states. An angry feeling can turn into an angry mood and come to dominate the whole field of the ego's experience. Jacobson emphasizes how a mood predisposition reflects a greater or lesser tendency to fixate for a period of time on certain concepts of the self and the world (1971, 71). Thus moods can be highly refined, idiosyncratic, and even linked to specific character traits—as in optimism or pessimism. Mood disorders also display a kind of rigidity, and in contrast to normal moods, are lacking in subtle shades and are monotonous. This monotony is one reason why chronically depressed or chronically hypomanic people "get on our nerves" (1971, 79).

For Klein, on the other hand, moods are not fixed affect states. Moods are the affective component of *strategic* responses to environmental signals. Thus an environmental signal that evokes pleasurable reminiscences leads to anticipation of future success and rewards which produces a good background mood. With this goes an increased willingness to take risks. Affects for Klein do not lead to moods but are *tactical* responses that occur within particular moods. Klein would thus emphasize that chronically depressed or hypomanic people "get on our nerves," because they are plugged into the environment in an insensitive, unstrategic way which precludes a mutually gratifying exchange. Klein emphasizes that moods are adaptive responses to standard situations that face the species over the course of its evolution. The role of "psychic reality" in shaping moods is not emphasized in a discussion that has more to say about the species than the individual, more to say about the blues in general than about the blue-grays, the off-greens, and the mauves of moods that we experience.

Jacobson points out that moods are regulated by existing self- and object representations. Particularly important is the relationship between the self-representation and the wished-for self-image (Jacobson 1964; Milrod 1982). A psychological experience can cause a change of mood only "if it can bring about qualitative changes in the representations of the self and of the object world" (1971, 73). Thus particular moods can be triggered by any number of self, object, and affect configurations. Insofar as defensive activity also plays a role as to which cognitive affective unit (self-representation, object representation, and mediating affect) is in consciousness at a give time (see Kernberg 1980, 55, and below), it too can influence mood.

The converse is also true, psychoanalytically speaking: moods influence defensive activity. In discussing a patient whose defenses were modified by his disappointment in love, Jacobson notes: "Once a mood has established itself, it affects all patterns of responses to stimuli or objects of the most diverse kind, including, as in my example, typical, individually acquired emotional responses to specific stimuli; e.g. reaction formations, such as shame or pity" (1971, 69).

Given Jacobson's description of moods as regulators of the self and object world, one should not be surprised that psychopharmacologists such as Klein (1987) and Liebowitz and co-workers (1988) have been increasingly claiming that mood-stabilizing drugs influence the self-esteem and self-representations of their patients, particularly in a group of rejection-sensitive patients.

Psychological Theory and Medication Effects

As stated, this discussion points toward a model for integrating psychodynamics with mood-stabilizing or altering medication effects. The claim of psychopharmacologists that mood-altering medications seem to influence key psychic functions—in some way—is not altogether farfetched. Yet analysts have been few to describe how defenses, mental representations, fantasies, and self-esteem might be influenced by medications or biological disorders or processes. Rado (1926, 1933, 1969), Lewin (1950), and Ostow (1965, 1975) have been among the few even to venture speculation, but this work has not been updated either with psychoanalytic clinical theory or psychopharmacology.

Until now, analytic thinking has generally focused on what it means to the patient to be taking mood-altering or stabilizing medication. Attention has been paid to how giving medication alters the transference, the medication being a gift, an introject, a sign of failure, and so on: If prescribed, to which kind of patient and in which treatments should it be prescribed? In such discussions, there has been little focus on how specific medications influence the patient's mood and hence his psyche—which is the reason, after all, for which medications are given. The medications are treated almost as though they were placebos, that is, with general, nonspecific positive effects, rather than as highly specific instruments. The absence of theoretical bridges between these two areas remains an important problem for practitioners who have patients on medication, and in effect, serves to restrict needlessly the application of psychoanalytic thought.

The Dual Track Method

It is now a truism to observe that the discovery of the *Project for a Scientific Psychology* and the unearthing of Freud's neurological education (Bernfeld 1944, 1949; Amacher 1965; Holt 1965; Sulloway 1979) gave rise to a thirty-year intellectual paternity suit against "antiquated neuroscience" within psychoanalysis that led Holt (1965) to say, "I believe that many—perhaps most—of the obscurities, fallacies and internal contradictions of psychoanalytic theory are rather direct derivatives of its neurological inheritance." By what method do we hope to avoid the same errors with a slightly more up-to-date neuroscientific albatross?

The prototype for the methodology presented here is the dual track method (Reiser 1984). In it, the separate languages of neuroscience and psychoanalysis are applied to a single clinical phenomenon. Though the concepts of neurobiology and psychoanalysis cannot often be translated into each other, they can be looked at simultaneously to raise important questions. An interaction between mind and body is assumed, but speculations as to how this occurs are not generally known and hence are deferred (see Smith and Ballenger on psychophysical parallelism, 1981, for a similar discussion). Thus to observe, as Freud did, that the patterns of paralysis in hysterical patients are symbolically but not anatomically credible is consistent with dual tracking. To say that conversion symptoms are caused by the flow of a psychic excitation or energy into the body is a speculation as to how mind becomes body, and as such is inconsistent with the dual track approach.[4]

4. This dual track approach is not inconsistent with the argument that psychoanalysis proper must not go beyond its own expertise, which importantly includes the study of "the subjective experiences and meanings that are constructed by human beings" (Warme 1982). Warme argues that even if our experiences are "biological or ethological events," they can only be represented "uniquely, personally and privately." Yet, the species-specific components of our cognitive or affective responses pose limits upon our "personal" meaning-making, at least insofar as they influence the mental status. In fact, the dual track approach grew out of the same soil that gave rise to intentionality, upon which rests in part the work of Ricoeur, Schafer, and others of a hermeneutic bent. Brentano pioneered the study of intentionality (see Ricoeur

Biological Developments

Klein's Theory of Appetitive and Consummatory Pleasures

Klein's (1987) theory of appetitive and consummatory pleasures, briefly stated, asserts that there are at least two broad, independent pleasure systems. One regulates appetitive pleasure and in normal situations acts to boost energy for the pleasurable pursuit of a goal. A second system of consummatory pleasure underlies the pleasurable enjoyment of food, sex, and other interests already obtained. Each system has its own underlying neurochemical basis that can be modified by exogenous psychoactive drugs. Klein postulates that stimulants, such as cocaine and amphetamines, act by turning on the appetitive pleasure system while opiates, such as heroin, morphine, and the endorphins, turn on the consummatory pleasure system.[5]

Klein first got interested in this division through the work of the ethologists (see, for example, Lorenz 1957; Hinde 1966). According to Lorenz, appetitive behavior strives toward a stimulus situation that releases a consummatory act. Appetitive behaviors are environment responsive and affected by learning. Consummatory activities, such as feeding or sexual orgasm, are species specific, highly stereotyped activities that are directly involved with species survival. The higher the organism, the more variable is its appetitive behavior in relation to its goal. Klein's work attempts to relate this division of activities to physiological substrates, psychopathology, and psychopharmacology.

In the 1950s Klein noted that some drug addicts had specific "taste preferences" for stimulants which led to an exciting, nonsatiating euphoria, while others preferred opiate derivatives which led to a satiating euphoria accompanied by decreased arousal. These different preferences led Klein to "question the existence of a single functional pleasure response."

Klein then drew the analogy between positive feedback and negative feed-

---

1970, 363, 379) which, through Husserl, inspired phenomenology and phenomenological psychiatry (Spiegelberg 1972). Freud was also Brentano's student at the University of Vienna in 1874, and it was Brentano who first exposed him to the mind-brain problem when he was studying philosophy and medicine simultaneously. McGrath (1986) has reviewed the unpublished letters of Freud to Eduard Silberstein that demonstrate the profound influence that the philosopher Brentano had on Freud's understanding of the mind-brain question. In his *Psychology from an Empirical Standpoint,* which was published in 1874, Brentano divided all the data of consciousness into the physical and the mental, both subject to different laws: "Not only may physical states be aroused by physical states, and mental states by mental, but it is also the case that physical states have mental consequences and mental states have physical consequences" (1973, 6). He also emphasized that the mental and physical occur parallel in time, and the most effective means of study is by supplementation of mental and physical sciences—not by reducing one to the other.

5. Klein regards this division into two systems as a parsimonious way of accounting for observed differences; in fact, he suspects that each pleasure system consists of component systems with different neurochemistries. For example, the consummatory pleasures of eating and intercourse likely share a common neurochemistry of consummatory pleasure but also have their own specific component neurochemistries (pers. com., 1987).

back loops and satiation. Cocaine intoxication is nonsatiating. It gives rise to an exciting pleasure that makes one want more and more cocaine. Hence it functions like a positive feedback loop. The language of the addict captures much of this: a cocaine addict "goes on a run" and gets high, takes a snort, gets higher, and takes another snort until he runs out of cocaine. In contrast, morphine is satiating, hence taking morphine appears to function like a negative feedback loop. Following a shot, a heroin or morphine addict becomes sedated, sleepy, and indifferent to the world. This is called "going on the nod." He becomes emotionally "cool" if not indifferent to external or internal changes. An opiate addict appears to be satiated and satisfied while on the drug and shows less physiological arousal or drug-seeking behavior. He experiences a peaceful euphoria in contrast to the augmented activity induced by stimulants. Thus, even though both stimulants and opiates can, over the long term, be addictive and lead one to want more of the drug, in the short term while one is intoxicated, each drug-induced euphoria is different with respect to satiation.[6]

Klein during this time was also working with seriously depressed patients. Depression may be seen, in part, as an impairment of the ability to obtain pleasure. In the 1950s, while looking for alternative biological treatments to ECT for melancholics, Klein observed the effects of amphetamines on depressed patients. When given amphetamines, some depressed patients showed a temporary mood improvement, while others went from retarded to agitated depressions. Klein wondered if these patients had different problems with pleasure. Klein speculated that melancholics (that is, patients with lowered self-esteem and decreased sleep, appetite, and energy) had problems experiencing both appetitive and consummatory pleasure. He observed that they did not pursue pleasure, nor could they consummate it even if the usual sources of pleasure— such as food, sex, and friendship—were presented to them on a silver platter. Most of these melancholic patients, when given imipramine, showed not only improved mood, sleep, and appetite but also a renewed ability to engage in appetitive pursuit and consummation of pleasure.

Some of these imipramine-treated melancholic depressives, however, showed an improved ability only to consummate pleasure; they still would not pursue pleasure. Klein reasoned that these patients were left with an appetitive deficit. Yet this appetitive deficit often improved when a stimulant was added to the imipramine. Observing this two-phased response again led Klein to wonder whether there were two neurochemically distinct pleasure systems rather than just one.

Klein next turned his attention to a second group of depressives, called "atypical depressives," which appeared to have a different biological syndrome.

6. The notion that different addicts have different taste preferences is not inconsistent with the work of Khantzian (1985), who asserts, on the basis of longitudinal psychodynamically oriented case studies, that "cocaine has its appeal because of its ability to relieve distress associated with depression," whereas opiates are the drug of choice for those who desire "muting action on the disorganizing and threatening affects of rage and aggression."

Atypical depressives, like melancholics, have lowered self-esteem, depression, and decreased interest in pursuing pleasure. In contrast to the melancholics, however, they eat more and sleep more when depressed. Klein noted that though they complained that no pleasure could interest them, they were cheerful and animated if amusements or friends came their way, again, on a silver platter. These atypicals seemed to have an appetitive but not a consummatory deficit. In general, the atypicals do not improve on imipramine but respond to mono-oamine oxidase inhibitors (MAOIS). This positive drug response of atypicals to MAOIS has since been replicated in a double-blind study (see Liebowitz et al. 1988).

Finally, a third group of patients, very much like the atypicals, also had a good response to MAOIS and actually got worse on imipramine. This seemed further to suggest a discrete appetitive pleasure system deficit. Klein called these patients "hysteroid dysphorics" (after the descriptions by Easser and Lesser 1965). They are described as histrionic, seductive, unstable personalities with many borderline features. They respond to rejection with acute sensitivity, decreased self-esteem, lethargy, overeating, and oversleeping. In effect, they have a "crash" that is indistinguishable from a brief atypical depression or an amphetamine withdrawal. Yet, in their normal state, hysteroid dysphorics are highly energetic, expansive, and outgoing people.[7]

This work led Klein to ponder what neurochemical action MAOIS, which have structural resemblances to amphetamines, were having. Klein has since hypothesized that phenylethylamine (or PEA) functions as an endogenous amphetamine-like substance (ALS) and is part of the appetitive pleasure system.[8]

The Appetitive Pleasure System

The appetitive pleasure system, once turned on, gives rise to a nonsatiating pleasure. This state is a *desirable* state of desiring, triggered by a sense of imminent satisfaction and accompanied by hopeful thoughts. It is quite different from the yearning kind of desire that is based upon an awareness of a lack of something. Klein postulates that the appetitive system is a feed-forward system,

7. Subsequent studies (Klein et al. 1980; Klein 1987; Davidson et al. 1988; Kayser et al. 1985) have shown that hysteroid dysphorics also respond preferentially to the MAOI, phenelzine. The classification of hysteroid dysphoria remains controversial (see Spitzer and Williams 1982; Klein and Liebowitz [in reply] 1982).

8. This is not to imply that the mechanism of action of MAOIS is stimulation. Klein and Davis (1969, 450) distinguish between "compensatory" drugs, which affect normal physiology similar to their effect on pathophysiological states, and "reparative" drugs, which correct only abnormal states. Amphetamines are compensatory—they have a similar effect on depressed and nondepressed groups; MAOIS and tricyclics are reparative—they work only on certain depressed subgroups. MAOIS affect the enzyme monoamine oxidase, which is involved in catecholamine regulation. Monamine oxidase B also regulates PEA, which differs by only one methyl group from amphetamine. Many atypical depressives seem to have discovered that stimulants help their condition and have been self-medicating with addictive stimulant drugs and nosesprays before MAOI treatment.

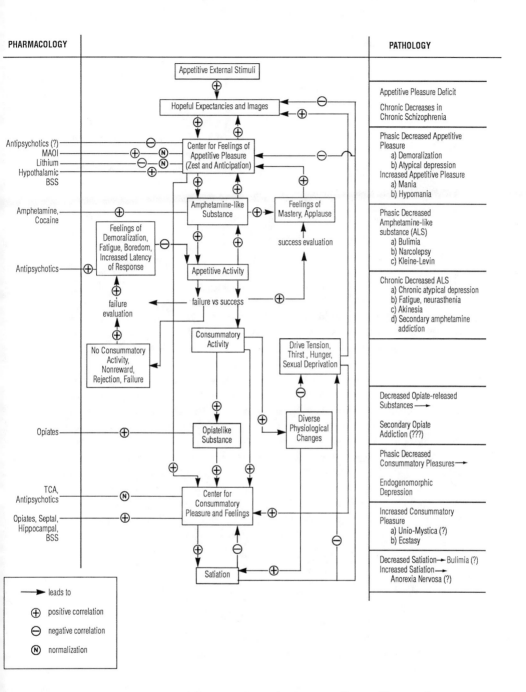

Figure 7.1 Processes of pleasurable hedonically regulated activity. (Source: Nunes and Klein 1987. Reprinted by permission of Brunner-Mazel.)

turned off only when the goal is achieved and the consummatory system is turned on. Presumably with Freud's early theories of tension reduction in mind, Klein describes appetitive activities: "These activities are primarily in the foraging, hunting, searching and socializing area. A very good example of a pleasurable activity that often produces a crescendo of massive joyful excitation is sexual foreplay. This is a good example of pleasure in an excitatory situation and seems to contradict the belief that all pleasure derives from excitation reduction" (1987, 3).

It is important to keep in mind that the term "appetitive pleasure" does not refer to the consummatory pleasure it eventually brings about. Appetitive pleasure is anticipatory but constitutes pleasure nonetheless: "Hopeful expectancies and images are generated when one is confronted with appetitive stimuli. Further, there is a positive feedback loop associated with the appetitive drive state. That is, if you're in a state of heightened drive it generates hopeful expectancies and fantasies. These hopeful expectancies then stimulate the center for feelings of appetitive pleasure. In other words, it makes you feel good when you are contemplating the possibility of consummatory pleasure, as any daydreamer can tell you. The appetitive center makes you feel good about both the initiation and pursuit of consummatory pleasure" (1987, 11).

In our civilization, a number of activities such as sports and challenging play substitute for hunting proper. However, the appetitive system can be involved in any goal-directed activity and is not restricted to aggressive behaviors. Klein hypothesizes that the activity of the appetitive pleasure system is associated with the release of an endogenous, yet to be discovered, amphetamine-like substance. This initiates increased energy for mental and physical activities, arousal, and a decreased need for sleep. If the pursuit is going well and the goal seems within reach, there is a crescendo of good feeling. Klein speculates that when the appetitive center's feed-forward loop is working too well, this is manifest clinically by a manic syndrome with increased goal directed activity, energy, and so on. Manics also have the sense that everything is looking marvelous, regardless of the negative signs that would normally turn off the appetitive center; the normal dips of energy following activity do not occur. Normally, if the pursuit is not going well, this is evaluated and inhibits the pleasure center—subjectively experienced as demoralization, loss of energy, and fatigue.

In contrast to the manics, in atypical depressives, the appetitive system does not seem to function well and requires much environmental priming and stimulation before it will work, leaving the person less able to initiate goal-directed behavior.

Romantic Attraction and the Appetitive System

In his discussion of hysteroid dysphorics Klein, in essence, proposes that in certain patients aspects of interpersonal relationships, such as rejection sensitivity, are medication responsive, and are thus in part a function of thresholds of neurotransmitter systems. Liebowitz (1983), who has worked extensively with

Klein, continues this trend and emphasizes that phenomena, such as tolerance, dependence, withdrawal, and crashing, reflect the properties of these underlying neurotransmitter systems and impose constraints upon the experiences of moods and pleasure. In the "psychopharmacology of everyday life," we are all aware that falling romantically in love is like a stimulant intoxication. In both we feel excited, energetic, may need less sleep, and are confident, elated, and optimistic even to the point that it can impair our judgment. Liebowitz hypothesizes that this is because the same underlying neurotransmitter systems are involved. Aspects of neurochemical "dependence" on the love object are seen most clearly when the object is lost or absent. What is called "working through" or mourning at a psychological level is associated with a necessary biochemical withdrawal syndrome, which can even be precipitated or undone by the *thought* of object loss or return.

> Certain parallels with drug withdrawal appear to occur during temporary separation from a husband, wife, boyfriend or girlfriend with whom one is intimate. Granted there are important psychological reactions, such as fear or feelings of abandonment. Nevertheless, what often happens is that one begins to miss deeply and, in fact, crave the other's presence. Feelings of anxiety may set in, coupled with a certain loss of energy, optimism, and enthusiasm, which has been likened to "running down one's battery." The thought of seeing the person again, a phone call or letter, and, best of all, a reunion, can be exciting, calming, or energizing events, perhaps in part because of the physical changes induced in us. (Liebowitz 1983, 64)

Cocaine, the Appetitive Pleasure System, and Freud

Comparisons between stimulant intoxication and enthusiastic appetitive states, such as romantic attraction, were made by Freud during his cocaine episode. Freud was initially interested in cocaine's purported ability to reduce fatigue but soon found it to be a magical drug that could relieve his neurasthenia and make him feel powerful, "like a wild man," and more. In his letter to Martha, 2 February 1886, he describes taking cocaine while writing the letter. Because cocaine is so quick acting, the letter, as it unfolds, gives a marvelous window into the subjective effects of the drug. He first describes how the cocaine makes him talkative and confessional. His initial self-deprecatory remarks vanish as the letter goes on, and soon he is speaking of his fearlessness in identification with his Jewish ancestors who defended the Temple. He likens cocaine's ability to cure his fatigue and neurasthenia to the magical cure he gets from being with Martha romantically. Elsewhere (18 January 1886), he speaks of how it reduces his shyness, and he describes his euphoria, enhanced energy and self-esteem, enthusiasm, and decreased depression. In *On Coca* ([1884] 1974), Freud published his famous account of the subjective effects of cocaine and documented the exhilaration, alterations in sense perception, and its physical effects on his muscular exertion; he also discussed its aphrodisiac effect.

Freud's cocaine episode was linked with many painful affects for him, such as those associated with the Fleischl-Markow affair, and his understanding of cocaine was never explicitly linked with psychoanalytic theory. The experience of pleasure occurring in the absence of the object, that is, autoerotically, may have been taken by Freud as support for an autoerotic state and the associated hedonic theory. Many now question Freud's privileging of the need for drive discharge over the need for the object tie as the primary motivational principle (Greenberg and Mitchell 1983).[9]

Needless to say Freud nowhere regards the cocaine experiences as refuting the Fechnerian notion that pleasure equals the reduction of excitement.

The Neurochemistry of the Cocaine High and Crash

Current reviews of the phenomenology of a cocaine high remain essentially unchanged from Freud's classic description. According to Nunes and Rosecan (1987) the best-known effect of cocaine is that it blocks presynaptic reuptake of the catecholamines norepinephrine, dopamine, and serotonin and may lead to the presynaptic release of norepinephrine and dopamine as amphetamines do. This release makes more of these neurotransmitters available and increases their effect in the short term. It is thought that the release of dopamine in the mesolimbic tracts and mesocortical tracts (both of which appear in normal functioning to have to do with reward systems) contributes to the euphoriant and energizing effect. Cloninger (1986, 1987) has recently proposed that midbrain dopaminergic cell bodies with projections to the forebrain form "a final common pathway for the behavioural activating system." This incentive system has important similarities with Klein's appetitive pleasure system. King and others (1986) report that the cerebrospinal fluid (CSF) dopamine level is higher than normal in extroverted, energetic sensation-seeking males. This also suggests the role of dopamine in energetic activity. Though no endogenous cocaine has been found, there are a number of very high affinity receptor sites on dopaminergic nerve terminals.[10]

9. As well, one may wonder if Freud's idea that neurasthenia was the result of the inadequate sexual discharge arose from his cocaine experience. Cocaine both "cures" neurasthenia in the short term and is an aphrodisiac (Taberner 1985). In *On Coca*, Freud stated that "among the persons to whom I have given coca, three reported violent sexual excitement." Did he assume cocaine cures neurasthenia by leading to improved sexual discharge? Freud did not seem to be aware that chronic cocaine use gives rise to an atypical depression syndrome indistinguishable from neurasthenia.

If one brings a fairly classical drive psychology to bear on such matters, as does Jürgen von Scheidt (1973), one can argue that cocaine loosened Freud's censorship, giving freer reign to aggressive and sexual feelings, and that this enabled him to come into contact with unconscious material he might otherwise not have. Freud continued to prescribe cocaine until 1895, the year he had the dream of Irma's injection. That dream as well as the dream of the botanical monograph make covert and overt references to cocaine.

10. The role of serotonin is more obscure, but there is growing evidence that it is needed for a vast array of inhibitory functions. Cocaine is thought to inhibit serotonin function, and this inhibition of inhibition is thought to allow further excitation of norepinephrine and dopamine functions.

If cocaine is taken repeatedly, the presynaptic stores of dopamine and norepinephrine are soon depleted—leading to a rebound depression. This rebound depression is thought to be related to long-term changes in the postsynaptic neurons. It is hypothesized that presynaptic dopamine synthesis cannot keep up with the cocaine-induced dopamine and norepinephrine release, leading to a depletion of presynaptic stores. The postsynaptic target receptors—in the absence of dopamine and norepinephrine—increase in numbers and become supersensitive. (This process is also called *up-regulation*. See figure 7.2.) Cocaine thus leads to a compensatory up-regulation of postsynaptic beta receptors. Both beta supersensitivity and the presynaptic depletion of norepinephrine and dopamine are associated with the cocaine crash: depression, lethargy, REM rebound, and drug craving.[11]

In summary, the work on cocaine and the work of Klein suggest that exogenous stimulants have the effect of turning on an internal appetitive pleasure system for placing the organism in high gear, increasing energy, the pleasures of pursuit, and apparently, self-esteem.

The Consummatory Pleasure System and the Putative Role of Opiates

Klein hypothesizes that the consummatory pleasures may at a neurochemical level have in common the release of some sort of endogenous opiatelike substance, such as an endorphin or enkephalin, which then turns off the appetitive system and turns on the satiation center. This gives rise to euphoria, bliss, peace, lack of anxiety, relative analgesia, and a happy indifference to the world. Important for Klein's hypothesis is the notion that the appetitive and the consummatory euphorias involve chemically different systems. Recent work by Koob and others (1986, 1987) demonstrates that the euphorias of cocaine and those of opiates are independent.[12]

Opiates reduce anxiety, as well, possibly by inhibiting norepinephrine release in the locus ceruleus (Gold and Rea 1983). Reiser (1984) has reviewed and

11. The fact that Bromocriptine, a dopamine agonist, seems to diminish craving in cocaine abusers is taken as possible evidence by some investigators that it is the high number of unoccupied postsynaptic dopamine receptor sites which underlie drug craving. Antidepressants, like cocaine, initially cause more norepinephrine and dopamine to be available in the synaptic cleft. However, they are widely thought to lead to a secondary down-regulation of the postsynaptic beta receptor populations.

12. Koob and co-workers (1986, 1987) have demonstrated this by giving dopamine receptor blockers to two groups of rats involved in self-administration paradigms. The first group had free access to cocaine, the second group to heroin. Both groups of rats were given a dopamine blocker, which altered the self-administration of cocaine only. This points to a dopamine-dependent system for cocaine euphoria. Next Koob and co-workers gave an opiate blocker, naltrexone, to rats on both cocaine and heroin self-administration. The opiate blocker affected only heroin self-administration. Again this suggests independent euphoria systems. In later work, Koob and his colleagues chemically obliterated the presynaptic dopamine stores in the nucleus accumbens. This blocking affected the cocaine but not heroin self-administration, which points to the role of a presynaptic mechanism in the nucleus accumbens in stimulant, but not opiate-induced euphoria.

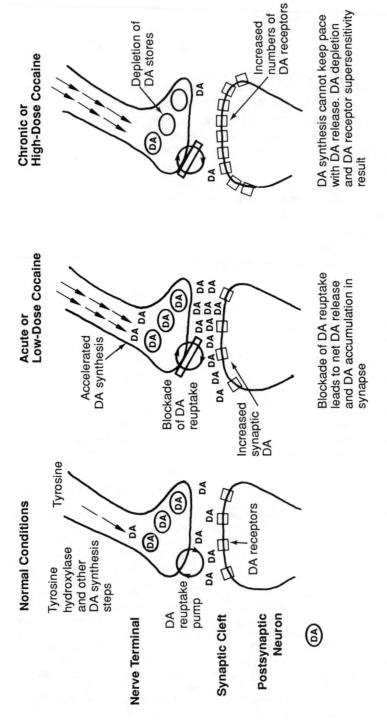

Figure 7.2 Effects of cocaine on dopamine (DA) neurons (similar for norepinephrine neurons). (Source: Nunes and Rosecan 1987. Reprinted by permission of Brunner-Mazel.)

dual tracked psychoanalytic and neurochemical concepts of the anxiety-regulating systems. Opiates have many other roles, and there are a number of different endogenous opiates. Opiates have been shown in experiments to lessen separation anxiety and reduce the separation calls of puppies, guinea pigs, and chicks separated from their mothers (Panksepp, cited in Liebowitz 1983). There is speculation that they are involved in the neurochemistry of attachment. Finally, it should be emphasized that the consummatory system plays a key role in gently turning off the appetitive system and helping one not to experience a stimulant-like crash. If Klein is correct that opiates are a substrate of the consummatory system, the transition from appetitive to consummatory activities may be an endogenous version of what cocaine addicts induce in themselves to avoid crashing—they mix some heroin with their cocaine. The term for this is "speedballing."

Lowering the Threshold of the Pleasure Centers

The final important biological concept that will form an important bridge in understanding how endogenous neurochemical activity might influence cognitive affective mental states is that of the pleasure threshold.

Holt (1965) and Rubenstein (1967) both have pointed out that the discovery of the localizable brain pleasure centers by Olds and Milner in the 1950s cast doubt upon the notion that pleasure was only the result of drive discharge. The assertion that pleasure was associated with falls in an inherently noxious quantity was less believable when animals seemed able to experience pleasure independent of any obvious instinctual drive discharge. (However, although these data are suggestive, one must caution that the stimulation of pleasure centers involves artificially turning on a component of an overall system. The existence of discrete pleasure centers does not rule out that they may be biologically wired sequentially or parallel with the drive systems. This wiring may be short-circuited by the direct implantation of electrodes.) Rubenstein (1967, 72) suggested that Olds's demonstration of primary hypothalamic reward systems would—if these applied to human beings—provide a "structural alternative to the need-reduction (energy discharge) theory of pleasure." His belief then was that "information may in a sense activate a structure . . . which operates on its own stored physicochemical energies."

Specifically, Olds and Milner in their well-known experiments discovered that rats that had electrodes implanted in their limbic systems appeared to work very hard to maintain an ongoing level of pleasurable electrical stimulation. This phenomenon is called intracerebral self-stimulation or ICSS. Those limbic areas that lead to pleasurable responses are dubbed pleasure centers, in contrast to other well-defined pain centers. These pleasure centers are thought to be part of normal brain reward systems. One can measure how often an animal with electrodes implanted in its pleasure center will press a bar switch that leads to the electrical stimulation of its pleasure center. Bar presses are a measure of how much work an animal will do for pleasure and are thus taken as an indirect indication of the intensity of the pleasure. One can also measure how few presses are required to make the center fire, which is taken as a measure of the lowest threshold at which a center will fire. For example, if an animal presses the bar thirty times and then stops, it appears to require thirty stimuli to turn on the pleasure center. This amount of stimulation, measured in bar presses, is called the *threshold of stimulation.*

Researchers (see Kornetsky 1985, for a review; Kornetsky and Bain 1987) set out to test the hypothesis that euphorogenic drugs of abuse work by making it easier for the pleasure centers to fire. Repeated experiments have shown that drugs of abuse or drugs with a known euphorogenic effect lower the threshold of stimulation, that is, the amount of electrical stimulation needed for the center to fire. An animal pretreated with cocaine or opiates presses the stimulation bar fewer times before it exhibits a pleasure response. For example, an animal that might otherwise have to press a bar thirty times a minute to turn on its pleasure center, if preinjected with amphetamine, will only press the bar four times before it displays a pleasure response. This model assumes that the number of bar presses corresponds to the threshold.[13]

In 1974 in animal experiments, Marcus and Kornetsky (reported in Kornetsky 1985) used an electroencephalogram (EEG) with electrodes placed simultaneously both in the pleasure centers (in the medial forebrain and hypothalamus) and aversive centers (in the brain stem) of a rat. They demonstrated that morphine (an opiate) lowered the threshold of the pleasure centers and raised the threshold of the aversive centers. Heath (reported in 1974) reported similar findings in human subjects. This phenomenon has been called *reciprocal inhibition.*[14] (Although the behaviorists have a very specific use of this term, the use in this chapter derives from the neurobiological sense.)

13. Kornetsky (1985) describes a refined version of this paradigm, which measures the threshold more directly than the number of bar presses. In the experiment, an animal is given an electrical stimulus at a particular intensity. If 7.5 seconds elapse and there is no bar pressing, this is considered a below-threshold response. After 15 seconds, the stimulus is repeated. If the animal presses the bar within the 7.5 seconds, this is an indication that the threshold has been reached or exceeded. This procedure is somewhat like asking the animal, "Do you wish to have another stimulus like the one you just received?" The next manipulation is to increase or decrease the level of stimulation. At high levels of stimulation, the animal responds positively to each stimulus, in effect requesting another one. At very low levels it does not respond at all. At certain levels of stimulation, the animal responds positively in a given period as many times as it responds negatively. This level of stimulation is defined as the threshold of stimulation.

14. Heath, who studied with Rado, tried to demonstrate the importance of hedonic regulation in the 1950s by implanting electrodes and cannulas in the brains of sixty-five patients with intractable, psychiatric illnesses and severe, unresponsive pain syndromes. These patients reported their subjective states when electrodes were inserted into various areas. Heath found that the pleasure system focused on the septal region, "extending caudally by way of the medial forebrain bundle through ventrolateral hypothalamus to the interpeduncular nuclei of the brain stem." This work also showed that when the pleasure system was enhanced, opposite changes were observed in brain sites identified for aversive behavior, suggesting "an inverse relationship between pleasure and pain" in that "physiologic induction of pleasure promptly abolished pain" (Heath 1974).

The notion of reciprocal inhibition is not inconsistent with the Freudian assertion that pleasure and pain appear to be on a continuum. However, Freud initially thought the continuum to be a function of changes in the amount of psychic energy or excitation (a rheostat model), and this model sees it as a function of reciprocally inhibiting, qualitatively different pleasure and pain systems (a cybernetic model). Klein (Klein and Davis 1969, 443) postulates that depression may show a loss of the normal reciprocal inhibitory balance between the pleasure and the pain centers.

Global Effect of Pleasure Center Changes

Klein argues that "in the manic state there is a pathological responsiveness of the pleasure center so that such patients frequently behave foolishly for immediate pleasures. Their anticipatory mechanism is also deranged in parallel form since they frequently are sure that everything will work out. . . . This self-deluding belief is due to their intense pleasure in anticipation and the consequent lack of self-criticism" (Klein and Davis 1969, 443). Klein extends this analysis and postulates that when cocaine and amphetamine are given, "the appetitive pleasure center threshold is lowered and can fire more easily" (Klein et al. 1980, 799). In effect he is saying that these drugs lower the threshold of stimulation. This has cognitive implications. Once pleasure center thresholds are lowered, images of the future more easily elicit hope. One can extend this analysis and say that the same happens in mania. Liebowitz (1983) applies this concept of "pathological responsiveness of the pleasure center" to not only stimulants and mania but also to romantic states and even pleasant memories of the beloved. All these can lower the threshold at which the pleasure centers will turn on. Thus, when one's pleasure center threshold is lowered, at a phenomenological level, it is not only "the rush" of the drug but the whole world of experience that gives one pleasure. As shall be discussed below, enthusiasm, romance, and related hypomanic states always confer a global optimism and sensitivity to pleasure (Greenson [1962] 1977). Needless to say, Klein's corollary to this concept is that depression involves an increase in activity in the pain center: "In a certain proportion of these patients, the inhibition of . . . an hypothesized pleasure center seems accompanied by disinhibition of an equally hypothetical pain evaluation center, resulting in marked fearful anticipations and agitation" (1974).

Dual Tracking Psychoanalytic and Psychopharmacologic Theories

For our specimen mood, I shall take a pleasurable and exciting one—enthusiasm. Greenson's paper on enthusiasm is an attempt to outline enthusiastic and related pathological states and to explain them in psychic energy terms. Greenson terms enthusiasm as a mood state, in which the entire self and object world is transformed. Enthusiasm is described as a passionate state of mind that has

some of the buoyancy of euphoria and the activity of mania. . . . It is exciting, active, and noisy—not quiet or passive like bliss. In this regard it resembles the hypomanias, only the activities are more realistic and adaptive.
. . . There is an air of extravagance and expansiveness about enthusiasm—
a readiness to use superlatives. The enthusiastic person does not merely
feel good or even very good, but great—in fact, "the greatest!" There is a
sense of exuberance, richness, an abundance of good fortune; yet with it
all, there is some awareness that one is exaggerating; but it is enjoyable,
and one is reluctant to give it up. Enthusiasm has the quality of an infatuation, and indeed is present when there is infatuation. However, enthusiasm can occur without romance and without sex, and in regard to an
inanimate object. But enthusiasm, too, contains a feeling of being capti-
vated, an awareness of folly, a loss of one's reason. It is characteristic for
both enthusiasm and infatuation to occur suddenly. . . . The wish to share
is urgent, even compelling. One cannot remain enthusiastic alone . . . one
needs cohorts. . . . For all its noisy busyness, enthusiasm is fragile and ca-
pricious. It can be punctured like a balloon. . . . The lack of response
from a "wet blanket" can easily smother its flame." (1962)

Greenson gives an example of how an object can lead to enthusiasm. He
describes how an adolescent girl patient receives the gift of a beautiful European
sports car and becomes enthusiastic, infatuated with it, and describes herself as
though she were a new person, and the world were now full of possibility. She
loses weight and emphasizes her European features, taking on a modified beauty
that, like the new object, is sophisticated. This feeling of being identified with
an idealized object is typical of early analytic explanations of mania (Lewin 1950;
Freud [1917] 1957; [1921] 1955). Typically, the new object also serves to ward
off unpleasant facts. In this case it is the patient's feeling of being unsophisti-
cated. Greenson also remarks that there is a regression of cognitive processes
in all of this, which is normal and reversible. However, "in pathological states
like the hypomanias, the fusion is with internal objects, and more denial is seen.
In enthusiasm, external objects are needed in order to perpetuate the state,
where the manias are relatively independent of external objects."

Energy and Enthusiasm
Greenson remarks that enthusiasm is a state of great activity: "An enthused
person seems suddenly to have acquired a great abundance of energy, and the
world seems pliable and accessible. There is a plethora of enterprise, talk,
gregariousness, and imagination." He goes on to explain this in psychic energy
terms:

A question that now arises is: where does this new quantity come from?
Freud (1921), Jacobson (1957), and others have noted the striking economic changes which occur in all joyous states. It is as though an abundance of psychic energy, which had been ordinarily consumed elsewhere,

has now become free and available. It has been hypothesized that the fusion of ego and superego in manic states is responsible for the liberation of this energy. The union with an idealized object does away with all tension between ego and superego; the superego temporarily gives up its functions. Thus, the id is free from pressure and is permitted greater discharge. . . . There is another reason for the surplus of energy. The process operating in enthusiasm is similar to what we see in laughter. The joke makes the ego's defenses unnecessary, and so does enthusiasm. The energy which has been used for defense can now be utilized for enthusiasm.

Thus he considers the energies that have been released in joyous states to be made up of (1) energy formerly consumed in superego functions, (2) energy formerly consumed by the ego for defensive activity and countercathexis, and (3) id energy, which can now be freely discharged.

Greenson's clinical portrait basically describes effector energy, and as Rubenstein would point out, Greenson takes an unwarranted leap when he assumes this energy corresponds to the psychic energy of the motivational structures (id, ego, and superego). Yet there is nothing inherently psychological—in the sense of pure psychology as dealing with personal meanings—in this leap. Let us therefore integrate the notion of an appetitive system and pleasure center changes to account for the energics of enthusiasm.

A Dual Tracking Sequence of Enthusiasm

In this dual tracking scheme, the cognitive affective unit will play the central conceptual role from the psychoanalytic side. Yet, on close inspection, it is in fact a concept that straddles the mind-body question insofar as both the mind and body are associated with it. Affects, for instance, have physiological and subjective components. As it is commonly used, the cognitive affective unit consists of a configuration of self-representation, object representation, and mediating affect (Kernberg 1976). This notion of the cognitive affective unit is a clinical one which states that the basic unit of phenomenological experience consists of these three components which are encoded together and which can be discerned in any fantasy or interpersonal interaction. With the capacity for organizing internal representations that begins at about eighteen to thirty months (Greenspan 1981), the child can organize self-representations and object representations, interacting with an associated affect. The notion of the cognitive affective unit expresses the fact that in the adult affects express dispositional states (Basch 1976) and are always directed in some way to an object, with a related concept of self vis à vis a particular situation. This approach is consistent with essential insights of phenomenology, Gestalt psychology, and Lewin's topological field theory. Studies (Lewis, Sullivan, and Michalson 1984) show that notions that see affect as always preceding cognition or vice versa are not empirically sound. Rather, microanalysis of states of mind based on facial expression shows a "cognitive-emotional fugue."

Kernberg adds that a pleasant cognitive affective unit can be used defensively to ward off an unpleasant one and vice versa: "Unconscious intrapsychic conflicts are never simple conflicts between impulse and defense; rather, the drive derivative finds expression through a certain primitive object relation (a certain unit of self- and object representation); and the defense, too, is reflected by a certain internalized object relation. The conflict is between these structures" (Kernberg 1980, 155). We shall use that assertion to show how pleasure states can be used for defensive reasons.

Interspersing the psychoanalytic and biological concepts, we can set up the following schema for enthusiasm:

Psyche (psychoanalytic track)
1. There is a perception of an imminently obtainable object or objective. This triggers

Psyche (psychoanalytic track)
2. An appetitive fantasy. The self-representation is seen as moving toward, or is in the state of, consummation. Such fantasies are associated not only with instinctual satisfaction, they are associated with fantasies in which the self is identified with, loved by, or positively gratified and modified by the desired object so that it lives up to the wished-for self-image. This leads to a general sense of well-being that extends toward the future because if one is beloved, one is good and entitled to consummate a host of desires. Memories of past good fortune enter preconsciousness and consciousness. This triggers

Soma (neuroscience track)
3. The appetitive pleasure system and associated neurochemical changes, possibly including the release of the hypothesized endogenous stimulant, ALS. The appetitive pleasure system functions as an effector structure (Rubenstein 1967) and mobilizes energy (defined as the increased capacity to do physical or mental work that can be measured in terms of speed, force, and intensity of all activities). This may be associated with a temporary decrease in the need for sleep, food, or other vegetative functions which are not immediately necessary, and with increased goal-directed activity, such as enterprise and gregariousness. The appetitive pleasure system also leads to a lowering of the threshold of stimulation for the pleasure centers and an increase in the threshold of the pain centers. The decreased pleasure threshold is experienced, simultaneously, at a psychological level as

Psyche (psychoanalytic track)
4. The evocation of specific, positively toned self- and object representations and associated pleasurable or euphoric affects and enhanced self-esteem.

As well, the lowered pleasure threshold triggers associatively linked cognitive affective units, which become consciously or preconsciously available. These can in turn trigger other pleasant memories, giving momentum to the change. As well, in the presence of a lowered pleasure threshold, perceptions that would normally have a more neutral or negative affective valence are now associated with pleasure. This might be termed *globalization* of the pleasure experience. What might be seen as a threat, is seen as a challenge. One becomes hopeful. Finally, the subjective experience of having increased energy at one's disposal bolsters a secondary fantasy of increased competence and a bouyant sense of mastery.

5. If the goal is obtained, consummatory release mechanisms turn on
Soma (neuroscience track)
6. The consummatory system, which leads to decreased arousal and changes in the pleasure threshold which trigger
Psyche (psychoanalytic track)
7. Consummatory cognitive affective units and fantasies of being at one with a good object.

If the goal is not obtained after step 4, a sequence of acute endogenous stimulant withdrawal from the appetitive system occurs—leading to the vegetative components of the experience of disappointment and a transformation of the self and object world that has both vegetative (biological) and psychological components.

To summarize, this sequence describes a psychologically triggered, biologically mediated, psychological change.

Cognitive Changes: The Global Transformation of the Self and Object World

Greenson and Jacobson emphasize that judgment is altered in enthusiasm, infatuation, and love: the world is "rich," one has an abundance of good fortune, and one's attitude is optimistic. Jacobson describes this as brought about by "a generalized transference of certain hypercathected pleasurable attributes" from the object of enthusiasm or infatuation to all objects (Jacobson 1971). In the model proposed here, one can add that such transferences occur in a particular context. The lowered pleasure threshold triggers memories of past pleasant experiences, and associated cognitive affective units come into preconscious awareness during enthusiastic states. Attributes of these units color here-and-now perceptions of self and other, and this accounts for the transference of past to present. However, as experience with cocaine and stimulants shows, in the context of a lowered pleasure threshold, all current perception is positively toned. These effects of globalization should not be called transference unless specific attributes of a specific object are imputed to another object.

Anticipatory Thought and Thought as Deferred Action

In Klein's model, anticipation leads to the imaging of the desired object. Imaging for Klein is a necessary part of obtaining objects, a *pre-taste* which precedes taste and further stimulates the appetitive pleasure system. It implies

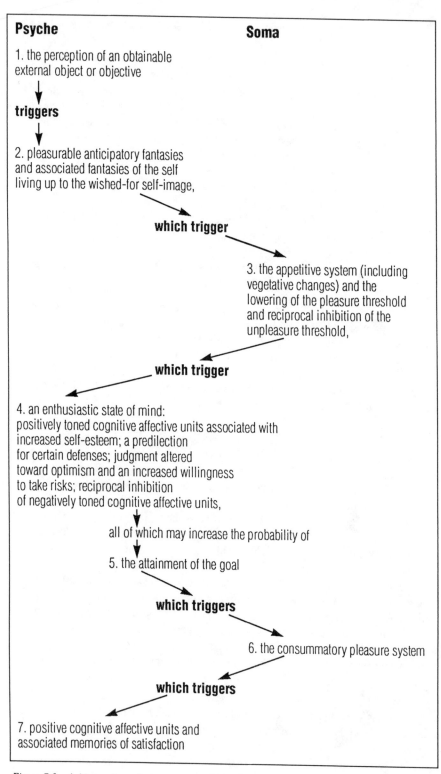

Psyche　　　　　　　　　　**Soma**

1. the perception of an obtainable
external object or objective

triggers

2. pleasurable anticipatory fantasies
and associated fantasies of the self
living up to the wished-for self-image,

which trigger

3. the appetitive system (including
vegetative changes) and the
lowering of the pleasure threshold
and reciprocal inhibition of the
unpleasure threshold,

which trigger

4. an enthusiastic state of mind:
positively toned cognitive affective units associated with
increased self-esteem; a predilection
for certain defenses; judgment altered
toward optimism and an increased willingness
to take risks; reciprocal inhibition
of negatively toned cognitive affective units,

all of which may increase the probability of

5. the attainment of the goal

which triggers

6. the consummatory pleasure system

which triggers

7. positive cognitive affective units and
associated memories of satisfaction

Figure 7.3 A biopsychoanalytic sequence for enthusiasm followed by the achievement
of a nonconflicted goal

an ongoing conviction that the goal is attainable. Anticipatory thought is not deferred action but preliminary action. This different emphasis derives in part from the fact that psychoanalytic theory has grown out of a tension reduction model. The absence of the object for Freud leads to an endogenous build-up of drive, affect, and associated thoughts or wishes. For Freud ([1911] 1958) hallucinatory imaging occurs in the absence of the object or when one is unable to act to bring about drive discharge.

There are other roots for the notion of thought as deferred action, notably Freud's recapitulationist understanding of evolution. For Freud, ontogeny recapitulates phylogeny, and therefore "lower" instinctual-affective processes are assumed to precede the "higher" cognitive ones in the life history not only of the species but of the individual. Frustration of the instinctual drives gives rise to thought. There are major problems with uncritical recapitulationism (Gould 1977) that cannot be taken up here except to say that higher functions, once evolved, may become supraordinate and relatively autonomous, as Hartmann's (1958) work emphasized. In Klein's model, the anticipatory imaging seen in appetitive behavior is not merely a result of "deferred" consummatory gratification; rather, anticipatory imaging has—presumably over the course of evolution—become a necessary part of the sequence of satisfaction. In an individual act, the appetitive component precedes the consummatory one, even though the appetitive component was likely a later development phylogenetically. Later, higher functions can dominate earlier, more instinctual ones (Lorenz 1957). Appetitive behaviors may come to take their place alongside the consummatory behaviors that follow.[15]

Reciprocal Inhibition, Altered Pleasure Threshold, and Defense

Defenses ward off painful affects and associated thoughts or negatively tinged cognitive affective units (Kernberg 1980). From a clinical point of view, this aspect of defenses is of primary importance. Defenses also lead to pleasure. One can ward off exhibitionistic tendencies with a shyness that brings attention to oneself, or fend off a lover in an enticing way. The notion that pleasure-gain, and not just anxiety-avoidance, plays an important part in defensive activity brings to mind the work of Schafer (1968). He emphasizes the dynamic constructive elements in defensive activity and sees each defense mechanism as making "negative and positive assertions" that provide libidinal and aggressive gratification, as well as a warding off of anxiety. In a similar vein, Sackeim (1983), in his empirical study of defenses, purports to show that defenses can sometimes be used primarily for positive self-representation enhancement. Sackeim argues that the wish-fulfilling distortion of one's self-image can occur

---

15. Those who prefer a quick consummation are often tempted to forego the niceties of appetitive courtship the moment they sense that the object of their affection is willing. Such suitors may find themselves surprised to learn that hasty advances are considered of low evolutionary order, or "brutish," by their more refined partners who temporarily dally with, rather than try to overcome, the appetitive pleasures.

purely to gain pleasure, not merely to ward off anxiety. In effect, he proposes that defenses can function as "offenses" that evoke pleasurable states de novo.

Applying this work to the model proposed here, one could say that some defenses turn on specific pleasure systems, lower the pleasure threshold, and lead to the reciprocal inhibition of pain centers and the raising of the pain threshold. Reciprocal inhibition of pain, and probably anxiety centers, gives a biological account for the general observation Freud made: pleasurable states create conditions in which it is "comparatively difficult" to experience unpleasure. This reciprocal inhibition reinforces the intended goal of the defense to ward off a negative affect state. Insofar as such changes involve underlying neurochemistries, changes in important defenses may lead to such phenomena as withdrawal. Working through such defenses would entail not only cognitive unlearning (Schwartz 1987; Sandler, Dare, and Holder 1973) but also undergoing miniwithdrawal states, which may be manifest clinically when pleasure-inducing defenses are modified.

Manic Defenses

Klein's theory of the appetitive system describes a feed-forward system. An external stimulus turns on the system. The increased energy available for work stimulates the psychological belief that one is more competent or able to live up to one's wished-for self-image ("Look how energetic I am—I'll get what I want!"), which further stimulates the appetitive pleasure system. The feed-forward loop involves the interaction of psychological and biological systems. The trigger is a meaning attached to an event that can often help the person deny some unpleasant aspect of themselves or the world (Greenson [1962] 1977). Insofar as this trigger turns on the appetitive system and lowers the pleasure threshold that gives an optimistic glow to everything, this denial is reinforced by a feed-forward system.

Manic and hypomanic defenses, as well as defensive feelings of control, triumph, and contempt (Segal 1975; Kernberg 1975, 32), make use of denial to ward off particular thoughts, feelings, or whole aspects of the self experience, including depressive states (MacKinnon and Michels 1971). Manic, enthusiastic, or hypomanic states impair judgment by mutually reinforcing psychological and biological mechanisms: (1) defenses lead to cognitive rigidity and distortion; (2) pleasure threshold alterations predispose to the inflexible use of particular cognitive affective units through globalization; and (3) appetitive feed-forward loops function as amplifiers of images of hopeful expectancy and lead to preoccupation with a particular goal, creating a mental climate that favors hypomanic defenses and that reciprocally inhibits negative cognitive affective states. In other words, wishful thinking has both biological and psychological reinforcers.

In groups with shared ego ideals, cognitive distortions become more pronounced. This is in part because reality testing is surrendered to the leader, and in part because the leader can manipulate these appetitive feed-forward mechanisms of the group members in concert. Enthusiasm is contagious. Once the appetitive system is turned on, it must run its course, often in destructive ways. A hypomanic crowd or mob is a group all in the same state with the same feed-forward cognitive set, which amplifies the distortion. This is manipulated by those who craft group events, military and political rallies, and rhetoric. The timing of appetitive arousal is very important. Astute political handlers for presidential candidates always attempt to lower expectations just before debates to avoid overstimulating the appetitive system prematurely.

Mania, Mood, and Medication

Klein postulates that manic states are caused by a dysregulation of an appetitive system that cannot be turned off once it is turned on, leading to a chronic lowering of the pleasure threshold and to the impairment in judgment described above. In the context of a lowered pleasure threshold, certain types of positively toned cognitively affective units and associated defenses are more likely to be used. The opposite would be the case for depression. Dysregulations would hamper the flow into consciousness of the full range of cognitive affective units.

According to Klein's model, medications repair dysregulations in pathological pleasure systems. In our model, this kind of repair can restore the normal flow into consciousness of existing cognitive affective units. But medications, while enlarging the repertoire available at a given time do not *directly* change the content of these units, or for that matter, the mental rules by which individual units are related. The latter is the province of dynamic psychotherapy or psychoanalysis. It should be noted as well that a chronic mood disorder can give rise to a laying down of specific cognitive affective units over a long period of time.

Wurmser (1974) has described how a drug of abuse can function as "an artificial or surrogate defense against overwhelming affects" (829). I believe the biopsychoanalytic model proposed herein, which takes into account pleasure threshold changes, globalization, and reciprocal inhibition of negative cognitive affective units, gives a biopsychoanalytic elaboration of the complexity of Wurmser's "affect defense."

On the Independence of Hedonic Valence

Although pleasure thresholds and systems function as biological givens, the link by association of a particular hedonic valence to a particular cognitive affective unit is influenced by developmental experience—something not emphasized in Klein's model. Henry Krystal, in a series of papers (1978, 1981, 1982, 1987) argues that the hedonic (pleasure-unpleasure) component of affects is something that is often attached to specific affects in the course of personal development. Krystal points out that "the assumption is commonly made that some emotions are intrinsically and invariably pleasurable and others equally constantly unpleasant and painful." He points out the existence of numerous exceptions to this observation. Such exceptions are often the province of psychoanalysis. The moral masochists, those wrecked by success, people who love

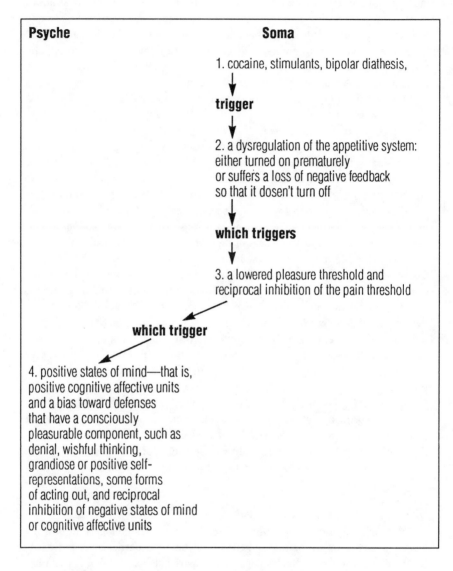

Figure 7.4 Pleasure threshold changes influence defensive activity

to hate, those thrill seekers who *libidinize anxiety*, are relevant examples. A tension reduction model cannot well account for how something like anxiety could be pleasurable.

If the hedonic quality of an affect is "separately derived, and only associatively linked with a particular affect" (Krystal 1987, 105), hatreds, despair, defeat, anxiety, and self-pity can, in certain cases, become major sources of pleasure for some by way of association during development. Krystal emphasizes that ideas, thoughts, or fantasies become pleasurable "only by mobilizing a reaction at an erotogenic zone, or a direct stimulation of hedonic centers of the brain, or by producing a pleasurable affect" (98). He adds that in day-to-day life "we are constantly involved in modifying and influencing our affective states" including "the modification of hedonic quality." This modulation is central to art. Certain states of sadness can be beautifully articulated and lead to a sublime artistic experience. Much of what is often described as drive fusion and defusion involves the coupling of various affective and hedonic valences. In fact, many neutralized or sublimated activities can be seen as appetitive activities that over time become associated with a positive hedonic tone, rather than as "disguised" drive discharge or deferred consummation. An example would be the shared pleasure of two parents who are investing financially in their child's future. Investment is not in itself obviously a form of drive discharge or a consummatory act. Yet it can be an exciting anticipatory pleasure, which is associatively linked to the instinctual wishes having to do with generativity.

Conclusion

The description of independent pleasure and unpleasure systems offers both a new way of thinking about and poses constraints upon the theories of pleasure regulation to which psychoanalysis has inevitable recourse.

1. *The appetitive system fills, in part, a gap in psychoanalytic theory that has been poorly filled by the psychic energy model.*

   There are at least two broad kinds of pleasure activities, appetitive and consummatory pleasures. In the language of ethologists, early Freudian theory described pleasure largely in terms of its consummatory aspects. The model discussed here sees exciting appetitive pleasures and behavior as gradually evolving to become more autonomous and independent from associated consummatory acts, to the point that they have their own neurochemistries and principles. The appetitive system is an effector system that can put the individual in high gear and lead to increased energy, as well as to threshold changes that predispose toward increased self-esteem.

2. *The pleasure threshold, through the process of globalization, acts as a gate that mediates the entry into consciousness or preconsciousness of various states of mind or cognitive affective units based upon hedonic valence.* This is not to say that hedonic valence is the only criterion of what enters consciousness.

Changes in the pleasure threshold lead to global changes in how perceptions are experienced. Some of what has been described as the transference of attributes of the good object, is in fact globalization. The term transference is important enough and need not be stretched more than it already has been.

3. *Reciprocal inhibition provides a model for explaining how certain states of mind defensively ward off other states.*

The notion of the reciprocal inhibition of pleasure and unpleasure centers is helpful in explaining our frequent experience of a subjective continuum of pleasure and unpleasure, without having any of the inadequacies of the psychic energy rheostat model. Reciprocal inhibition also gives us a model for understanding how certain defenses, such as denial and wishful thinking, might be biologically reinforced. In this new model, certain ideas lower pleasure thresholds and simultaneously raise pain thresholds, making it harder for negative cognitive affective units or states to flow into consciousness. This state change can be used defensively if necessary. A hypomanic flight into health is a typical example of this. As well, negative cognitive affective states can ward off exciting but dangerous cognitive affective states. Krystal's work, however, can be taken as a caveat that there are limits to reciprocal inhibition and that because pleasure and unpleasure systems are discrete systems, they can, under special circumstances, function together by way of association over the course of an individual's development. Krystal describes many situations of interest to the psychoanalyst where pleasure and pain co-exist.

4. *The pleasure threshold both influences and is influenced by mental activity.*

Certain ideas can raise or lower the threshold, which in turn influences which cognitive affective units from the existing repertoire will enter consciousness and which defensive strategies will be employed. Psychopharmacologists modify pathological thresholds that become fixed in certain positions. Psychoanalysts elucidate the content of cognitive affective units and the relation between them. Psychopharmacologists unglue the sticky pages of the dictionary while psychoanalysts work on altering and refining definitions and the relations between the definitions.

5. *The pleasure threshold both influences and is influenced by biological activity.*

Euphorogenic drugs, antidepressants, and mania all influence the pleasure threshold, and in so doing bias toward the triggering of specific cognitive affective units. The converse applies to depression that triggers specific, painfully tinged cognitive affective units and predisposes toward other kinds of defensive activity.

6. *Neurotransmitter systems influence our sensibilities and our subjective meaning states and vice versa.*

Freud's speculation in the opening quote of this paper that there are certain endogenous substances that govern our sensibilities and pleasure experience and which seem similar to those exogenous substances that induce mania probably very much derived from his cocaine experience. His notion is picked up in Klein's work, and while at this time, ALS remains elusive, there is gathering evidence that it, or something like it, plays a major role in our experience of exciting pleasure.

REFERENCES

Abraham, K. [1911] 1954. Notes on the psycho-analytical investigation and treatment of manic-depressive insanity and allied conditions. In *Selected Papers of Karl Abraham*. New York: Basic Books, 137–56.

Amacher, P. 1965. *Freud's Neurological Education and Its Influence on Psychoanalytic Theory. Psychological Issues*, monograph 16. New York: International Universities Press.

Applegarth, A., reporter. 1977. Psychic energy reconsidered. *Journal of the American Psychoanalytic Association* 24:647–57.

Basch, M. F. 1976. The concept of affect: A re-examination. *Journal of the American Psychoanalytic Association* 24:759–77.

Bernfeld, S. 1944. Freud's earliest theories and the school of Helmholtz. *Psychoanalytic Quarterly* 13:341–62.

———. 1949. Freud's scientific beginnings. *American Imago* 6:163–96.

———. 1953. Freud's studies on cocaine, 1884–87. *Journal of the American Psychoanalytic Association* 1:581–613.

Bibring, E. 1953. The mechanism of depression. In *Affective Disorders*, ed. P. Greenacre. New York: International Universities Press.

Brentano, F. 1973. *Philosophy from an Empirical Standpoint*. Trans. A. C. Rancurello, D. B. Terrel, and L. L. McCallister. New York: Humanities Press.

Cloninger, C. R. 1986. A unified biosocial theory of personality and its role in the development of anxiety states. *Psychiatric Developments* 3:167–226.

———. 1987. A systematic method for clinical description and classification of personality variants. *Archives of General Psychiatry* 44:573–88.

Davidson, J. R. T.; Giller, E. L.; Zisook, S.; and Overall, J. E. 1988. An efficacy study of isocarboxazid and placebo in depression, and its relationship to depressive nosology. *Archives of General Psychiatry* 45:120–27.

Easser, B. R., and Lesser, S. R. 1965. Hysterical personality: A re-evaluation. *Psychoanalytic Quarterly* 34:390–405.

Edelheit, H. 1976. Complementarity as a rule in psychological research: Jackson, Freud and the mind/body problem. *International Journal of Psycho-Analysis* 57:23–29.

Freud, S. [1884] 1974. Über Coca. In *Cocaine Papers by Sigmund Freud*, ed. R. Byck. New York: Meridian, New American Library.

———. [1911] 1958. Formulations on the two principles of mental functioning. *Standard edition*, 12:215–26.

———. [1914] 1957. On narcissism. *Standard edition*, 14:69–102.

———. [1917] 1957. Mourning and melancholia. *Standard edition*, 14:239–58.

———. [1921] 1955. Group psychology and the analysis of the ego. *Standard edition*, 18:67–143.

———. [1923] 1961. The ego and the id. *Standard edition*, 14:3–66.

———. [1924] 1961. The economic problem of masochism. *Standard edition*, 19:157–70.

———. [1927] 1961. Humour. *Standard edition*, 21:165.

———. [1930] Civilization and its discontents. *Standard edition*, 21:59–145.

Gold, M., and Rea, W. 1983. The role of endorphins in opiate addiction, opiate withdrawal, and recovery. In *Endorphins, The Psychiatric Clinics of North America*, vol. 6, no. 3, ed. S. Risch and D. Pickar. Philadelphia: W. B. Saunders.

Gould, S. J. 1977. *Ontogeny and Phylogeny*. Cambridge: Belknap Press of Harvard University Press.

Greenberg, J., and Mitchell, S. 1983. *Object Relations in Psychoanalytic Theory*. Cambridge: Harvard University Press.

Greenson, R. [1962] 1977. On enthusiasm. In *The World of Emotions*, ed. C. Socarides. New York: International Universities Press.

Greenspan, S. I. 1981. *Psychopathology and Adaption in Infancy and Early Childhood*. New York: International Universities Press.

Hartmann, H. 1958. *Ego Psychology and the Problem of Adaptation*. New York: International Universities Press.

Heath, R. 1974. Application of Sandor Rado's adaptational psychodynamic formulations to brain physiology. *Journal of the American Academy of Psychoanalysis* 2(1): 19–25.

Hinde, R. A. 1966. *Animal Behaviour: A Synthesis of Ethology and Comparative Psychology*. New York: McGraw-Hill.

Holt, R. 1965. A review of some of Freud's biological assumptions and their influence on his theories. In *Psychoanalysis and Current Biological Thought*, ed. N. S. Greenfield and W. C. Lewis. Madison: University of Wisconsin Press.

———. 1981. The death and transfiguration of metapsychology. *International Review of Psycho-Analysis* 8:129–43.

Horowitz, M. J. 1987. *States of Mind: Configurational Analysis of Individual Psychology*. New York: Plenum Medical Book Company.

Horowitz, M. J., and Zilberg, N. 1983. Regressive alterations of the self concept. *American Journal of Psychiatry* 140:3.

Hyman, S. E., and Arona, G. W. 1987. *Handbook of Psychiatric Drug Therapy*. Boston: Little, Brown.

Izard, C. E. 1978. On the ontogenesis of emotions and emotion-cognition relationships in infancy. In *The Development of Affect*, ed. M. Lewis and L. A. Rosenblum. New York: Plenum.

Jacobson, E. 1953a. The affects and their pleasure-unpleasure qualities in relation to the psychic discharge processes. In *Drives, Affects, Behavior*, vol. 1, ed. R. Loewenstein. New York: International Universities Press.

———. 1953b. Contribution to the metapsychology of cyclothymic depression. In *Affective Disorders*, ed. P. Greenacre. New York: International Universities Press.

———. 1957. On normal and pathological moods: Their nature and functions. *The Psychoanalytic Study of the Child* 12:73–113. New York: International Universities Press.

———. 1964. *The Self and the Object World*. New York: International Universities Press.

———. 1971. *Depression*. New York: International Universities Press.

———. 1975. The regulation of self-esteem. In *Depression and Human Existence*, ed. E. J. Anthony and T. Benedek. Boston: Little, Brown.

Kayser, A.; Robinson, D.; Nies, A.; and Howard, D. 1985. Response to phenelzine among depressed patients with features of hysteroid dysphoria. *American Journal of Psychiatry* 142:486–88.

Kernberg, O. 1975. *Borderline Conditions and Pathological Narcissism.* New York: Jason Aronson.

―――. 1976. *Object Relations Theory and Clinical Psychoanalysis.* New York: Jason Aronson.

―――. 1980. *Internal World and External Reality.* New York: Jason Aronson.

Khantzian, E. 1985. The self-medication hypothesis of addictive disorders: Focus on heroin and cocaine dependence. *American Journal of Psychiatry* 142: 1259–64.

King, R.; Mefford, I.; Wang, C.; Murchison, A.; Caligari, E.; and Berger, P. 1986. CSF dopamine levels correlate with extraversion in depressed patients. *Psychiatry Research* 19:305–10.

Klein, D. F. 1974. Endogenomorphic depression: A conceptual and terminological revision. *Archives of General Psychiatry* 31:447–54.

―――. 1987. Depression and anhedonia. In *Anhedonia and Affect Deficit States,* ed. D. Clark and J. Fawcett. New York: PMA Publishing, 1–14.

Klein, D. F., and Davis, J. M. 1969. *Diagnosis and Drug Treatment of Psychiatric Disorders.* Baltimore: Williams and Wilkins.

Klein, D. F.; Gittelman, R.; Quitkin, F.; and Rifkin, A. 1980. *Diagnosis and Drug Treatment of Psychiatric Disorders: Adults and Children,* 2d ed. Baltimore: Williams and Wilkins.

Klein, D., and Liebowitz, M. 1982. Hysteroid dysphoria. *American Journal of Psychiatry* 139(11): 1520–21.

Kohut, H. 1971. *The Analysis of the Self.* New York: International Universities Press.

Koob, G.; Vaccarino, F.; Amalric, M.; and Bloom, F. 1986. Neurochemical substrates for opiate reinforcement. In *Opiate Receptor Subtypes and Brain Function. NIDA Research Monograph 71,* ed. R. Brown, D. Clouet, and D. Friedman. Washington, D.C.: U.S. Department of Health and Human Services.

Koob, G.; Vaccarino, F.; Amalric, M.; and Swerdlow, N. 1987. Neural substrates for cocaine and opiate reinforcement. In *Cocaine: Clinical and Biobehavioural Aspects,* ed. S. Fisher, A. Raskin, and E. H. Uhlenhuth. Oxford: Oxford University Press.

Kornetsky, C. 1985. Brain-stimulation reward: A model for the neuronal bases for drug-induced euphoria. In *Neuroscience Methods in Drug Abuse Research, NIDA Research Monograph 62.* Washington, D.C.: Department of Health and Human Services.

Kornetsky, C., and Bain, G. 1987. Neuronal bases for hedonic effects of cocaine and opiates. In *Cocaine: Clinical and Biobehavioural Aspects,* ed. S. Fisher, A. Raskin, and E. H. Uhlenhuth. Oxford: Oxford University Press.

Krystal, H. 1978. Trauma and affect. *The Psychoanalytic Study of the Child* 33:81–116.

―――. 1981. The hedonic element in affectivity. *The Annual of Psychoanalysis* 9:93–115.

―――. 1982. The activating aspect of emotions. *Psychoanalysis and Contemporary Thought* 5:605–41.

―――. 1987. The hedonic element in affectivity. In *Anhedonia and Affect Deficit States,* ed. D. Clark and J. Fawcett. New York: PMA Publishing.

Lewin, B. 1950. *The Psychoanalysis of Elation.* New York: International Universities Press.

Lewis, M.; Sullivan, M. W.; and Michalson, L. 1984. The cognitive-emotional fugue. In *Emotions, Cognition and Behaviour,* ed. C. Izard, J. Kagan, and R. B. Zajonc. Cambridge: Cambridge University Press.

Liebowitz, M. 1983. *The Chemistry of Love.* Boston: Little, Brown.

Liebowitz, M., and Klein, D. 1981. Interrelationship of hysteroid dysphoria and borderline personality disorder. In *Borderline Disorders, Psychiatric Clinics of North America*, vol. 4, ed. M. Stone. Philadelphia: W. B. Saunders.

Liebowitz, M.; Quitkin, F.; Stewart, J.; McGrath, P.; Harrison, W.; Markowitz, J.; Rabkin, J.; Tricamo, E.; and Klein, D. 1983. Phenylzine v. imipramine in atypical depression: A preliminary report. *Archives of General Psychiatry* 41:669–77.

Liebowitz, M.; Quitkin, F.; Stewart, J.; McGrath, P.; Harrison, W.; Markowitz, J.; Rabkin, J.; Tricamo, E.; Goetz, D.; and Klein, D. 1988. Antidepressant specificity in atypical depression. *Archives of General Psychiatry* 45:129–37.

Lorenz, K. 1957. The nature of instinct. In *Instinctive Behavior*, ed. and trans. C. Schiller. New York: International Universities Press.

McGrath, W. 1986. *Freud's Discovery of Psychoanalysis*. Ithaca, N.Y.: Cornell University Press.

MacKinnon, R. A., and Michels, R. 1971. *The Psychiatric Interview in Clinical Practice*. Philadelphia: W. B. Saunders.

Milrod, D. 1982. The wished-for self image. *The Psychoanalytic Study of the Child* 37:95–120.

Modell, A., reporter. 1963. The concept of psychic energy. Journal of the American Psychoanalytic Association 11:605–18.

Nunes, E., and Klein, D. 1987. Research in cocaine abuse: Future directions. In *Cocaine Abuse: New Directions in Treatment and Research*, ed. H. Spitz and J. Rosecan. New York: Brunner-Mazel.

Nunes, E., and Rosecan, J. 1987. Human neurobiology of cocaine. In *Cocaine Abuse: New Directions in Treatment and Research*, ed. H. Spitz and J. Rosecan. New York: Brunner-Mazel.

Ostow, M. 1962. *Drugs in Psychoanalysis and Psychotherapy*. New York: Basic Books.

———. 1965. Psychic energies in health and disease. In *Psychoanalysis and Current Biological Thought*, ed. N. Greenfield and W. Lewis. Madison: University of Wisconsin Press.

———. 1966. The complementary roles of psychoanalysis and drug therapy. In *Psychiatric Drugs*, ed. P. Solomon. New York: Grune and Stratton.

———. 1975. Psychological considerations in the chemotherapy of depression. In *Depression and Human Existence*, ed. E. J. Anthony and T. Benedek. Boston: Little, Brown.

Peele, S. 1985. *The Meaning of Addiction: Compulsive Experience and Its Interpretation*. Lexington: Lexington Books.

Peterfreund, E., and Schwartz, J. 1971. *Information, Systems, and Psychoanalysis: An Evolutionary Biological Approach to Psychoanalytic Theory. Psychological Issues, monograph 25 / 26*. New York: International Universities Press.

Plato 1945. *Plato's Examination of Pleasure (The Philebus)*. Trans. R. Hackforth. Indianapolis, Ill.: Bobbs-Merrill.

Pribram, K. H., and Gill, M. M. 1976. *Freud's "Project" Re-assessed: Preface to Contemporary Cognitive Theory and Neuropsychology*. New York: Basic Books.

Radó, S. 1926. The psychic effects of intoxicants: An attempt to evolve a psycho-analytical theory of morbid cravings. *International Journal of Psycho-Analysis* 7:396–413.

———. 1933. The psychoanalysis of pharmacothymia (drug addiction). *Psychoanalytic Quarterly* 2:1–23.

———. 1969. *Adaptational Psychodynamics: Motivation and Control*, ed. J. Jameson and H. Klein. New York: Science House.

Reiman, E.; Raichle, M.; Robins, E.; Butler, F.; Herscovitch, P.; Fox, P.; and Perlmutter,

J. 1986. The application of positron emission tomography to the study of panic disorder. *American Journal of Psychiatry* 143(4): 469–77.

Reiser, M. 1984. *Mind, Brain, Body: Toward a Convergence of Psychoanalysis and Neurobiology*. New York: Basic Books.

Ricoeur, P. 1970. *Freud and Philosophy: An Essay on Interpretation*, trans. D. Savage. New Haven: Yale University Press.

Rubenstein, B. 1967. Explanation and mere description: A metascientific examination of certain aspects of the psychoanalytic theory of motivation. In *Motives and Thought: Psychoanalytic Essays in Honor of David Rapaport. Psychological Issues, monograph 18 / 19*, ed. R. Holt. New York: International Universities Press.

Sackeim, H. 1983. Self-deception, self-esteem, and depression: The adaptive value of lying to oneself. In *Empirical Studies of Psychoanalytical Theories*, vol. 1, ed. J. Maisling. Hillsdale: Analytic Press.

Sandler, J.; Dare, C.; and Holder, A. 1973. *The Patient and the Analyst*. New York: International Universities Press.

Schafer, R. 1968. The mechanisms of defense. *International Journal of Psycho-Analysis* 49:49–62.

———. 1976. *A New Language for Psychoanalysis*. New Haven: Yale University Press.

———. 1983. *The Analytic Attitude*. New York: Basic Books.

Schwartz, A. 1987. Drives, affects, behaviour—and learning: Approaches to a psychobiology of emotion and to an integration of psychoanalytic and neurobiologic thought. *Journal of the American Psychoanalytic Association* 35:467–506.

Segal, H. 1975. *Introduction to the Work of Melanie Klein*. London: Hogarth Press and the Institute of Psycho-Analysis.

Siever, L., and Davis, K. 1985. Overview: Toward a dysregulation hypothesis of depression. *American Journal of Psychiatry* 142:1017–31.

Smith, J., and Ballenger, J. 1981. Psychology and neurobiology. *Psychoanalysis and Contemporary Thought* 4:407–21.

Spiegelberg, H. 1972. *Phenomenology in Psychology and Psychiatry*. Evanston, Ill.: Northwestern University Press.

Spitzer, R. L., and Williams, J. B. W. 1982. Hysteroid dysphoria: An unsuccessful attempt to demonstrate its syndromal validity. *American Journal of Psychiatry* 139:1286–91.

Spitzer, R. L., and Williams, J. B. W. 1982. Drs. Spitzer and Williams reply. *American Journal of Psychiatry* 139(11): 1521.

Sulloway, F. 1979. *Freud, Biologist of the Mind*. New York: Basic Books.

Taberner, P. V. 1985. *Aphrodisiacs: The Science and the Myth*. Philadelphia: University of Pennsylvania Press.

Von Scheidt, J. 1973. Sigmund Freud und das Kokain. *Psyche* 5:384–430.

Warme, G. 1982. The methodology of psychoanalytic theorizing: A natural science or personal agency model? *International Review of Psycho-Analysis* 9:343–54.

Wender, P. H., and Klein, D. F. 1981. *Mind, Mood and Medicine: A Guide to the New Biopsychiatry*. New York: Farrar, Straus, Giroux.

Wurmser, L. 1974. Psychoanalytic considerations of the etiology of compulsive drug use. *Journal of the American Psychoanalytic Association* 4:820–43.

III

The Clinical Situation:
The Patient, the Analyst,
and the Importance
of Pleasure

8

Hatred as Pleasure

OTTO F. KERNBERG, M.D.

The psychoanalytic situation offers us a unique way to explore all kinds of affects, from primitive affect states (such as rage and messianic or sexual excitement) to complex, cognitively differentiated, toned-down feelings; it also offers us an opportunity to study moods—those transitory but diffuse, temporarily fixed emotional states. As Brierley (1937) and Jacobson (1953) have pointed out, affects are complex structures, psychophysiological in nature. They include a basic subjective experience of a rewarding, painful, or frightening quality. The subjective experiences of pleasure and pain are usually differentiated from each other but may, under certain conditions, be combined in complex ways.

In addition to these qualitative differences among affects there are quantitative differences: the intensity of subjective experience varies, as is usually observable in physiological "discharge" patterns and psychomotor behavioral manifestations. These latter also serve a communicative function. In fact, the communicative functions of affects are usually as central to the transference as the patient's subjective experience of affects in conveying to the analyst the patient's total experience, and in permitting the analyst to empathize with and internally respond emotionally to that experience. Affects also have an ideational content, an observation that may seem obvious but has importance in relation to the psychoanalytic exploration of, especially, primitive affects, which may at first impression appear devoid of cognitive content. The psychoanalytic exploration of intense affect storms in regressed patients regularly demonstrates that there is no such thing as a "pure" affect without cognitive content.

Not only do the affects we observe in the psychoanalytic situation always have cognitive content, but—and this is, I think, a crucial finding—they always have an object relations aspect as well; that is, they express a relation between a total or partial aspect of the patient's self and a total or partial aspect of one or another of his object representations. Moreover, the immediate communicative function of the affect in the psychoanalytic situation either directly reflects or complements a reactivated internal object relation implied in the subjective quality and the ideational content of the affect.

In the transference, then, an affect state actualizes a significant past object relation of the patient. Nor have I ever observed the actualization of an object relation in the transference that did not contain a certain affect state as well.

In earlier work I proposed that, from a clinical point of view, the manifestations of impulse/defense configurations in the psychoanalytic situation may be conceptualized as the activation of certain object relations in conflict, the one defensive, the other repressed, dissociated, or projected, reflecting the impulse or drive-derivative side of the conflict (Kernberg 1984, chap. 13). The masochistic suffering of a hysterical patient who experiences the analyst as frustrating and punitive may serve as a defense against the patient's underlying sexual excitement, fantasies, and implied positive oedipal strivings. The mixture of sadness, rage, and self-pity reflects a complex affect state with defensive functions directed against repressed sexual excitement. This example illustrates the function of affects on both sides of the impulse/defense configuration. In fact whenever, clinically speaking, we point to the defensive use of one drive against another, we are actually referring to the defensive function of one affect against another.

Frequently, however, the defensive process disrupts the affect state itself, thus obscuring the predominant object relation in the transference and interfering with a patient's full awareness of his own subjective experience as well as with the analyst's capacity for empathic understanding. Consider, for example, an obsessive patient's ruminating sexual thoughts while their affective, sexually excited qualities remain in repression; or a hysterical patient's intense and dramatic affect storm that obscures the cognitive content of the experience or permits the continued repression of such cognitive aspects of the affect; or a narcissistic patient's speaking in an apparently affective way while his or her behavior bespeaks a total absence or unavailability of any emotional communication. This dissociation of various components of affects in the service of defense may give the impression that the subjective experience of affects is separate from their cognitive, behavioral, communicative aspects, particularly in the initial stages of treatment or when resistance is high.

Under the impact of this defensive dissociation, the patient seems to illustrate the traditional psychological view that affect, perception, cognition, and action are separate functions. When defensive operations are worked through, however, and as the deeper layers of the patient's intrapsychic experience gradually emerge, the psychoanalyst also encounters, with growing clarity, the integration of these various components of affects. The more archaic or primitive the nature of the unconscious conflict that develops in the transference, the more affects appear as full-blown, complex processes centered upon a subjective experience, but with a full complement of cognitive, physiological, behavioral, and communicative aspects, and expressing a specific relation between the patient's self and the corresponding object representation in the transference.

These observations represent specific psychoanalytic contributions to contemporary neuropsychological research on affects that has evolved in the same direction—namely, to contradict the traditional belief that affects, cognition, communicative behavior, and object relations develop separately (Emde et al. 1978; Hoffman 1978; Izard 1978; Plutchik 1980; Plutchik and Kellerman 1980; Stern 1985; Emde 1987). Affects thus can be seen as complex psychic structures, indissolubly linked to the individual's cognitive appraisals of his immediate situation, which contain a positive or negative valence with regard to the relation of the subject to the object of the particular experience. Affects therefore have a motivational aspect. Arnold's (1970a, 1970b) definition of emotions—that they are a felt action tendency based on appraisal—is relevant here. Her concept of emotion corresponds to that of affect used in this chapter. (I reserve the term *emotion* for the mature side of the affective spectrum—that is, for affects with highly differentiated cognitive contents and relatively mild or moderate psychomotor and neurovegetative components; primitive affects have opposite characteristics.) Arnold described two components of emotion: one static, the appraisal; and one dynamic, the impulse toward what is appraised as good or the impulse away from what is appraised as bad. If Arnold's idea reflects, as I believe it does, a general trend of contemporary neuropsychological research on affects, this trend is remarkably concordant with the clinical findings on affects in the psychoanalytic situation spelled out by Brierley (1937) and Jacobson (1953).

When intense affect states are activated, a gratifying or frustrating corresponding past object relation is recalled, together with the effort to either reactivate the object relation if it was gratifying or escape from it if it was painful.

This process, in fact, defines the origin of fantasy—namely, the juxtaposition of an evoked remembered state with a future desired state in the context of a current perception that motivates the desire for change, a juxtaposition that reflects the simultaneity of past, present, and future, which characterizes id functions and predates the awareness and acceptance of objective space-time constraints that characterize the differentiated ego (Jacques 1982). From such a primordial integration of primitive affective memory linking "all good" or "all bad" peak affect states stems the development of more specific wishful fantasies linking self and object that characterizes unconscious fantasy in general.

The Effects of Hatred in the Psychoanalytic Situation

Max Gitelson has been quoted as once having said that many people believe in psychoanalysis, except for sex, aggression, and transference. It is, of course, well known that hatred, a derivative of rage, may give rise to highly pleasurable aggressive behaviors: sadistic enjoyment in causing pain, humiliation, and suffering; and the glee derived from devaluating others. Each of these behaviors might be rationalized as an expression of righteous indignation or even expressed in unmitigated, explosive violence that obscures its very origin—sadistic pleasure—in the act of destroying the object of its hatred. But to acknowledge the depth of the roots of hatred in a biology of aggression that would parallel the acknowledgment of the biological sources of erotism and love runs counter to firmly established cultural biases that emerge, again and again, in psychoanalytic theorizing.

At the level of clinical theory, it has taken an entire generation of psychoanalysts dedicated to the treatment of severe character pathology and the borderline conditions, regressive types of perversions, and psychosis to clarify the role of regressive forms of aggression, of hatred in its many clinical manifestations, thus gradually mapping out a vast territory boldly circumscribed in Freud's dual drive theory. In the realm of empirical research on psychoanalysis and psychoanalytic psychotherapy, the focus is still almost exclusively on the constructive, as opposed to the destructive, aspect of the patient-therapist interaction. Infant research is carried out largely in periods of "alert inactivity" (Kaplan 1987), which means its subject is a basically contented infant. Most impressively, the work of some key contributors to the study of hatred in the psychoanalytic situation tends to be neglected in comparison with other aspects of their work. For example, Fairbairn's (1954) stress on the central importance of the internalization of bad objects and the predominance of severely destructive object relations in the transference at advanced stages of treatment is rarely mentioned; in contrast, emphasis is given to his object relations theory, which eliminates aggression as a basic drive. Winnicott's (1965) "holding function" of the analyst in the transference as a source of resolution of severe regressions is often quoted, but his stress on the analyst's capacity to remain alive as an object in spite of the patient's aggression is neglected, as is his analysis of normal hatred in the countertransference (1949). The same may be said regarding Sullivan's (1953) description of malevolent transformations in the patient's engagement in the treatment, and Jacobson's (1971, chap. 13) contribution to the relationship between paranoid features and betrayal.

Origins of Primitive Hatred

André Green, in a review of the psychoanalytic conceptions of affect, proposes to differentiate "affect with a semantic function as an element in the chain of signifiers (chaine signifiante), and affect overflowing the spreading as it breaks the links in the chain" (1977, 208). I believe he is saying that at a certain level of primitivization of affect, typically in borderline and psychotic patients, affective experience itself is so disruptive that ordinary ego functioning is subverted, the communicative process is destroyed, and the very differentiation between self and object, between love and hatred, is temporarily lost. This catastrophic condition brings about primitive defenses against affect that are more disruptive, more difficult to diagnose and manage than the ordinary "neurotic" defensive disorganization of affects as reflected in obsessive, hysterical, phobic, and depressive patients. In agreement with Green, I propose that secondary defensive disruptions of primitive aggressive affect may distort or fragment the complex psychological and psychophysiological structure of the affect, similar to but with very different clinical characteristics from the defensive disruption of affective structure at a higher-level functioning referred to before. In his book on affective theory, Green (1973) warns against the genetic fallacy of attributing the most intense and primitive affects to the earliest stage of life. He stresses the difference between actual past traumatic experiences and the retrospective investment of them with new meanings and affective experience. For example, the resurgence of oedipal fantasies and conflicts in adolescence might differ vastly from the original oedipal fantasies during the oedipal stage of development. He also warns against premature closure in the investigation of affects by the analyst's efforts to frame a patient's affective experience before its cognitive implications have been fully explored by the patient himself.

In what follows, I explore the clinical manifestations of pleasure in the experience and expression of primitive hatred, a complex affect derived from primitive rage, with particular emphasis on the secondary defenses against hatred in the transference.

In my experience, primitive hatred may be differentiated from rage in the transference by its relatively stable, enduring, and characterologically anchored qualities. Regardless of its origin and the concrete unconscious fantasies encompassed by such hatred, its most impressive characteristic is, as Bion (1970) has pointed out, the intolerance of reality on the part of the patient controlled by such hatred. Primitive hatred predominates in the psychopathology of severe personality disorders, both in patients who are analyzable—particularly, narcissistic personalities—and in those with indication for psychoanalytic psychotherapy—that is, the majority of patients with borderline personality organization and some psychotic patients.

A strange process occurs in the patient under the domination of primitive hatred: a common defense against the awareness of such hatred is the very destruction of the patient's capacity to be aware of it, so that the patient's mind can no longer "contain" the awareness of a dominant emotion. Thus, the defense is at the same time an expression of the impulse against which it is directed. In practice, intolerance of reality becomes hatred of psychic reality directed against the self and against the hated object.

Hatred against the self shows directly in self-destructive impulses, such as self-mutilating or suicidal behavior, or in severely masochistic perversions. Intolerance of psychic reality also brings about a self-directed attack on the patient's cognitive functions, so that the patient is no longer able to use ordinary means of reasoning, to listen to ordinary reasoning from the analyst; under the sway of intense hatred, the patient may present the combination of focused curiosity, arrogance, and pseudostupidity described by Bion (1957). In essence, the patient attempts to destroy the means of communication between himself and the therapist to erase the awareness of his own hatred. The intolerance of the object is reflected in the patient's intense fear and hatred of the analyst perceived as a persecutor. This leads to paranoid developments in the transference, which may go so far as to result in transference psychosis, with what amounts to a desperate display on the part of the patient of projective identification. By means of this defense, the patient attempts to locate his aggression in the analyst by provocative behaviors reinforcing the projection, omnipotent control, and intolerance for any interpretations from the analyst at that point.

The intolerance of the analyst as a good object, evidenced in periods when paranoid mechanisms are not in effect and the analyst is perceived as a potentially good object is reflected in the patient's inordinate greed, the voracity with which the analyst's attention, time, and interpretive comments are solicited, but with a concomitant, unconscious destruction of what is received: whatever the analyst contributes the patient experiences as inadequate and triggers further greed and voracity.

A major question is, why can the patient not tolerate the awareness of the intensity of his rage? Why does he have to deny the pervasive, constant, overwhelming quality of his hatred? Ultimately, this intolerance is the expression of the deepest fears of losing the object of love, the good mother endangered by the very destructiveness of the patient's hatred. But immediately, as the very consequence of the intolerance of his hatred, the patient is threatened by the fantasy of his own destruction as a consequence of pathological projective mechanisms that transform the frustrating and hated object (the "bad" mother) into a powerful, dangerous, overwhelming enemy who might well annihilate the patient. The fantasied threat of annihilation, of bodily and mental destruction, is the immediate source of attempts desperately to fight off both the influence of the object and the awareness of the self under the impact of hatred.

The analyst's own hatred in the countertransference, a product of the patient's projective identification and omnipotent control—or more concretely, the natural consequence of the patient's consistently provocative behavior, his active destruction of meaning and of everything he receives in the therapeutic relationship—may generate in the analyst a wish to cut through the madness that invades the hours, to free himself from the endless entanglement in trivial bones of contention that seem to drown all opportunities for the patient's authentic learning in the hours, and in simple terms, to escape from this destructive relationship.

The psychoanalyst has several well-traveled escape routes from this situation. The first one, of course, is not to treat patients with severe borderline character pathology, paranoid personalities, antisocial features, and the syndrome of malignant narcissism.

A second one is the temptation to enter into a tacit agreement with the patient in the sense that the patient's extreme destructiveness as well as his fear of destructiveness in others are understandable and justified in view of the patient's terrible experiences in his past. If the analyst can convey to the patient that he understands how the patient could not but become what he is under the impact of the savage aggression from significant others in the past (*au fond,* mother), then both may gradually come to terms on how to decrease the impact of that aggression on the present relationship, turn it back upon the past, and establish firmer dissociative boundaries between an idealized present relationship in the transference and a persecutory, reprojected one in the past. This approach may also facilitate the patient's eventual acknowledgment of the intense pleasure he experiences in his revengeful attack on the frustrating and aggressive object, now perceived not only safely in the past but also in other experiences in the present as well (particularly, of course, in the transference). Sadistic enjoyment may thus become more tolerable to the patient, and if it is also tolerable to his analyst, while splitting and projective mechanisms remain in place, a significant diminution in the pressure of unacknowledged aggression may ensue.

A third escape route is to treat the patient as a frustrated and vulnerable infant whose wishes need to be catered to within the limits of the possible, with a tactful, gradual explanation to the patient of what such ultimate limits are. The patient treated as a "special" human being—symbolically as "his offended majesty," the baby—may, in the hands of a patient and gifted therapist, transform the chaos and violence of the ordinary borderline patient into the superficial calm of the compensated narcissistic personality. Psychotherapy becomes a safe haven that protects the patient from the rigors of ordinary life and protects the therapist from the onslaught of the patient's unacknowledged hatred.

The question may be asked, to what extent is the patient's intolerance of reality of self and other and its concomitant destruction of the communicative process a defense against, rather than a direct expression of, primitive hatred? In my experience, what is typically being defended against under such conditions is the patient's direct experience of hatred as an affect, of the derivative affect states of gleeful, sadistic enjoyment of the destruction of the object, and the enjoyment of disgust, contempt, cruelty, and humiliation expressed toward the object. For if and when the patient can tolerate the conscious experience of sadistic pleasure in the transference, a first step in the containment of hatred has been achieved. At this point, the patient is characteristically less afraid of the destructive effects of his aggression; his need to project aggression diminishes, and there is therefore a decrease in his perception of the analyst as a bad object. The patient may now begin to be aware that the object of his love and of his hatred is one.

Claude Lanzmann, the producer and director of the film *Shoah,* described in an interview with the French psychoanalyst François Gantheret (1986) the sense of his film as the depiction of total and atemporal hatred, a type of "hallucinating intemporality or atemporality." In a statement that may be transferred directly to the task of the psychoanalyst in dealing with primitive hatred, Lanzmann says, "But this is not the real problem; the real problem is incarnation. Not to transmit bits of information, but to incarnate them." I would say that the analyst's task is to permit the patient to incarnate his hatred and to tolerate the awareness of this incarnation.

Hatred exists in a dialectic relation with love. Hatred implies an intense involvement with an object of past or potential love, an object that, at some time, was or is deeply needed. Hatred is, first of all, hatred of the frustrating object, but at the same time, it is also hatred of the loved and needed object from whom love was expected and from whom frustration is unavoidable. In its origins, hatred is the consequence of the incapacity to eliminate frustration through rage, and it goes beyond rage in a lasting need to eliminate the object.

But hatred also has a differentiating aspect; if love is associated with attempts at fusion or merger, hatred attempts to differentiate the self from the object. Insofar as hatred cannot be tolerated and is projected onto the periphery of or outside the self, hatred contributes to differentiating self from object and counteracts the urge to merge. Thus, hatred may contribute to differentiation, the experience and testing of personal strength, self-affirmation, and autonomy; hatred may evolve into serving the sublimatory functions of aggression as healthy self-affirmation.

Primitive hatred at a sustained, intense level, however, creates a vicious circle that not only perpetuates but pathologically increases hatred itself. By projective mechanisms, particularly projective identification, the rage with the frustrating object brings about distortion of the object, and the frustration is now interpreted as a willful attack. This sense of being attacked by a formerly needed and loved object is the most primitive experience of love betrayed, which brings about powerful resonances through the entire sequence of preoedipal and oedipal stages of development.

The experience of love betrayed further increases hatred with even further amplification of hatred through projective identification, and now the object is perceived as extremely cruel and sadistic. The internalization of this distorted object relation perpetuates the experience of an enraged, humiliated, debased self and a cruel, sadistic, contemptuous object, with corresponding derivative ego and superego identifications that bring about a general distortion of internalized object relations. The identification with the aggressive, triumphant object in this dyadic relation in turn triggers cruelty and contempt in the expression of hatred toward the object when the intolerable, debased concept of the self can be projected onto it, and in identifying with the object, it also triggers aggression toward the self.

Now the state described earlier has been reached: hatred is destroying external and internal object relations; the defensive process of destroying the perceiving self to eliminate both pain and dangerous hatred is a major feature in these patients' defensive organization. Projective identification may be replaced by generalized splitting mechanisms, leading to the fragmentation of affective experience and of cognitive processes as well, a development described by Bion (1959). Or less severe forms of splitting may preserve a divided world of idealized and persecutory objects, and of an idealized and a bad self, with alternating behavior patterns clinically reflected in chaotic object relations, in destructive and self-destructive acting out alternating with defensively idealized relations with objects.

What I have been describing might well go far in explaining the affective experience and behavior of the borderline patient. Under more favorable circumstances, a more normal type of resolution may be achieved that prevents the full development of the vicious circle just described.

Sadomasochism and Higher Levels of Aggressive Affects

When the patient is able to tolerate some degree of direct expression of hatred other than simple rage attacks, he may experience pleasure with the discharge of hatred and even acknowledge this pleasure. Although the analyst as "outside" observer of the patient's pleasure in inflicting pain may suspect the existence of a direct condensation of hatred and sexual excitement—that is, sadism as a condensation of aggression and sexuality—the underlying mechanisms are usually more complex.

The experience of hatred against the object that brings about frustration and rage first goes through a stage in which the experience of being the passive victim of the object's hatred become subtly infiltrated with pleasure. By mechanisms that are still largely unexplored, the biological predisposition to experience pleasure with physical pain is transformed into the psychological process by which an external persecutor becomes an internal one with moral overtones. Here we are in the realm of the psychology of the battered child, whose attachment to the battering parent is intensified, and in the realm of extreme masochism where physical suffering acquires a dimension of psychological submission, moral gratification, and physical pain in one.

Fairbairn (1954) has pointed to the primitive mechanism he called "the moral defense," by means of which internalized bad objects that are perceived as "unconditionally" bad are turned "conditionally" bad in the sense that their attack on the subject is justified by the subject's badness. Hence a primitive sense of justice and order is returned to the inner world, at the cost of an internal submission to rationalized but essentially irrational suffering: the relation with the needed though bad object is maintained by transferring the badness upon the self.

Punishment endured under such circumstances, particularly if it is condensed with sexual excitement, opens a road toward absorption of aggression within and against the self, toward masochism as a defense against hatred. Suffering now condenses aggression with an expression of love, and love triumphs in the relation with the mistreating object. In clinical practice, it is amazing to observe how patients who are aggressive, paranoid, and accusatory may respond with a quiet sense of reassurance to interactions in which the analyst, acting out his own hatred in the countertransference, in fact criticizes or attacks the patient. It is as if the analyst's anger is experienced as a sign of love and caring, a more effective demonstration of his or her commitment to the patient than thoughtful, impassive interpretive interventions.

A patient's overtly sadistic pleasure in attacking the object—in contrast to "righteous indignation"—implies his or her identification with the aggressor at a primitive level of psychic functioning. This identification condenses tolerance of hatred and the wish to destroy the object in punishment for the frustration endured from it with the underlying experience of masochistic pleasure now projected onto the attacked and mistreated object. Between the impulsive ruthlessness of the normal infant and the pleasurable sadism of the patient with a perversion lies the intermediary structure of the masochistic condensation of hatred and sensuality. At a more advanced level of development, behind the righteous indignation that permits the full flourishing of the sadist's aggression is the secret expiation of the unconscious guilt of a masochist.

Lanzmann (in Gantheret 1986) has described the unmitigated joyful hatred in the faces of Polish peasants who, jokingly, made warning signals with their hands to the Jews who were entering the Treblinka concentration camp in sealed trains, warning signals graphically indicating that their throats would be cut. To this day, the jocular quality of those warnings can be experienced in the film *Shoah* (Lanzmann 1985, 23–38). The intimate connection between the primitive forms of sadism and masochism is illustrated in the life of the Marquis de Sade (Barry 1987, chap. 6). De Sade's sexual orgies included whipping prostitutes as well as forcing them to whip him with equal savagery, and he was particularly eager to sniff their anus while they were breaking wind. His thoughtless, self-destructive provocation of the criminal system landed him in jail in spite of his political influence, and his gradual deterioration in jail was marked by the continuing provocation of those who potentially might mitigate his suffering while he was increasingly losing touch with reality.

I have described the containment effects of the condensation of hatred and sensuality. That condensation may evolve in two directions. One, a healthier direction, continues the transformation of gleeful hatred into righteous indignation in the form of an aggressive investment of moral aims and ethical convictions, a road leading eventually to courageous self-affirmation and also to courageous self-sacrifice at the service of one's ideals. In the sexual realm, this same road leads to the progressive erotization of physical suffering and psychological submission, the neurotic types of sexual masochism, and finally, to the usual sadistic and masochistic components of sexual fantasy and play. Here, in summary, aggression is absorbed by libido, hatred by love, and the pleasure with hatred becomes the ordinary pleasure in aggressive self-affirmation, in sexual conquest, and in surrendering emotionally and erotically to the loved object.

A regressive evolution proceeds in the opposite direction, namely, a condensation of love and hatred in which, in contrast to the recruitment of hatred by love, love is recruited by hatred, and perversity replaces perversion (Kernberg 1985). Clinically, we find here the most severe types of characterological sadism in the form of rationalized cruelty—that is, a condensation of self-idealization with a sadistic self-concept in which ruthless aggression is "morally" justified. Severe, potentially life-threatening forms of sexual sadism and masochism are the counterparts of this psychological structure. At an even more extreme level, nonidealized characterological sadism is expressed in the purposeless cruelty of the psychopath and the sexual forms of sadistic torture. The political torturer often combines this extreme form of guiltless sadism with sadistic sexual rituals.

At advanced levels of personality organization—in neurotic patients with a well-integrated tripartite psychic structure and a predominance of oedipal conflicts without undue infiltration by preoedipal aggression—more complex relations may evolve between hatred as an expression of revengefulness and sadism and the erotic aspects of merging in polymorphous perverse sexual encounters and of idealization of the love object. Sadomasochistic interactions with the partner may serve as a defense against the feared positive oedipal implication of a good sexual relationship, similar to the functions of masochistic character and masochistic perversion as an expression of and defense against oedipal guilt. Hatred and efforts to destroy an oedipal rival, the joyful triumph over such a rival, and the revengeful rejection of an unfaithful love object include differentiated levels of hatred. From the viewpoint of the vicissitudes of affects, all of these patients have a much higher tolerance for both loving and hating in the transference and present a dominance of repression of affects, in contrast to the predominance of dissociated or split-off affects in acting out, hypochondriacal somatization, and the defensive fragmentation or intolerance of affective experience of more primitive psychopathology.

In all cases, the secondary defenses against full experience of hatred need to be resolved before the patient is able to consciously experience hatred in the transference, including the sadistic pleasure that would permit the analyst to explore fully the nature of the object relation activated at such points.

REFERENCES

Arnold, M. B. 1970a. Brain function in emotion: A phenomenological analysis. In *Physiological Correlates of Emotion*, ed. P. Black. New York: Academic Press, 261–85.

———. 1970b. Perennial problems in the field of emotion. In *Feelings and Emotions*, ed. M. B. Arnold. New York: Academic Press, 169–85.

Barry, J. 1987. Pain and pleasure: The Marquis and the Marquise de Sade. In *French Lovers: From Heloise and Abelard to Beauvoir and Sartre*. New York: Arbor House, 145–75.

Bion, W. R. 1957. On arrogance. In *Second Thoughts: Selected Papers on Psycho-Analysis*. New York: Aronson, 1967, 86–92.

———. 1959. Attacks on linking. In *Second Thoughts: Selected Papers on Psycho-Analysis*. New York: Aronson, 1967, 93–109.

———. 1970. *Attention and Interpretation*. London: Heinemann.

Brierley, M. 1937. Affects in theory and practice. In *Trends in Psychoanalysis*. London: Hogarth Press, 1951, 43–56.

Emde, R. 1987. Development terminable and interminable. Plenary Presentation at the

Thirty-fifth International Psycho-Analytical Congress, Montreal, Canada, 27 July. Manuscript.

Emde, R.; Kligman, D.; Reich, J.; and Wade, T. 1978. Emotional expression in infancy: 1. Initial studies of social signaling and an emergent model. In *The Development of Affect*, ed. M. Lewis and L. Rosenblum. New York: Plenum, 125–48.

Fairbairn, W. D. 1954. *An Object-Relations Theory of the Personality*. New York: Basic Books.

Gantheret, F. 1986. Les non-lieux de la memoire: Entretien avec Claude Lanzmann. In *L'Amour de la haine*. Nouvelle Revue de Psychanalyse, 33. Paris: Editions Gallimard, 11–24.

Green, A. 1973. *Le discours vivant*. Paris: Universitaires de France.

————. 1977. Conceptions of affect. In *On Private Madness*. London: Hogarth Press, 1986, 174–213.

Hoffman, M. L. 1978. Toward a theory of empathic arousal and development. In *The Development of Affect*, ed. M. Lewis and L. Rosenblum. New York: Plenum, 227–56.

Izard, C. 1978. On the ontogenesis of emotions and emotion-cognition relationship in infancy. In *The Development of Affect*, ed. M. Lewis and L. Rosenblum. New York: Plenum, 389–413.

Jacobson, E. 1953. On the psychoanalytic theory of affects. In *Depression*. New York: International Universities Press, 1971, 3–47.

————. 1971. Acting out and the urge to betray in paranoid patients. In *Depression*. New York: International Universities Press, 302–18.

Jacques, E. 1982. *The Form of Time*. New York: Crane, Russak.

Kaplan, L. 1987. Discussion. *Contemporary Psychoanalysis* 23(1): 27–44.

Kernberg, O. F. 1984. Character analysis. In *Severe Personality Disorders: Psychotherapeutic Strategies*. New Haven: Yale University Press, 210–26.

————. 1985. The relation of borderline personality organization to the perversions. In *Psychiatrie et Psychanalyse: Jalons pour une fecondation reciproque*. Quebec: Gaetan Morin Editeur, 99–116.

Lanzmann, C. 1985. *Shoah: An Oral History of the Holocaust*. New York: Pantheon Books.

Plutchik, R. 1980. *Emotions: A Psychoevolutionary Synthesis*. New York: Harper and Row.

Plutchik, R., and Kellerman, H., eds. 1980. *Emotion*. Vol. 1, *Theory, Research, and Experience*. New York: Academic Press.

Stern, D. N. 1985. *The Interpersonal World of the Infant*. New York: Basic Books.

Sullivan, H. S. 1953. *The Interpersonal Theory of Psychiatry*. New York: Norton.

Winnicott, D. W. 1949. Hate in the countertransference. In *Collected Papers*. New York: Basic Books, 1958, 194–203.

————. 1965. *The Maturational Processes and the Facilitating Environment*. New York: International Universities Press.

9

On Pleasurable Affects

CHARLES BRENNER, M.D.

The present state of affect theory in psychoanalysis is such that any discussion of pleasurable affects is best introduced by some consideration of affects in general. The whole subject of affects has been relatively little discussed by psychoanalysts because of the way Freud viewed them. He looked upon affects as accompaniments of drive discharge, as part of one's conscious reaction to the gratification or nongratification of drive derivatives. He explicitly ruled out the possibility of affects being unconscious (Freud 1920, 1923), a position that took affects out of the realm of ideation. Thought and affect, for Freud, were contrasting concepts rather than similar or identical ones, as they had been thought to be throughout the centuries.

One of the first to question Freud's dictum that affects cannot be unconscious was Pulver (1971). Without directly addressing the question of the relation between thought and affect, he pointed out on the basis of compelling clinical observations that if one uses the same criteria for affects that one does for fantasies or wishes, one must conclude that affects can be and often are unconscious.

As the contents of this volume demonstrate, there are at least three ways of studying affects. One is through neurophysiology, another is developmentally, and a third is psychologically, or better, psychoanalytically. Because certain vegetative and behavioral patterns are so obviously and frequently associated with affects, many investigators have focused on them in their research into the topic. Indeed, one theory of affect goes so far as to assert that one's emotion is a consequence of one's behavioral reaction. One does not cry because one feels sad, for example; one feels sad because one is aware that one is crying.

The importance of neurophysiological and neuroendocrine mechanisms for the affective life of all mammals, including humans, is obvious. There is not, however, the clear and simple relation between the two that one may be tempted to assume. Patterns of behavior—for example, crying, laughing, or hypermotility—are no doubt constitutionally determined by the structure of the central nervous system. They are inborn just as are the neural mechanisms that control heart rate, sweating, respiratory rate, vomiting, and intestinal motility. One can confidently assert that the existence of such neural mechanisms is independent of experience, that it is a behavioral given. This is not to say that their relation to what we recognize as affects or emotions (I use the words synonymously) in mental life is either simple or constant. Tears of laughter are as common as tears of grief; cries and tears of rage or pain are equally familiar. Anxiety may be associated with syncope or with hyperalertness, with flight or with attack, with defecation or with vomiting. Indeed, what is striking about the relation between affects and neurophysiological mechanisms in humans is that it is so far from a simple, unambiguous one. Since a single behavioral or vegetative pattern that is accessible to observation is so uncertain an index of the affective state of a person one is observing, one is well advised not to conclude from neurophysiological and behavioral observations on species other than humans that the affects associated with the observable patterns are necessarily the same. The simpler the central nervous system, the farther removed is its mental life from that of humans. The tendency to anthropomorphize is ever present, and one must be constantly on the alert against it.

Somewhat similar considerations govern the conclusions to be drawn from observation of the behavior of neonates. Recent studies have demonstrated in fascinating detail the many unsuspected capacities of the central nervous system in neonates. Such new knowledge is welcome, but it carries with it the danger of neglecting the well-known facts concerning the great differences between the structure and functional capacity of the central nervous system at birth and after a few years of growth. The brain, the organ of the mind, is anatomically very different at birth from what it is months or years later, as any microscopist knows. Not only does it have fewer cells, it has much less myelin and many fewer synaptic connections as well. To take a simple well-known example, the area of the cerebral cortex just anterior to the central sulcus, the so-called motor gyrus, does not begin to control the motoric activity of the extremities until some weeks after birth, when the corticospinal tracts connecting the gyrus with the anterior horn cells of the spinal cord begin to be myelinated. Until the age of a year, a human infant's Babinski reflex is positive, as it is in an adult who has suffered a stroke that has functionally interrupted the corticospinal tracts. If the future motor cortex of a neonate has any function, its nature is unknown at present. The most reasonable assumption is that, at birth, it has none. Moreover, as the brain—in particular, the neocortex—develops anatomically and functionally, its functional capacity changes so markedly at certain points in the course of development that its development can best be described as discontinuous.

Prior to a certain stage of development, to choose once more a familiar example, an infant, as the word itself implies, is unable to comprehend or to use language. After that stage has been reached, she is no longer *infans,* or "speechless." The baby has become an organism whose brain has the capability of acquiring language, an organism whose brain is very different in its functional capability from what it was before. Since language is of such unique importance to all that is subsumed under the headings "the mind" and "mental life," it is especially incumbent on psychologists and psychoanalysts to pay attention to the difference between the brain of the child before and after the development of the capacity to acquire language. That the two stages of development have much in common is clear and explicitly recognized by all analysts. That they are in many ways very different is equally clear but too often overlooked or denied.

In what follows I shall discuss affects as psychological phenomena studied by the psychoanalytic method in subjects who have already acquired language. It is interesting to consider how such conclusions about affects can best be supplemented by and integrated with the conclusions reached by neurophysiologists, by ethologists, and by students of neonatal behavior, conclusions presented in other chapters in this volume. Interesting as it would be to make the attempt, however, I shall forbear. I note only that the considerations outlined above must be taken into account by whoever, reader or editor, is bold enough to try. Whatever their neurophysiology, whatever their behavioral and developmental features, whatever their correlates in other species, affects are unquestionably psychological phenomena; they are part of the mental life of every person. Indeed, our interest in them derives from their subjective importance to each of us in daily experience. Long before psychoanalysis was thought of, affects (emotions) have been objects of study, as witnessed by the elaborate attempts to distinguish one emotion from another by giving each a separate name.

Early efforts to classify affects and to study them systematically were based on introspection, since for a very long time that was the only method available for studying any psychological phenomenon of real subjective importance. But the unreliability of introspection as a method of studying a psychological phenomenon, affects included, has long been evident on an empirical basis—so much so that the words *subjective* and *unreliable* are nearly synonymous. It was not until the advent of psychoanalysis that a rational explanation was available for what had previously been simply an empirical fact. What psychoanalytic investigations have shown is that the fundamentally decisive reason adult human beings do not know all that they think and feel is that, throughout their lives, they go to considerable lengths to deceive themselves with respect to many of their most important thoughts and feelings. To depend on an adult subject's introspection for one's data, therefore, is to depend on data that are incomplete and that have in addition been deliberately and systematically falsified and concealed by the reporter-observer. It is only when the reporter and the observer are two, not one, that it becomes possible (though never easy) to detect and undo omissions and falsifications.

Simply stated, it is the development of the psychoanalytic method that has made it possible to understand the reasons for the unreliability of introspection as a way of investigating psychological phenomena and that has, in addition, made it possible to overcome those obstacles satisfactorily. By applying the psychoanalytic method under suitable circumstances—in an analytic situation—one gains access to subjective psychological data that are complete and reliable enough to serve as a satisfactory basis for theories of many previously obscure aspects of mental life, including the aspect we call affects or emotions.

In practice, psychoanalysts are largely concerned with psychic conflicts, since it is the consequences of conflict, the pathological compromise formations resulting from conflict, that bring patients to seek treatment. Conflicts are triggered by unpleasurable affects, in particular, by anxiety and depressive affect, and analysts have thought and written much more about them than about pleasurable affects. My own first efforts in the field of affect theory, in fact, had to do with anxiety (Brenner 1953). Careful attention to clinical data during the years since that time has led me to the conclusion that the formulation I suggested then for anxiety and related unpleasurable affects can be legitimately broadened to include the entire range of affects. I believe that every affect, whether pleasurable or unpleasurable, is a complex mental phenomenon that includes (1) sensations of pleasure, unpleasure, or a mixture of the two, and (2) thoughts, memories, wishes—in a word, ideas. As a psychic phenomenon, an affect is a sensation of pleasure, unpleasure, or both *plus* the ideas associated with that sensation. Ideas and sensations *together*, both conscious and unconscious, constitute an affect.

From the developmental point of view, what we know of ego development in general suggests that each affect has its beginnings early in life when ideas first become associated with sensations of pleasure and unpleasure. Such sensations are most frequently and most importantly associated with the instinctual drives. They arise in connection with drive tension and drive discharge or, in other words, in connection with the satisfaction and lack of satisfaction of instinctual wishes—that is, of drive derivatives. It is reasonable to assume that, for the most part, sensations of pleasure and unpleasure are not too different in adult life from what they are in childhood, that they undergo no special process of development. This assumption, to be sure, is open to question, since the pleasurable experience of orgasm is, as a rule, not part of sexual life before puberty. There is no doubt that the pleasurable sensation that is part of orgasm differs from other and earlier sensations of pleasure in its extraordinary intensity. Whether it differs in some other, qualitative way, is very difficult to say. All one can say with assurance is that there is at present no evidence that it does so.

It seems fair to say, therefore, that at present we have no evidence that sensations of pleasure and unpleasure change in any qualitative way during the course of physical and mental development. By contrast, it is obvious that the ideas that are part of every affect do develop as one's mind develops and matures. Such ideas, like any others, are wholly dependent on ego development and ego functioning with respect to their content and their complexity. It follows from this that the evolution of affects and their differentiation from one another depend on ego (and superego) development. To go a step further, one may say that the evolution of affective life is an aspect of ego development, an aspect that can serve as one very important measure of the level of ego functioning on any scale of developmental lines.

One feeling of pleasure or of unpleasure, then, can be differentiated from another only by its intensity and by the ideas associated with it. It is reasonable to assume that pleasure and unpleasure are physiological givens in an individual's psychological development. Whenever it is during the first weeks or months after birth that mental life as such may be said to begin, the sensations of pleasure and of unpleasure of that early age are the undifferentiated matrix from which the entire gamut of the affects of later life develops.

The theory of affects I have just outlined first appeared in the psychoanalytic literature in 1974 (Brenner 1974). I shall not attempt a comprehensive review of the literature on the subject of affects, but I shall mention several earlier contributions that are significantly related to this theory.

In 1947 Glover proposed that one useful way in which affects may be classified is into primary affects, which he thought of as innate, and secondary affects, which he viewed as depending at least in part on ego and superego development. He noted also that affects can be usefully classified according to whether they are pleasurable or unpleasurable.

Novey (1959) noted the close relation between affect and ideas. He concluded that the two intermingle and overlap to such an extent in the data derived from clinical psychoanalytic observations that, at least in adults, it is impossible to say which is cause and which is effect.

Lewin (1961, 1965) made two contributions to the subject that are of interest. He was concerned with the question, Is there such a thing as "pure affect," that is, affect without any ideational content? In 1961 he dealt with the question only with respect to the emotion of sadness. He concluded that, though sadness may be felt without any conscious ideational concomitant, it is never without unconscious concomitant ideas. Thus, even though this affect may *seem* to be without ideational content, in fact the affect and the idea, as he put it, are inseparable. In 1965 he enlarged his discussion to include affects in general and asserted that, whatever the emotion, an affect always has ideational content. The apparent exceptions, he wrote, are instances in which the ideational content has been repressed and is therefore unconscious.

Schur (1969) essentially echoed Lewin's view. Feeling, or affect, he said, is always inseparably linked with some idea or ideas.

Katan (1972) noted the difference between *distress* and *anxiety* in children. She asserted that one can properly speak of anxiety—that is, of an affect, as opposed to a mere sensation of unpleasure—only after a certain level of ego development has been attained.

It will be seen that each of the authors cited has offered one or more suggestions or conclusions that support the concept of the nature and development of affects I have proposed. Thus, Glover and Katan emphasized the developmental aspect of affects, and Novey, Lewin, and Schur shared the view that ideas are a part of, indissolubly linked with, or inevitably associated with affects; to summarize:

1. Affects are complex mental phenomena that include (a) sensations of pleasure, unpleasure, or both, and (b) ideas. Ideas and pleasure-unpleasure sensations together constitute an affect as a mental or psychological phenomenon.
2. The development of affects and their differentiation from one another depend on ego and, later, on superego development. The development and differentiation of affects is, in fact, an important aspect or measure of ego development.
3. Affects have their beginning early in life when ideas first become associated with sensations of pleasure and unpleasure. Such sensations are most frequently and most importantly associated with drive tension (lack of gratification) and drive discharge (gratification). They constitute the undifferentiated matrix from which the entire range of affects of later life develops.

This theory of affects offers a rational basis for defining various affects and for distinguishing among them. To illustrate with respect to pleasurable affects, what we call happiness is a feeling of pleasure in connection with an experience or fantasy of instinctual gratification, no matter whether the gratification is wholly or in part unconscious. If the pleasure is intense, the affect is called ecstasy or bliss; if the ideas have to do with having defeated a rival or rivals, the affect is called triumph. Variants of triumph are called omnipotence, self-satisfaction, mild superiority, or smugness, depending on the intensity of the pleasure and the nature of the associated ideas. As one can see, in general any attempt to define affects in psychological terms and to distinguish them can be done only by (1) specifying the experience of pleasure or unpleasure and its intensity and (2) making some reference to the content and origin of the associated ideas. Since the most significant ideas are often unconscious, it is also important to remember that a patient's own label is by no means always reliable. It may or may not be. Only a successful application of the psychoanalytic method can decide.

It will be noted that I have followed Freud in attributing pleasurable affects to satisfaction of one or more drive derivatives. The question arises whether such a view is not too limited. Are there also pleasurable affects that are related to self-definition and self-organization, to self-esteem and to memory and cognition—what might be called ego, or even, superego pleasures?

Sandler (1960) and later Joffe and Sandler (1968), for example, postulated a wish for safety rather than fear of calamity (anxiety) as operative in triggering psychic conflict. By doing so they attributed the seeking for and gaining of pleasure to that aspect of ego functioning called defense. In effect they said that when a person eliminates or mitigates unpleasure by one or several defenses, what the individual achieves is pleasure of a sort, pleasure that has resulted from ego functioning rather than from drive gratification. Although this proposal is descriptively true, it has always seemed to me to be at best a quibble with Freud's idea that the functioning of the mental apparatus proceeds according to what he called the pleasure-unpleasure principle. The mind functions, said Freud, in such a way as to achieve the pleasure associated with gratification of drive derivatives, insofar as that is possible, and to avoid or minimize whatever unpleasure is associated with those drive derivatives. What Sandler and Joffe proposed is different from Freud's idea only in leaving out any explicit mention of unpleasure. Defense, they said, is pleasurable in that it provides relief from unpleasure.

I cannot see an advantage in the proposed change, and I do see a possible disadvantage. To think of defense without reference to anxiety (and depressive affect) is to run the risk of overlooking or minimizing the significance of an aspect of a patient's conflicts that is of vital importance. One cannot analyze to best advantage if one does not interpret the ideational content of a patient's fear and misery. *What* the patient is afraid of or made miserable by is an essential part of analysis.

Another attempt to conceptualize pleasure that is not associated with instinctual gratification took its origin from the concept of pleasure in function, an idea put forward some years ago by developmental psychologists (Bühler 1930). The idea was viewed with favor by Hartmann, who saw in it some support for his concept of autonomous ego energy. As far as I know, however, Hartmann did not attempt to incorporate pleasure in function into psychoanalytic theory. Hendrick (1942, 1943) did adopt it in a somewhat altered form. In order to avoid having to say that there are sources of pleasure other than drive gratification, Hendrick postulated a drive or instinct for mastery, an idea that had some vogue for several years among analysts.

Pleasure in function as a conscious phenomenon is something everyone has experienced many times. When such pleasure can be studied by the psychoanalytic method, however, one invariably discovers unconscious determinants of what is consciously felt to be purely pleasure in function or mastery. One discovers, for example, unconscious fantasies of triumphing over one's rivals, of being loved for one's competence, of being cheered by one's audience, all of which suggest that at least part of what passes for pleasure in function is in fact related to the unconscious gratification of drive derivatives.

As for superego pleasures, by which is presumably meant the glow of virtue that one may feel at having resisted temptation, when one is able to examine its unconscious determinants as well as its conscious ones, a more complex picture will surely emerge there as well. Morality is, in its origins and in its unconscious dynamics throughout life, motivated by a desire to win parental approval as well as parental forgiveness. Pleasure in being virtuous derives, at least in part, from the fantasy of having won one's parents' love—that is, from an instinctual source.

Insofar as self-regulation is derived in the first instance from the ability in childhood to regulate urination and defecation, sleep and waking, a need to eat, and the like, I think that pleasure in self-regulation in adult life has unconscious sources, just as pleasure in function and pleasure in being moral have.

It seems to me, finally, that the following is the most that we, as analysts, can say about the question of whether there is or is not pleasure other than drive-related pleasure. Every aspect of conscious mental life and behavior that is felt by each of us to be significant is a compromise formation that has arisen from childhood instinctual wishes. Everything we think and do, in other words, gratifies instinctual wishes to a greater or less extent and is to that extent a source of pleasure. There may be other, additional sources of pleasure in connection with thought and behavior, but we are not in a position to decide one way or the other with the methods of study available to us. What we can say is that there are always important instinctual sources of pleasure and that often enough their nature and origin are discoverable only through analysis. Even when there seem to be no instinctual sources of the pleasure one consciously feels, analysis will show that there really are. What we, as analysts, cannot say about the matter may be more important than we suspect. But what we can say about sources of pleasure in mental life is surely of major significance to any understanding of the role of pleasure in the functioning of the human mind.

REFERENCES

Brenner, C. 1953. An addendum to Freud's theory of anxiety. *International Journal of Psycho-Analysis* 34:18–24.

———. 1974. On the nature and development of affects: A unified theory. *Psychoanalytic Quarterly* 43:532–56.

Bühler, K. 1930. *The Mental Development of the Child.* New York: Harcourt Brace.

Freud, S. 1920. Beyond the pleasure principle. *Standard edition*, 18:1–64.

———. 1923. The ego and the id. *Standard edition*, 19:1–59.

Glover, E. 1947. Basic mental concepts: Their clinical and theoretical value. *Psychoanalytic Quarterly* 16:482–506.

Hendrick, I. 1942. Instinct and ego during infancy. *Psychoanalytic Quarterly* 11:33–58.

———. 1943. Work and the pleasure principle. *Psychoanalytic Quarterly* 12:311–29.

Joffe, W. G., and Sandler, J. 1968. Comments on the psychoanalytic psychology of adaptation with special reference to the role of affects and the representational world. *International Journal of Psycho-Analysis* 49:445–54.

Katan, A. 1972. The infant's first reaction to strangers: Distress or anxiety? *International Journal of Psycho-Analysis* 53:501–3.

Lewin, B. D. 1961. Reflections on depression. In *Selected Papers of Bertram D. Lewin*, 147–57. New York: *Psychoanalytic Quarterly*.

———. 1965. Reflections on affect. In *Selected Papers of Bertram D. Lewin*. New York: Psychoanalytic Quarterly.

Novey, S. 1959. A clinical view of affect theory in psycho-analysis. *International Journal of Psycho-Analysis* 40:94–104.

Pulver, S. 1971. Can affects be unconscious? *International Journal of Psycho-Analysis* 52:347–54.

Sandler, J. 1960. The background of anxiety. *International Journal of Psycho-Analysis* 41:352–56.

Schur, M. 1969. Affects and cognition. *International Journal of Psycho-Analysis* 50:647–53.

10

Anhedonia and Its Implications for Psychotherapy

MICHAEL H. STONE, M.D.

Introduction

Freud, in his 1895 "Project for a Scientific Psychology," strove to comprehend mental phenomena as particular functions of the brain whence these phenomena originated. He pursued this task as far as the neurophysiology of his era permitted, concentrating for the remainder of his life upon purely psychological matters. Because of the interplay that nevertheless exists between the mind and its substrate, the brain, it behooves us at appropriate intervals to examine whatever new neurophysiological data may in the meantime have become available, in the hope that some of them might serve to modify or embellish existing psychoanalytic theory. This obligation is felt all the more keenly as we approach the centennial of Freud's project. Indeed, our 1995 "Project" will be more sophisticated than its predecessor. Mercifully, we will not be witness to how simplistic our refurbished model might appear in the eyes of those privileged to celebrate the Project's bicentennial.

This chapter focuses on only one element of the psychobiologic material out of which our model of "mind" is constructed—namely, anhedonia. In my efforts to expand traditional psychoanalytic ways of thinking about pleasure as an organizing principle, I have found it useful to examine first the more severe psychiatric disorders—those that lie beyond the pale of psychoanalysis as a *therapy*—the neurophysiological abnormalities of which may shed some light upon the more subtle disturbances that constitute the domain of analytic treatment.

Anhedonia connotes, etymologically, the absence of pleasure. Clinically one uses the term to signify a patient's inability to experience pleasure. Fortunately, few patients are so lacking in this capacity as to merit the appellation literally. One encounters instead varying degrees of *diminished* capacity—for which *hypohedonia* might be the more accurate, albeit more cumbersome, label (see Clark and Fawcett 1987).

198

Two broad categories of patients tend to exhibit anhedonia: depressives and those situated along the schizophrenic continuum. The latter manifest what Radó (1956) and later Meehl (1962) spoke of under the heading of "schizoidia," referring to the presumed genetic liability for schizophrenia. Radó went so far as to place anhedonia at the center of his explanatory model of schizophrenia. For Radó, anhedonia was one of the most important phenotypic expressions of schizoidia, reflecting some central dysregulation of hedonic control, such that the "schizotype" suffers a serious defect in the ability to experience pleasure. The limbic system was terra incognita thirty years ago; Radó could offer no more than a guess as to the nature of this "central dysregulation."

The psychological consequences of anhedonia are much less mysterious. Whatever underlying mechanism it is that affects the pleasure-capacity adversely will tend to upset the balance in human relationships between joy and frustration. Love relationships in particular illustrate the peculiar trade-offs nature imposes upon us: our keenest pleasures (those for which we reserve the special vocabulary of *ecstasy, bliss, rapture,* and so on) come within the context of passionate love. But this joy is fragile, since it can turn into misery if the beloved abandons one, has a cruel streak, or becomes petulant or jealous. Since some degree of frustration is inherent in all love relationships, it seems fair to claim that only those individuals with an unimpaired pleasure capacity can experience the bliss that allows them to endure the inevitable rebuffs and disappointments. One could analogize this balance to a cost-benefit mathematics. As an example, consider the young man who gets the phone number of an attractive girl he meets in a classroom. In calling her later for a date, he must enter a win-lose situation, since she can either accept or decline. Let -5 equal the degree of disappointment should she refuse the date. If the maximum anticipated pleasure from the encounter is, say, $+10$, the young man will call and take his chances. If the maximum pleasure is considerably less, say, $+3$, he may consider the risk unacceptable and leave the number in his pocket. We may view the anhedonic person as someone for whom the maximum anticipated pleasure, particularly in intimate relationships, is characteristically less, by a wide margin, than the anticipated pain. This leads, over time, to superficiality in such relationships (where the potential for pain is reduced through the trivialization of the relationship) or to outright avoidance.

If anhedonia is not total, less intense and more controllable pleasures (such as those involving nonhuman objects) will take the place of sexual love. Suppose, to expand the above analogy, the young man (for whom acceptance by the girl would yield only $+3$) estimates the pleasure of owning and driving a sports car as $+2$ and the possible displeasure (worrying about the payments, worrying about an accident) as -0.5. Clearly, he will find it advantageous to eschew the hazards of the dating game and to invest his hopes in the car.

Before introducing some clinical examples illustrating various facets of anhedonia, I would like to emphasize that in most patients who show this trait to a pronounced degree, adverse temperament (that is, innate factors) appears to combine with adverse early experience in producing the clinical picture we eventually recognize. Lacking any litmus paper for genetic influences, I offer this not as a fact but as an article of faith: one does encounter certain anhedonic patients whose parents and early environment were almost surely "good enough" in Winnicott's sense (1965) and whose hedonic dysregulation has little, if anything, to do with psychodynamics. Or rather, psychodynamic patterns do emerge in the course of psychoanalytic therapy, but they related far less to abnormal parent-child interactions than to nonparental factors. Conversely, one also encounters anhedonic patients whose temperament seems in no way abnormal but whose early lives were either unrelievedly bleak or else marred by chronic verbal and corporal abuse, such that the inborn capacity for pleasure became extinguished through disuse, much as one's vision could become permanently impaired were one raised until age twelve in a darkroom.

The vignettes that follow will, I hope, demonstrate the various avenues that lead to anhedonia. They represent the main bands in the spectrum of hedonic dysregulation. Enhanced awareness of these pathways will in turn enlighten the reader with respect to therapeutic strategies. The neurophysiological underpinnings of hedonic control, though far from being completely elucidated, are better understood than they were in Radó's time. I will address this topic as well further on.

Clinical Vignettes

A Patient with Endogenomorphic Depression and Marked Anhedonia

A twenty-one-year-old single man had been admitted to a psychiatric hospital because of a suicide gesture (overdose of an antidepressant) in the wake of a romantic disappointment. He had been at college when the breakup occurred. Following the rebuff by his girlfriend, he quickly lost all enthusiasm for his schoolwork. He began to feel sad, tearful, and confused about his goals. Simultaneously he lost the capacity for both consummatory and appetitive pleasure: his weight decreased, he could no longer pursue his artistic hobbies, and so on. His condition had the quality of a "double depression" inasmuch as the acute symptoms were superimposed on a *depressive temperament,* noticeable since childhood. The latter included such traits as hypochondriasis, irrational guilt, extreme fear of exams, lack of initiative, self-doubt, sexual inhibition, indecisiveness, and no more than a meager pleasure-capacity at best.

While in the hospital, his mood brightened within several weeks. Although tricyclics had been given, he became cheerful sooner than could be ascribed to the medication. In the protected setting he actually flourished, resuming his hobbies, making friends, becoming a leader among his fellow patients. Ten weeks later he seemed ready for discharge. He then moved from his parents' house to a sheltered residence, maintained his medication at a high level, and structured his week with group therapy, day hospital, and thrice-weekly psychotherapy sessions.

His therapist encouraged him to engage in his favorite artistic interests during the evenings, as a way of further structuring his time. For a while, this program succeeded. But within a few weeks, his old social inhibitions and hypersensitivity resurfaced. He asked a girl for a date, but when he was with her, he panicked and could think of nothing to say. He lost interest in all his leisure-time pursuits, the mildest criticism by other members of his group seemed malignant, and all his self-confidence and enthusiasm vanished. He became agoraphobic, but even returning home did not restore his equilibrium. He tried volunteer work but could not talk on the same "wave-length" as the other workers, felt isolated and afraid, and quit precipitously. His interest in sex dropped to zero, and in fact no activity or person could provide him with any enjoyment. The world now appeared hopelessly gray to him, and his suicidal thoughts recurred. All psychotherapeutic and psychopharmacologic efforts to restore his pleasure capacity in the hopes that this would serve as an antidote to his downward slide were unavailing, and he was rehospitalized.

Endogenous Depression in a Cyclothymic Patient with Normal Hedonic Capacity

A thirty-seven-year-old physician, married with three small children, had led a successful career since graduating from his surgical residency. He had always been ambitious, intense, and hardworking. His marriage was reasonably satisfactory, although his sexual drive was stronger than his wife's, and he had begun to grow irritable with the (rather ordinary) demands of his children. Others experienced him as extroverted, almost excessively generous, raucous in his laughter, and at times brusque. Several relatives of the maternal line had bipolar illness. At about thirty-four, as he began to dig out of the indebtedness accumulated from his training days, and without obvious precipitants, he grew depressed, at times so severely as to interfere with his work. He lost some confidence in his abilities, found the noises and distractions of the family intolerable, lost interest in sex, and felt progressively more hopeless. He spoke of his condition as a black shroud that someone had mysteriously pulled over his life. He no longer ventured out to social gatherings and parties and became humorless and morose. He took to self-administering morphine, upon which he became increasingly dependent. The opiate normalized his mood, though he was left with fears of being caught by the authorities for his drug abuse.

He was referred for psychotherapy, but it was soon clear that his drug habit took precedence over his underlying depression and that the habit could not be conquered by therapy alone. Treatment consisted of an opiate-antagonist, which nullified the effects of the morphine, along with a tricyclic antidepressant and supportive therapy. Later, he responded better to a monoamine oxidase inhibitor (MAOI). Psychotherapy was directed toward freeing him of his negative self-image. He had grown to feel "bad" or "worthless" because of the drug abuse. When it was pointed out to him that his reliance on the morphine constituted a self-defeating but otherwise understandable effort on his part to cure himself and to remain at work for the sake of his family, he became less self-critical and more relaxed. His old capacity for pleasure gradually reasserted itself. For a time he became hypomanic; he bought an expensive new home and a big diamond for his wife and took the family on a lengthy trip. For the past two years he has been euthymic on a regimen of MAOIs and once-weekly psychotherapy and has not returned to opiate abuse.

Anhedonia in a Manic-Depressive with Bulimia: Double Depression

A twenty-six-year-old single woman was hospitalized after a suicide attempt. She had been bulimarexic since age fourteen. In addition, she was a chronic wrist cutter, who for years had periodically made superficial razor cuts in her wrists to relieve tension.

She had grown up as one of three children in a family marred by intense marital discord. The father had numerous affairs with other women, which the patient had known about since she was five or six. She was fond of her father but sided with her mother, who eventually divorced that father when the patient was fifteen. The patient had by that age already been subject to depressive episodes and regarded her life as essentially joyless since age twelve. She worked as a bookkeeper after finishing high school and never had a boyfriend or even a casual date up to the time of her latest hospitalization. There had been no sexual molestation or physical abuse during her early years. She was usually amenorrheic because of anorexia, and she could not recall any connection between her menses and her mutilative or suicidal behavior.

In recent years, treatment with psychotherapy and with tricyclic antidepressants made no dent in her chronic anhedonia. She was intolerant of MAOIs because these drugs made her feel "like a zombie." After a suicide attempt five months before her last hospitalization, she was treated with six electroconvulsive treatments (ECTs). She felt much better afterward and recaptured a pleasure capacity she had lost fourteen years before. One month later, however, after a friend committed suicide, she tried to hang herself. Although rescued, she has reverted to her anhedonic state ever since.

Anhedonia in a Patient with Chronically Traumatic Background

An unmarried man of twenty-five was referred for psychotherapy at the urging of his father. The patient had a master's degree in chemistry but had a menial laboratory job, cleaning the bottleware in preparation for the next day's experiments. Apart from this he lived a hermetic existence, spending his leisure hours alone watching television or, occasionally, a movie. He had no friends of either sex. His parents had divorced when he was fifteen, his mother subsequently remarrying. She and the man's older sister lived in a different part of the country and rarely saw him. His father lived nearby and visited him with some regularity. Appalled at his son's constricted life, he arranged for psychiatric treatment in the hope that this would help his son to "come out of his shell."

Treatment consisted of twice-weekly sessions of analytically oriented psychotherapy. The patient was markedly anhedonic, avoidant, schizoid, rarely looking in the direction of the therapist or broaching any spontaneous remarks. He lived in a state of emotional anesthesia, claiming to feel nothing even in response to his dreams. The latter, ironically, were dramatic and electrifying in the same proportion as his outward life was barren and emotionally dead.

His early life had been traumatic, largely as a result of his mother's verbal and physical abusiveness. She taunted him with his scholastic mediocrities and punished any peccadillos with extreme harshness: washing his mouth out with soap, locking him in a dark closet for a whole night without food, and so on. His sufferings were all the more poignant for having been inflicted by his German mother, who had married his Jewish father shortly after World War II and who had then proceeded to continue in private, so to speak, what the Nazis had previously inflicted on a more public scale.

When the patient was about fourteen, his mother had a "nervous breakdown" (perhaps schizoaffective in nature). His father divorced her shortly afterward.

The only consistently warm relationship he could recall was with his paternal grandmother, who had died when he was twelve. This fact emerged in connection with a dream in the second month of his treatment: "I was Superman. Two men attack me, but I escape. I try to get to my grandmother's house in the city. I felt if I could get back to the city, they couldn't find me. I look for a shortcut but there doesn't seem to be any. I walk through some school where there were pictures of starving Biafran children and venereal disease sores. I thought those were part of some sex-education course, warning the pupils about the dangers of sex."

At first, he said, he thought of hitchhiking, but abandoned the idea, saying "I hate to have to get to know people or to strike up conversations with them." To my suggestion that the "school" might have to do with his treatment—something unpleasant he had to go through to get to where it was safe—he said, "No, there was nobody else there, just me; whatever is to be done I have to do myself." ("Like Superman.") "Yeah, I have no rapport with you." ("So whatever improvement you might experience has to come through your own superhuman *strength*, not through relatedness to anyone?") "Yes, I don't know if I want friends at all anyway. They seem revolting." ("Like V.D.") "Yeah, like V.D."

Shortly thereafter he reported another dream: "A wart on my foot turned cancerous. Blood came out. They try to get me to a hospital." His associations began with his annoyance at his father (whom he had seen the night before) for once again insisting that he continue his therapy. Then he recalled seeing a movie about a man who bullies a woman into going to his apartment. She tries to seduce him in an attempt to get free, but he condemns her as a "dirty slut." The patient was disgusted by the movie but made no connections between the "dirty slut," the dangerous sore on his foot, and the allusion to V.D. and the dangerousness of sex from the earlier dream. Mostly he maintained a dull silence throughout the session.

His general fear of "depth therapy" came through in a subsequent dream in which he found himself in a submarine traversing the waters around the city, wondering, "What if we're depth-bombed? How will I ever get back to the surface?" Later on, he mentioned, in another context, "My parents never enjoyed life. My mother used to say—never expect any fun in life; life is miserable."

After five months of therapy—which he experienced as an entree to intimacies for which he had neither the skills nor the enthusiasm—he quit. Just before, he shared with me a dream: "My sister and I walk in a garden. Poisonous snakes attack her and then tiny roaches were all over her hands." He said, with his usual ennui, "The dream doesn't seem important." He did mention having felt intense love for his sister when he was younger. As he put it, "That was in a different life," as though the events belonged to a time so distant as to be altogether disconnected to his present burned-out self. The dream portrayed a kind of reverse paradise, where the protagonists were also in reversed roles: instead of the apple (breast) ruining Adam, the snake (penis) ruined Eve. His sexual interest in her was loathsome and unacceptable: the roaches were "insects," to which he then associated (by similarity of sound) "incest."

His aversion to sex and avoidance, not only of sex but of all human closeness, appeared to stem partly from the extraintense prohibition against incestuous feelings in his joyless and judgmental family, partly from the mistrust engendered by his sadistic mother. There may have been an innate component to his lifelong anhedonia, but the predominant factor appeared to be the bleak and traumatic early environment. He had, in effect, been taught to be anhedonic. Psychotherapy, for him, held out only a false promise: the replacement of his barren but no longer tortured existence with the disease-ridden and fatal "joys" of closeness. With no *experiences* of intense pleasure anywhere in memory, he could only regard the "cure" that awaited him through psychotherapy as so much misleading advertising.

A Schizotypal Patient with Anhedonia

A thirty-three-year-old divorced woman was referred for psychotherapy by a therapist with whom she had worked while living in a different part of the country.

She had married at twenty-one and borne a child that her husband had made clear he did not want. They soon divorced, and the child was raised by distant relatives with whom she has had little contact. Her mother had been hospitalized several times for a paranoid schizophrenic psychosis and ultimately committed suicide when the patient was in her mid-twenties. Her father developed cancer not long afterward and subsequently also took his life. These events left her with an intolerable sense of guilt, which, superimposed upon the aridity and abusiveness of her early life, intensified the already marked impairment in her pleasure capacity. As a child, for example, she was often abandoned for brief periods by her mother, who was becoming increasingly preoccupied with bizarre thoughts and seemed at times to forget all about having a daughter. The patient, as a six-year-old, invented an imaginary companion consisting of herself as she then imagined she might be at eighteen or nineteen. This older version of herself constituted a kind of illusory caretaker to replace her erratic mother. Her father was irascible and overindulgent by turns, sometimes showering her with expensive gifts, sometimes flicking lit matches at her in a contemptuous kind of punishment.

The patient had few friends while she was growing up. She had some sources of pleasure, such as music lessons and hiking, but mostly kept to herself. She met her husband when both were students at the university. They had political views in common, along with a love of the outdoors. Both tended to be irritable and hypercritical. Following the divorce, her personality hardened along paranoid lines. Her sense of humor was all but absent. Habitually mistrustful and referential, she eschewed small talk and was known by her co-workers as solitary and dour. Most potentially pleasurable situations she avoided, on the ground that she must constantly atone for her parents' deaths.

Despite her psychological handicaps, she was highly motivated for therapy and worked diligently in her sessions with me. These have been thrice weekly for the past eighteen years. This patient has made slow but substantial progress throughout this unusually lengthy process, which has by now encompassed nearly three thousand meetings.

Analytically oriented at the outset, the therapy had emphasized exploration of the central dynamics and the meticulous differentiation, through the transference work, of her parents' personalities from my personality (upon which their images had, in her mind, become almost inseparably veneered). During a subsequent phase of therapy, the emphasis was upon entitlement: I actively fought against the notion that she bore any realistic responsibility for her parents' morbid evolution and encouraged her to exercise her privilege to enjoy various small pleasures, such as weekend trips and foreign travel. In recent years, she has mellowed enough to make several lasting relationships. Currently, she has been living with a man for three years—the longest time she has ever spent in one relationship. Both she and her friend are stubborn and querulous, but thanks in part to the problem-solving direction in which our sessions have now begun to point, she has come to understand better when it is realistic and when it is self-defeating to challenge her friend's desires and patterns of behavior. Her pleasure capacity has subsequently grown greater in this important *interpersonal* realm, whereas until lately her gains were mainly in the "narcissistic" realm related to solitary hobbies and travel.

Anhedonia and Anorgasmia in a Patient
with "Moral Masochism" and Anaclitic Features
A twenty-seven-year-old married woman, the mother of two small children, was referred for psychotherapy because of irritability and tension connected with psychological problems with her older child. The boy had become enuretic

and disobedient, both tendencies infuriating the patient to the point of striking him on several occasions. These episodes quickly ushered in feelings of intense remorse, shame at being a "bad mother," and ultimately depression with insomnia and suicidal ruminations. Her attitude toward the boy had been markedly ambivalent from the outset, partly because he was conceived out of wedlock. This violated her family's (most especially her mother's) values and left her with feelings of sinfulness. The labor had been unusually difficult as well, so that the boy came to symbolize both her own "badness" and a menace to her health. She had never been able to respond sexually and was so inhibited in the area of sex in general as to be unable to utter the names of the sexual organs. Thus, when her son developed a small pustule on his penis, she could not bring herself to tell the pediatrician on the phone for what ailment she was seeking an appointment. At our first consultation she made it a precondition of the therapy that she never discuss sex. I accepted this, with my own proviso that should she later change her mind, I would be quite willing to hear her out on the subject.

She had grown up on the West Coast in a well-to-do family, where she was the eldest of three daughters. Their mother raised the girls in a strict Catholic tradition, although the father was a Presbyterian and was much less strict in his handling of the children. The patient was the father's favorite. The mother had suffered postpartum depression at the births of the two younger children. One of her sisters became addicted to amphetamines during her twenties.

The personality features most apparent during the early phases of therapy were the "infantile": the patient was dependent, irritable, easily moved to tears, histrionic, and prone to panic. She made many emergency calls. Anhedonia was not confined to the sexual life: she took no pleasure in child rearing, socializing with friends, the marital relationship, or various entertainments and hobbies. This trend had not been apparent during her earlier years, when she had had a bubbly personality (especially in the presence of her father), enjoyed horseback riding and other sports, dancing, and so on. As it began to surface in her sessions, marriage was the (negative) turning point. Once past the altar, her husband became demanding, hypercritical, and demeaning. The mildest examples of assertiveness in this otherwise submissive woman met with sharp rebuke. A typical instance: she mentioned a certain fact (about an exotic animal species) she had gleaned from some magazine. Her husband shot her down with "you don't know what you're talking about!" Three days later, chancing to peruse the same article, he enthusiastically told her the same fact. He had been raised in an atmosphere in which a woman doing or knowing anything outside the acceptable sphere of Kinder, Kirche, Küche meant "wearing the pants" in the family—the worst evil that could befall a grown man.

Therapy, which consisted of thrice-weekly psychoanalytically oriented sessions, alongside mild anxiolytics on an as-needed basis, focused initially on her sexual inhibitions. Themes of aggression, mutilation, and dangerousness predominated. She saw, for example, in an early dream, "blood gushing out of a hole in the backside of my older boy, who fell out of his stroller as I was pushing him along in the street." Her associations were to her menstrual periods and to a serious hemorrhage that followed a miscarriage before this boy was conceived. Subsequently, she was terrified of labor and delivery, had actually had a difficult delivery, and required a large episiotomy.

In a dream two months later: "I swim across a lake. Floating in the water is a bag with jaws and teeth in it. I was afraid someone would hurt me if they found out I'd seen it. The scene shifts to a bus trip. Planes were strafing the bus. Jackie Kennedy was on the bus and they were trying to kill her. Two women next to her were killed. There was fire and blood all over. I'm back in the lake, and a crocodile grabs hold of my leg and won't let go."

She spoke of recent conflicts in her marriage: her husband's demands for sex, her compliance and mute acceptance. She was caught in a situation that stifled and imprisoned her. The male and the male organ (the crocodile), instead of providing a woman pleasure, bruised and entrapped her.

These themes were elaborated further in connection with another dream two months later: "We were picnicking someplace. A bum accosted us trying to touch my leg with his dirty towel and I slap him. My friend Carol had her arm amputated as a result of a snake-bite." Here she mentioned her intense guilt over premarital sex and went on to recall having gotten her period the night before the dream: "We don't usually have sex when it's my period" (period = having the rag on = dirty towel = something dirty).

Shortly thereafter, as she was expressing the conflictual feelings she had about birth control, bemoaning the impossibility for a good Catholic of using anything but the rhythm method, she reported a dream: "I was in Hell, with fire and crowds of other sinners all around me. I'd done something sexual . . . not sure what. My mother stood behind me and whipped me with a long set of rosary beads."

This dream led to a turning point for the better, as she realized that her compunctions about sex, especially premarital sex, "kinky" sex, and birth control, stemmed not so much from the church in the abstract as from the particular and not necessarily representative personification of the church that had raised her—her joyless and puritanical mother. More on this theme surfaced later, toward the end of her treatment, with this dream: "Mother tried to kill me and was insane. I had to escape because Daddy was reluctant to put her into an institution. The scene changed to our home, where there was a maid who was mentally ill. I was afraid she'd kill my children. I didn't want to ruffle her feelings, yet I knew we'd have to get rid of her."

By the third and last year of her therapy, she had become far less inhibited sexually and was now orgastic. She recaptured her capacity for pleasure in other realms of life also—for instance, in preparing gourmet meals, in socializing, in organizational work. She grew less submissive as well as less guilt-ridden and matured in a way that put her ahead of rather than behind her husband. She moved with him to a different city where, within the next year, she divorced him. She returned to college for postgraduate work, remarried (to a man much more similar to herself in cultural pursuits and much less chauvinistic), and went on to achieve a top position in an academic institution. Over the past twenty years, she has kept in touch with me through letters, from which it is clear that she has remained well (including hedonically) and high functioning.

Anhedonia in this case did not appear to be the expression of innate factors. Her early environment was free of the severe and chronic physical abuse that often leads to the perpetual bitterness, gloom, and mistrust seen in these "post-traumatic" states (see Kolb 1987). Hers was the "hypohedonia" of neurotic (conflict-engendered) inhibition of pleasure. To this extent it seemed—and was—more remediable by conventional psychoanalytic interventions. Her central conflicts reemerged in the transference situation with a distinctive layered pattern. For her the easiest, hence most superficial, layer concerned negative feelings toward her mother. More threatening were the warm feelings toward her father, since she soon came to recognize the forbidden erotic overtones with which these feelings were charged. Next came negative feelings toward her father (for being unfaithful to her mother and, in effect, to his favorite daughter, or "little wife"). Finally, she was able to reach the most disturbing layer of all: her warm, homoerotically tinged feelings toward her mother. Throughout most of the first year of her therapy, the transference work took on the quality of a tug-of-war between herself, as an ultraconservative Catholic (through identification with her mother), and myself, as the perfidious infidel, the Jewish analyst who would lure her into a relinquishment of her childhood values. It was only after the rosary dream that she could begin to see that I was inviting her to reexamine not her attachment to a particular religion but her blind loyalty to her mother's excessively harsh and ultimately maladaptive attitudes toward sex. As she successfully worked through this superego conflict, she regained her capacity for pleasure.

Discussion

As adumbrated in the introductory remarks, anhedonia conveys the notion denotatively of a generally reduced pleasure capacity, even though across-the-board impairment is clinically rare. Instead, the potentially most intense pleasures are the most vulnerable. Freud (1911) commented on the apparently diminished pleasure-capacity and sexuality in dementia praecox cases—most notably, that of Schreber. Radó (1956) also mentioned the schizophrenic's lack of interest in sex. In recent years Chapman, Edell, and Chapman (1980) have developed questionnaires for the methodical assessment of "physical anhedonia." These authors found that schizophrenics with poor premorbid adjustment were particularly prone to show high scores on their anhedonia scale. Akhtar and his colleagues (1977) reported around the same time a noticeable decrease in overt sexuality among hospitalized schizophrenic patients compared with other groups of hospitalized patients.

Analgesia, the reverse side of the coin of anhedonia, had also been claimed for schizophrenics—as though they were, when compared with normals, as insensitive to painful stimuli as to pleasurable. This impression received some corroboration in a study by Buchsbaum, Davis, and Van Kammen (1980), who demonstrated this reduced pain sense not in all schizophrenic subjects but in a subgroup consisting of about a quarter of the original patients. Added to this problem of heterogeneity is the problem of nonspecificity alluded to above: anhedonia is not limited to the schizotype but is noted with equal prominence in depression. With the increased attention to the "negative signs" of schizophrenia during the past ten years, anhedonia has often been lumped together with apathy, affect constriction, asociality, and attentional defects (Andreasen 1982). But these same "five A's" of negative symptoms are also encountered in serious depression, as well as in those with akinesia induced by neuroleptic drugs (Johnstone 1986).

The clinical situation has become complicated in recent years by the realization that *self-reported* anhedonia cannot always be taken at face value. Brown and his co-workers (1979) noted that the self-report of pleasure tends to be decreased, along expected lines, in schizophrenics, even more than in depressives. Yet if one relied instead on observers' estimates of pleasure, judged from the patients' facial expressions, and so on, the schizophrenics' pleasure ability seemed to exceed that of the acutely depressed patients. From a practical standpoint, nevertheless, one should keep in mind that many schizotypes (including certain schizoid and schizotypal patients, along with the schizophrenics; see Fairbairn 1941), though not devoid of pleasure-sense, show fairly marked degrees of anhedonia throughout life, whereas many patients with a major depressive episode, who may be totally anhedonic while ill, have enjoyed adequate pleasure capacities pre- (and post-) morbidly. The schizotype is more in the situation of the color-blind person, who can see no reason a Fauve painting might be more enjoyable than an etching, whereas the acutely depressed patient might be compared to someone temporarily blinded, who can at least recall colors easily and can perhaps look forward to experiencing them once again.

Another irony is implicit in the preoccupation of the psychiatric profession with efforts to ameliorate the admittedly flashier "positive" symptoms of schizophrenia—something the neuroleptics accomplish with reasonable efficacy—even though the schizophrenic may experience his illness as consisting not so much of (for him, often ego-syntonic) hallucinations and delusions as of apathy and anhedonia. As Carpenter and Hanlon (1986) point out, however, alleviation of the positive symptoms is usually purchased at the price of intensified negative symptoms: medications customarily diminish the schizophrenic's already enfeebled spontaneity and pleasure capacity.

Despite the subtle differences in the intensity and relative chronicity of anhedonia in schizotypes versus depressives (see Harrow at al. 1977), most recent investigators would agree that anhedonia in these patient groups harks back to some innate defect. Psychodynamic theory alone, in other words, cannot account for the phenomenon except in certain instances of chronic abuse, familial joylessness, or, as in the last case discussed above, chronic guilt provocation. For this reason, an *arousal* theory has developed alongside dynamic theory, as a supplementary model with some explanatory power vis-à-vis anhedonia in either schizophrenics or depressives. Berardi and Garske (1977), for example, understand schizophrenia as a function of factors that diminish the threshold for behavioral disorganization. The schizophrenic adapts by means of a detour around potentially disorganizing stimuli. He may at times try to lower the intensity of a stimulus (such as keeping a date with a girl, but talking and behaving in such a way that "nothing happens") or at other times try to avoid the upsetting stimuli altogether (by remaining alone). Sexual stimuli in particular are vulnerable to these detour mechanisms, since the schizophrenic typically experiences intimacy and sexuality as maximally bewildering from the standpoint of stimulus processing and maximally disturbing from the standpoint of psychic equilibrium.

Contemporary theory regarding anhedonia may better be understood, at this point, by adopting a systems-analytical approach. This allows us to assign otherwise isolated and seemingly disconnected findings to their proper places on several hierarchical levels, beginning with the molecular level and ending at the level of clinical observation. Depending upon their particular areas of interest, various authors have, as already noted, looked at anhedonia from the perspective of schizophrenia; others, from the vantage point of depression. Still others have tackled the subject in a more general way, unrelated to specific diagnostic entities. In table 10.1, I have summarized the relevant data within a hierarchical framework encompassing five levels.

TABLE 10.1   A Systems-Analysis View of Anhedonia

Level	General	Schizophrenic/ Schizotypal Patients	Depressed Patients
Clinical	Social isolation; decreased interest in sex, communication skills. Increased likelihood of future psychopathology (Simons 1982). Increased pleasure-avoiding defenses in moral masochism (Krystal 1981). May lead to abuse of alcohol or of cannabis euphoriants. May lead to opiate (cocaine) abuse.	Other "negative" symptoms. Decreased sex activity among hospitalized patients (Akhtar et al. 1977). SZ more anhedonic than other diagnostic groups (Harrow et al. 1977). Decreased ability to experience love. Decreased seeking for sexual gratification. Increased insensitivity to pain (Buchsbaum et al. 1980).	Decreased consummatory and appetitive pleasure capacity in endogenomorphic depression (Klein 1980). Increased percent recovery in depressed patients with anhedonia (though some anhedonia persists) compared with normal hedonic depressed patients (Clark et al. 1984).

Psychopharma-cological	Special medications may be necessary to combat drug dependence (e.g., naloxone, Anta-buse).	May be aggravated by neuroleptics (Carpenter and Hanlon 1986). Decreased self-report (though in-creased observer report) of pleasure (Brown et al. 1979). Amphetamines not helpful (Crow 1985).	Responsiveness to tricyclic MAOI anti-depressants or to ECT. Occasionally leads to opiate abuse.
Psychological	Pathological defenses against normal pleasures may lead to moral maso-chism (Krystal, 1981). Decreased notice of novel stimuli (Miller 1986). Addicts start out with hedonic capacity but lose it through chronic failure in intimacy. Ennui (Reil 1803).	Patient may seek to reduce stimulation via avoidance of contact with others (Berardi and Garske 1977). Decreased avidity for opiates as euphor-iants because of decreased history of keen pleasure experiences (Sny-der 1980).	Demoralization, perennialization of belief that life situ-ation will never get better. Some de-pressives are tem-peramentally anhedonic; others, not.
Neurophysio-logical	Abnormality in CNS self-stimulation centers of the lim-bic system. Slow cortical re-sponses (Simons et al. 1982).	Frontal lobe abnor-malities may un-derlie "negative" signs (including anhedonia), whereas hippo-campal dopamin-ergic tracts may underlie "positive" signs (Crow 1985).	Smaller P-300 com-ponent in event-related potential tests (Miller 1986).
Molecular	? Disturbances in opioid-receptors (Snyder 1980). ? Disturbances in certain noradren-ergic and/or do-paminergic tracts.	? Damage to norad-renergic reward system by 6-hydroxydopamine (Stein and Wise 1971).	? Disturbances in noradrenergic tracts.

The Molecular Level

Most satisfying to the researcher would be the discovery of one or perhaps a small number of neurotransmitters, operating within a few well-defined tracts, abnormality of whose function correlated closely with the clinical phenomenon of anhedonia. One-to-one relationships of this sort have yet to be demonstrated, however, despite certain promising leads. Opioid receptors, sensitive to enkephalin-endorphin compounds, may be involved in certain pleasure-pain phenomena (Snyder 1980) as well as in the related phenomena of orgasm and sleep. Enkephalin tracts in the limbic system may, for example, regulate certain emotional states; specifically, they may mediate the euphoriant effects of opiates and play a prominent role in the mechanism of pain perception. At the psychological level, of course, pleasure is a complex phenomenon (compare the paradoxical pleasure of the horror-show devotee or of the masochist) and is not likely to be subserved entirely by one set of receptors along one narrow pathway. Others have suggested the importance of noradrenergic and dopaminergic tracts. Stein and Wise (1971) postulated that in schizophrenia, an abnormal gene leads to reduced dopamine-beta-hydroxylase activity, such that dopamine is not all converted to norepinephrine in the nerve terminals: some is oxidized to (the potentially toxic) 6-hydroxydopamine. This might in turn damage the noradrenergic "reward" system. The authors speculated that this abnormality in the ventral limbic system might underlie anhedonia not only in schizophrenia but also in manic-depression. Schizophrenia and manic-depression emerge as rather too similar in the Stein and Wise hypothesis, as though both stem somehow from a common neurotransmitter defect whose clinical expression is anhedonia.

What may we take from current investigation at the molecular level? Only, I believe, that the data tend to support Radó's hunch in ways that are nevertheless still nonspecific and in need of further clarification.

The Neurophysiological Level

Subjects who score high on Chapman questionnaires that tap physical anhedonia, perceptual aberration, and psychosis-proneness tend to show schizotypal and affective symptoms indicating vulnerability to psychosis (G. A. Miller 1986). These features include poor communication skills, social isolation, low heterosexual interest, psychoticlike Rorschach responses, deviant word associations, and mild forms of Schneiderian "first-rank" symptoms. During tests on these subjects of auditory discrimination tasks, Miller found differences in event-related brain potentials (especially a diminished P-300 component) that suggested a deficit in the use of memory templates by anhedonics. Given adequate stimulus input, the anhedonics tended to compensate, but in general they appeared to resist noticing novel stimuli or else to treat every stimulus, even a familiar one, as though novel (1986, 111). Earlier, Simons (1982) had reported that anhedonics, compared with normal subjects, showed an insufficiency in their orienting responses to novel stimuli.

Simons, MacMillan, and Ireland (1982) tested anhedonic and normal control subjects for their physiological responsivity to neutral versus high-interest stimuli (the latter consisted of color slides of attractive centerfolds). Anhedonics showed less differential responsivity to the two types of stimuli, especially in relation to the slow cortical potential (303). This group of investigators understood this failure of differentiation as a manifestation of dysfunction in the anhedonic's CNS reward or pleasure system. In their view, this dysfunction seemed more related to schizophrenia than to depression. As they mention, "while depressed *patients* do score high on the Physical Anhedonia Scale, depressed undergraduates (as measured by the Beck Depression Inventory) do not" (307). Anhedonic college students produce Rorschach protocols reminiscent of schizophrenia (Edell and Chapman 1979). The results of Simons's study pertain more to sexual aspects of hedonic capacity, given the emphasis on sexual stimuli in the initial tests. The generalizability of their observations needs to be tested in relation to other types of customarily pleasurable stimuli.

Other recent studies have focused on anhedonia in chronic schizophrenia and have interpreted their results as indicating two schizophrenic syndromes— one characterized by negative symptoms (including anhedonia-asociality), and the other, by positive symptoms (Crow 1985). The positive-symptom variant is more responsive to neuroleptic drugs and appears to be a neurochemical disorder associated with increase in numbers of D_2 dopamine receptors. The anhedonic syndrome is associated with intellectual impairment, chronicity, and a degenerative process eventuating in CNS cell loss. The last may be detectable by changes in ventricular size neuroradiologically and by similar signs of cortical atrophy on computerized tomography (CT) scan (Johnstone et al. 1976). The sites of cell loss or damage remain unclear and are perhaps not localized to any one narrow region. Crow mentions abnormalities in the hippocampus and amygdala in patients with negative symptoms, though Levin (1984) emphasizes abnormalities in the *frontal lobes*, particularly in relation to severe negative symptoms such as social withdrawal and flat affect. The hypothesis of a frontal lobe abnormality is in line with Kraepelin's original belief that frontal cortex dysfunction might underlie the loss of integrative functions in dementia praecox (1919). Other authors who favor a frontal lobe hypothesis in relation to negative symptoms have also cautioned against accounting for all these clinical signs by localized neuropathology (Seidman 1983; Wing 1980), given the diversity of neurological "soft signs" and neuropsychological deficits (eye tracking and attentional disturbances) also found in chronic schizophrenia. Perhaps what is important in determining the balance between positive and negative (including anhedonic) signs is the "degree of deficit in a corticosubcortical arousal-attention system that includes brain stem, limbic [see Schmajuk 1987] and frontal/temporal cortical regions" (Seidman 1983, 227).

The Psychological Level

Anhedonia is not all of a piece with respect to its outward manifestations. There is variety in the psychological experience of anhedonia as in the diagnostic groups within which anhedonic patients are found.

In the realm of affective disorder, for example, one encounters persons with what Kraepelin (1921) called the "depressive temperament," whose pleasure capacity is below normal all through their lives. The depressive tends to reach out toward others, however, albeit with the primary aim of developing a clinging ("anaclitic") dependency. Sexual interest is low and is subordinated to the over-arching need for maternal protection. The schizotype, outwardly anhedonic in a similar degree and fashion, seeks to reduce what for him is excess stimulation through avoidance of contact with others (Berardi and Garske 1977). Anhedonia may be so pervasive that the schizotype sees little point in opiate abuse. Euphoria is a foreign experience: there is nothing to "recapture" through substance abuse (compare Snyder 1980).

Many depression-prone persons, such as bipolars experiencing a downturn, are not chronically anhedonic. They may abuse opiates (as in the second case above) or alcohol. Endogenomorphic depressions are accompanied by diminished capacity for consummatory and appetitive pleasures, along with certain "vegetative" signs (Klein et al. 1980, 234); some evidence suggests that there may be separate centers for consummatory and appetitive pleasures, which may find parallels in the effects of opiates and cocaine, respectively. One must also distinguish between the anhedonia associated with depression and the state of demoralization. Depression and anhedonia may occur without obvious precip-itants or may be ushered in by irreplaceable loss (such as the death of a spouse); demoralization may follow upon the heels of a loss or reversal that is more easily rectified (an inventor fails to obtain a patent, feels demoralized, but obtains the patent after making a revision—whereupon the feeling of demoralization quickly dissipates). There are different shades of gray in these varieties of anhedonia, a different clinical course with different implications for therapy.

Overlapping, but lying largely outside, the domains of depressive and schi-zotypal anhedonia are several subtle forms of impaired pleasure-capacity, such as those associated with the abuser of opiates, the moral masochist, and the once-hedonistic, sensation-seeking person who becomes burned out and chron-ically bored.

Krystal (1981) has drawn attention to the pathological defenses erected against normal pleasures in the moral masochist (as in the last case above). Pleasure capacity is not innately defective but becomes impaired within the context of relationships that are either pain-dependent or characterized by pro-hibition against pleasure (as in the case of patients with puritanical parents).

The bored hedonist was apparently a well-recognized figure (especially among the "idle rich") in bygone times, as witness the following description by Reil: "Many suicides had been unmarried and in a state of excessive lust, becoming finally so indifferent as no longer to be able to find interest in anything. In cases of this sort, where ennui developed through excessive use and feigned desire, it will usually be quite difficult to instill in such lost souls any renewed interest for life" (1803, 353; my translation).

The Psychopharmacological Level

When anhedonia is associated primarily with moral masochism or with en-nui, response to psychopharmacological agents is apt to be negligible. The same is true in other situations where pleasure capacity is subnormal predominantly on a characterological or temperamental basis. Schizotypal patients seldom experience any improvement in hedonic potential after receiving phenothiazines. The anhedonia in patients with "characterological depression" (Kraepelin's depressive temperament) seldom responds to tricyclic or MAOI antidepressants. Endogenomorphic depression, either by itself or superimposed on characterological depression, may lead to a temporary anhedonia ("state") or may intensify the anhedonia associated with the temperament ("trait"). This anhedonic component may respond to the customary medications or to ECT. The anhedonia of schizophrenic patients with prominent negative symptoms usually does not respond to amphetamines (Crow 1985) and may be aggravated by neuroleptics (Carpenter and Hanlon 1986).

Depressed patients who attempt to self-medicate through opiate abuse may require naloxone to help them conquer the substance abuse but may then be left with their original anhedonia. This condition, along with the underlying depression, requires an effective regimen of its own, often consisting of antidepressants and supportive psychotherapy. Similarly, in those who abuse alcohol, partly to make themselves feel more "alive" (that is, to enhance their pleasure capacity), treatment of the alcoholism is the first priority. Antabuse may be helpful in selected cases, and anhedonia may reemerge in the process. Here, impairment in pleasure capacity may be the reflection of deeply embedded characterological problems, not amenable to antidepressants and yielding only slowly to psychotherapy. This will be particularly true for the shy, sullen alcoholic who uses alcohol as a specific to overcome anxiety in social situations.

The Clinical Level

As we have noted, "endogenous" anhedonia represents a region of overlap between schizophrenia and characterologic or endogenomorphic depression. Constricted affect and anhedonia in schizophrenia predict a poor long-term outcome (Knight et al. 1979). Not all schizophrenics show negative symptoms, but in those who do, scores on a scale of negative-symptom assessment (Andreasen 1981) are in the same range as the scores of severely depressed patients (Kulhara and Chadda 1987). Subtle clinical differences might include poor eye contact, inappropriate affect, and a scanty history of friendships among schizophrenics with anhedonia in contrast to greater fixity of facial expression, physical anergia, and a better history of friendship and intimate relationships among anhedonic depressed patients. Again, anhedonia is likely to be milder and briefer in secondary (reactive) depressives than in those with unipolar depression and the depressive temperament (see R. E. Miller 1987). Depressives with less impaired pleasure capacity are usually those with the least psychomotor retardation and the least feeling of hopelessness (Clark et al. 1984). The endogenous components and accompaniments of anhedonia are likewise less in evidence in the moral masochist and the jaded hedonist, where the clinical abnormalities tend to remain at the level of personality.

Treatment Considerations

Differences in the origin and natural history of anhedonia among various types of patients justify different treatment strategies and predict differences in outcome.

In general one works *with* the anhedonia in reactive depression and moral masochism; one works *around* the symptom in schizophrenia, schizotypal personality, and depressive temperament. In the former, one strives to restore or enhance a pleasure capacity that was once clearly present but became temporarily enfeebled. In the latter situations, one strives to inject variety and depth of experience into the lives of chronically joyless persons as substitutes for the permanently underdeveloped pleasure capacity (see the fifth case described above). Anhedonia in severely traumatized patients—those who have been the victims of extreme corporal or sexual abuse—often acquires the tenacity of endogenous anhedonia, probably because of near-permanent alterations in neuroregulatory feedback mechanisms. Such patients need sealing-over and adroit supportive therapy rather than an uncovering therapy, since the latter will usually (as in the fourth case above) prove too threatening.

The potential for suicide is greater in patients with a depressive temperament or severe endogenous depression, and less worrisome in schizotypals. Chronic negative-symptom schizophrenia is associated with an intermediate, although still substantial, risk of suicide (Stone, Stone, and Hurt 1987).

The anhedonia associated with some cases of moral masochism or mild obsessional neuroses with sexual inhibition usually lifts when the core conflicts are resolved or the inhibitions lifted. Psychoanalysis or psychoanalytically oriented psychotherapy is often effective in these clinical situations. Krystal (1981) makes a similar point in relation to the moral masochist, who, he states, can eventually dispense with pleasure-avoiding defenses once he learns to identify past defensive patterns, explore the underlying fantasies, and develop more adaptive patterns of behavior. The masochist has generally developed strong dependent attachments to persons (usually a parent) who set in motion a pain-dependent relationship or who vehemently interdicted all indulgence in pleasurable (especially sexual) activity (as in the last case above).

Anhedonic patients of all diagnostic categories (but particularly the schizotypal) tend to be exquisitely sensitive to criticism, disappointment, and frustration. Sexual gratification, which often acts as a kind of physiological clearinghouse for petty frustrations, unresolved personal conflicts, and the like, is usually not keen enough or not even available to anhedonics, who are thus left more vulnerable than average people to the negative aspects of life. The more the anhedonia derives from temperament, the less it can be made to evaporate through exploratory psychotherapy. Supportive measures, including environmental manipulation, may be helpful in diminishing the likelihood of criticism, and so on. Patients of this sort, for example, may need a suggestion about the advisability of changing to a low-profile job or of shifting their allegiances to less critical or otherwise intimidating friends, and the like. Chronically hypo-hedonic patients may benefit greatly from education about the advantages of the less intense pleasures they *can* experience in the nonhuman realm (from travel, pets, collecting, music) over the intense pleasures of intimate life, which may remain problematic or beyond their reach.

REFERENCES

Akhtar, S.; Crocker, E.; Dickey, N.; Helfich, J.; and Rheuban, W. J. 1977. Overt sexual behavior among psychiatric inpatients. *Diseases of the Nervous System* 38:359–61.

Andreasen, N. C. 1981. *The Scale for the Assessment of Negative Symptoms* (SANS). Iowa City: University of Iowa Press.

———. 1982. Negative symptoms in schizophrenia. *Archives of General Psychiatry* 39:784–88.

Berardi, A. L., and Garske, J. P. 1977. Effects of sexual arousal on schizophrenia. *Journal of Clinical Psychology* 33:105–9.

Brown, S. L.; Sweeney, D. R.; and Schwartz, G. E. 1979. Differences between self-reported and observed pleasure in depression and schizophrenia. *Journal of Nervous and Mental Disorders* 167:410–15.

Buchsbaum, M. S.; Davis, G. C.; and Van Kammen, D. P. 1980. Diagnostic classification and the endorphin hypothesis of schizophrenia. In *Perspectives in Schizophrenia Research*, ed. C. F. Baxter and T. Melenchuk. New York: Raven Press, 177–94.

Carpenter, W. T., Jr., and Hanlon, T. E. 1986. Clinical practice and the phenomenology of schizophrenia. In *Handbook of Studies on Schizophrenia*, ed. G. D. Burrows, T. R. Norman, and G. Rubinstein. Amsterdam: Elsevier, 123–30.

Chapman, L. J.; Edell, W. S.; and Chapman, J. P. 1980. Physical anhedonia, perceptual aberration and psychosis proneness. *Schizophrenia Bulletin* 6:639–53.

Clark, D. C., and Fawcett, J. 1987. *Anhedonia and Affect Deficit States*. Great Neck, N.Y.: PMA Publishing.

Clark, D. C.; Fawcett, J.; Salazar-Grueso, E.; and Fawcett, E. 1984. Seven-month clinical outcome of anhedonic and normally hedonic depressed inpatients. *American Journal of Psychiatry* 141:1216–20.

Crow, T. J. 1985. Two syndromes in schizophrenia? In *Neurotransmitters in Action*, ed. D. Bousfield. Amsterdam: Elsevier, 279–85.

Edell, W. S., and Chapman, L. J. 1979. Anhedonia, perceptual aberration, and the Rorschach. *Journal of Consulting and Clinical Psychology* 47:377–84.

Fairbairn, W. R. D. 1941. A revised psychopathology of the psychoses and psychoneu-roses. *International Journal of Psychoanalysis* 22:250–79.

Freud, S. 1895. Project for a scientific psychology. *Standard Edition*, 1:283–397.

———. 1911. Notes on a case of paranoia. *Standard Edition*, 12:3–79.

Harrow, M.; Grinker, R. R., Sr.; Holzmann, P. S.; and Kayton, L. 1977. Anhedonia and schizophrenia. *American Journal of Psychiatry* 134:794–97.

Johnstone, E. C. 1986. Schizophrenia: Measurement and assessment. In *Handbook of Studies on Schizophrenia*, ed. G. D. Burrows, T. R. Norman, and G. Rubinstein. Amsterdam: Elsevier, 159–67.

Johnstone, E. C.; Crow, T. J.; Frith, C. D.; Husband, J.; and Kreel, L. 1976. Cerebral ventricular size and cognitive impairment in chronic schizophrenia. *Lancet* 2:924–26.

Klein, D.; Gittelman, R.; Quitkin, F.; and Rifkin, A. 1980. *Diagnosis and Drug Treatment of Psychiatric Disorders: Adults and Children,* 2d ed. Baltimore: Williams and Wilkins.

Knight, R. A.; Roff, J. D.; Barnett, J.; and Moss, J. L. 1979. Concurrent and predictive validity of thought disorder and affectivity: A 22-year follow-up of acute schizophrenics. *Journal of Abnormal Psychology* 88:1–12.

Kolb, L. C. 1987. A neuropsychological hypothesis explaining posttraumatic stress disorders. *American Journal of Psychiatry* 144:989–95.

Kraepelin, E. [1919] 1971. *Dementia Praecox,* trans. R. M. Barclay. Edinburgh: E. S. Livingstone.

———. 1921. *Manic Depressive Insanity and Paranoia.* Edinburgh: E. S. Livingstone.

Krystal, H. 1981. The hedonic element in affectivity. *Annual Review of Psychoanalysis* 9:93–113.

Kulhara, P., and Chadda, R. 1987. A study of negative symptoms in schizophrenia and depression. *Comprehensive Psychiatry* 28:229–35.

Levin, S. 1984. Frontal lobe dysfunctions in schizophrenia-II: Impairments of psychological and brain functions. *Journal of Psychiatric Research* 18:57–72.

Meehl, P. 1962. Schizotaxia, schizotypy, schizophrenia. *American Psychologist* 17:827–38.

Miller, G. A. 1986. Information processing deficits in anhedonia and perceptual aberration: A psychophysiological analysis. *Biological Psychiatry* 21:100–115.

Miller, R. E. 1987. Method to study anhedonia in hospitalized psychiatric patients. *Journal of Abnormal Psychology* 96:41–45.

Radó, S. 1956. *Psychoanalysis of Behavior,* Vol. 1. New York: Grune and Stratton.

Reil, J. C. 1803. *Rhapsodien über die Anwendung der psychischen Curmethode auf Geisteszerrüttungen.* Halle: Curt.

Schmajuk, N. A. 1987. Animal models for schizophrenia: The hippocampally lesioned animal. *Schizophrenia Bulletin* 13:317–27.

Seidman, L. J. 1983. Schizophrenia and brain dysfunction: An integration of recent neurodiagnostic findings. *Psychological Bulletin* 94:195–238.

Simons, R. F. 1982. Physical anhedonia and future psychopathology: An electrocortical continuity? *Psychophysiology* 19:433–41.

Simons, R. F.; MacMillan, F. W.; and Ireland, F. B. 1982. Anticipatory pleasure deficit in subjects reporting physical anhedonia: Slow cortical evidence. *Biological Psychology* 14:297–310.

Snyder, S. H. 1980. Brain peptides as neurotransmitters. *Science* 209:976–83.

Stein, L., and Wise, C. D. 1971. Possible etiology of schizophrenia: Progressive damage to the noradrenergic reward system by 6-hydroxydopamine. *Science* 171:1032–36.

Stone, M. H.; Stone, D. K.; and Hurt, S. W. 1987. Natural history of borderline patients treated by intensive hospitalization. *Psychiatric Clinics North America* 10:185–206.

Wing, J. K. 1980. Social psychiatry in the United Kingdom: The approach to schizophrenia. *Schizophrenia Bulletin* 6:556–65.

Winnicott, D. 1965. *The Maturational Processes and the Facilitating Environment.* New York: International Universities Press.

IV

Aesthetic and Philosophic Inquiries on the Nature of Pleasure

11

Reflections on Psychoanalysis and Aesthetic Pleasure: Looking and Longing

ELLEN HANDLER SPITZ

"a Mosaic glance at the Promised Land of the real"
—Roland Barthes, 1972

We gaze at art, we listen to music, we attend theatrical performances, we read and recite poetry because these experiences give pleasure. Here I shall offer one of many possible psychoanalytic approaches to aesthetic pleasure, focusing particularly on the art of painting. Although for reasons of space I shall not distinguish among the qualities of experience afforded by the different arts,[1] I believe that what is presented here can be ascribed, with variations, to other media. Furthermore, from the perspective I adopt here, efforts to dissect, describe, and classify the pleasure(s) of art fail necessarily to capture its special qualities; they are doomed in the same way and for the same reasons that Monsieur G, prefect of the Paris police and his men, in Edgar Allan Poe's "Purloined Letter," are barred from finding the missing document (we shall return in the end to Monsieur G)—doomed for reasons best expressed by parable.

I shall thus begin by recounting an allegory—a Talmudic story in the somewhat embellished version I recollect from childhood.[2] It concerns the sage Rabbi Joshua ben Hananiah, known and respected for his great wisdom. Rabbi Joshua, as the story goes, was a guest at the palace of the emperor Hadrian, who

In addition to thanking Professor Steven Z. Levine and my colleagues in the Symposium on Art History and Psychoanalysis (College Art Association, Boston, 1987), in which several of these ideas began to take shape, I would like to express my appreciation to Rabbi Jeffrey Sirkman, Professor Priscilla Wald, Julie Klein, and Nathaniel Geoffrey Lew for their bibliographic assistance during the writing of this chapter and to Professor Michael Fried, who gave the final manuscript a generous reading at the NEH Summer on Image and Text (Johns Hopkins University, 1988).

1. For illuminating discussions of these differences, see, e.g., Langer 1953; Goodman 1976.

2. For the source of this tale, see *The Babylonian Talmud*, Tractate Shabbat 119A.

requested him one day to describe how to prepare the Sabbath meal so that the emperor might experience the wondrous tastes and exquisite pleasures he had often observed among the Jews as they ate their Sabbath dinner. At the emperor's command, Rabbi Joshua instructed the royal chefs, explaining in detail how each dish was prepared, describing with care each ingredient and procedure. When, however, the resulting meal was served to the eager emperor, he could discern no difference in taste between these dishes and his ordinary fare. Disappointed, he sent for Rabbi Joshua and, in the rabbi's presence, interrogated his cooks to ascertain whether the instructions had been carried out precisely. Clearly, they had. Nevertheless, unlike the Sabbath Jews, the emperor had experienced no bliss, no desire to sing aloud with each mouthful. Surely, he cried, some *special* spice, some extra substance must have been omitted! The Sabbath food *must* have a special taste, for this was manifest in the expressions of the Jews when they were eating it. Unperturbed, Rabbi Joshua listened to the emperor and smiled. Yes, he responded patiently, there *is* a special taste, a unique spice, if you like, but the recipe cannot be given, for it comes of itself to those who love the Sabbath.

My essay is concerned with just this—that is to say, with a spice or taste for which no recipe can be given and for which no classificatory system composed of the characteristics of objects can account. This is because, as the parable reveals, desire and what I shall call the *pleasure of desire* are located *in the subject.* Not unique to, but exquisitely apposite to, the realm of the aesthetic, this quality of experience, this spice or *pleasurable desire,* is the element I hope to trace in what follows.

Whereas at least some traditional aesthetics[3] is committed to a view of aesthetic pleasure that privileges the apprehensible properties of objects—begins, that is, with an examination of works of art themselves[4]—psychoanalysis locates aesthetic pleasure in the subject and in a dynamic in which the spectator-subject may become object to the aesthetic object qua subject. In other words, the beholder of a painted image, drawn into what Gombrich (1960) has called the "magic circle of creation," may experience himself or herself as being radically determined by, as becoming the object of, the illusory gaze of that image. In a parallel phrase of Roland Barthes: "The text you write must prove to me that it desires me" (1975, 6). I believe, therefore, that one unique contribution of psychoanalysis to a discourse on aesthetic pleasure is to take up a position

3. Exclusions would, of course, have to be made for existential and phenomenological authors.

4. I feel that this is the case even with respect to the work of Suzanne Langer (1953), who, while emphasizing the relationship between viewer and art object, etc., always begins with an examination of the object. In the case of sculpture, for example, she speaks of "virtual space," and of music, "virtual time," categories that have to do with perceptual qualities of the different arts that, as she sees it, *match* certain aspects of human psychic experience as it is mapped under the Kantian categories. She sees the object not as radically structuring the subject but as mirroring it and thus affording a kind of recognition pleasure.

radically other than that offered by those aestheticians whose project it has been to study external objects as if they were identical with the causes of pleasure. Further on, I shall discuss the work of one contemporary aesthetician who has written both on the disjunction between the objects and causes of pleasure and on the possibility of their elision and, in so doing, has provided an aesthetic discourse that complements the psychoanalytic approach I propose here.

The psychoanalytic texts that ground my thesis are Freud's *Interpretation of Dreams* (1900–1901), his works of 1905—*Three Essays on the Theory of Sexuality* and *Jokes and Their Relation to the Unconscious*—and his *Beyond the Pleasure Principle* (1920). Three major precepts can be extracted from these texts. First: An object found is an object refound, and the refinding rather than the intrinsic properties of the found or chosen object is of prime significance. Second: The relations of joke/teller/listener (work of art/artist/spectator) imply a dynamic characterized by subtle reversals, complex alignments, and shifts of position. Third: Subjectivity, born of loss, stages the replicative recovery of its object through links with a symbolic system that radically determines this very subjectivity.

Thus, psychoanalytically speaking, we have in aesthetic experience the staging of a peculiar drama in which the presence of an object intensely engages a subject. The object's presence figures an absence, induces a lack (desire) in the subject which it (the object), in an imaginary way, fulfills. This dynamic can be both reversed and replayed. The subject thus experiences fulfillment and want— a *pleasure in desiring*—which constitutes the special quality of aesthetic experience. Capturing the beholder in this dynamic (which is staged in different ways in all the arts), the painting, for example, offers an imaginary completion to the subject while simultaneously engaging him or her on the symbolic level. It thus provides the conditions for pleasure while keeping desire in play.

Curiously, many anthologies of articles on aesthetics currently in university use omit the topics of "pleasure" and "aesthetic pleasure."[5] Not only are these headings absent, but in many cases the editors have not even bothered to index them. Research into papers published over a six-year period in leading journals shows that one prominent American periodical published only three articles that use "pleasure" in their titles, none of them a contribution that has sparked continuing debate in the literature.[6] This neglect or avoidance of the pleasure of art as a subject for academic discourse itself raises questions and rouses

5. See, e.g., *Aesthetics Today*, ed. M. Philipson and P. J. Gudel (New York: New American Library, 1980); *Philosophy Looks at the Arts*, ed. J. Margolis (Philadelphia: Temple University Press, 1978); and *Art and Philosophy*, ed. W. E. Kennick (New York: St. Martin's Press, 1979). Topics include: Aesthetic Judgment, the Nature of Art, Aesthetic Qualities, Representation in Art, and Style: Form and Content.

6. *Journal of Aesthetics and Art Criticism* (1980–86).

speculation.[7] After all, if art did not provide a measure of delight (if not rapture and desire), there would seem little point in exploring the more rarified aesthetic issues that *are* extensively treated by academic discourse, such as the ontology of art and its representational conventions, communicative possibilities, expressive qualities, and ideological underpinnings.

Because my task here is to play an interdisciplinary role, always precarious and fraught with territorial imperatives, it seems worthwhile to note that, like the daughter of Pharaoh, I have seized an opportunity to rescue (temporarily) a virtually abandoned issue. All but disowned by aestheticians since the eighteenth century, languishing in (con)temporary exile, aesthetic pleasure moans for recognition and embrace (even if not psychoanalytic embrace) and for adoption. It thus seems legitimate if not actually helpful to pursue my course in spite of the risks—to attempt to blend, gently, notions of aesthetic pleasure with a psychoanalytic perspective on desire.

One notable exception, however, to the rule of philosophers' neglect deserves more than cursory mention: an elegant and comprehensive work on aesthetics by Mary Mothersill (1984) that treats pleasure at length.[8] Her view forms a compelling complement to the psychoanalytic perspective I develop here.

Mothersill reinstates the notion of pleasure in aesthetic discourse by asking whether aesthetics as a philosophical discipline can lay claim to any primitive questions. She poses this query in the course of an attempt to counter the charge of fellow philosopher Stuart Hampshire (1952) that aesthetics is devoid of such questions and hence lacks a basic subject matter. Questions may be considered primitive with respect to a theory, Mothersill explains, when, first, they can be asked by and are of interest to persons who are naive about the theory and can therefore be put in terms that do not involve the theory, and when, second, the theory yields consequences that delimit the range of acceptable answers. Examples include: "Why is the sky blue?" (primitive for optics) and "What would be the right, the reasonable, thing to do?" (primitive for ethics). In her effort to find a comparable question for aesthetics, Mothersill turns to pleasure: "Why does this work of art please me?" she asks. Immediately, however, she identifies a problem with this question—namely, that it may all too easily generate answers that make it sound like a primitive question not for aesthetics but for psychology. The difficulty of finding answers that either fail to go beyond the personal and

7. Richard Howard, in his introduction to Barthes's *Pleasure of the Text* (1975), makes the point that, unlike French culture, American culture tends to consider pleasure as a state that is unspeakable, beyond words. The fear seems to be, as he puts it, that "what can be said is taken—is likely—to be no longer experienced, certainly no longer enjoyed" (vi). Howard contrasts this position with that of the French, who have "a vocabulary of erotism, an amorous discourse which smells neither of the laboratory nor of the sewer" (v) and which allows them to speak of pleasure without necessarily being either coarse or clinical.

8. It is important to say that Mothersill (1984) offers an analysis of the concept of beauty and is not restricted to a discussion of beauty as it is found in works of art. Mothersill holds the view that whereas twentieth-century aesthetics has been restricted largely to the philosophy of art, the problems of beauty and aesthetic pleasure ought not to be so delimited.

subjective or exclude them leads her to a discussion of pleasure centered around philosophical psychology. At the risk of oversimplification, one might read her argument as an erudite and at times supremely witty effort to save this particular primitive question for aesthetics and, implicitly, to wrest it from the imperialistic purview of psychology—to show, among other things, that properties inhering in objects may and do legitimately count as a source of aesthetic pleasure. She supplies, as an important, even central, step in her argument, a definition of aesthetic properties based on indistinguishability: "The aesthetic properties of an individual O are those that define the class of items which, for a particular subject, S, under standard conditions, etc., are indistinguishable from O" (1984, 364). This definition foregrounds the particularity of objects while implying (as well as granting) a significant subjective element—*indistinguishable* being an adjective derived from the verb *to distinguish*, which presupposes a subject. In other words, the statement defines a situation wherein a subject ascribes his or her pleasure to properties of a work of art that, by the indistinguishability clause, cannot be transferred or generalized—the object itself is thus privileged, and the possibility of deriving general laws or rules of taste from pleasure is obviated.

To cover for cases in which the subject attributes personal pleasure to the aesthetic qualities of a work but is mistaken, Mothersill adds to the first definition a second as follows: "Someone finds an individual [work of art] beautiful if and only if the individual pleases him and he believes that it pleases him in virtue of its aesthetic properties *and his belief is true*" (347, emphasis added). Here, drawing on the distinction between belief and knowledge, Mothersill adds a strong objective element to her first definition. The role assigned to the object in the experience of pleasure is fortified. Her third definition, which binds the first two, states: "Any individual [work of art] is beautiful if and only if it is such as to be a cause of pleasure in virtue of its aesthetic properties" (347).

The thrust of her effort is to seek a solution to the double bind articulated by Kant ([1790] 1978) in the so-called antinomy of taste.[9] Kant here poses as a problem the juxtaposition of two theses that appear mutually contradictory but true. These are: that although judgments of taste are genuine (O is pleasing to S), they are not based upon concepts, for if they were they would be open to dispute (which, clearly, they are not: *de gustibus non disputandum est*). Surely, however, the opposite is also true: namely, judgments of taste *are* based on concepts, for if they were not there would be no place for contention, not even for claims to the necessary agreement of others with a particular judgment.

9. See Kant [1790] 1978, 206. The following passage, which occurs much earlier in the text, is also helpful: "There can . . . be no rule according to which any one is to be compelled to recognize anything as beautiful. Whether a dress, a house, or a flower is beautiful is a matter upon which one declines to allow one's judgement to be swayed by any reasons or principles. We want to get a look at the Object with our own eyes, just as if our delight depended on sensation. And yet, if upon so doing, we call the object beautiful, we believe ourselves to be speaking with a universal voice, and lay claim to the concurrence of every one, whereas no private sensation would be decisive except for the observer alone and *his* liking" (56).

In addressing this problem, Mothersill works out her ideas in part by elaborating on a text of Aquinas, the famous "*'Pulchrum dicatur id cujus apprehensio ipsa placet'*—'Let us call that beautiful of which the apprehension in itself pleases'" (quoted in Mothersill 1984, 323). This dictum corresponds roughly to her third definition. She is thus deeply concerned with an aesthetic that can offer compelling reasons for the position that, in her words, some judgments of taste are genuine, that pleasure is, albeit with important caveats, caused by the aesthetic properties of the works perceived—and *perceived* means, importantly, that subjectivity is not omitted.

To define this position more clearly, Mothersill addresses problems introduced by theorists who have sought to separate the objects of pleasure from its causes. For example, we might imagine a beholder who, while attending the Miró retrospective at the Guggenheim Museum, experienced particular pleasure while gazing at the *Portrait of Mrs. Mills in 1750 (After Constable)*. Taking it as the object and cause of her pleasure, she failed to remember that the last time she saw the painting, she was in the company of her now deceased mother. An analogous philosophical/psychological issue can be extracted from the following three sentences in Freud: "[Dora] remained *two hours* in front of the Sistine Madonna, rapt in silent admiration. When I asked her what had pleased her so much about the picture she could find no clear answer to make. At last she said: 'The Madonna'" (1905a, 116).

Some theorists would argue that the object of pleasure (the painting) is noncontingently related to the subject's pleasure, in that she *heeds* the painting and it is the *target* of her gaze. The cause of her pleasure, however, is only contingently related to that pleasure in that it may or may not be (consciously) available to her. Mothersill gives her own example, as follows: "The object of his pleasure might be what he perceives to be a compliment or joke; the cause might involve physiological factors such as his reaction to the vodka he had been absent-mindedly sipping" (1984, 280). A related, slightly different, example might be introduced: an opera buff who states that although he adores *Traviata*, he regularly weeps at Violetta's death *because* it reminds him of his young wife's death years ago from cancer. At stake here, psychoanalytically speaking, is the issue of granting subjective status to unconscious trends (as in notions of the split subject, divided self, and others).

Mothersill herself, for completely nonpsychoanalytic reasons, rejects a dualistic view that would separate objects from causes of pleasure. She points to the subjective element in the notion of "object of pleasure." This phrase is, as she puts it, "an ellipsis that allows us to speak of the cause of someone's pleasure *as it appears to him, relative to his beliefs, attitudes*, etc." (283, emphasis added). In a cogent discussion she points out that objects of pleasure are not only not equivalent to ordinary objects but in fact serve only the minimal function of being referents for such phrases as "what S saw."

Her staunch refusal to bypass, deny, or eliminate subjectivity as an essential element in aesthetic pleasure situates her discourse closer to the psychoanalytic than that of many predecessors.[10] This position is implied by her rejection of a dualistic theory of pleasure that entails two logically independent entities: namely, an object specified by a subject, and a causal hypothesis requiring evidential support. About such a theory she says: "Thus we have an island of Cartesian certainty in a sea of complex, contingent, psychological fact" (287). Her preference, as I read her, is for a theory that inscribes the subjective/ objective disjunction so that each position is implicated in the other.

Mothersill's work stands as a unique effort in contemporary aesthetics to grapple with the issue of pleasure in art.[11] In the course of her announced project, to clarify what we mean when we call an object beautiful, she addresses what she calls "the cloudy issues" surrounding the relation of "subjective" to "objective" (347). Her work models an attempt to thread through a maze of seemingly unavoidable intellectual inconsistencies rather than either accept them as inevitable or collapse one set of terms into another. In so striving, she addresses, by implication, the fundamental dichotomy of mind and body that lies at the heart of the issue of pleasure.

Psychoanalysis, by contrast, problematizes the status of objects in a radical way. It poses the question of aesthetic pleasure from the shifting positions of subject and signifier (rather than of perceptual object) and may even conceive of the aesthetic object dialectically as subject.

In deriving aesthetic pleasure from sexuality, Freud postulates a set of stratagems for channeling energy and substituting both aims and objects. Yet the cherished psychoanalytic theory of sublimation is riddled with paradox. As Bersani (1986) has pointed out, sublimation is described as a psychic maneuver that not only denies (bypasses) and transcends sexuality but at the same time appropriates, extends, and elaborates it—is, thus, coextensive with desire. In formulating this theory and introducing, *pari passu,* the notion of displacement, Freud implicitly holds, contra aesthetics, that to ascribe intrinsic attractiveness to an object (sexual in the first instance, but by contiguity or displacement, metonymy or metaphor, aesthetic) is to commit a fundamental conceptual error[12]

10. I realize that it would be possible to counterargue that the theory which severs objects of pleasure from its causes is actually closer to psychoanalysis in that it mirrors the radical psychic split between what Freud called id and ego. The position I take here, however, is based on the notion of split subjectivity and/or a divided self.

11. See n. 8, above. Although aspects of Mothersill's discussion are here applied to aesthetic pleasure in the context particularly of visual art, the scope of her work is broader.

12. That Freud himself was not immune to such "errors" has been explored with increasing frequency in the literature; see M. Balmary (1979), J. Masson (1984), L. Bersani (1986), and A. I. Davidson (1987). For, though he consistently reintroduces in his clinical, applied, and technical as well as theoretical papers the pivotal notion of the variability and inconstancy of the object, Freud almost as consistently undercuts his own conceptual innovation—"clearly reluctant," as Bersani puts it, "to accept the psychic and social consequences of the sexual and ontological floating which he describes" (1986, 45). These hesitations on Freud's part, especially those in Part I of *Three Essays,* where the problem of the object is posed relative to the sexual perversions, are laid out in detail and analyzed from a slightly different but also Foucaultian perspective in a fine essay by Davidson (1987).

(like adherence to a seduction theory)—since what is supremely important about finding any object is that, in fact, this object has been refound.[13]

In addition to the problematic status of the object, the nature of pleasure eludes Freud. Puzzling over the enigmas of forepleasure, endpleasure, and unpleasure, and the increase, decrease, and surcease of sexual tension, he opines not only that "psychology is still so much in the dark in questions of pleasure and unpleasure that the most cautious assumption is the one most to be commended" (1905c, 49) but that "everything relating to the problem of pleasure and unpleasure touches upon one of the sorest spots of present-day psychology" (1905c, 75). Out of such gestures of despair, however—out of the position of not knowing (of lack)—fascinating new questions are born.

In Part III of *Three Essays*, for example, the roles played by forepleasure and endpleasure suggest analogies with visual and plastic as opposed to performing and literary arts. In the latter, fixed temporal dimensions may be seen as entailing a pleasure that comes to a specific end or climax, a moment of satisfaction— for which each art provides a convention, a physical counterpart to the psychological process: a curtain falling, a conductor turning, a book closing. In the visual arts, by contrast, as in sexual pleasures that do not result in discharge, there is no definite limit to the experience—no particular duration of time one must linger before the painting or sculpture, no expectable conventions to structure or release the tension built up in the spectator. One remembers Dora's "*two hours*" in the Dresden Gemäldegalerie before the Raphael.

What happens in these stretched (or compressed) moments before a painted image? Is there any danger here analogous to the danger Freud perceives in the forepleasure? Freud speaks about lingering over such moments of pleasure as dangerous in that they may become an end in themselves, thus a perversion; they may perhaps become what Yeats describes in the lines: "players and painted stage took all my love, / And not those things that they were emblems of" ("The Circus Animals' Desertion"). Yet countervailing forces are provided by the presence of spatial, as opposed to temporal, structure, by the limits of various framing devices, as well as by the powerful presence of verbal texts (labels) that tame the perilous image and stem the tide of its regressive pull.

Psychoanalysis, I propose, offers an account of aesthetic pleasure that acknowledges risk and incorporates danger. The long look at any artistic image poses an implicit question as to why the spectator is *moved* or *held* thus to linger. Seeing, our metaphor par excellence for knowing, is shown to be riddled with desire. Thus, the long(ing) look of aesthetic contemplation is demarcated from rapid, focused, teleological perception dictated by need. The two verbs chosen for the subtitle of this chapter inscribe both the active and the passive elements inherent in these moments. The work of art—neither an object appropriate for the satisfaction of instinctual drive, nor an object merely redolent and evocative

13. The famous statement is made by Freud at the end of the first paragraph under "[5] The Finding of an Object" in "Section III: The Transformations of Puberty." See Bersani 1986, 30–40.

of desire, nor "a mere thing" (see Heidegger 1971)—comes into being at the intersection of the reflex arc of (sexual/scoptophilic) satisfaction; attenuated experience marked by frustration, delay, and disguise; and the values, expectations, and beliefs imposed by a culture. This triple registration of the work of art in the realms of the real, the imaginary, and the symbolic is exquisitely encoded in the paintings of René Magritte, who plays simultaneously with images and words. Long looks at his seductively enigmatic works have contributed incalculably to the thesis of this chapter.

But in such cases, surely art informs psychoanalysis as well as the other way around. Perhaps art teaches psychoanalysis something about the dynamics of desire. In a recent paper, Bernstein (1987) extends and elaborates Freud's account of the relations of joke/artist, object/painting, and secondary object/ (listener/spectator) to analyze several paintings of Edouard Manet, among them *Olympia* (figure 11.1). She demonstrates that Manet constructs similar but even more subtle and labile structures of relation. These both parallel and reverse the paradigm of the joke so that (in part) what was originally meant to be the exposure of the object (in *Olympia*, the image of the nude woman) is reversed into the exposure of the would-be subject (the beholder of the painting) as object of the gaze of the intended object now turned subject.

In Bernstein's analysis, the riveting gaze of *Olympia* marks out a privileged place for an absent spectator that each beholder is lured to fill. Olympia's carefully posed nudity, accentuated by the barest traces of dress and her dramatized display, are calculated to arouse in each (male) beholder the desire to fill this place—the place of her desire. Yet, as Bernstein intimates, that dyadic relation is complicated by a triadic resonance—the implicit imminent approach of a rival, another admirer, signaled by the bouquet held in the servant's arms. The beholder is thus confronted by an invisible double—who, we may imagine, waits to emerge from behind the curtain. Meeting Olympia's gaze, the beholder reexperiences her allure and seduction as transformed now into frozen unavailability. Invitation becomes rejection (what the upper half of the body promises, the lower half refuses; what the right hand offers, the left revokes). The beholder gradually becomes aware of himself as merely an infinitely replaceable object of Olympia's gaze. Brought face to face with his own lack, he circles again, trying to close the gap between himself and the painted image.

In this dynamic, the painted image serves a mirroring function, reflecting to the beholder his own gaze; compelled to behold himself beholding and struggling to avoid a confrontation with his own self-alienation, he is both *moved* and *held*—spellbound, bewitched—by the painting. The ambiguous collusion of joke teller/artist with listener/spectator has thus shifted toward a new (but equally ambiguous) collusion between spectator and painted image—a collusion that circles back into a version of the earlier configuration. Thus, the painting radically (re)constitutes its subject. As Barthes has put it: "The text is a fetish object, and *this fetish desires me*. The text chooses me" (1975, 27).

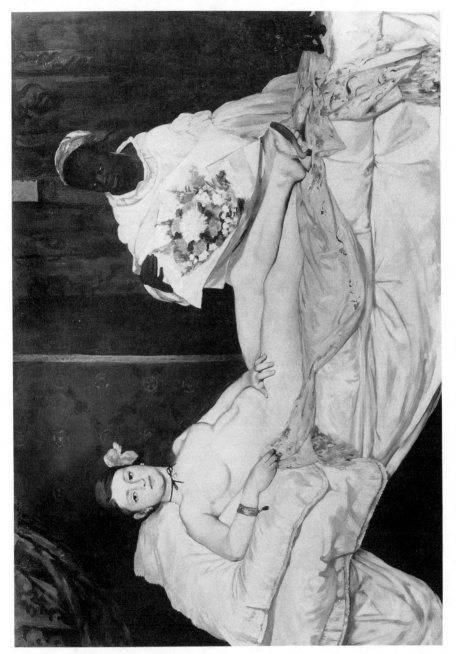

Figure 11.1 Edouard Manet, *Olympia*, 1863. Courtesy of Giraudon/Art Resource, New York

Bernstein's analysis of the subtle interactions among the terms of image, artist, and beholder is applicable, in my view, well beyond *Olympia* and the oeuvre of Manet. The invisible circling relations of desire bespeak a psychoanalytic approach to imagery in general. And, with respect to the original Freudian text upon which the interpretation rests, I would suggest that these sliding, eliding cross-identifications that compel interminable deferrals of satisfaction illuminate something about the artfulness of art as distinguished from the craft of joke—a distinction Freud made little effort to clarify. Bernstein's work offers clues as to why (at least for adults) even the best joke is good for only a couple of retellings, whereas the *Olympia* exerts a lasting fascination.

A similar dynamic is activated by Magritte's painting *Le Mois des vendanges* (1959). Multiple bowler-hatted men stare in through an open window. Paradoxically, although they look inside the window, their gaze is simultaneously directed out, at the spectator, thus drawing us into the space of the image. As is usual for Magritte, the title is crucial: "The Month of the Harvest." Harvest brings food (grapes)—that which is eaten or drunk—and, typically, Magritte here introduces a characteristic substitutive metaphor, suggesting a harvest for the *eyes* rather than the *mouth*—a harvest that can never truly nourish—an awareness both signified and suppressed by the multiplicity of eyes depicted.

In a similar way, Caravaggio's paradigmatic rendering of Medusa (figure 11.2) both evokes and denies castration by its multiple snakes and brilliantly figures the splitting of consciousness by conflating subject and object. Medusa, the sight of whose snakelike hair turns men to stone, is portrayed on the surface of a mirrorlike shield and given a visage that itself expresses the horror of her victim. As the destroyer bleeds, sadism and masochism are, with the snakes, entangled.

Magritte's painting also conflates the aims of looking, of voyeurism, with those of exhibitionism. Like the spectator of the picture, the bowler-hatted men, personae of the artist, are simultaneously seeing and being seen while remaining anonymous. The painting captures that moment when we suddenly realize that we are not only subjects but objects for the consciousness of others—who are also not merely the objects of our gaze but subjects in their own right. In this way, the image exploits the uncanny—the repressed returns as beholders reexperience before it the enforced splitting of their own subjectivity and behold themselves beholding the painting—much as, on occasion, we realize that we are dreaming.

In like manner, Fried's (1978, 1987, 1988) work on Gustave Courbet relies on the psychoanalytic text but also raises questions about the dichotomies it embodies. Fried interprets masculinity and femininity as merging in Courbet's images in ways that follow from, elaborate, and problematize some of the standard oppositions (as activity/passivity) associated with gender. Obliged to reconsider these terms in the light of imagery that probes and blends them, we are warned against colluding in any interpretive exercise that would transfix a reality more fluid than what they can represent. Fried features the bisexuality

Figure 11.2 Caravaggio, *Head of Medusa*, c. 1600–1601. Courtesy of Alinari/Art Resource, New York

of Courbet's imagery—its merging not only generally of the sex of the beholder with that of the beheld, but specifically in this case of the male painter-beholder with the female sitter-beheld—and, especially, Courbet's sensual replications and displacements of the physical act of painting. Fried sees this act as an intense bodily experience that figures ubiquitously in the artist's imagery. In what he has called "fantasmatic conflations," phallus, brush, and distaff are evoked together (see figure 11.3, *The Sleeping Spinner*, 1853), sword and blood may figure brush and pigment (as in *The Wounded Man*, 1844–54), and in other images, a flowering branch and a woman's hair are linked to both the phallus and the painter's brush.

Like Bernstein, Fried goes far beyond the specific paintings he addresses to adumbrate deeply disturbing and pleasurable and disturbingly pleasurable qualities of painted images per se and to highlight their fundamental incommensurability with (any) words. His sexual readings of Courbet reveal the ways in which images both transfix and unsettle the equilibrium of the beholder, induce pleasure with anxiety, destabilize the preconditions for maintenance of control, and set in motion a lability that words cannot arrest.

Against the critique that psychoanalysis ignores the artfulness of art, that it honors the totality of works only in the breach by digging for more than surface coherence (Meltzer 1987), I have tried to demonstrate that, at least from the point of view presented here, it is not just superior wholeness or complexity of organization that distinguishes the art object but, paradoxically, its structured inducing of an experience of lack—lack that compels the long(ing) look we identify with the aesthetic. And the task of psychoanalytic critics is in part to reveal the artfulness required in creating the very absence that awakens desire.

The difference between Marcel Duchamp's bicycle wheel (*Ready-made*, 1913) and the one in my garage, the difference between Jeff Koons's Hoover vacuum cleaner (*New Hoover Dimension 1000*, 1986) and the one in any department store, is, psychoanalytically speaking, that whereas one object signifies—attracts, frustrates, compels a search—the other, if and when it becomes focal, does so because it directly satisfies a practical need.

I now return, as promised, to Monsieur G, prefect of the Paris police, and close, for symmetry's sake, with another parable, actually another reading of a reading: an interpretation of Poe's "Purloined Letter," a text that illuminates with exquisite clarity the different way of looking implied by the aesthetic I have tried to convey.[14] My objective is not to interpret the story generally but to consider it from just this vantage point.

You will recall that a letter of great (though unspecified) value is *found missing*. That we never discover its contents or the identity of its sender constitutes one of the greatest sources of (pleasurable) frustration for the reader. If

14. The thematic reading that follows is based on J. Lacan's "Seminar on 'The Purloined Letter.'"

Figure 11.3 Gustave Courbet, *The Sleeping Spinner*, 1853. Courtesy of Giraudon/Art Resource, New York

the story is taken as a parable for psychoanalysis, this fact indicates that its objective is not to unmask a hidden content—a notion that does, however, animate certain misapplications of psychoanalysis to art.

The narrative of the story, carried, interestingly, via conversations among the narrator, his friend Dupin, and Monsieur G, concerns the vicissitudes of the search for this letter, stolen apparently by a certain Minister D from the "Queen." As the search proves increasingly fruitless, the letter increases in importance and value—a metaphor for desire. Many wonderful and ingenious replications have been noted by other critics,[15] but I shall stress only the different modes of *looking* figured in the story.

Monsieur G, the realist, describes his search as follows: He and his squad search the entire building from which the letter was presumably purloined. They examine all the furniture; they open every drawer (including "secret drawers"). They probe the cushions with fine needles. They remove the tops of tables. They excavate the rungs of every chair, the joinings of every piece of furniture. They dismantle the mirrors and test the beds, linens, curtains, carpets. Finding nothing, they finally divide the entire surface into numbered compartments and scrutinize every square inch with the aid of a powerful microscope. And so it goes, even to the point of opening every book. Not content with a shake, they turn over every leaf in each volume, probing the bindings with needles. All efforts prove fruitless.

Dupin, however, finds the letter, by employing a completely different method. He discovers it soiled, crumpled, and placed carelessly in a card rack among some visiting cards. It has been turned inside out, its edges frayed. In what can be taken as a metaphor for the critical/analytical enterprise, upon finding it he replaces it with a facsimile. In just such a manner, Minister D had earlier replaced the original with a facsimile when he had perceived its significance and had stolen it from the queen. Dupin, asked by Poe's narrator why he bothered to replace the letter with a duplicate, replies that by so doing he will assure that D, who has the original no longer, will nevertheless proceed as though he did—that he will be duped by the facsimile into continuing his previous (and apparently, ruinous) course of action, the precise nature of which is never made known to the reader.

Instead of describing his method of finding the letter, Dupin draws an analogy (a tactic that I of course replicate): "'There is a game of puzzles . . . which is played upon a map. One party playing requires another to find a given word—the name of a town, river, state, or empire—any word, in short, upon the motley and perplexed surface of the chart. A novice in the game generally seeks to embarrass his opponents by giving them the most minutely lettered names; but the adept selects such words as stretch, in large characters, from one end of the chart to the other. These, like the overlargely lettered signs and

15. In addition to Lacan's analysis, I am indebted to commentaries by J. Mehlman (1980), J. Derrida (1975), B. Johnson (1977), N. Holland (1980), E. Wright (1984), and J. P. Muller and W. J. Richardson (1988).

placards of the street, escape observation by dint of being excessively obvious.'"
Dupin goes on to point out that *visual oversight* here is a precise counterpart of
that inapprehension which causes the mind to bypass unnoticed those considerations that are too obtrusively and palpably self-evident.

A *different mode of looking* is intimated. The painstaking researches of the
police fail to get at, fail to represent, the essentials of our experience (fail to
find the letter). This must continue unless and until these researches can be
reconnected with a signifying chain of linked meanings that will bind all the
events, orient them, and relate them to the letter perceived not as a "thing,"
not as a piece of paper that fits a certain fixed description, but as a *significant
object of desire*. Desire, which cannot be expressed openly because of the inevitable gap between the body and culture, between the thing and any representation of that thing, is subject to multiple disguises and subterfuges. Unless this
purloined letter is perceived as a symbol or signifier, it will be missed, passed
over; it will not be seen. To put it another way, some *thing* will be perceived
and we can assume *was* perceived by the police, but *its significance will not be
perceived* (just as, although Hadrian *ate* the Sabbath spice, he could not *taste* it).
Psychoanalysis has to do with perceiving significances—with restoring links to
chains of meaning.

Dupin describes the letter he finds as greatly altered in appearance: "To be
sure, it was, to all appearance, radically different from the one of which the
Prefect has read us so minute a description." So the shift involves looking with
an awareness of the *mechanisms of disguise*—mechanisms Freud detailed in *The
Interpretation of Dreams*. Enactment and repetition are also crucial issues. Dupin
does not merely see but actually replicates the ruse of disguise upon Minister
D that the minister had practiced on the queen. The interpreter thus partakes
in the action.

The shift I wish to highlight with this allegory involves perceiving that what
we take to be hidden or lost is always *really* there. The psychoanalytic project
is to restore to the object its significance or, in other words, to recognize it *as
a signifier*. Visible all along, it is not perceived because it is disguised by displacement (it was in the most obvious place, the card rack, where it was expected
not to be found, and therefore was not in its place). Other mechanisms operate,
too, as we have seen—for example, reversal: the letter is turned inside out. To
the police, therefore, it is rendered invisible. The letter, furthermore, has no
intrinsic meaning. Meanings are conferred on it by its location in a context, by
its place—both in the sense that its presence evokes an absence (it is not what
it seems) and in the sense that its invisibility, its disappearance, indicates merely
that it is out of place.

Psychoanalysis is equally concerned with tracing the signifier back to the
body and back to the earliest human relationships in which one's body and that
of the other are not differentiated. The longing looks evoked by works of art
are in part a response to the ambiguous lure of an image that promises a fantasy

of narcissistic completion but terrifies by its regressive pull to a place where the law no longer holds sway.

I think here of Exodus 20:4, which has profound and insufficiently explored meaning both for the aesthetics of the visual arts and for psychoanalysis. The Second Commandment of the Mosaic Law bespeaks our latent terror of the image, labile and alluring, devalued as a mute and inferior sign,[16] but harboring secrets, temptations, and forbidden pleasures. Necessary to object and image is the word. Necessary to perception is culture. As the Talmudic legend teaches, the Sabbath spice can be tasted only by those who observe the law. But perhaps to love a work of art is rather more to stand like Moses on Mount Nebo—gazing into the promised land of Judah.

REFERENCES

The Babylonian Talmud, Tractate Shabbat 119A.

Balmary, M. 1979. *Psychoanalyzing Psychoanalysis: Freud and the Hidden Fault of the Father.* Trans. N. Lukacher. Baltimore: Johns Hopkins University Press.

Barthes, R. 1975. *The Pleasure of the Text.* Trans. R. Miller. New York: Hill and Wang.

———. 1982. *A Barthes Reader.* Ed. S. Sontag. New York: Hill and Wang.

Bernstein, J. W. 1987. "Enframing the Gaze: A Psychoanalytic Exploration of Edouard Manet's Works." Paper presented at the Art History and Psychoanalysis Symposium, College Art Association, Boston, February 14, 1987.

Bersani, L. 1986. *The Freudian Body: Psychoanalysis and Art.* New York: Columbia University Press, 1986.

Davidson, A. I. 1987. "How to Do the History of Psychoanalysis: A Reading of Freud's *Three Essays on the Theory of Sexuality.*" *Critical Inquiry* 13(2): 252–77.

Derrida, J. 1975. "The Purveyor of Truth." *Yale French Studies* 52: 31–114.

Felman, S., ed. 1982. *Literature and Psychoanalysis: The Question of Reading: Otherwise.* Baltimore: Johns Hopkins University Press.

Freud, S. 1900. *The Interpretation of Dreams. Standard edition,* 4, 5.

———. 1905a. "Fragment of an Analysis of a Case of Hysteria." *Standard edition,* 7:7–122.

———. 1905b. *Jokes and Their Relation to the Unconscious. Standard edition,* 8.

———. 1905c. *Three Essays on the Theory of Sexuality. Standard edition,* 7:125–243.

———. 1920. *Beyond the Pleasure Principle. Standard edition,* 18:3–64.

Fried, M. 1978. "The Beholder in Courbet: His Early Self-Portraits and Their Place in His Art." *Glyph* 4 (Baltimore: Johns Hopkins Textual Studies), 85–129.

———. 1987. "Courbet's Femininity." Paper presented at the Art History and Psychoanalysis Symposium, College Art Association, Boston, February 14.

———. 1988. "Courbet's 'Femininity.'" In *Courbet Reconsidered,* ed. Sarah Faunce and Linda Nochlin. Brooklyn, N.Y.: Brooklyn Museum, 43–53.

Gombrich, E. H. 1960. *Art and Illusion.* Princeton: Princeton University Press.

Goodman, N. 1976. *Languages of Art.* Indianapolis: Hackett.

---

16. For illuminating studies of the relations between images and words, see W. J. T. Mitchell (1978, 1986); see also E. H. Spitz (1988).

Hampshire, S. 1952. "Logic and Appreciation." In *Art and Philosophy*, ed. W. E. Kennick. New York: St. Martin's Press, 1979, 651–57.

Heidegger, M. 1971. *Poetry, Language, Thought*. Trans. A. Hofstadter. New York: Harper and Row.

Holland, N. 1980. "Re-Covering 'The Purloined Letter': Reading as a Personal Transaction." In *The Reader in the Text*, ed. S. R. Suleiman and I. Crossman. Princeton: Princeton University Press.

Johnson, B. 1977. "The Frame of Reference: Poe, Lacan, Derrida." *Yale French Studies* 55–56: 457–505.

Kant, I. [1790] 1978. *The Critique of Judgement*. Trans. J. C. Meredith. Oxford: Clarendon Press.

Lacan, J. 1980. "Seminar on 'The Purloined Letter.'" In *Aesthetics Today*, ed. M. Philipson and P. J. Gudel. New York: New American Library, 382–412.

Langer, S. 1953. *Feeling and Form: A Theory of Art*. New York: Charles Scribner's Sons.

Masson, J. 1984. *The Assault on Truth: Freud's Suppression of the Seduction Theory*. New York: Farrar, Straus, and Giroux.

Mehlman, J. 1980. "Poe Pourri: Lacan's Purloined Letter." In *Aesthetics Today*, ed. M. Philipson and P. J. Gudel. New York: New American Library, 413–33.

Meltzer, F. 1987. "Editor's Introduction: Partitive Plays, Pipe Dreams." In *The Trial(s) of Psychoanalysis*. *Critical Inquiry* 13(2): 215–21.

Mitchell, W. J. T. 1978. *Blake's Composite Art: A Study of the Illuminated Poetry*. Princeton: Princeton University Press.

———. 1986. *Iconology: Image, Text, Ideology*. Chicago: University of Chicago Press.

Mothersill, M. 1984. *Beauty Restored*. Oxford: Clarendon Press.

Muller, J. P., and W. J. Richardson, eds. 1988. *The Purloined Poe: Lacan, Derrida, and Psychoanalytic Reading*. Baltimore: Johns Hopkins University Press.

Poe, E. A. 1956. "The Purloined Letter." In *Great Tales and Poems of Edgar Allan Poe*. New York: Pocket Library, 199–219.

Spitz, E. H. 1988. "The Artistic Image and the Inward Gaze: Toward a Merging of Perspectives." *Psychoanalytic Review* 75:111–28.

Wright, E. 1984. *Psychoanalytic Criticism: Theory in Practice*. London and New York: Methuen.

Yeats, W. B. 1960. *The Complete Poems of William Butler Yeats*. New York: Macmillan.

12

The Subdominance of the
Pleasure Principle

EDWARD S. CASEY

It remains a question of the highest theoretical importance, and one that has not yet been answered, when and how it is ever possible for the pleasure principle to be overcome.
—Freud, *An Outline of Psychoanalysis*

The genuine mystery lies in that surface into which the nerve-activity projects forms as pleasure and pain.
—Nietzsche, *The Philosopher*

It is tempting to regard Freud's *Beyond the Pleasure Principle* as an epitome of audacity and dogmatism. It is easy to presume that in this 1920 article (SE, 18) Freud indulges in speculations that are at once empirically unwarranted and intellectually irresponsible. In this skeptical vein, the death instinct is a natural target of doubt or opprobrium. More than a mere hypothesis, it seems to be set forth in a spirit of an assertoric polemic—much as Freud had earlier proclaimed the exceptionless reign of the pleasure principle. Disciplined readers (including many of Freud's otherwise faithful adherents) have concluded that the pleasure principle itself has been here replaced by a mere article of faith—one that is most implausible and highly unlikely.

But is this really the case? Is Freud in *Beyond the Pleasure Principle* as sheerly dogmatic as his critics have claimed? Might there be another way of reading this controversial text that is less dismissive? I believe that there is and that Freud himself provides the clues to this new reading—clues, however, that are sometimes concealed within the text itself.

In considering Freud's metapsychological essay in a different light, I shall not appeal to clinical practice as such or to any empirical or experimental findings. Instead, I will focus on the presentation of the text itself in its extant published form. To this form I will apply a species of what is currently termed "deconstruction," understood as an effort to show how a given text ends by

239

undermining itself. In Freud's case, a deconstructive (or, as it can also be called, an *auto-deconstructive*) reading will illustrate how *Beyond the Pleasure Principle* undoes its own dogmatic point of departure in a set of self-qualifying and self-questioning moves—some of which are expressly set forth by Freud, but some of which become apparent only upon close scrutiny.

Going Back Before

We need to notice first of all that Freud's title, *Beyond the Pleasure Principle*, is distinctly misleading. It is as misleading as Nietzsche's *Beyond Good and Evil*. Neither Nietzsche nor Freud goes *beyond* his respective subject matter; neither thinker enters fully into the far side of morality or pleasure, into its *jenseits*, its "other side." Each is engaged in his subject matter in such a way as to go *back* of it rather than beyond it: back to its genealogical or instinctual roots. We could also say that each seeks to position himself decidedly *before* his topic of concern. For it is only when one manages to stand before what one is writing about, gaining an advance position, that one is in a position to master it. This is especially true of the topics treated by Freud and Nietzsche. The very power, in fact the domination, of pleasure and morality in our lives leads both thinkers to moves of counterdomination. They go back before the austerity of morality or the lure of pleasure, not just to gain a privileged view; they also wish to attain a position of new power from which they can subvert the reigning principle.

It is striking that Freud speaks precisely of the "dominance of the pleasure principle in mental life" in the fourth paragraph of the opening section of *Beyond the Pleasure Principle*. *Dominance* is Strachey's translation of *Herrschaft*, which also connotes control, authority, command, and mastery (*herrschen* means to be master of, to dominate, to rule). It is an issue, from the very beginning of Freud's text, of the literally *pre*dominant position of pleasure, of its always already having mastered us. That Freud attempts in the very next paragraph to qualify this masterful dominance by claiming that "there exists in the mind a strong *tendency* towards the pleasure principle"[1] does not alter his basic perception of pleasure's authority. Late in the text, he adopts the compromise term "dominating tendency" (55) to describe the constancy principle, adding "a tendency which finds expression in the pleasure principle" (56). But as the pleasure principle itself preceded the constancy principle—"the latter principle was inferred from the facts which forced us to adopt the pleasure principle" (9)—it follows that pleasure is indeed the dominating force in our minds. (And in our lives as a whole: a later text will stipulate that "the pleasure principle [is] the watchman over our life rather than merely over our mental life."[2])

---

1. Sigmund Freud, *Beyond the Pleasure Principle*, SE [1955], 18:9, emphasis in original.
2. "The Economic Problem of Masochism," SE, 9:159.

The Hegemony of Pleasure

The undoing of the dominion of pleasure does not take place in a simple series of measured steps. The undoing is at first quite indirect, proceeding in a way which Freud fails to specify as such but which, for this very reason, it behooves us to notice as his readers. It is a matter, in short, of the turning back of a text upon itself. Freud's essay takes itself apart before our very eyes. This self-dismantling leaves us before, out in front of, the pleasure principle. No longer subject to its exclusive dominance, we come out from under it. In this way, Freud's essay, for all of its perplexities, represents a liberation from the *Herr-schaft* of pleasure. It holds out promise as indicating a path around from under pleasure's all-encompassing embrace.

That pleasure is a literally, that is, textually, predominant force in Freud's metapsychology is evident from the first two sentences of *Beyond the Pleasure Principle*:

> In the theory of psychoanalysis we have no hesitation in assuming that the course taken by mental events is automatically regulated by the pleasure principle. We believe, that is to say, that the course of these events is in-variably set in motion by an unpleasurable tension, and that it takes a di-rection such that its final outcome coincides with a lowering of that tension—that is, with an avoidance of unpleasure or a production of plea-sure. (7)

What is remarkable about this opening passage is not merely its doctrinal continuity with Freud's earliest metapsychological speculations but the very tone of assured self-confidence with which Freud, early and late, announces the dominance of pleasure. Already in the "Project for a Scientific Psychology" Freud had affirmed unequivocally that "we have certain knowledge of a trend in psychical life towards *avoiding unpleasure*" (SE, 1:312, emphasis in original). Notice the comparable rhetorical force of these two clauses, which were written twenty-five years apart: "we have no hesitation in assuming," and "we have certain knowledge." Such gestures reflect Freud's own certainty and invite that of the reader as well. They are tantamount to the claim that the pleasure principle is entirely self-evident, so much so that to question it would be to question the very foundation of human experience.

When Freud underlines the phrase "avoiding unpleasure," he is once more pointing to its self-evidence. It is as if he were to say, What else do we do but avoid unpleasure in the course of our lives? Is this not completely obvious? Here the appeal is to the observation of everyday conduct. But Freud's confidence in the universality of the pleasure principle could not rely on such fallible and partial observation alone. Hence Freud goes on to propose that the pleasure principle is axiomatic in status; it obtains everywhere, whatever is happening at the phenomenological level: "the course taken by mental events is automatically regulated by the pleasure principle" (7). To be *automatically regulated* is to be regulated in such a way that no exceptions can occur, despite significant variations in appearance. It is thanks to such an axiom—Freud, following Fechner, prefers the less geometrical term *principle* stemming ultimately from Kant—that Freud can invoke the seemingly incontrovertible claim that "unpleasure corresponds to an *increase* in the quantity of excitation and pleasure to a *diminution*" (8; emphasis in original).

We therefore witness, from the very beginning, the express assertion of the predominance of pleasure, its pervasiveness in our lives, affirmed as phenomenologically self-evident and as axiomatically inescapable. It is difficult to imagine a more powerfully fortified starting point of a theoretical treatise that aims to fathom the foundation of human existence.

Not only at the opening of Freud's 1920 essay but throughout, there is a continuing affirmation of the primacy of pleasure. Perhaps the major way in which this affirmation occurs is by an insistence on pleasure's originality, its literal predominance in the psyche. For example, pleasure already dominates in the primary processes. "The primary processes are the earlier in time," remarks Freud, "and we may infer that if the pleasure principle had not already been operative in *them* it could never have been established for the later ones" (63, emphasis in original). It follows that the pleasure principle logically and chronologically precedes the reality principle, thanks especially to its being "the method of working employed by the sexual instincts" (10). But the pleasure principle is not only there from the first; its dominance even *increases* over time. If the search for pleasure is more intense in early development, later on "the dominance of the pleasure principle is very much more secure" (63). The reality principle itself is nothing but the postponement of assured pleasure; in this respect it is only "a step on the long indirect road to pleasure" (10). The secondary processes are no exception; they, too, inhabit this long and indirect road insofar as the binding of energy on which they depend is said to occur "on *behalf* of the pleasure principle" (62, emphasis in original). In fact, the binding itself, which represents a curtailment of the more intense pleasure of the primary processes, is by no means outside the realm of pleasure. Freud conceives binding as "a preparatory act which introduces and assures the dominance of the pleasure principle" (62). In the end, the dominance of pleasure is unlimited; it is found, as Freud adds, even "in the ego itself" (10).

There can be no question, then, as to the dominion of the pleasure principle. Whether construed as a quasi-physiological axiom or as the result of the observation of human behavior, whether it is viewed as being developmentally prior or as pervasive of *all* development (including the later, or logically posterior, stages), the hegemony of pleasure appears to be intact and supreme. No wonder that Freud can be so serenely self-confident at the beginning of his essay (and at a number of subsequent points as well) in setting forth this hegemony. He appears to be setting up a situation in which to question the dominance of pleasure would be to question the very basis of our lives. For how can we call into question that which is so formative of human existence and so characteristic of it—and, by the same token, so universally explanatory of it?

Quantity and Quality

Yet Freud's own text calls the primacy of pleasure into question. It does so not just by celebrated recourse to the compulsion to repeat and to the death instincts. These notions cap a set of tacit steps that, like the death instincts themselves, "seem to do their work unobtrusively" (63). They do this work by a process of auto-deconstruction, subtly, but nonetheless forcefully, dismantling the predominance of the pleasure principle. In this section and the next, I shall trace out several of these auto-deconstructive moves, moves that often share the very same pages as those in which Freud still avers the pleasure principle's putative supremacy.

Auto-deconstruction is not to be confused with outright self-contradiction. When a text auto-deconstructs, it does not turn upon itself in a simple self-canceling maneuver. Instead, it complicates or qualifies itself in such a way as to put into question a thesis already announced expressly in that same text. It undoes the thesis by an action that may seem at first glance to be marginal or even trivial. Yet just this marginality or triviality can be intrinsic to the accomplishment of auto-deconstruction. A mere remark in passing, a qualifying phrase, a moment of hesitation, a footnote, may end by slaying the Goliath of the express thesis—or more exactly, by bringing the gigantic idea to subdominance from a former position of dominance. In *Beyond the Pleasure Principle*, more than in any of his other major texts, Freud reveals himself to be a master at David's game, albeit an often unwilling and even unwitting master.

Take, for example, the sentences that immediately follow Freud's proclamation (in the first two paragraphs of *Beyond the Pleasure Principle*) as to the unquestionable autarchy of the pleasure principle. No sooner has he asserted this autarchy and told us of its resolutely quantitative basis (that is, the ties between unpleasure and an increase of excitation and between pleasure and the diminution of excitation) than he adds:

> What we are implying by this [correlation between pleasure and level of excitation] is not a simple relation between the strength of the feelings of pleasure and unpleasure and the corresponding modifications in the quantity of excitation; least of all—in view of all that we have been taught by psychophysiology—are we suggesting any directly proportional ratio: the factor that determines the feeling is probably the amount of increase or diminution in the quantity of excitation *in a given period of time.* (8, emphasis in original)

This passage not merely disclaims allegiance to Fechner's psychophysical law whereby there is a logarithmic relation between changes in stimulus intensity and the resultant sensations, a law to which Freud had subscribed in the "Project" (see SE, 1:315). It also does something much more radical than this, for it introduces a dimension that is foreign to any sheerly quantitative paradigm. This dimension is that of *time* and in particular cyclical, periodical time. As if to underline the importance of this importation, Freud repeats it on the last page of his essay: "the pleasure and unpleasure series indicates a change in the magnitude of the cathexis *within a given unit of time*" (63; emphasis in original). Periodical time is critical, because it is the basis of all that is qualitative in experience, all that can be considered a matter of consciousness or feeling. More exactly, as Strachey puts it in commenting on Freud's first ruminations on such time in the "Project," the idea of a temporal period is that of a "qualitative characteristic" of a stimulus which, when it attains consciousness, "*becomes* quality" (SE, 1:313n., emphasis in original).

The issue that concerns us is not whether Freud is correct psychophysiologically speaking in his recourse to the notion of *period* as essential to feelings of pleasure or unpleasure. What is of most interest is his twofold questioning of the primacy of pleasure regarded as an exclusively quantitative matter. On the one hand, he denies any "directly proportional ratio" between quantities of excitation and the feelings attendant upon these quantities, which is in effect to open the doors to a nonquantitative assessment of the relation between excitations and feelings. On the other hand, he introduces an explicitly qualitative factor, the period of time, into his account. However regular it may be, periodicity is not altogether quantifiable.

This first, self-questioning (if not directly self-undermining) move points to the difficulty of reconciling the pleasure *principle*—which is strictly quantitative in its conception—with *pleasure* itself, which is a qualitative matter. "No doubt the essential point," says Freud unguardedly in a footnote added to the text in 1925, "is that pleasure and unpleasure, being *conscious feelings,* are attached to the ego" (11n., emphasis added). But precisely as "conscious feelings"—the phrase itself is pleonastic in Freudian metapsychology, despite Freud's occasional interest in "unconscious affects"[3]—pleasure and unpleasure cannot be assessed by quantitative criteria. Yet such criteria are the sole allowable criteria of the pleasure principle in its "economic" formulation, the main formulation at stake in *Beyond the Pleasure Principle.* Freud invokes the economic point of view in the first paragraph of this text,[4] and in the very next paragraph he introduces the apparently innocent phrase "in a given period of time." This phrase, in its inherent implication of the qualitative, calls into question the imperialism of the quantitative. It deconstructs this imperialism by showing that we cannot stay with quantitative considerations alone if we are to understand the nature of pleasure and unpleasure; we must also take something qualitative into account. Since the qualitative factor of periodicity emerges from the quan-

3. On this topic, see "The Unconscious," section 3, and *The Ego and the Id,* chap. 2.

4. "[In considering the pleasure principle], we are introducing an 'economic' point of view into our work" (SE, 18:7).

titative substratum itself and is not merely superadded to it, it appears that the purely economic dimension gives rise to something that exceeds its own means of determination—that is, to something foreign to its own nature.

Since Freud himself does not yet see the issue as problematic, his text only marginally reflects the tension between the quantitative and the qualitative, the economic and the affective. He still believes, as he first believed in the "Project," that the two dimensions can be encompassed in one overarching metapsychological matrix, that provided by Fechner's *principle of stability*, renamed by Freud (with contributions from Breuer) as the *principle of constancy*. But this latter is held to be equivalent to the pleasure principle in the text of 1920. Constancy, says Freud confidently, "is only another way of stating the pleasure principle" (9); thanks to the conceptual equivalence, he can also state the converse: "the pleasure principle follows from the principle of constancy" (ibid.). But if this is true, then the quantitative wholly pervades pleasure, leaving the undeniably qualitative character of the latter an unexplained excrescence on the body of the former. In this view, pleasure becomes metapsychologically opaque.

It is hardly surprising that Freud's writing reflects the unresolved tension between the qualitative and the quantitative within the principles of constancy and pleasure regarded as convertible into each other. We detect this tension in his earliest official treatment of quantity. In his 1894 article "The Neuro-Psychoses of Defense" he concludes triumphantly: "In mental functions something is to be distinguished—a quota of affect or sum or excitation—which possesses *all the characteristics of a quantity (though we have no means of measuring it)* which is capable of increase, diminution, displacement, and discharge, and which is spread over the memory-traces of ideas somewhat as an electric charge is spread over the surface of a body" (SE, 3:60, emphasis added). The mention of increase, diminution, and discharge assures us that we are in the land of pleasure (and unpleasure). But the sole conceptuality by which we may grasp the nature of pleasure is that of a "sum of excitation" which is thoroughly quantitative in its characteristics, except for the alarming fact that "we have no means of measuring it." A strange quantity this! An immeasurable quantity is an oxymoronic, if not downright self-defeating, notion. Freud's delicate (and quite auto-deconstructive) parenthesis at once signals and veils the problematic notion that will continue to haunt his textual asides and margins for another quarter of a century: a quantity that must be qualitative if it is to account for pleasure and unpleasure as feelings—which is to say, a quantity which is no quantity at all.[5]

In the "Project," written little more than a year after the composition of the sentence just examined, Freud wrestles more fully with the dilemma in ques-

---

5. An exemplary instance of such a quantity that is nevertheless not to be considered a quantity but a quality occurs in the text of *Beyond the Pleasure Principle* itself: the idea of *amplitude*. Freud writes that the "excitatory process" has "more than one *quality* (in the nature of amplitude, for instance)" (31, emphasis in the original; compare also ibid., 29, where amplitude is said to be a "qualitative" aspect of stimuli).

tion.[6] He devotes an entire section of his hastily written manuscript to it, appropriately located just after his discussion of quantity and pain in the two previous sections. "The Problem of Quality" is as notable for its confrontation with the issue of the qualitative as it is for its failure to resolve it. He states the issue forthrightly: "Our consciousness furnishes only *qualities*, whereas science recognizes only *quantities*. . . . It would seem as though the characteristic of quality (that is, conscious sensation) comes about only where quantities are so far as possible excluded" (SE, 1:309, emphasis in original). It is just here that Freud first introduces the notion of the period as a solution to the problem of how consciousness feels qualities—and *only* qualities—while all of its sources of stimulation, internal as well as external, are quantities or sums of excitation. As he puts it, "I can see only one way out of the difficulty: a revision of our fundamental hypothesis about the passage of [quantity]. . . . I speak of this as *period* for short" (SE, 1:310, emphasis in original). The ω neurones that Freud posits at this point are said to "appropriate" the period of an otherwise exclusively quantitative set of excitations. Sense organs conspire in the process; acting as "sieves," they "allow the stimulus through from only certain processes with a particular period" (ibid.). The result of this rather elaborate operation is a situation in which originally quantitative entities—"stimuli"—attain consciousness as the qualities that inhere in periodicities.

The candor of the unpublished text is refreshing and stands in contrast to the allusive asides and passing self-qualifications in Freud's published work. In the "Project," Freud admits his engagement in "complicated and far from perspicuous hypotheses" (SE, 1:311) instead of concealing this engagement behind the polish of the published surface. But he is no less caught up in difficulties from which he fails to extricate himself. In what exact way are periods qualitative and not quantitative? Is not positing them a move of desperation, an invocation of a gratuitous deus ex machina? Must we not say the same of his freshly minted ω neurones, as he himself comes to suspect in a subsequent letter to Fliess?[7] How do either periods or neurones resolve the major mystery of how quantity is transformed into quality? To say, as Freud does in a later section of the "Project," that "the stimuli which actually reach the [perceptual] neurones have a quantity *and a qualitative characteristic*" (SE, 1:313, emphasis added) is only to deepen the mystery of how a characteristic of something strictly quantitative comes to be experienced *as a quality*.[8]

6. In a remarkable passage in a letter to Wilhelm Fliess, he admits begrudgingly the importance of his endeavor: "The 'Psychology' is really a cross to me. Anyhow, scuttles and mushroom-hunting are far healthier. After all, I wanted to do no more than explain defence, but I was led from that into explaining something from the center of nature. I have had to work through the problem of quality, sleep, memory—in fact the whole of psychology. Now I want to hear no more about it" (letter 27 of 16 August 1895).

7. See letter 39 of 1 January 1896, in which ω neurones are in effect assimilated to ψ neurones.

8. Strachey's above-cited remark only reexpresses the same mystery: "only a qualitative *characteristic*—'period'— . . . *becomes* quality" (SE, 1:313n., emphasis in original). Here we must ask, By what alchemical process does quantity become quality?

The mystery is still very much present twenty-five years later in *Beyond the Pleasure Principle*—where, suitably camouflaged in a major pronouncement, its shadow is detectable in the auto-deconstructive maneuver of denying direct proportionality between quantity of excitation and quality of feeling, while maintaining nonetheless that "the factor that determines the feeling is probably the increase or diminution in the quantity of excitation" (SE, 18:8). Moreover, the invocation of periodicity occurs immediately afterward in the form of the phrase "in a given period of time," added to the just-cited sentence. The italicizing of this phrase in the text makes it stand out like a symptom once we are aware of how unsatisfactory it is to recur to the stopgap notion of period, itself perhaps a belated remnant of the influence of Fliess on Freud's early thinking. To write the string of words "the amount of increase or diminution in the quantity of excitation *in a given period of time*" is to rewrite the problematic idea of having "a quantity and a qualitative characteristic." The only progress, if we can speak of progress in such a stalemate, lies in Freud's self-conscious underlining of the auto-deconstructive phrase. But this bare signal points only indirectly to the persisting mystery.

By the time of writing *The Ego and the Id* in 1923, Freud could at least *name* the mystery and point to it directly: "Let us call what becomes conscious as pleasure and unpleasure a quantitative and qualitative 'something' in the course of mental events" (SE, 19:22). "A quantitative and qualitative 'something'": this deliberately ambiguous phrase at least puts quantity and quality on a par in matters of pleasure and unpleasure. Quality is no longer a cryptic by-product of quantity; it has a standing of its own, albeit a standing in an unknown *etwas*, a substrate withdrawn from human cognition.

Freud attempts to remove definitively the shroud of mystery in his 1924 essay, "The Economic Problem of Masochism," whose opening pages deal directly with quality and quantity in the life of pleasure. Declaring that the pleasure principle is "the watchman over our life" (SE, 19:159), he enters into an explicit self-critique. His identifying of the pleasure principle with the constancy principle gives rise to the prediction that "every unpleasure ought . . . to coincide with a heightening, and every pleasure with a lowering, of mental tension due to [an internal or external] stimulus" (ibid., 159–60). Yet, in fact, some tensions, especially sexual ones, can be pleasurable, and some relaxations of tension unpleasant. From this straightforward observation—which contradicts "the facts" that Freud claimed had forced him to adopt the pleasure principle in the first place—Freud is led to an apparently momentous conclusion:

> Pleasure and unpleasure, therefore, cannot be referred to an increase or decrease of a quantity (which we describe as "tension due to stimulus"), although they obviously have a great deal to do with that factor. It appears that they depend, not on this quantitative factor, but on some characteristic of it which we can only describe as a qualitative one. If we were able to say what this qualitative characteristic is, we should be much further advanced in psychology. (SE, 19:160)

Despite the promise of this passage—a promise that is based on Freud's first explicit dissociation of pleasure and unpleasure from augmentation or diminution of sheer quantity and thus (as an immediate consequence) of the pleasure principle from the constancy principle—we find ourselves disappointed by Freud's effort to tell us what the qualitative factor is that ultimately underlies pleasure and unpleasure. Just as the term "qualitative characteristic" itself is lifted directly from the "Project," so is Freud's final estimate of what this characteristic consists in: "Perhaps it is the rhythm, the temporal sequence of changes, rises and falls in the quantity of stimulus. We do not know" (ibid.). Not only are the inherent difficulties in the notion of periodicity still unfaced by Freud in this later passage—he has merely redescribed the idea of period in the more expressly temporal language of "rhythm" and "sequence"—but he even reintroduces, as if by a compulsion to repeat, the very idea of "quantity of stimulus" that he is professedly eschewing in the supposedly new direction of his thought.

All that is new in the end is the toning down of the dogmatism that had prevailed from the writing of the "Project for a Scientific Psychology" to the publication of *Beyond the Pleasure Principle*. The un-self-questioning proclamations that "we have certain knowledge" and that "we have no hesitation in assuming" have been replaced in the "Economic Problem of Masochism" by the more modest language of "perhaps" and "we do not know." Nevertheless, even if this language is not accompanied by genuinely new thinking as to the relation between quality and quantity in the generation of pleasure and unpleasure, even if it is *conceptually* stultified, it does represent a new and significant *textual* turn. For it means that Freud is no longer indulging in sub-rosa moves of the kind that we have discerned in *Beyond the Pleasure Principle* and before that, in "The Neuro-Psychoses of Defense," Freud's first essay on the subject. The auto-deconstruction of his own text, its sinuous and indirect self-undoing, has given way to self-questioning and a sense of limitation. The latent has been made patent as Freud attempts to come to more adequate terms with the problem of understanding pleasure as a quantitative-qualitative phenomenon.

As to what these more adequate terms, by which to grasp pleasure and unpleasure, might be, I can only allude to a promising strategy strangely overlooked by Freud. We should avoid pitting quantity and quality against each other, an oppositionalist tactic that is foredoomed to failure. Once we assume that the two terms are irrevocably opposed (for Freud, quantity belongs only to matter, quality solely to mind), the only meaningful connection we can provide for them is by a conceptual hat trick, whereby an intermediate term such as a "qualitative characteristic [of quantity]" appears as magically as a rabbit from a hat. Freud, however, might have considered other, more conciliatory models for the relation between quantity and quality. One of these models is proposed by Plato, for whom the scale of "Forms" represents a conceptual ladder in which differences of degree and differences of kind merge instead of being simply opposed. For Plato, when a belief about something turns into knowledge of it, the belief is altered both quantitatively *and* qualitatively, and this happens all at once.[9] Could this not be the case in regard to pleasure and unpleasure as well? Might they not be different both in kind and in degree from their exciting causes? If so, they would be at once continuous with these causes (that is, differing only by degree, thereby relating to causal conditions even if not existing in direct proportion to them) and discontinuous as well (that is, distinctly different in kind from such conditions, being something actually felt and not merely posited). The advantage of this Platonic model is evident. It allows one to retain both the intrinsic overlap and the equally intrinsic discrepancy between the two factors that Freud found so difficult to connect: the "stimuli" or "exciting causes" on the one hand and the "conscious feelings" of pleasure and unpleasure on the other. If Freud's metapsychology is to work at all, it must succeed in bringing these two groups of factors into communication, without having to resort to the conceptual sleight-of-hand that he was driven to employ in early and late texts alike.

Alternatively, we could consider an idea that stems from Kant, that of "intensive magnitude." In his discussion "Anticipations of Perception" in the *Critique of Pure Reason*, Kant is led to distinguish between a purely "extensive" and an "intensive" magnitude. The former is appropriate to description and explanation in the world of physics, that is, the strictly numerable world of quantity proper. The latter, in contrast, bears on the actually felt sensations that register that same quantitatively determinable world. As the Greeks had already observed in their notion of *aisthesis*, such sensations are experienced in ways that defy exact numeration. They are felt in terms of their comparative intensity—their "sting" as William James was wont to put it. This intensity is a measure of the impingement of the external (or internal) physical world on our senses. As such, it cannot be said to be measureless; but its units of measurement are not the conventional ones of arithmetic, not even in the elegant logarithmic extensions that were devised by G. T. Fechner. The units are uniquely *aesthetic* and differ only by degree, a degree to which no precise number can be attached, but which is felt clearly enough for differentiations to be made between one degree of influence and another—in effect, between one feeling and another.[10] Could it be that feelings of pleasure and unpleasure represent just such intensities of magnitude? Might not their environing causes represent extensive magnitudes? If so, we would once again have a means of understanding how feelings can be both disparate from their causes—as disparate as "intensive" is from "extensive"—and yet intimately related to them (since each is nevertheless a form of magnitude and is measurable as such).

9. For this model, see Collingwood, *An Essay in Philosophical Method*, 54–91.

10. For Kant's idea of intensive magnitude, see *Critique of Pure Reason*, 201–8, 373, 374n. "Degree of influence" is discussed at p. 202. Freud himself once alludes to the factor of intensity: "The excitations coming from within are, however, in their intensity . . . more commensurate with the system's method of working than the stimuli which stream in from the external world" (SE, 18:29). But for Kant, external as well as internal stimuli possess intensive magnitude.

The advantage of engaging in such strategic moves—and doubtless still others, for example, the idea of "tacit knowledge" as developed by Michael Polanyi, or of "pre-reflective knowledge" in the work of Merleau-Ponty—is that we would not have to make such self-defeating pronouncements as Freud made in 1894 concerning a quantity for which we have no means of measurement and in 1920 when he had to deny a determinate proportionality between things that are nonetheless quantitative in character. Nor would we have to resort to the kind of textual subplot that we have seen to characterize Freud's writings on pleasure and constancy before 1924, a subplot that is detrimentally deconstructive of his own manifest text. Nor would we, finally, have to explain the obscure by the more obscure, as Freud is led to do in his 1923 positing of "a quantitative and qualitative 'something'," a notion that Kant would have consigned to the world of unknowable noumena or things-in-themselves. Instead, we could begin to deal with pleasure and unpleasure and with their causes—indeed, with the constancy principle to which they are so closely if so ambivalently related—in their own phenomenally given states, employing terms that reflect such states more sensitively than Freud's own terms permit.

Pleasure and Death

Freud's self-masking idiom—a combination of rhetorical bravado and conceptual unclarity—calls for close analysis. The unclarity affects the foundations of the pleasure principle itself and is manifested only obliquely by the printed text. This text twists about itself and begins to speak against itself by a sinuous process of auto-deconstruction. It erects a seemingly impenetrable facade of theoretical confidence based on "the quantitative conception" that the "Project" had promoted as the "first principal theorem" of a truly "scientific psychology."[11] But cracks appear almost immediately in this same facade when the text denies any "simple relation" between human feelings and sums of excitation, much less "any directly proportional ratio between them." The text also strikes at the structure itself of the facade itself by alluding to the pseudoexplanatory notion of "a given period of time." By tracing the cracks in the wall of Freud's discourse, we have placed ourselves in a position that is not so much beyond the pleasure principle as in front of it, leaving us standing in its conceptual foreground, able to look upon it in its inherent problematicity. Viewed from this pre-position, the vaunted "dominance" of the pleasure principle begins to disestablish itself before our very eyes.

In this new section we shall take a quite different tack. Instead of looking for subversion from within, we shall consider contestation from without. The pleasure principle will be questioned not in terms of its internal architecture

11. Section 1 of Part 1 of the "Project" was promoted as the "First Principal Theorem—The Quantitative Conception." It is in this section that Freud announces "the principle of neuronal inertia," i.e., "that neurones tend to divest themselves of Q [quantity]." This principle is, of course, the same as the principle of constancy. (See SE, 1:295–97.)

but concerning its presumed dominion over other aspects of psychical life. This dominion will be displaced and delimited by the discovery of items and processes over which it does not, after all, rule. Although such displacement and limitation may not seem at first to be a dramatic restriction of the pleasure principle, it is in the end deeply subversive of the dominance that Freud continues to claim for it. Moreover, the subversion is more patent and is more often part of Freud's manifest text than was the case with the conceptual undermining examined just above. Now Freud himself will be his own overt critic. His auto-deconstruction will be explicit and self-directed rather than buried in the text. In short, Freud will begin to dismantle Freud—in that res publica called a "published text"— and he will take more complete responsibility for what he says in print. The uneasy squint of the system-builder is replaced by the open-eyed look of the self-critic.

Freud's strategy is straightforward from now on. It consists in locating exceptions to the hegemony of the pleasure principle, exceptions indicating factors that are genuinely independent of this principle. In pursuing this strategy, Freud begins by sorting out apparent exceptions from real exceptions. An apparent exception is scrutinized immediately after his ambivalent discussion of the relation between the pleasure and constancy principles in section 1 of *Beyond the Pleasure Principle*. I refer to the "reality principle." Given its very different criteria of operation and its often unconcealed opposition to the pursuit of pleasure, it might seem to be a prime, if not the leading, contestant of the primacy of pleasure. Freud's own first formulation in this 1920 essay contributes to this impression: "under the influence of the ego's instincts of self-preservation, the pleasure principle is replaced by the reality principle" (10, emphasis of last two words deleted). Pleasure must be replaced if preservation is to occur. The language of "replacement" (*Ablösung*, a word that also connotes "supersession") is emphatic, and Freud repeats the word in the next paragraph. Nevertheless, he refuses to accord to the reality principle any strict independence of the pleasure principle. The dominance of the latter is still present in it, albeit in a diffuse and deferred form. Whatever austerities it may impose upon us, the reality principle "does not abandon the intention of ultimately obtaining pleasure" (ibid.). On its "long indirect road" (ibid.), we are still pursuing pleasure in the end. In this light, the reality principle, far from replacing the pleasure principle, helps to realize pleasure all the more effectively and is thus, metapsychologically regarded, a "modification" of this principle.[12]

A second apparent exception to the rule of pleasure is formally identical with the first. The "neurotic unpleasure" that ensues from the repression of a forbidden impulse or wish is a disguised possibility of pleasure that has been forced to tread a "roundabout path" (11) to satisfaction. It is nothing but a "pleasure that cannot be felt as such" (ibid.). Similarly, the many instances of

12. The term "modification" comes from Freud's assessment of the reality principle in "The Economic Problem of Masochism": "The modification of the [pleasure principle], the reality principle, represents the influence of the external world" (SE, 19:160).

ordinary unpleasure in our lives—of "perceptual unpleasure" (ibid.) as Freud calls it—in no way undermine, or even limit, the reign of the pleasure principle: "their presence," Freud says unhesitatingly, "does not contradict the dominance of the pleasure principle" (ibid.).

It is with the rejection of such apparent exceptions to the dominion of the pleasure principle that section 2 of Freud's essay comes to a close. If he has surreptitiously deconstructed this principle in the opening pages of the section, he has given convincing support to its ubiquity in the last pages. Now he must turn to more serious candidates for exception, candidates whose consideration will occupy him for the remaining six sections of the text. To follow Freud's own roundabout path in these sections would call for a monumental labor (Jacques Derrida has recently devoted 250 pages of *La carte postale* to such a labor)[13] and is in any case not necessary for my purposes. I shall restrict consideration to a few of the "many processes [that] take place in mental life independently of the pleasure principle" (62). Here we shall meet genuine exceptions to the principle, so genuine that this principle can no longer claim the originality and universality that Freud had imputed to it as a matter of course.

Take, for example, the celebrated discussion of the *fort-da* game devised by Freud's grandson. Among several ways of interpreting the ultimate motivation of this game, the notion of active "mastery" presents itself as most tempting to Freud's thinking. The child's ingenious efforts "might be put down to an instinct for mastery that was acting independently of whether the memory [of his mother's departure and return] was in itself pleasurable or not" (16). Freud includes the cautionary "might" in this statement because he cannot rule out the possibility that the child's repeated engagement in the game may bring an unsuspected "yield of pleasure" that is nonetheless (unlike a neurotic symptom) "direct," for example, when the child in the game is also experiencing a rivalrous father as absent (see ibid.). As in the case of traumatic dreams that he has discussed earlier in section 2, Freud declares the matter moot: "We are therefore left in doubt as to whether the impulse to work over in the mind some overpowering experience so as to make oneself master of it can find expression as a primary event, and independently of the pleasure principle" (16).

But the matter is less moot than Freud here declares it to be. First of all, he reinforces his hypothesis of mastery by observing that almost everything children repeat as having made a special impression on them is done to "make themselves master of the situation" (17), including the effort to play at being grown-up. Then he makes (in section 5) the general point that mastery, as a form of binding, precedes the dominance of the pleasure principle. Although fully bound or mastered excitations subserve this principle, the process of binding or mastering proceeds independently of it: "until then [that is, the moment of full binding] the other task of the mental apparatus, the task of mastering or

13. See Derrida, *La carte postale,* 277–524 ("Spéculer—sur Freud"). This text is now available in an English translation by Alan Bass: *The Post Card* (University of Chicago Press, 1987).

binding excitations, would have precedence—not, indeed, in opposition to the pleasure principle, but *independently of it* and to some extent in disregard of it" (35, emphasis added). By the time Freud is ready to enter into summation in section 7, he can take a still further step on the road to independence. For by this time he has brought all of the component instincts—among them mastery— under the aegis of the urge to reinstate an earlier condition, an urge that pre-exists the pleasure principle.[14] It follows a fortiori that the component instinct of mastery itself shares in "matters over which the pleasure principle has as yet no control" (62). Thus it stands *before* the pleasure principle in the literal and temporal sense of preceding it.

When we consider the case of dreams—set forth in section 2 as having a status as moot as that of the *fort-da* game—it is striking to discover that Freud's return to the question of traumatic dreams brings with it an explicit avowal of this same "before," an avowal that is furthermore linked with the issue of mastery. Near the end of section 4, he speculates:

> We may assume . . . that dreams are here [that is, in the case of a person suffering from traumatic neuroses such as those incurred in wartime] helping to carry out another task, which must be accomplished *before the dominance of the pleasure principle can even begin.* These dreams are endeavoring to master the stimulus retrospectively, by developing the anxiety whose omission was the cause of the traumatic neurosis. They thus afford us a view of a function of the mental apparatus which, though it does not contradict the pleasure principle, is nevertheless independent of it and seems to be more primitive than the purpose of gaining pleasure and avoiding unpleasure. (32, emphasis added)

Here independence is explicitly linked with being *before* in a temporal sense, with being "more primitive," that is to say, more original. Freud picks up on the theme of originality in a second passage in which the theme of the "before" again figures. The wish-fulfilling function of dreams, he posits, "is not their *original* function," and "if there is a 'beyond the pleasure principle,' it is only consistent to grant that there was also a time before the purpose of dreams was the fulfillment of wishes" (33, emphasis in original). This is a time of *predom-*inance, a time of the *before*.

With this last claim, Freud has deconstructed the first part of his two-part characterization of the pleasure principle as both aboriginal—there from the start—and universal, all-pervasive. Moreover, he has done so by invoking the very factor that will also undo pleasure's pretension to universality. In this regard, dreams remain the *via regia* of Freud's metapsychological thinking. As he gently reminds us in section 2, when he is in the very midst of his own perplexity, "the study of dreams may be considered the most trustworthy method of investigating deep mental processes" (13). When he goes on to say that traumatic

14. On this development, see especially p. 39.

dreams arise *"in obedience to the compulsion to repeat"* (32, emphasis added), he names the very factor that acts to undermine the ubiquity of the pleasure principle. Through its consideration and by its extension to the idea of death instincts, Freud's auto-deconstruction of the dominance of the pleasure principle will be complete. Henceforth, this principle will be neither predominant nor pandominant. It will instead be subdominant: the dominance of pleasure is made subordinate to the dominance of death.

With the move to repetition and to death, we move from the assertion of mere independence of the pleasure principle—such as can be claimed effectively of the component instincts, and, ineffectively, of the reality principle and of neurotic symptoms—to an active contestation of this principle. Whereas even the instinct of mastery, insofar as it is allied with binding, can still be said to operate *"on behalf of* the pleasure principle" (62, emphasis added), this cannot be said of the compulsion to repeat or of the death drive. These latter are independent not merely in the sense of arising and functioning in separation from the pleasure principle—a separation that in the case of the binding involved in mastery proves to be *preparatory* to eventual domination by the principle. They are *altogether* independent, that is, from beginning to end and at every intermediate stage. It is a matter, in other words, of an independence so complete that the putative primacy of pleasure is *never* restored.

It would be useless and sterile to rehearse this argument step by step. Suffice it to say that everything follows from the premise that, as Freud states it in triumphant italics in section 5, *"an instinct is an urge inherent in organic life to restore an earlier state of things*; that is, it is a kind of organic elasticity, or, to put it another way, the expression of the inertia inherent in organic life"* (36, emphasis in original). Pronounced precisely halfway through his essay, this remarkable statement brings together repetition (as restoration), death (as the inorganic state that is the *earliest* state of things, and constancy (under the guise of "inertia," Freud's preferred way of speaking about constancy in the "Project"). And, with the same stroke, he draws pleasure into the drama as well: if, as we have seen, the constancy and pleasure principles are interchangeable, then pleasure itself is finally just another expression of that "demonic force" (35) whose most visible form is the compulsion to repeat, but whose invisible working is death. Hence Freud's bold and dire conclusion that "the pleasure principle seems actually to serve the death instincts" (63). It does so because of its own irrepressible tendency to operate by reducing excessive stimulation, by "avoiding unpleasure" in the laconic formula of the "Project" that still obtains at the end of *Beyond the Pleasure Principle*,[15] where Freud puts it this way: "The pleasure principle, then, is a tendency operating in the service of a function whose business it is to free the mental apparatus entirely from excitation or to keep the

15. Once again, we encounter this equivalence early as well as late. The "Project" states that "we are tempted to identify that trend [of avoiding unpleasure] with the primary trend of inertia" (SE, 1:312), while we read in *Beyond the Pleasure Principle* that "the pleasure principle follows from the principle of constancy" (SE, 18:9).

amount of excitation in it constant or to keep it as low as possible" (62). Pleasure's alliance with constancy, with what Breuer called the "tendency to keep intracerebral excitation constant" (SE, 2:197, italicized in the text), proves to be not just fateful but fatal. For the ultimate constancy, the very lowest level of excitation possible (the "Project" had spoken admiringly of a state of "zero excitation," SE, 1:297), is that of death itself.[16]

The quiescence that is the aim of all pleasure is the quintessence of death. It is also the aim of the binding that marks the transformation of primary into secondary processes, and thus of the mastery that requires binding. What Freud had called prophetically "the primary trend toward inertia" in the "Project" (SE, 1:312) is the common bond between pleasure, binding, and death. But in this inertial equilibrium, death is given the upper hand; it is placed before binding and pleasure, both of which become (along with the instincts of self-preservation and self-assertion) "the myrmidons of death" (39). Like the bellicose followers of Achilles, the original *myrmidons*, they trace a trajectory of Thanatos. From this trajectory not even Eros, "the preserver of all things" (52), can save them. For Eros, or the life instinct, itself exhibits "a need to restore an earlier state of things" (57, italicized in the text). Despite the aggrandizing and unifying power of Eros, it too, as Freud argues in section 6, manifests the regressive character of all instincts.

The primary trend toward inertia prevails everywhere, and there are in the end no exceptions whatsoever. Life itself, like the reality principle upon which it relies for bare survival, is "no more than a lengthening of the road to death" (40). The "long indirect road to pleasure" has been replaced by a *via dolorosa* of death: the latter route stands ineluctably *before* the former as its own primary path. If it is true that "what we are left with is the fact that the organism wishes to die only in its own fashion" (39), this primal fact has replaced the primordiality of "the facts which forced us to adopt the pleasure principle" (9), facts from which the constancy principle was also "inferred" (ibid.).[17]

In other words, the inertial-regressive trend has taken the place of pleasure; it has moved in front of it, or more exactly, it has been found to occupy a permanently prior position. This trend, in its (d)alliance with death, also replaces (in the strong sense of supersedes) pleasure in its two most generic characters. It is at once more original—being "inherent in organic life," it is there from the beginning of life itself, indeed before life even begins—*and* more universal: Freud twice calls the urge or need to restore an earlier, inorganic state of things "universal" (compare pages 36 and 62). Pleasure is in this way doubly out-

16. In this light it is somewhat ironic that Freud's first reference to the constancy-*cum*-pleasure principle allies it to *health*: "Now in every individual there exists a tendency to diminish [a disturbing] sum of excitation . . . in order to preserve his health" (SE, 3:36, from Freud's lecture of January 1893, "The Mechanisms of Hysterical Phenomena").

17. Fechner, from whose "tendency towards stability" Freud and Breuer derived their own principle of constancy, already envisaged the intimate tie between stability and death in his *Geschichte der Organismen*, 90–91.

flanked, twice subordinated to what now dominates it, both from afar and from close by.

Back Before Pleasure

It does not matter greatly that in a last bold maneuver Freud attempts in "The Economic Problem of Masochism" to ally the pleasure principle with the life instincts. Even if it were true that "the pleasure principle represents the demands of the libido" (SE, 19:160), it remains under the sign, if not under the direct dominion, of death. Despite this late reorientation, which is also taken up in Freud's *Outline of Psychoanalysis* (1938), the pleasure principle is ultimately in death's thrall as much as is its former twin, the constancy principle, which, renamed the "Nirvana principle," is said to be "entirely in the service of the death instincts" (SE, 19:160). This must be so if the basic inertial trend is indeed universal. Moreover, even if this were *not* the case, if the life instincts were in fact free from the death instincts (as Freud hints is just barely possible at the close of *Civilization and Its Discontents*), the dominance of pleasure would still be undermined—this time by Eros, whose subject pleasure would now in turn become. Perhaps this is a more hopeful or desirable prospect; it is certainly a more pleasant one! But it leaves the pleasure principle in a subordinate position once again.

In this paper I have had to ignore issues of fundamental importance in Freud's treatment of pleasure and of the pleasure principle. For example, the role of memory in the repetition of a pleasure-giving experience is crucial, as Freud himself suggests in one passage from *Beyond the Pleasure Principle*: "Even under the dominance of the pleasure principle, there are ways and means enough of making what is in itself unpleasurable into a subject to be recollected and worked over in the mind" (17). Freud has in mind theatrical experiences, such as Greek tragedies, in which intrinsically unpleasant events are nonetheless felt to be enjoyable in the spectator's recollective working over of them. That the place of memory in the experience of pleasure or unpleasure may be of still more general significance is not, however, pursued by Freud—even though the very idea of temporal periodicity, which we have seen to be so critical (and so problematic) for his theory of pleasure as quality, entails memory. We only grasp a cycle or period *as* a cycle or period insofar as we remember a previous such unit, which is now being repeated. If Freud is curiously negligent in this area (curious because of his otherwise acute sensitivity to memory in therapy and in theory) Plato was not so. Plato's conception of pleasure in the *Philebus* is that of an experience that is dependent on prior experiences of like pleasure: "When hoping for replenishment [of a given need or desire], we feel pleasure *through what we remember*" (*Philebus* 36b, emphasis added); and in the pursuit of pleasure "memory is what leads us on to objects of our desire" (ibid., 35d). Freud, who also conceives of the satisfaction of desire as a form of replenishment, might here have taken a second crucial clue from Plato.[18]

Another area that calls for exploration concerns the relation between repetition and regression. Despite Freud's blending of the two concepts in *Beyond the Pleasure Principle*, they should not be confused. In repetition, a twofold action of (a) a return to an original state, and (b) a reenactment of itself, is added inevitably to the original condition. As Kierkegaard said, "What is repeated has been, otherwise it could not be repeated, but precisely the fact that it has been gives to repetition the character of novelty."[19] Regression, on the other hand, involves nothing intrinsically new; it is uniformly backward moving: in the instance that preoccupies Freud, it is a movement backward to the purely inorganic state. The distinction between repetition and regression, whose importance has been underlined by Lichtenstein and by Sulloway,[20] threatens to unhinge Freud's later metapsychology in yet another auto-deconstructive twist. It is intriguing to think that it might be memory which could heal the split, since in remembering both regression (as the backward grasping of the past) and repetition (as the recall that takes place at the present moment) are intrinsically involved.

In this chapter, I have moved from detecting a covertly auto-deconstructive moment in Freud's text of 1920 when the presumed predominance of the pleasure principle begins to come apart at the seams, given that quantity and quality fail to combine in a consistent and unitary whole, to a consideration of much more overtly self-dismantling phases of the same text in which Freud himself expressly undercuts the dominance of pleasure which he posited to begin with. These latter phases are various in kind, ranging from the establishment of a mere difference of operation in the case of the component instincts to the laying down of a more deeply disturbing trend in the case of the death instincts. This trend, one of regression to an unliving inorganic state, proves to be lethal indeed to the pleasure principle, whose only recourse is to become the minion of Thanatos. At that late point, when the proud dominion of pleasure has been made distinctly subdominant, Freud's text comes to a close that is not so much beyond pleasure as back before it in death. As Freud adds wryly: "What we cannot reach flying we must reach limping."[21]

18. For Plato, "the satisfaction of a desire . . . contains the seeds of the desire's return [i.e., via a memory of its former satisfaction]" (Gosling and Taylor, *The Greeks on Pleasure*, 138).

19. Kierkegaard, *Repetition: An Essay in Experimental Psychology*, 52. This point is developed subtly by Loewald in his article "Some Considerations on Repetition and Repetition Compulsion," reprinted in his *Papers on Psychoanalysis*, 87–101.

20. See Lichtenstein, "Zur Phänomenologie des Wiederholungszwanges und des Todestriebes," *Imago* 21 (1935): 446–80; and Sulloway (who draws on Lichtenstein's article), *Freud, Biologist of the Mind*, 401–9.

21. This line, along with another ("The Book tells us it is no sin to limp"), is cited by Freud at the end of his essay (64) from the *Maqâmât* of al-Hariri. I would like to thank David Olds, M.D., for his careful reading of my own text in an early stage of preparation.

SELECT BIBLIOGRAPHY

References to Freud's works are cited in the text using the abbreviation SE for the *Standard Edition of the Complete Psychological Works of Sigmund Freud,* trans. J. Strachey (London: Hogarth Press, 1953–).

Collingwood, R. G. *An Essay in Philosophical Method* (Oxford: Oxford University Press, 1933).

Derrida, Jacques. *La carte postale: de Socrate à Freud et au-delà* (Paris: Flammarion, 1980).

Fechner, Gustav Theodor. *Einige Ideen zur Schöpfungs- und Entwicklungsgeschichte der Organismen* (Leipzig, 1873).

Gosling, J. C. B., and Taylor, C. C. W. *The Greeks on Pleasure* (Oxford University Press, 1982).

Kant, Immanuel. *Critique of Pure Reason,* trans. N. K. Smith (New York: St. Martin's Press, 1950).

Kierkegaard, Søren. *Repetition: An Essay in Experimental Psychology,* trans. W. Lowrie (New York: Harper and Row, 1941).

Lichtenstein, Heinz. "Zur Phänomenologie des Wiederholungszwanges und des Todestriebes," *Imago* (1935).

Loewald, Hans W. *Papers on Psychoanalysis* (New Haven: Yale University Press, 1980).

Merleau-Ponty, Maurice. *Phenomenology of Perception,* trans. C. Smith (New York: Humanities Press, 1964).

Nietzsche, Friedrich. *Beyond Good and Evil,* trans. W. Kaufmann (New York: Vintage, 1966).

Plato. *Philebus,* trans. R. Hackforth (Cambridge: Cambridge University Press, 1972).

Polanyi, M. *Tacit Knowledge* (Chicago: University of Chicago Press, 1972).

Sulloway, Frank J. *Freud, Biologist of the Mind: Beyond the Psychoanalytic Legend* (New York: Basic Books, 1979).

13

The Pleasures of Repetition

JUDITH BUTLER

Originally published in 1920, Freud's *Jenseits des Lustprinzip* marks a significant departure from his earlier speculations on the primacy of pleasure in human motivation. In this work, Freud refers to certain experiences of compulsive repetition that cannot be understood in the service of the pleasure principle, and so disjoins the pervasive phenomenon of repetition from the wish for satisfaction. The effect of *Beyond the Pleasure Principle* is to displace the monistic theory that posited the achievement of real or conjectured pleasure as the primary goal of human activity with a dualistic theory which claims that the drive toward pleasure is always interrupted and thwarted by a rival drive, that of death or Thanatos. Toward the end of this speculative treatise, it appears that Thanatos supersedes Eros, that the drive toward death not only regulates but dominates the drive toward pleasure.

Freud introduces himself as a speculative metaphysician in this controversial text, employing a vocabulary which recalls the philosophical debates of the Enlightenment, the various high speculations on the passions and ends of human life that we might expect of Spinoza's *Ethics* or Descartes's *Passions of the Soul*. In keeping with his role as metaphysician, Freud seeks recourse to a vocabulary of "principles," "instincts," and "drives," which are understood to structure and impel human action, are manifest in that action, but which, strictly speaking, can never be intuited or known outside of the various human acts, utterances, and gestures in which they are discerned. The problems associated with a vocabulary of principles, instincts, and drives are well rehearsed, but one dimension of that problematic vocabulary will deserve reconsideration within the context of this chapter, namely, the way in which it distorts and limits the possibilities of interpreting repetitive pleasures.

Critically considered, the ontological integrity of an ostensibly universal principle of Thanatos becomes questionable when the only demonstration we have for it are the various phenomena it is meant to explain. Freud reviews for his reader instances of compulsive repetition to show that (a) they cannot be construed as instances of pleasure and (b) they all exhibit a common impulse or drive toward the restoration of an earlier stage and, hence, a restoration of the earli*est* stage, namely, the time before birth and before the development of the ego itself. Freud considers a stasis equivalent to death to be the telos of this drive. Hence, repetition compulsion is a strategy not merely to stop present time or to return to a "better" time, but to negate time altogether, and with it life itself. But what grounds do we have for claiming that this wish is (a) thoroughly separate in origin from pleasure and (b) a universal principle of human motivation that, in some sense, informs *all* compulsively repetitive experiences? The logical point insists itself here as well: if this principle can be shown only through the various phenomena of repetition, and if those phenomena are precisely what have to be explained, then Freud's argument appears circular at best. But the added philosophical confusion appears when we note that the "death instinct" is posited as a universal principle which conditions and structures various particular, empirical manifestations. Here we see that it in no way follows that because some repetitive behavior reveals a wish to restore an earlier time or, indeed, the time before time itself, that *all* repetitive behavior is engaged in a similar project of restoration; nor, most significantly, does it follow that such compulsive repetitions engage a fantasy of restoring that earlier time to achieve a pleasure that had previously been denied.

Although one might discount Freud's postulation of the death instinct from the outset, maintaining that it is a purely speculative notion that cannot be justified, it seems wiser to concede Freud the speculative license he claims and to question instead whether this principle and instinct does the explanatory work that he claims it does. The challenge to that explanatory power that I wish to pursue here is embodied in those experiences that are both pleasurable *and* repetition-compulsive. If Freud is right, then repetition compulsion is not motivated by pleasure, but by the Thanatic wish for a complete regression to a time before life. But what do we make of *the pleasures of repetition* themselves, the compulsive and defeated pleasures that not only accompany various forms of neurosis, but nourish and sustain them as well? In *Beyond the Pleasure Principle*, Freud searches for a manifestation of the death instinct that will support his point, and the example he lights upon is sadism. By claiming that sadism is not motivated by pleasure, Freud is forced to revise the theory articulated in *Three Essays on the Theory of Sexuality* (1905) and "Instincts and Their Vicissitudes" (1914), that sadism is a strategy of self-preservation and not, as he comes to claim, a strategy of self-annihilation. Although this article will consider some of the key shifts within his theory that culminate in this view of sadism as emblematic of the death instinct, it will in no way represent a comprehensive summary of Freud's various insights into the psychosexual meaning of sadism. Instead, we will consider the ways in which sadism as pleasurable repetition might well disprove the very construct of the death instinct that Freud assumes it will confirm. I will suggest how the phenomenon of compulsively repetitive pleasures confounds and challenges some of the speculative notions that lead Freud's theory astray, and I will sketch an alternative point of departure based on phenomenological grounds. The invocation of phenomenology is not intended to displace the psychoanalytic framework—indeed, points of comparison between the doctrine of intentionality and the psychoanalytic school of object relations will be explored—but to ground psychoanalytic insights in experience rather than in wholly speculative constructs. Indeed, the phenomenological approach offered here is one which in fact characterizes much of Freud's own analytic work to understand those peculiarly (self-)destructive postures of pleasure as the dramatized fantasies of traversing time in order to repeat and repair a history that one wishes never was.

Pleasure or Repetition?

When Freud argues that compulsive repetition appears to stem from an origin other than pleasure, Freud refers to dreams which re-present a frightening experience and which, compulsively repeated, cannot be construed as *pleasurable* experiences. This kind of nonpleasurable repetition is manifest, according to Freud, even in those forms of playful repetition that psychoanalysis itself has identified as pleasurable. The *"fort-da"* game that Freud reviews in some detail in *Beyond the Pleasure Principle* initially appears to be a case of repetition in which the young child playfully repeats the separation from the mother by alternately throwing his toy from his crib and retrieving it. The game allows the young child to gain a sense of mastery over the experience of separation from his mother, first by substituting the toy for the mother, and second, by gaining control over the conditions under which the departure and return of the toy occurs. Though this game does provide an indisputable pleasure for the young boy, Freud wants to argue that even this pleasure of acquiring mastery over a situation in which one was originally without control is not primarily governed by the pleasure principle. Indeed, Freud's controversial claim is that the drive toward pleasure is itself invariably subordinate to the drive toward death and that this latter is an overriding compulsion of organic life that is stronger and more fundamental than self-preservative instincts as a whole. Hence, even the compulsion to repeat which seems, on a first analysis, to serve the project of the imaginary acquisition of mastery is subject to the death instinct or principle and this motivation is not only free of pleasure but antithetical and superogatory to it. In Freud's words:

> Seen in this light, the theoretical importance of the instincts of self-preservation, of self-assertion and of mastery greatly diminishes. They are component instincts whose function it is to assure that the organism shall follow its own path to death, and to ward off any possible ways of return-

ing to inorganic existence other than those which are immanent in the organism itself. . . . the organism wishes to die only in its own fashion. (51)

Throughout *Beyond the Pleasure Principle* Freud is aware that his theory is
speculative and represents a significant departure from the theory of instincts
he previously developed. At the close of his text, he asks his reader not to fault
him for changing his position, and throughout the text he defends the speculative
nature of his inquiry. In a remark of characteristic intellectual bravado, Freud
maintains that "in the obscurity that reigns at present in the theory of instincts,
it would be unwise to reject any idea that promises to throw light on it" (73).
Although one might conclude that the move toward greater speculative license
is precisely what ought to be discouraged when a theory is already mired in
obscurity, Freud suggests even more generalized constructs, such as the death
instinct, to explain the variety of repetition compulsions that seems to contradict
the claims of pleasure.

Among the more problematic of such compulsively repetitive behaviors are
sadism and *masochism,* configurations of sexual pleasure that are not primarily
governed by the motivation for pleasure. Indeed, Freud asks rhetorically, "Is it
not plausible to suppose that this sadism is in fact a death instinct which, under
the influence of the narcissistic libido, has been forced out of the ego and has
consequently emerged in relation to the object?" (BPP, 73). Only six years
earlier, Freud interpreted sadism as an "impulsion to mastery" (I, 102) which
manifests the self-preservative instincts characteristic of the ego instincts. At
that point, sadism is understood as an effort not only to inflict pain, but also to
effect a "subjection and mastery of an object" (I, 93) that is deemed dangerous
to the ego. Masochism is the inversion of the sadistic instinct whereby the
subject assumes the passive role and "institutes" another subject in the role of
the sadist. In either case, the overriding project of this drama is to effect mastery
over a potentially dangerous and painful situation.

I write "potentially" with unease for, at least in 1914, Freud maintained that
sadism and masochism were not primarily defenses against pain, but rather
efforts to eroticize a present and actual pain and, through that eroticization, to
subordinate pain to a pleasurable sexual fantasy. Note that in this earlier speculation on sadism and masochism, Freud maintains that certain kinds of pain
can become sources of pleasure: "We have every reason to believe that sensations of pain, like other unpleasant sensations, extend into sexual excitation and
produce a condition which is pleasurable, for the sake of which the subject will
even willingly experience the unpleasantness of pain" (I, 93). In *Beyond the
Pleasure Principle,* Freud moves to a theoretical position that discounts sadism
as an effect of self-preservation, and he asks, "How can the sadistic instinct,
whose aim it is to injure the object, be derived from Eros, the preserver of life?"
(BPP, 73). Earlier, Freud was content to answer that the desire to overpower
and injure the object constitutes a self-preserving defense against an object
perceived as dangerous or debilitating to the ego, but here Freud clearly dis-

sociates sadistic defense from the wider aims of self-preservation. Freud earlier distinguished between the ego instincts, characterized as self-preserving, and the sexual instincts, which are fundamentally concerned with the achievement of pleasure. From the point of view of the developed ego, these latter emerge antecedent to the former: "At the very beginning," Freud writes, "the external world, objects and that which was hated were one and the same thing" (I, 100); only later are objects discovered that present the possibility of pleasure and that the ego endeavors to incorporate into its own structure. This distinction between self-preserving or "hateful" instincts and sexual instincts is recast in *Beyond the Pleasure Principle* as the polarity between the death instincts and the sexual instincts, whereby self-preservation is now understood as a regressive effort to recapture earlier stages of ego development and, indeed, stages of libidinal organization prior to the development of the ego itself. The practical consequence of this expanded notion of "ego instincts" is that repetition compulsion is no longer to be interpreted as a project of mastery or self-preservation but instead as a regressive effort which neither the principles of pleasure nor self-preservation can explain.

In 1914, Freud understood the hateful relation to the love-object as "a tendency ... to repeat in relation to the former the primordial attempt at flight from the external world and its flow of stimuli" (I, 100). Hence, sadism is understood as a repetition of a primary urge toward self-preservation, of a primary encounter with the external world as an endangering and, hence, as a hateful field of objects. That sadism is eroticized is a sign of its admixture with the sexual instincts and also underscores the pleasurable experience of gaining mastery over a situation in which one originally felt oneself to be the victim. The pleasure of mastery, which is always in some sense the pleasure of a contemporary victory over the past, represents an ambivalent organization of sexual and ego instincts.

Yet it seems necessary to ask whether these two kinds of "instincts" are as ontologically discrete as Freud here suggests. After all, he maintains that the ego instincts are primary and that sexual relations appear as an extension and manifestation of the former. If an object is found pleasurable, the first and primary response of the ego is to *incorporate* it, to instate that object as part of the self. Hereafter, the relation to that pleasurable object is but an extension of narcissism or self-love, and one endeavors to "preserve" this object *as if it were one's own self*. Hence, the sexual instincts emerge, according to Freud, as elaborations of the ego instincts and come to work against the ego instincts only in the later course of instinctual development when the explicit object of pleasure is denied or lost and the ego discovers the limits of its own incorporative strategy of self-preservation. As Freud notes, the first response to the object is hate, followed by consumption or incorporation, followed then by mastery; sadism clearly belongs to this last stage of instinctual development. In effect, sadism is the effort to reconcile the demand for pleasure with the demand to be protected from danger, but this latter is an affective memory of danger that poses now as a contemporary threat. Hence, for the sadist, sexual pleasure is organized and marked by the repetition and representation of the "primordial" hatred of all things external.

The theoretical shift that occurs between 1914 and 1920 effects a distinction between the repetition as *mastery* and repetition as *regression*. In the former instance, repetition signals a fantasized return to the past for the purposes of repairing an injury there incurred. One may well interpret the strategy of return as an effort to rewrite or reconstruct a history that remains painful in contemporary experience. Hence, return is always linked with the desire to redo or repair; repetition is wishful reparation, the assimilation of the present to the past in order to inhabit that past within the terms of the present and effect its fantasized reconstruction.

In 1920, however, Freud interprets repetition less as a return to the specific injuries of the personal past than as a more generalized return to a time before the distinction has emerged between the ego and the external world. The death instinct is not primarily future-oriented, but rather it effects an identification of death with the "boundary-less" state of the ego before individuation. Although this primary condition is interpreted in 1914 as an experience of *pleasure,* it is associated with the absence of pleasure by the time Freud develops his theory of the death instinct in 1920. What accounts for this significant transition?

Freud explains the death instinct as a tendency toward conservation which comes to subordinate the ego instincts, characterized as self-preservative, to the death instincts themselves. While pleasure is always characterized as excitation or stimulation, the absence of pleasure is marked by a state of equilibrium and rest. In distinguishing between Eros, the life-affirming sexual instincts, and Thanatos, the death-driven instincts, Freud understands himself to be accounting for the bipolar dynamism of human life. Repetition compulsion reveals a primary urge to return to a state in which the problem of pleasure and its satisfaction cannot even be posed; neither the temporary respite from excitation, nor the fantasized reconstruction of the past as a legacy of pleasure, repetition designates the thorough obliteration of the problematic of pleasure itself. In other words, repetition compulsion signifies the desire not merely for death, but for the possibility of *never having been born.* In 1914, Freud regarded the external world as prompting an originally hostile response on the part of the ego. For this world, external and, hence, beyond the ego's control, represents the permanent possibility of dissatisfaction, pain, and literal endangerment. The thorough negation of that external world would effect a permanent protection, and we might understand the logic of Freud's transition from ego to death instincts within the terms of this fantastic desire to be rid of the dangers of externality. In effect, the final triumph of the ego instincts would be the death of the ego itself, for if the ultimate goal of the ego is self-preservation, then this aim would be realized fully only upon the negation of the distinction itself between ego and the world. Indeed, the ultimate protection of the ego from the world consists in its own self-obliteration. Along these lines, we might consider suicide not primarily as the effort to rid oneself of oneself but to stamp out the world that makes the experience of being a self, an ego, so unbearably endangering.

Significantly, Freud refuses to identify this state of worldlessness with a state of pleasure. As neither excitation nor equilibrium, this state is neither pleasurable nor living, but rather it represents an irrevocable foreclosure of both the pleasures and dangers of externality. As a conjectured peace, it would remain within a binary opposition to excitation and to the pleasure-danger axis, but as death, it transcends bipolar dynamism altogether. Freud thus established the death instinct, and its regressive functions, outside of the sexual instincts and, hence, of the dynamism of life itself. But he makes a move that is significantly more radical as well: he subordinates the sexual instincts to the death instincts, thus promoting the death instinct as the overriding teleological principle of human existence:

> Let us make a sharper distinction than we have hitherto made between function and tendency. The pleasure principle, then, is a tendency operating in the service of a function whose business it is to free the mental apparatus entirely from excitation or to keep the amount of excitation in it constant or to keep it is as low as possible. . . . It is clear that the function thus described would be concerned with the most universal endeavour of all living substance—namely to return to the quiescence of the inorganic world. (BPP, 86)

Later, Freud suggests that "the pleasure principle seems actually to serve the death instincts" (87), a formulation that contests the rival status of these two instincts. As tendencies that are subordinate to a function, the sexual instincts are always confined within the overall plan of the death instinct's strategy to return to "the quiescence of the inorganic world." Hence, sexual instincts no longer appear as independent, ontologically discrete libidinal manifestations, but instead they are subordinate tendencies within an instinct or function which both integrates and overrides them. This theoretical joining of the sexual and death instincts suggests that the theory of rival instincts, along with its dualistic ontology, becomes questioned by the terms of Freud's own theory. The distinction is further challenged, however, by his explicit discussion of sadism in *Beyond the Pleasure Principle.*

Although Freud uses the language of instincts to describe this impulse toward death, understood as the irrevocable stasis of libidinal activity, the description of this instinctual activity inadvertently puts the very theory of rival instincts into question. Not only is the ontological status of an instinct with an internal teleology questioned, but the dualistic account of sexual and death instincts is similarly undermined. The result, I would suggest, is a return to the theory of sadism as wishful mastery over the past, although this conclusion in no way undermines the existential contributions implicit in Freud's account of sadism as a contradictory or self-defeating expression of sexuality. Relieved of the theoretical burden of his theory of instincts, Freud's analysis suggests that sadism is a specific strategy of the ego. According to this revised theory, one which makes tentative gestures in the direction of object relations theory, the body that serves as the focus of sadistic desire comes to represent the history of unrepaired injuries, as well as the world itself, as a scene of perpetual endangerment.

Sadism and the Desire for Death

As an expression of the instinct to return to a prior organic state, sadism would be yet another "circuitous path ... to death" (BPP, 51). Its "aim," strictly speaking, would be to reinstate this primary condition of quiescence and to subordinate thereby the future of the organism to the task of recreating the conditions of its origins. As mentioned above, sadism is the "example" of the death instinct that Freud thinks confirms his speculations (74), and as such it would also manifest this cyclical teleology in which the original state of an organism reemerges as its implicit and governing telos.

The sadism Freud considers is explicitly sexual sadism and, as noted earlier, it manifests the joint operation of both sexual and death instincts. If the sexual instincts, however, are conceived as life-affirming and life-creating, then it would appear that these instincts suffer a reversal of aim when subordinated to the death instincts. What in the usual course of sexuality is an urge to establish cathexis is, in the case of sadism, rechanneled into a strategy of distantiation. The paradox of sadism as a sexual expression consists in its capacity to undermine every accomplished cathexis. The binding or cathecting possibilities of sexuality are interrupted and repealed, as it were, by the death instinct, which seeks a return to a condition prior to need, pleasure, and sexuality itself. Understood within the framework, sadism emerges as a configuration of sexuality turned against itself, the "k/not" of sexuality, as it were, a sexual instinct compelled to achieve its own defeat.

In *Three Essays on the Theory of Sexuality* (1905) and in other earlier writings, Freud held that masochism is derived from sadism; the originally hateful relation to the Other becomes internalized as a hateful relation to oneself. Although sadism is derived from primary narcissism, the masochism that is itself derived from sadism constitutes a thorough reversal of that primary condition. But in *Beyond the Pleasure Principle*, Freud begins to argue that perhaps sadism signifies a reflexive instinct at its origins that is *not* that of narcissism but the instinct toward self-negation which, existentially broader than mere masochism, serves as the condition for sexual sadism. According to this view, sexual sadism manifests the urge to die, although, in Freud's words, this urge "has been forced out of the ego" (74). Hence, the death instinct occasions sadism as its externalized, sexual manifestation; this sadism then achieves a second-order reflexivity in the form of masochism, which must be understood as a regression, already under the sway of the death instinct. Freud speculates that perhaps there is such a thing as primary masochism, a possibility he previously discounted. In this context, however, it is clear that the meaning and scope of masochism has changed decisively. By making the desire to die foundational to the ego, Freud precludes an inquiry into how such a desire is constituted in the first place. In other words, sadistic action is traced back to a primarily self-negating relation which is, strictly speaking, both universally invariant and non-specific. Hence, whatever concrete relations become internalized as part of the psyche are themselves reducible to universal causes, which reveal those concrete relations as instruments or occasions of primary instincts. In the case of sadism, the analysis would be able to explain the propensity to injure oneself not as an *internalized* punishment but rather as an *externalized* instinct. Moreover, sadism could not readily be interpreted as a strategy to gain wishful mastery over the past, that is, the recreation of an earlier scene of punishment in which the original roles are now felicitously reversed. Sadistic action would now be interpreted within a more generalized framework, manifesting not simply the peculiar history of the sadistic individual but rather the general history of the organism. As the manifestation of a quasi-biological instinct, sadism would, in effect, represent the desire of the organism; analytically considered, it would only be fully explained through recourse to its universal and nonspecific origins.

As an explanatory principle, the notion of an instinctual drive toward death is no doubt comprehensive. But the problem of establishing the ontological validity of such a construct is notoriously difficult. Freud knows his inquiry to be speculative, and he knows as well that the usefulness of his theoretical constructs consists in their capacity to illuminate those aspects of repetition compulsion that have previously remained opaque. Indeed, he suggests at the end of his inquiry that his theory of instincts belongs to "the figurative language peculiar to psychology" (83). The question, however, is whether the intellectual breadth afforded by this avowedly speculative construct diminishes the analytic practicability of his theory. In developing this instinctual theory of sadism, Freud moves away from a position which took the desire for mastery and reparation as the key to understanding the origins and strategies of sexual sadism. That the sadist now manifests the generalized urge of the organism to return to its original stasis leaves the interpretation of the sadist at a generalized level.

But consider the possibility that Freud's reversal of his own position might well require a further reversal, in order that its analytic usefulness be restored. We might go along with Freud and argue that the sadist first seeks his or her own death, albeit unconsciously; that this aim conflicts with the sexual instinct, which seeks cathexis and hence life-affirming connections; and that the resolution of this conflict is achieved through the subordination of the sexual strategy to the overall plan of restoring the stasis characteristic of the organism prior to its individuation. As such, the sexual dimension of sadism would always be considered a mere channel or vehicle for the death instinct, its instrument and cover, as it were. In Freud's own words, this death instinct, first "forced" out of the ego, "has pointed the way for the libidinal components of the sexual instinct, and . . . these follow after it to the object" (74). This tagging along of sexuality suggests its inadvertent and unnecessary function in the strategy of sadism and suggests as well that both the sexual and the sadistic dimensions might be understood as organized and regulated by the death instinct.

This explanation has impressive existential dimensions, and one might also account for a variety of religious experiences on the basis of this universally human urge to restore the organism to its original state. But though we have explained the phenomenon of sadism through recourse to a universal principle, it seems that we have lost the capacity to explain it on the level of the individual. Indeed, what framework is left to us to explain the specificity of sadistic strategies in the biographical context of the individual? Inasmuch as human beings are sadists, are they sadists for the same reasons? It appears that Freud's move to a universal grounding of sadism deprives his theory of the capacity to discern the particular forms of sadism, their origins, and the specific content of their aims. Is it purely tangential that sadism takes a sexual form, or is the relation between pleasure and pain more closely interrelated than Freud at this point in his theory seems ready to acknowledge?

As was suggested above, we might well reverse Freud's ever-reversible theory yet another time and ask: What conditions within the biographical experience of the individual occasion both the desire to die and the externalization of this desire in the form of sadism? Clearly, I have already reinterpreted Freud's vocabulary, renouncing the naturalistic lexicon of instinct for the more phenomenologically familiar notion of desire. But this reworking of Freud's vocabulary is crucial, if we are to retain the experiential insights he offers and yet to escape the unfortunate implications of his speculative naturalism. We might well concur with Freud that there is a significant connection between a desire for death and the sadistic effort to master or injure another human being, but we might remain skeptical with regard to the ontological primacy attributed to the death instincts and the subsidiary, even inadvertent, role assigned to the sexual instincts. In his earlier theory, he suggested that sadism is the effort to master the love-object that has resisted and escaped the strategy of appropriation and incorporation. Indeed, if I cannot make the object into a part of me, then I will subdue it through force or coercion, and thereby I will make it into an instrument of my will. Sadism would then appear as the failure of incorporation, the effort to maintain the Other as an extension of my will, a refusal to grant the Other its Otherness. Moreover, in both the earlier theory and in *Beyond the Pleasure Principle*, Freud maintains that sadism is structured by repetition, that sadistic acts are efforts to recover a time past in order to gain satisfaction for a wish previously unsatisfied. Here Freud suggests the crucial link between sadism and *reparation* that is lost from the theory developed in 1920, unless of course we understand life itself as a damage for which one seeks reparation.

According to the theory of primary narcissism, all externality provokes a hostile reaction on the part of the established ego, and Freud said as much in 1914. But what of the peculiar history of hostilities that comes to structure the sadistic aims of an individual's sexual desire? How does hostility become incorporated into desire, if it was not always there, and does a schematic rendering of the universal basis of hostility do enough to explain the particular forms of sadism that appear in human sexual behavior?

As a repetitive pleasure, sadism is both cathexis and regression at once; it is a binding activity that regularly unbinds itself, a connection that reasserts distance, a sexual act that seeks to repudiate sexuality. The paradoxical character of sadism reveals the conflict that it expresses, but there is no good reason to assume that this conflict rests in instinctual life per se. The negation of pleasure at the heart of sadism may not readily be equated with the desire to die; what is intended is primarily the death of pleasure in the midst of pleasure. We may subsequently interpret this effort to negate pleasure as an effort to negate life and this attempt to negate life as a regressive effort to recover a time before the anxieties and hostilities associated with pleasure, sexuality, and loving emerge. But the latter two conclusions in no way follow necessarily from the phenomenological description of the paradoxes of sadism. We can further conclude that the effort to subdue or even injure the body of the Other in and through sexual acts is an externalized relation of the ego to itself, that the body which is being subdued and repudiated is only *secondarily* the body of the Other, but it is primarily the body of the sadist himself. But here again, to argue on behalf of the primary reflexivity of the sadistic relation in no way compels an acceptance of any postulation regarding the instinctual basis of sadism.

Toward a Phenomenological Interpretation of Repetitive Pleasures

Freud's route for providing a universal basis for sadism is through the theory of instincts, a theory he knows to be speculative, but one that he considers to be part of the necessarily "figurative language of psychology." Although Freud occasionally wrote that he hoped to ground that theory of instinct in a neurophysiological framework, he also appeared to be prepared to settle for a certain necessary ambiguity in the language that describes psychic and affective life. Rather than enter into the debate over whether Freud intended psychoanalytic theory to be a science and, if so, in what its scientific character consists, I would like to suggest an alternative point of departure for understanding the particular phenomenon under investigation here: the pleasures of repetition. In claiming that this alternative point of departure is phenomenological, I mean simply that it takes its bearings within experience and that it subscribes to a view of psychic life as *intentional.* Although the term "intentional" is often equated with the mental disposition of having a clear and conscious intention to do *x* or *y,* its usage within phenomenology is significantly different. As Edmund Husserl has argued, the intentional character of consciousness is its *relatedness* to the world in which it is found and which offers up the various objects of its experience. In Husserl's words, "consciousness is always consciousness of," meaning that consciousness is never wholly self-referential, that it can only take itself as its object once that "self" is projected or determined in a countervailing world.

With the presumption of *intentionality*, philosophical and psychological theories can no longer claim that our various ways of being conscious or aware of the world are merely mental representations that have no bearing or relation to an objective field. Our conscious thoughts and various modalities of awareness are related to an exterior field, whether it is existent or not. This relationship is characteristic of human existence. Indeed, it constitutes the primary structure of human experience and consequently all interpretations of psychological life must in some way presuppose this relationship.

The phenomenological doctrine of intentionality is comparable to that tenet of object relations theory which assumes that concrete relationships, whether in memory or fantasy, provide the point of departure for psychological interpretation. According to Jean-Paul Sartre, within a phenomenological framework it is no longer possible to describe a human being as solely concerned with himself or herself. Even the most reclusive or monastic of human beings maintains a relation to the world, even if in the mode of denial. The refusal to be in the world is but one way of maintaining a relation to that world, as the "negation" of others is still a vital and significant way of being related to them. This effort to deny connection emerges within Sartre's analysis as a connection that is specified as denial. According to Sartre's psychological extension of phenomenological philosophy, human beings are inevitably and, indeed, unbearably *in the world*. Whether in a posture of rejection, hatred, or indeed, sadism, the individual endeavors to break the intentional bond with the world that constitutes the ineradicable structure of his or her experience. Turning against intentionality itself, the individual attempts to deny its own connectedness but necessarily fails. Not unlike Freud's view of Eros, the doctrine of intentionality assumes a primary and difficult connectedness with the external objects of the world. Indeed, if sadism is, as Freud argues, a turning of Eros against itself, the phenomenological explanation is not far afield: sadism would be the effort to break a connection which, in effect, can never be broken precisely because connection is, as intentional, constitutive of human experiences itself. Freud's view of Eros as *cathexis* appears to be reaffirmed by Maurice Merleau-Ponty, another twentieth-century French phenomenologist, who argued that intentionality ought to be understood as the mundane manner in which we continuously *embrace* the world.

Note that for the phenomenological point of view articulated by Sartre, the connections with specific objects and Others and the connection with "the world" are purposefully confused. Sartre argues in *Outline of a Theory of Emotion* (1939) that in every specific emotional relationship to something external, a more generalized, universal relationship to the world is implicitly at work. Indeed, in our various specific loves, hatreds, and fears, we manifest not merely the affective orientation toward the object at hand, but a more generalized relationship to the world. Sartre's early phenomenological work fails to incorporate a psychoanalytic understanding of how the objects of attachment are formed with reference to the concrete psychobiography of the individual, and it also fails to consider how our various conceptions of the world constitute displaced and false generalizations of the object relations specific to the individual's personal past. Sartre's theory may well strike a psychoanalytic audience as too abstract and formal to be of any interpretive use. But let us consider what a phenomenological interpretation of the pleasures of repetition might offer as an experientially based framework to psychoanalytic insights freed of Freud's speculative quandary regarding the dualistic theory of instincts.

Repetitive pleasures are a contradiction in terms only when pleasure is understood exclusively as the drive toward *cathexis,* and repetition, exclusively in the service of the drive toward *decathexis.* From the point of view of experience, we may well note two opposing directions to human longings, the movement toward greater connectedness and engagement and a movement that militates against connectedness. The phenomenological description of these two movements does not presuppose that each emerges from an ontologically separate origin. Indeed, the phenomenological task at hand is to understand a structure of human longing that is fundamentally at odds with itself, a pleasure that regularly defeats itself and thus necessitates its own repetition. In addition, however, the phenomenological interpretation rejects the notion that pleasure can be conceived as a *state* or free-floating *energy* that can be said to exist prior to its object. In other words, it makes no sense from a phenomenological point of view to conceive of pleasure as ontologically separable from an object. As an intentional relation, pleasure is necessarily pleasure "about" some exterior object or event, imagined or real. In contrast with the view that the meaning of pleasure is discoverable in its somatic origins, the doctrine of intentionality maintains that the meaning of pleasure is to be discerned in its *intentional object.* The intentionality of pleasure in no way discounts the somatic and physiological basis of pleasure, but it merely implies that pleasure becomes significant only within lived experience, becomes felt, known, and interpretable when it takes on an object of some kind. In other words, pleasure is not a substance or state that has any meaning outside of the context in which it is related to an object. Indeed, the physiological or somatic preconditions of pleasure are not identifiable with pleasure itself, for pleasure denotes an experience, and hence, an intentional relation. The consequence of this view is that we cannot meaningfully speak of pleasure as a principle or instinct that maintains ontological integrity before experience itself; the attribution of pleasure to a pre-experiential set of processes is an inappropriate transposition of a term applicable only to lived and knowable experience to the physiological conditions of that experience. Although Sartre's argument relies unfortunately on a refutation of the unconscious, his theory makes some more general points about the applicability of terms such as "pleasure," "desire," and "emotion" that do not require us to corroborate his misunderstanding of unconscious processes. At its best, his theory offers an insight which object relations theory specifies and demonstrates in terms of early childhood: that the structure, aim, and strategies of pleasure are developed in relation to the earliest objects of love. The consequence of this claim is that pleasure is only and always understandable in relation to an object, that it is referential and intentional in its ontology, that it is neither instinct nor state but a relation to an object repeated and elaborated over time.

Because intentionality, according to Husserl, is a polyvalent structure, the intentional structure of pleasure may well have a variety of objects. The problem of compulsively repeated pleasures that Freud describes in *Beyond the Pleasure Principle* might be described, then, as maintaining at least a twofold intentional object: the uncathected object of love and temporality itself. For the individual who suffers this repeated and frustrated effect of pleasure, it is not only the object of the past that cannot be recovered, nor the relation that cannot be restored or reconstructed, but it is time itself that resists the human will and proves itself unyielding. Between pleasure and satisfaction, a prohibition or negation of pleasure is enacted which necessitates the endless repetition and proliferation of thwarted pleasures. The repetition is a vain effort to stay, or indeed, to reverse time; such repetition reveals a rancor against the present which feeds upon itself.

Resisting the present is, from a phenomenological point of view, a useless effort to exercise control over the structure of temporality as necessarily expressed in time past, time present, and time future. The effort to stop or break this temporal continuity is, in effect, the self-defeating strategy of the individual. To be an individual is to be *in time*: to be subject to the exigencies of time; to refuse the temporal continuity of experience is to refuse the very structure of the self.

From the viewpoint of phenomenology, then, pleasure is polyvalent in its intentional structure; it relates not only to an object—present, past, or both— but to temporality and to the world as such. These last two objects of pleasure constitute the existential dimension of the intentionality of pleasure. The Sartrian question—what kind of relation to the world is expressed in this posture of self-defeat?—suggests that the selfsame agency that pursues pleasure also interrupts and rejects that pleasure and that this fundamental ambivalence is an intentional relation rather than a phenomenal expression of a wholly instinctual source. Again, to claim that this ambivalence emerges from a relationship is not to offer a causal account of the origins of pleasures and their repetitive character. Indeed, such a claim merely designates the operative intentional relationship as an ambivalent one and poses the question of what sort of necessarily failed effort to eradicate the ineradicable structure of intentionality is here under way. The primacy of intentionality suggests that connectedness is insuperable and that the effort to deny connection is always and only a manner of being engaged in the world in the mode of denial. Clearly, the phenomenological conclusion to the problem of repetitive pleasures is to assert as primary what Freud would have called Eros, the intimate involvement with exteriority which, despite its best efforts, the human subject cannot overcome within the confines of lived experience.

From the terms of Sartre's phenomenology, then, the pleasures of compulsive repetition constitute a crisis of intentionality but not its refutation. Only through the contention that a nonintentional break with exteriority is possible does the problem of rival drives or instincts become possible. In other words, only if we fail to understand disconnection as a mode of connection does the question of opposing human drives or tendencies become possible. With intentionality as the theoretical point of departure, however, we can understand the negation of pleasure and connection as its own kind of connection and, in psychoanalytic terms, its own peculiar kind of pleasure.

The consideration of repetitive pleasures might well extend beyond those experiences of repetition that are clearly compulsive. For Freud in 1924, pleasure appears to be associated with the satisfaction of a drive and the consequent release of libidinal energy. This release is associated with a decathexis that paves the way for a new cathexis, the ushering in of new bonds and, implicitly, new experience. In effect, repetition is associated with the re-presentation of the past, and hence, it indicates a way in which the ego fails to inhabit present time. In contrast, pleasure is associated with the new, the transcendence of the past, the possibility of new connections, and hence, the temporal domain of futurity. But what is to preclude a pleasure of repetition, of reminiscence or recollection that is not at once a refusal of present or future time? Or the pleasure associated with jokes that have been told myriad times when the punch lines are no surprise, or the simple pleasures of musical rhythm or poetic alliteration, assonance, or internal rhyme which give pleasure through the repetition of sound? Are these repetitions indicative of a pleasure wholly past? Perhaps they serve in part to bind the past and future together, to provide ritualized and sensuous occasions for the invocation of the past and the convocation of the present. Indeed, what other route than repetition instates *the pleasure of temporal continuity* between the irrecoverable past and the unknowable future?

If instinct generally, and the death instinct in particular, no longer functions as an explanatory construct, it may be a shorthand for an experience that does admit of explanation. In pondering the conflict between pleasure and repetition, Freud is aware that certain pleasures are thwarted by compulsive acts which seem not to originate in pleasure. Sadism is the example he provides, so we return to a consideration of his views to see whether we might redescribe the phenomenon within the terms of phenomenology.

The Specific Needs of Theory

Neither the postulation of a death instinct nor the doctrine of intentionality provides a way to understand the specific strategy of self-defeat that characterizes the conjunction of pleasure and compulsive repetition that concerns Freud in *Beyond the Pleasure Principle*. If the sadist dramatizes the desire to die, why is death sought, why is it externalized in the form of dominating or injuring another? And why does it take a sexual form? There are other kinds of explanations, more specific to the history of the individual, that account for this radical turning against pleasure within the very act in which pleasure is most clearly expected.

The desire to die might well signify a desire for a return to an enclosure that effectively forecloses the anxious possibility of a hostile external world. As a yearning for the protection associated with the womb, this yearning which we call the death instinct may be less a desire for literal death than a call for a radical protection within the terms of life. Indeed, we run the risk of overlooking the concrete precipitating reasons for the emergence of such a yearning when we attribute its primary cause to an inexorable and universally available instinct. The interpretation of the desire to die may be taken as emblematic of a species desire or it may be the response to a perceived situation that seems preferable to any other. Indeed, we might inquire, rather death than what? In the response we might find the noninstinctual basis for the desire, the specific danger that is feared that makes death a preferable option.

The repetitive nature of sadism suggests the dissatisfaction at its core. The sadistic act must be repeated because it can never accomplish the aim it sets for itself—namely, the literal recovery of radical safety through the immobilization of the Other. As repetitive, the sadistic act seeks time and again to break the veil of the present, to break the surface of the Other's body in an effort to penetrate the insistent facticity of the temporal present. In the convergence of the temporal present and past that characterizes the experience of the sadist in his or her vain repetitions, the body of the Other becomes the impenetrability of time itself. In this sense, the Other's body becomes the sign of the present which forecloses the recovery and reparation of the past; injury to that body is conceived as an injury inflicted against the contemporaneity of life. Similarly, the Other's body becomes resistance itself, the *externality* of the world which deprives the ego of both pleasure and protection. But this externality is not simply the existential fact of the world's fundamental alterity, but the legacy of specific hostilities and deprivations that have at various times characterized the particular emotional worlds of that ego. In this sense, the body of the Other can represent the history of loss, defeated desire, hostility, and deprivation, and the effort to negate that body can be the effort to negate those very negativities and thereby to produce a positive compensatory fantasy—to rewrite that history of deprivation as a history of satisfaction and fullness. Hence, the effort to injure or subdue that Other might well be the displaced and ill-fated strategy to do violence to a history that has, in effect, done violence to the ego itself. Through the externalization of this primarily reflexive relation, the body of the Other becomes the sign of that lost self, and the desire to subdue, to injure, indeed, to eradicate that body bespeaks the more fundamental desire to rid oneself of a history, a life, that has produced this posture of self-negation. Just as Freud maintained that sadism maintains hostility toward external objects per se, Sartre would argue that sadism exemplifies an unresolved quarrel with exteriority, and hence, with the intentional structure of pleasure itself.

In reversing his earlier position, which argued that masochism was but the internalization of a primarily sadistic relation, Freud opened the way for a consideration of sadism as an externalized relation to oneself. Here it is clear that for Sartre, sadism signifies a rebellion against intentionality that can never wholly succeed (even in the desire to obliterate the object, it is still the object whose obliteration is sought). Freud's theory in *Beyond the Pleasure Principle* does not entail a controversial rehabilitation of primary masochism as a way of explaining the reflexive relations, those which the ego maintains toward itself, characteristic of sadistic acts. In postulating the death instinct as the primary basis of sadism, Freud suggests that sadism is inadvertently sexual only in its expression and that this destructive urge is conditioned by the innate physiological constitution of human beings. By relinquishing the postulation of an instinct as the origin of sadism, we free the analysis to consider whether sadism, although grounded in a posture of self-hatred, might be further explained as an internalized relation, the repetition of an originally external abuse as a self-inflicted injury, that is, the internalization of abuse as self-punishment. Moreover, by disputing the dualistic account of sexual instincts and death instincts, we allow for the possibility that pleasure is not arbitrarily associated with sadism, neither tagging along behind it as a separate instinctual force nor serving as a mere channel for the expression of a death instinct. On the contrary, the unhappy repetitions of sadistic acts bear out a useless desire to repeat and repair a history of dissatisfaction. The effort to comprehend this pleasure that goes nowhere, that repeats itself endlessly as the infinite stutter of desire, requires a turn: not to instinct but to the particular history of injury which, internalized then externalized, becomes the focus of a sexual battle.

REFERENCES

Two works frequently cited have been identified in the text by the following abbreviations.

BPP   Beyond the Pleasure Principle, Sigmund Freud (New York: Liveright), 1950.
I   "Instincts and Their Vicissitudes," Sigmund Freud, *General Psychological Theory* (New York: Macmillan), 1963.

Note: This chapter was written in 1987. It is dedicated to the memory of Patricia Emerson Owen.

Contributors and Editors

STANLEY BONE, M.D. Associate clinical professor of psychiatry, Columbia University College of Physicians and Surgeons; faculty, Columbia University Center for Psychoanalytic Training and Research; director of education, Washington Heights Community Service, New York State Psychiatric Institute.

CHARLES BRENNER, M.D. Training and supervising psychoanalyst, New York Psychoanalytic Institute; clinical professor of psychiatry, State University of New York; lecturer in psychiatry, Yale University School of Medicine.

JUDITH BUTLER, PH.D. Associate professor of humanities, Johns Hopkins University.

EDWARD S. CASEY, PH.D. Professor of philosophy, State University of New York at Stony Brook.

NORMAN DOIDGE, M.D. Candidate, Columbia University Center for Psychoanalytic Training and Research; research fellow, New York State Psychiatric Institute; instructor of clinical psychiatry, Columbia University College of Physicians and Surgeons.

ROBERT A. GLICK, M.D. Associate clinical professor of psychiatry, Columbia University College of Physicians and Surgeons; associate director, Columbia University Center for Psychoanalytic Training and Research.

STANLEY I. GREENSPAN, M.D. Clinical professor of psychiatry and behavioral sciences and child health and development, George Washington University Medical Center; supervising child psychoanalyst, Washington Psychoanalytic Institute.

MYRON A. HOFER, M.D. Professor of psychiatry, Columbia University College of Physicians and Surgeons; director, Department of Developmental Psycho-biology, New York State Psychiatric Institute.

OTTO F. KERNBERG, M.D. Professor of psychiatry, Cornell University Medical College; training and supervising psychoanalyst, Columbia University Center for Psychoanalytic Training and Research; associate chairman and medical director, New York Hospital Cornell Medical Center, Westchester Division.

EUGENE MAHON, M.D. Faculty, Child and Adult Programs, Columbia University Center for Psychoanalytic Training and Research; assistant clinical professor of psychiatry, Columbia University College of Physicians and Surgeons.

DONALD L. NATHANSON, M.D. Clinical associate professor of psychiatry, Hahneman University; senior attending psychiatrist, Institute of Pennsylvania Hospital.

ANDREW SCHWARTZ, M.D. Candidate, Baltimore-Washington Institute for Psychoanalysis; faculty, Department of Psychiatry, Overholser Division of Training, St. Elizabeths Hospital.

ELLEN HANDLER SPITZ, PH.D. Visiting lecturer of aesthetics in psychiatry, Cornell University Medical College; Getty Scholar in the History of Art and the Humanities (1989–90).

DANIEL N. STERN, M.D. Professor, Department of Psychiatry and Human Behavior, Brown University; professor, Faculty of Psychology and Science of Education, University of Geneva.

MICHAEL H. STONE, M.D. Professor of clinical psychiatry, Columbia University, College of Physicians and Surgeons; professor of clinical psychiatry, Cornell University Medical College; director, Psychotherapy Service, Extended Treatment Division, New York Hospital-Cornell Medical Center, Westchester Division.

Index